Funk & Wagnalls WORLD ATLAS

Maps created by

GeoSystems Global Corporation

GEOSYSTEMS

K-III Reference Corporation

A K-III Communications Company

K-III Reference Corporation Staff

Director of Editorial Production Andrea J. Pitluk

Director–Purchasing and Production Edward A. Thomas

Deputy Editor William A. McGeveran, Jr.

Managing Editor Eileen O'Reilly

Associate Editors Ileana Parvulescu, Lori Wiesenfeld

Vice President & Editorial Director Robert Famighetti

GeoSystems Staff

Project Manager Keith Winters

Project Coordinator *(Encyclopedia map set)* Nancy Hamme

Associate Project Coordinator *(Encyclopedia map set)* Andrew DeWitt

Project Coordinator *(Atlas)* Andrew Green

Associate Project Coordinator *(Atlas)* Matt Tharp

Layout & Design
Jeannine Schonta, Andy Skinner

Research & Compilation
Marley Amstutz, John Clements, Ron Haag, Laura Hartwig, Bill Truninger

Research Librarian Luis Freile

GIS
John Fix, Mark Leitzell, Mike Marino, Brad Sauder, Dave Folk, Larry Meyers, Darrin Smith

Cartographers
Kumar Chaudhari, Wendy Crumbaugh, Sherri Cumberledge, Zach Davis, Linda Dows-Byers, Nicole Emmich, Michael Gadd, Brian Goudreau, Chris Gruber, Marc Hershey, Kendall Marten, Todd Martin, Jeff Martz, Tara McCoy, Justin Morrill, Tracey Morrill, Linda Peters, Hylon Plumb, Robert Rizzutti, West Rowles

Editors
Robert Harding, Dana Wolf

Production Support
Jill Luettgens, Nina Luettgens, Shawna Roberts, Brenda Stackler

Imagesetting/Proofing
Fred Hofferth, Ron Rittenhouse, Robin White

ISBN 0-8343-0110-5

Printed and manufactured in the United States of America

TABLE OF CONTENTS

LEGEND

POLAR REGIONS

UNITED STATES

General

- National Capital
- Territorial Capital
- Other City
- International Boundary (subject area)
- International Boundary (non-subject)
- Internal Boundary (state, province, etc.)
- Disputed Boundary
- Perennial River
- Intermittent River
- Canal
- Dam

U.S. States, Canadian Provinces & Territories

(additions and changes to general legend)

- State Capital
- County Seat
- Built Up Area
- State Boundary
- County Boundary
- National Park
- Other Park, Forest, Grassland
- Indian, Other Reservation
- Point of Interest
- Mountain Peak
- Continental Divide
- Time Zone Boundary
- Limited Access Highway
- Other Major Road
- 90 Highway Shield

PROJECTION

The only true representation of the earth, free of distortion, is a globe. Maps are flat, and the process by which the geographic locations (latitude and longitude) are transformed from a three-dimensional sphere to a two-dimensional flat map is called a Projection.

For a detailed explanation of Projections, see ***MapScope*** in Volume 2 of ***Funk & Wagnalls New Encyclopedia.***

This example is used on pages 20, 21 for India, Bangladesh, and Pakistan.

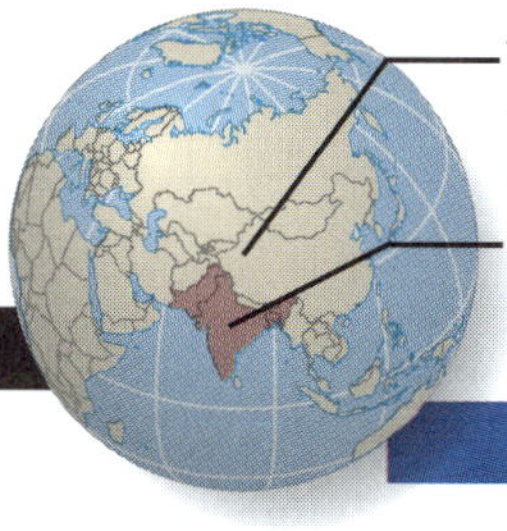

The Globe is centered on the continent of Asia, as shown on pages 6, 7.

The subject countries are shown in a stronger red/brown color.

LOCATOR

TYPES OF SCALE

Visual Scale

Every map has a bar scale, or a Visual Scale, that can be used for measuring. It shows graphically the relationship between map distance and ground distance.

Miles

One inch represents 1 mile

Kilometers

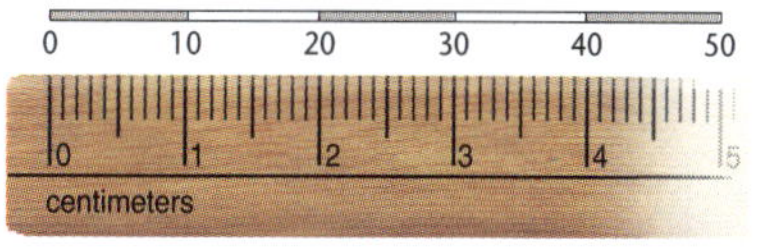

One centimeter represents 10 kilometers

Representative Fraction

The scale of a map, expressed as a numerical ratio of map distance to ground distance, is called a Representative Fraction (or RF). It is usually written as 1/50,000 or 1:50,000, meaning that one unit of measurement on the map represents 50,000 of the same units on the ground.

The World

Scale at the equator
1:116,400,000

0 1000 2000 3000 mi
0 1000 2000 3000 4000 km

Robinson Projection

1:30,000,000

0 250 500 750 mi
0 250 500 750 1000 km

Bipolar Oblique Conic Conformal Projection

ARCTIC OCEAN
GREENLAND (KALAALLIT NUNAAT) (Denmark)
Svalbard Is. (Norway)
Franz Josef Is. (Russia)
Jan Mayen (Norway)
ICELAND
Arctic Circle
Faeroe Is. (Denmark)
See inset below
EUROPE
ALPS
URAL MOUNTAINS
RUSSIA
ASIA
KAZAKHSTAN
MONGOLIA
Kuril Is. (Russia)
Azores Is. (Portugal)
GEORGIA
ARMENIA
TURKEY
UZBEKISTAN
KYRGYZSTAN
TURKMENISTAN
TAJIKISTAN
CHINA
NORTH KOREA
SOUTH KOREA
JAPAN
LEBANON
SYRIA
AZERBAIJAN
IRAN
AFGHANISTAN
HIMALAYAS
BHUTAN
MOROCCO
TUNISIA
ISRAEL
IRAQ
JORDAN
Canary Is. (Spain)
ALGERIA
KUWAIT
BAHRAIN
PAKISTAN
NEPAL
W. SAHARA (Morocco)
SAHARA
LIBYA
EGYPT
QATAR
SAUDI ARABIA
UNITED ARAB EMIRATES
INDIA
TAIWAN
International Date Line (Monday)
CAPE VERDE
MAURITANIA
MALI
NIGER
CHAD
SUDAN
OMAN
BANGLADESH
BURMA
LAOS
MACAU (Portugal)
SENEGAL
THE GAMBIA
GUINEA-BISSAU
GUINEA
SIERRA LEONE
LIBERIA
CÔTE D'IVOIRE
BURKINA FASO
GHANA
TOGO
BENIN
NIGERIA
AFRICA
ERITREA
YEMEN
DJIBOUTI
THAILAND
VIETNAM
PHILIPPINES
MARSHALL ISLANDS
Guam (U.S.)
ETHIOPIA
CENTRAL AFRICAN REP.
CAMEROON
SRI LANKA
CAMBODIA
PALAU
MICRONESIA
BRUNEI
MALAYSIA
SÃO TOME AND PRÍNCIPE
EQUATORIAL GUINEA
GABON
UGANDA
KENYA
SOMALIA
MALDIVES
SINGAPORE
KIRIBATI
RWANDA
REP. OF THE CONGO
DEM. REP. OF THE CONGO
BURUNDI
SEYCHELLES
NAURU
INDONESIA
PAPUA NEW GUINEA
SOLOMON ISLANDS
TANZANIA
INDIAN OCEAN
TUVALU
ANGOLA
MALAWI
COMOROS
ZAMBIA
MOZAMBIQUE
Cocos Is. (Australia)
VANUATU
FIJI
MADAGASCAR
MAURITIUS
ZIMBABWE
NAMIBIA
BOTSWANA
Réunion (France)
Tropic of Capricorn
New Caledonia (France)
AUSTRALIA
ATLANTIC OCEAN
SOUTH AFRICA
SWAZILAND
LESOTHO
NEW ZEALAND
N
Prime Meridian
Kerguelen Is. (France)
Antarctic Circle
ANTARCTICA
40° 20° 0° 20° 40° 60° 80° 100° 120° 140° 160° 180°
80° 60° 40° 20° 0° 20° 40° 60° 80°

FINLAND
NORWAY
SWEDEN
ESTONIA
IRELAND
GREAT BRITAIN
DENMARK
LATVIA
LITHUANIA
RUSSIA
NETHERLANDS
BELARUS
BELGIUM
GERMANY
POLAND
ATLANTIC OCEAN
LUXEMBOURG
CZECH REPUBLIC
UKRAINE
FRANCE
SLOVAKIA
SWITZERLAND
AUSTRIA
MOLDOVA
HUNGARY
SLOVENIA
CROATIA
ROMANIA
BOSNIA AND HERCEGOVINA
YUGOSLAVIA
PORTUGAL
SPAIN
ITALY
BULGARIA
Black Sea
GEORGIA
ALBANIA
F.Y.R. MACEDONIA
Gibraltar (Br.)
Mediterranean Sea
GREECE
TURKEY
MOROCCO
ALGERIA
TUNISIA
MALTA
CYPRUS
LEBANON
SYRIA
N
50° 40° 10° 0° 20° 30°
1:43,000,000
0 250 500 750 mi
0 250 500 750 1000 km
Azimuthal Equal Area Projection

MAJOR CITIES

Afghanistan	
Kabul	1,424,000
Bahrain	
Manama	151,000
Bangladesh	(metro)
Dhaka	3,459,000
Bhutan	
Thimphu	8,900
Brunei	
Band. Seri Begawan	51,000
Burma (Myanmar)	
Rangoon	2,513,000
Cambodia	
Phnom Penh	800,000
China	
Shanghai	7,500,000
Beijing	5,700,000
Tianjin	4,500,000
Shenyang	3,600,000
Wuhan	3,200,000
Guangzhou	2,900,000
Chongqing	2,700,000
Harbin	2,500,000
Chengdu	2,500,000
Zibo	2,200,000
Xi'an	2,200,000
Nanjing	2,091,000
Cyprus	(metro)
Nicosia	167,000
India	(metro)
Bombay	12,572,000
Calcutta	10,916,000
Delhi	8,375,000
Madras	5,361,000
Hyderabad	4,280,000
Bangalore	4,087,000
Indonesia	
Jakarta	8,200,000
Surabaya	2,400,000
Bandung	2,000,000
Medan	1,700,000
Iran	
Tehran	6,043,000
Mashhad	1,464,000
Iraq	
Baghdad	3,841,000
Israel	
Jerusalem	544,000
Japan	
Tokyo	8,164,000
Yokohama	3,220,000
Osaka	2,624,000
Nagoya	2,155,000
Sapporo	1,672,000
Kobe	1,477,000
Kyoto	1,461,000
Fukuoka	1,237,000
Kawasaki	1,174,000
Hiroshima	1,086,000
Jordan	
Amman	936,000
Kazakhstan	
Almaty	1,147,000
North Korea	
P'yŏngyang	2,300,000
South Korea	
Seoul	10,628,000
Pusan	3,798,000
Taegu	2,229,000
Kuwait	
Kuwait	78,000
Kyrgyzstan	
Bishkek	628,000
Laos	
Vientiane	377,000
Lebanon	
Beirut	475,000
Malaysia	
Kuala Lumpur	920,000
Maldives	
Male	55,000
Mongolia	
Ulan Bator	536,000
Nepal	
Kathmandu	419,000
Oman	
Masqat	85,000
Pakistan	(metro)
Karachi	5,181,000
Lahore	2,953,000
Faisalabad	1,104,000
Islamabad	204,000
Philippines	(metro)
Manila	1,895,000
Qatar	
Doha	236,000
Russia (Asian)	
Novosibirsk	1,442,000
Yekaterinburg	1,371,000
Omsk	1,169,000
Chelyabinsk	1,143,000
Krasnoyarsk	925,000
Saudi Arabia	
Riyadh	1,300,000
Jiddah	1,200,000
Singapore	
Singapore	2,818,000
Sri Lanka	
Colombo	615,000
Syria	
Damascus	1,451,000
Halab (Aleppo)	1,445,000
Taiwan	
Taipei	1,770,000
Tajikistan	
Dushanbe	602,000
Thailand	
Bangkok	5,876,000
Turkey (Asian)	
Ankara	2,559,000
İzmir	1,757,000
Turkmenistan	
Ashgabat	407,000
United Arab Emirates	
Abu Dhabi	722,000
Uzbekistan	
Tashkent	2,094,000
Vietnam	
Ho Chi Minh City	2,900,000
Hanoi	1,090,000
Yemen	(metro)
Sana	427,000

International comparability of city population data is limited by various data inconsistencies.

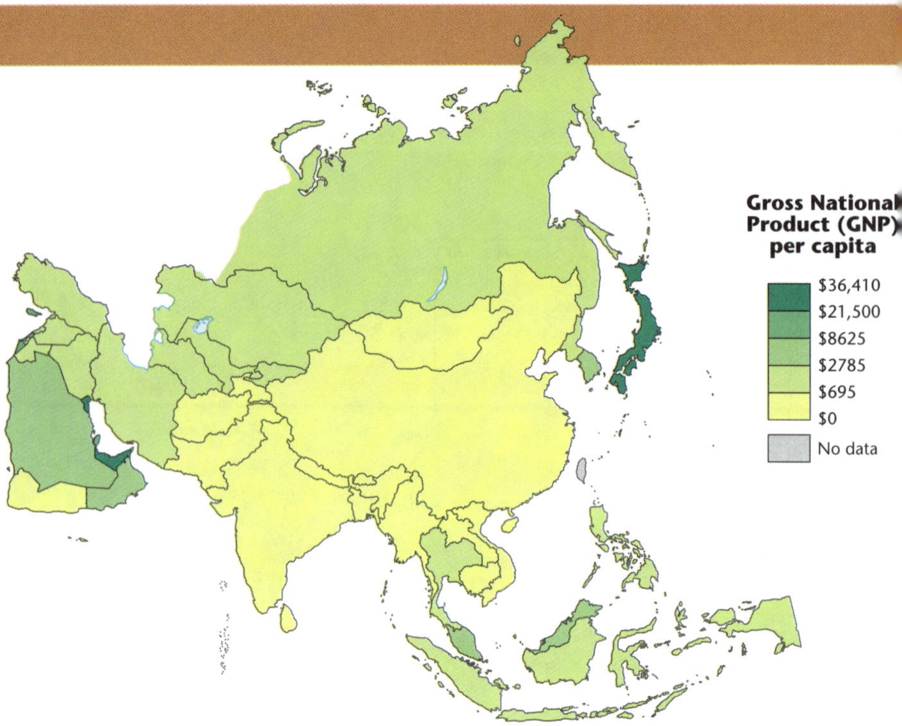

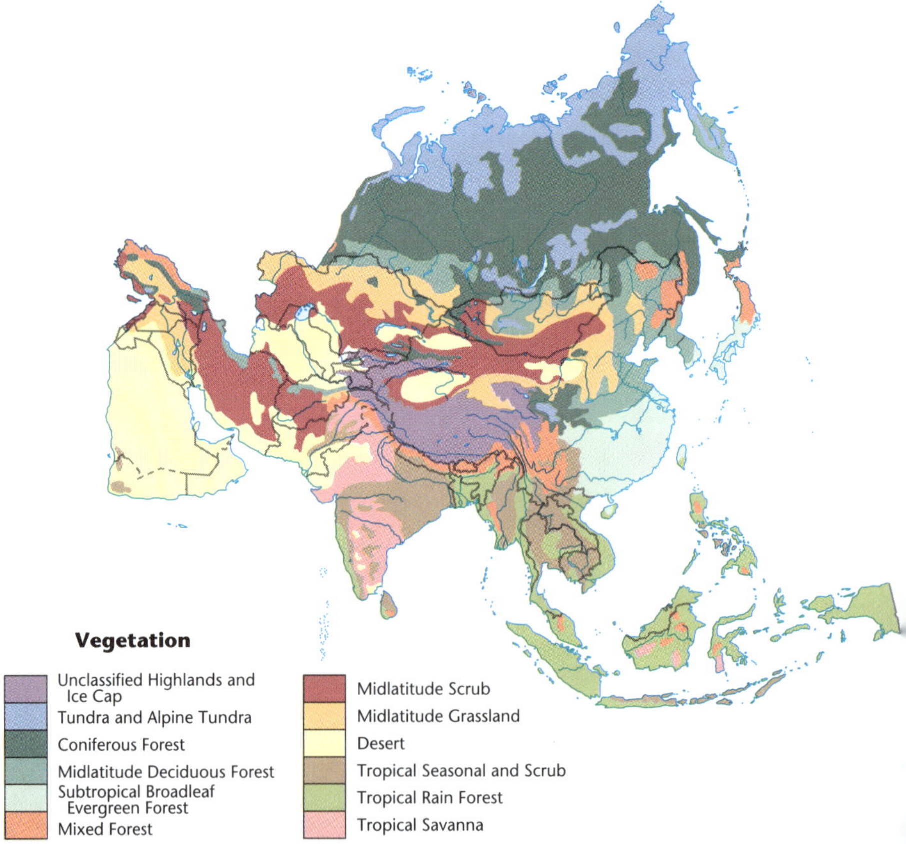

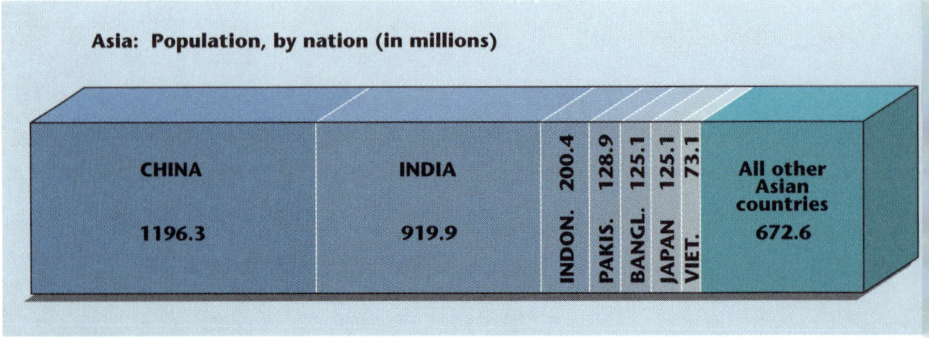

ARCTIC OCEAN
PACIFIC OCEAN
INDIAN OCEAN
RUSSIA
CHINA
MONGOLIA
KAZAKHSTAN
INDIA
JAPAN
PHILIPPINES
INDONESIA
MALAYSIA
THAILAND
VIETNAM
CAMBODIA
LAOS
BURMA (MYANMAR)
PAKISTAN
AFGHANISTAN
IRAN
IRAQ
SAUDI ARABIA
TURKEY
YEMEN
OMAN
SRI LANKA
NEPAL
BHUTAN
BANGLADESH
TAIWAN
N. KOREA
S. KOREA
UZBEKISTAN
TURKMENISTAN
SYRIA
JORDAN
LEBANON
ISRAEL
CYPRUS
KUWAIT
BAHRAIN
QATAR
UNITED ARAB EMIRATES
MALDIVES
BRUNEI
SINGAPORE
HONG KONG
MACAU (PORT.)
PLATEAU OF TIBET
Mt. Everest 8848 m (29,028 ft)
HIMALAYAS
GOBI DESERT
TAKLA MAKAN DESERT
KUNLUN MTS.
URAL MTS.
ZAGROS MTS.
HINDU KUSH
TIEN SHAN
RUB AL-KHALI
WESTERN GHATS
EASTERN GHATS
Bering Strait
BERING SEA
SEA OF OKHOTSK
SEA OF JAPAN
EAST CHINA SEA
SOUTH CHINA SEA
PHILIPPINE SEA
Yellow Sea
Celebes Sea
Sulu Sea
Banda Sea
Arafura Sea
Timor Sea
JAVA SEA
BAY OF BENGAL
ARABIAN SEA
Andaman Sea
Gulf of Thailand
Gulf of Aden
Gulf of Oman
RED SEA
Black Sea
Caspian Sea
Aral Sea
L. Balkhash
L. Baikal
Laptev Sea
Kara Sea
East Siberian Sea
Chukchi Sea
Wrangel I.
Franz Josef Land
Severnaya Zemlya
Novaya Zemlya
Sakhalin
Kuril Is.
Hokkaido
Honshu
Kyushu
Ryukyu Is. (JAPAN)
Luzon
Mindanao
Borneo
Celebes
Sumatra
Java
Timor
New Guinea
Hainan
Andaman Is. (INDIA)
Nicobar Is. (INDIA)
Laccadive Is. (INDIA)
Socotra (YEMEN)
Norilsk
Yakutsk
Magadan
Anadyr
Petropavlovsk-Kamchatskiy
Yekaterinburg
Chelyabinsk
Omsk
Novosibirsk
Tomsk
Krasnoyarsk
Bratsk
Irkutsk
Ulan-Ude
Chita
Novokuznetsk
Pavlodar
Semey
Qaraghandy
Komsomol'sk-na-Amure
Blagoveshchensk
Khabarovsk
Vladivostok
Harbin
Changchun
Shenyang
Ulan Bator
Dund-Us
Ürümqi
Beijing
Tianjin
Hohhot
Taiyuan
Jinan
Qingdao
Dalian
P'yongyang
Seoul
Pusan
Sapporo
Sendai
Tokyo
Yokohama
Kyoto
Kobe
Osaka
Kitakyushu
Shanghai
Nanjing
Wuhan
Zhengzhou
Xi'an
Lanzhou
Chengdu
Chongqing
Changsha
Nanchang
Fuzhou
Taipei
Kunming
Nanning
Guangzhou
Macau
Hanoi
Vientiane
Da Nang
Bangkok
Phnom Penh
Ho Chi Minh City
Manila
Quezon City
Davao
Kota Kinabalu
Bandar Seri Begawan
Kuching
Kuala Lumpur
Medan
Singapore
Padang
Palembang
Jakarta
Bandung
Surabaya
Banjarmasin
Ujung Pandang
Manado
Jayapura
Rangoon
Mandalay
Dhaka
Calcutta
Thimphu
Kathmandu
Lucknow
Kanpur
Delhi
New Delhi
Jaipur
Ahmadabad
Bombay
Nagpur
Hyderabad
Bangalore
Madras
Madurai
Colombo
Male
Lahore
Faisalabad
Islamabad
Karachi
Kabul
Kashi
Dushanbe
Tashkent
Bishkek
Almaty
Ashgabat
Mashhad
Tehran
Esfahan
Tabriz
Baghdad
Basra
Kuwait
Riyadh
Manama
Doha
Abu Dhabi
Masqat
Jiddah
Mecca
Sana
Aden
Damascus
Amman
Jerusalem
Beirut
Nicosia
Ankara
İzmir
0 500 1000 1500 mi
0 500 1000 1500 2000 km
N
ELEVATIONS
Feet Meters
13,120 4000
6560 2000
1640 500
656 200
0 0
Below sea level
CITIES
National Capital
Territorial Capital
Other City

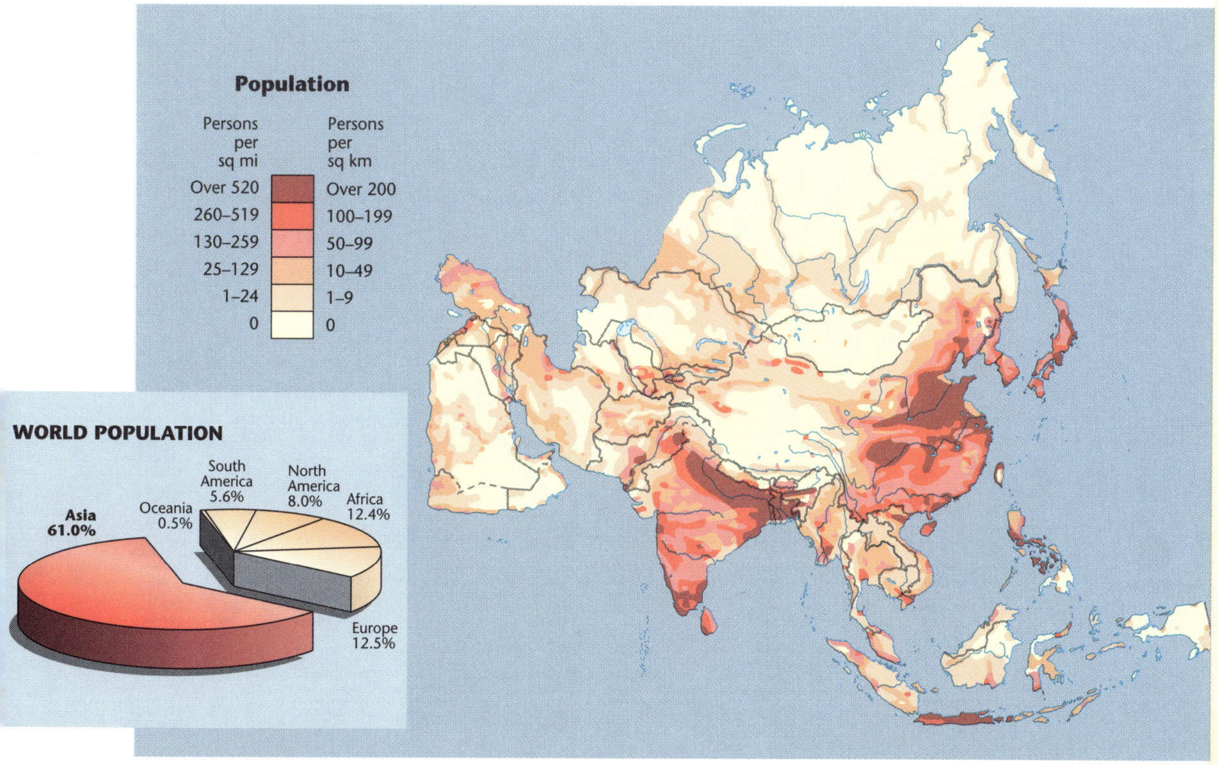
Population
Persons per sq mi
Persons per sq km
Over 520 Over 200
260–519 100–199
130–259 50–99
25–129 10–49
1–24 1–9
0 0
WORLD POPULATION
Asia 61.0%
Oceania 0.5%
South America 5.6%
North America 8.0%
Africa 12.4%
Europe 12.5%

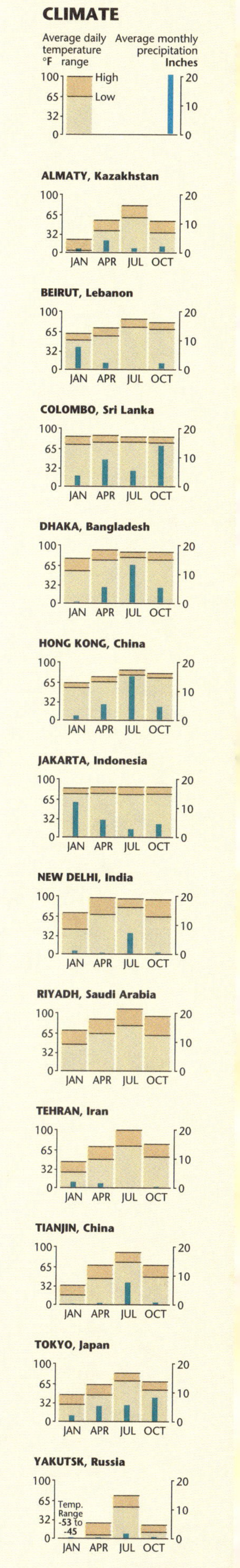
CLIMATE
Average daily temperature °F range
Average monthly precipitation Inches
High
Low
ALMATY, Kazakhstan
BEIRUT, Lebanon
COLOMBO, Sri Lanka
DHAKA, Bangladesh
HONG KONG, China
JAKARTA, Indonesia
NEW DELHI, India
RIYADH, Saudi Arabia
TEHRAN, Iran
TIANJIN, China
TOKYO, Japan
YAKUTSK, Russia
Temp. Range -53 to -45
JAN APR JUL OCT

Japan

Capital: Tokyo
Area: 145,850 sq. mi.
377,850 sq. km.
Population: 125,107,000
Largest City: Tokyo
Language: Japanese
Monetary Unit: Yen

Japan: Map Index

Prefectures

Aichi	C3
Akita	D2
Aomori	D1
Chiba	D3
Ehime	B3
Fukui	C3
Fukuoka	A3
Fukushima	C2
Gifu	C3
Gumma	C2
Hiroshima	B3
Hokkaido	D1, Inset I
Hyogo	B3
Ibaraki	D2
Ishikawa	C2
Iwate	D2
Kagawa	B3
Kagoshima	A4
Kanagawa	C3
Kochi	B3
Kumamoto	A3
Kyoto	B3
Mie	C3
Miyagi	D2
Miyazaki	A3
Nagano	C3
Nagasaki	A3
Nara	B3
Niigata	C2
Oita	A3
Okayama	B3
Okinawa	Inset II
Osaka	B3
Saga	A3
Saitama	C2
Shiga	C3
Shimane	B3
Shizuoka	C3
Tochigi	C2
Tokushima	B3
Tokyo	C3
Tottori	B3
Toyama	C2
Wakayama	B3
Yamagata	C2
Yamaguchi	A3
Yamanashi	C3

Cities and Towns

Aizuwakamatsu	C2
Akashi	B3
Akita	D2
Amagasaki	B3
Aomori	D1
Asahikawa	Inset I
Ashikaga	C2
Awaji	B3
Chiba	D3
Chitose	Inset I
Fujisawa	C3
Fukue	A3
Fukui	C2
Fukuoka	A3
Fukushima	D2
Fukuyama	B3
Funabashi	D3
Gifu	C3
Gotsu	B3
Gushikawa	Inset II
Haboro	Inset I
Hachinohe	D1
Hachioji	C3
Hakodate	D1, Inset I
Hamamatsu	C3
Higashiosaka	B3
Himeji	B3
Hirakata	B3
Hirara	Inset II
Hirosake	D1
Hiroshima	B3
Hitachi	D2
Ibaraki	B3
Ichihara	D3
Ichikawa	D3
Ichinomiya	C3
Ise	C3
Ishinomaki	D2
Iwaki	D2
Iwakuni	B3
Izuhara	A3
Joetsu	C2
Kagoshima	A4
Kanazawa	C2
Kashiwa	D3
Kasugai	C3
Kawagoe	C3
Kawaguchi	C3
Kawasaki	C3
Kitakyushu	A3
Kitami	Inset I
Kobe	B3
Kochi	B3
Kofu	C3
Komatsu	C2
Koriyama	D2
Koshigaya	C3
Kumamoto	A3
Kurashiki	B3
Kure	B3
Kurume	A3
Kushiro	Inset I
Kyoto	B3
Machida	C3
Maebashi	C2
Maizuru	B3
Masuda	A3
Matsudo	C3
Matsue	B3
Matsumae	D1, Inset I
Matsumoto	C2
Matsuyama	B3
Mito	D2
Miyako	D2
Miyakonojo	A4
Miyazaki	A4
Mombetsu	Inset I
Morioka	D2
Muroran	D1, Inset I
Mutsu	D1
Nagano	C2
Nagaoka	C2
Nagasaki	A3
Nagoya	C3
Naha	Inset II
Nara	B3
Naze	Inset II
Nemuro	Inset I
Neyagawa	B3
Niigata	C2
Niihama	B3
Nikko	C2
Nishinomiya	B3
Nobeoka	A3
Numazu	C3
Obihiro	Inset I
Oita	A3
Okayama	B3
Okazaki	C3
Omiya	C3
Omuta	A3
Osaka	B3
Otaru	Inset I
Otsu	B3
Ryotsu	C2
Saga	A3
Sagamihara	C3
Sakai	B3
Sapporo	Inset I
Sasebo	A3
Sendai	D2
Shimizu	C3
Shimonoseki	A3
Shizuoka	C3
Suita	B3
Takamatsu	B3
Takatsuki	B3
Tanabe	B3
Tokorozawa	C3
Tokushima	B3
Tokuyama	A3
Tokyo, *capital*	C3
Tomakomai	Inset I
Tottori	B3
Toyama	C2
Toyohashi	C3
Toyonaka	B3
Toyota	C3
Tsuruga	C3
Tsuruoka	C2
Ube	A3
Urawa	C3
Utsunomiya	C2
Uwajima	B3
Wakayama	B3
Wakkanai	Inset I
Yamagata	D2
Yamaguchi	A3
Yao	B3
Yatsushiro	A3

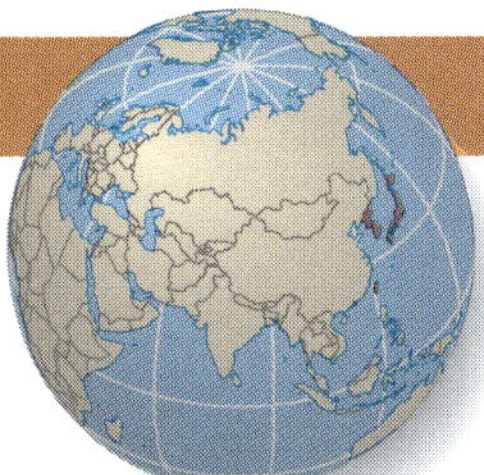

Japan: Map Index
Yokkaichi C3
Yokohama C3
Yokosuka C3
Yonago B3
Yubari .... Inset I

Other Features
Akuseki, *island* A4
Amakusa, *islands* A3
Amami, *island* .... Inset II
Amami, *islands* .... Inset II
Asahi Dake, *mt.* .... Inset I
Asama, *mt.* C2
Ashizuri, *cape* B3
Aso, *mt.* A3
Awaji, *island* B3
Biwa, *lake* B3
Bonin, *islands* .... Inset III
Boso, *peninsula* D3
Bungo, *channel* B3
Chichi, *island* .... Inset III
Chugoku, *mts.* B3
Dogo, *island* B2
Dozen, *island* B2
East China, *sea* A4
Erimo, *cape* .... Inset I
Fuji, *mt.* C3
Fukue, *island* A3
Hachijo, *island* C3
Haha, *island* .... Inset III
Henashi, *cape* C1
Hidaka, *mts.* .... Inset I
Hino, *cape* B3
Hokkaido, *island* .... D1, Inset I
Honshu, *island* C2
Iki, *island* A3
Inland, *sea* B3
Iriomote, *island* .... Inset II
Ise, *bay* C3
Ishigaki, *island* .... Inset II
Ishikari, *river* .... Inset I
Ishinomaki, *bay* D2
Ishizuchi, *mt.* B3
Iwo Jima, *island* .... Inset III
Izu, *islands* C3
Izu, *peninsula* C3
Japan, *sea* B2
Japanese Alps, *mts.* C3
Kakeroma, *island* .... Inset II
Kamui, *cape* .... Inset I
Kii, *channel* B3
Kii, *peninsula* B3
Kita, *island* .... Inset III
Kitakami, *river* D2
Kitami, *mts.* .... Inset I
Korea, *strait* A3
Koshiki, *islands* A4
Kozu, *island* C3
Kuchino, *island* A4
Kume, *island* .... Inset II
Kyushu, *island* A3
La Pérouse, *strait* .... Inset I
Mikura, *island* C3
Minami, *island* .... Inset III
Miyake, *island* C3
Miyako, *island* .... Inset II
Mogami, *river* D2
Muko, *island* .... Inset III
Muroto, *cape* B3
Nakadori, *island* A3
Nakano, *island* A4
Nemuro, *strait* .... Inset I
Nii, *island* C3
Nishino, *island* .... Inset III
Nojima, *cape* D3
Noto, *peninsula* C2
Okhotsk, *sea* .... Inset I
Oki, *islands* B2
Okinawa, *island* .... Inset II
Okinawa, *islands* .... Inset II
Okino Erabu, *island* .... Inset II
Okushiri, *island* .... C1, Inset I
Oshima, *peninsula* .. D1, Inset I
Osumi, *islands* A4
Osumi, *peninsula* A4
Osumi, *strait* A4
Ou, *mts.* D2
Rebun, *island* .... Inset I
Rishiri, *island* .... Inset I
Ryukyu, *islands* .... A4, Inset II
Sado, *island* C2
Sagami, *bay* C3
Sakishima, *islands* .... Inset II
Sata, *cape* A4
Satsuma, *peninsula* A4
Senkaku, *islands* .... Inset II
Shikoku, *island* B3
Shimonoseki, *strait* A3
Shinano, *river* C2
Shiono, *cape* B3
Shirane, *mt.* C3
Shiretoko, *cape* .... Inset I
Soya, *point* .... Inset I
Suwanose, *island* A4
Takara, *island* A4
Tanega, *island* A4
Tenryu, *river* C3
Teshio, *river* .... Inset I
Tokachi, *river* .... Inset I
Tokara, *islands* A4
Tokuno, *island* .... Inset II
Tone, *river* C2
Tosa, *bay* B3
Towada, *lake* D1
Toyama, *bay* C2
Tsu, *island* A3
Tsugaru, *strait* .... D1, Inset I
Uchiura, *bay* .... Inset I
Volcano, *islands* .... Inset III
Wakasa, *bay* B3
Yaku, *island* A4
Yariga, *mt.* C2
Yonaguni, *island* .... Inset II
Yoron, *island* .... Inset II
Yoshino, *river* B3
Zao, *mt.* D2

© GeoSystems Global Corp.

North Korea: Map Index

Provinces
Chagang B2
Kaesŏng B3
Kangwŏn B3
Namp'o A3
North Hamgyŏng C1
North Hwanghae B3
North P'yŏngan A2
P'yŏngyang A3
South Hamgyŏng B2
South Hwanghae A3
South P'yŏngan B3
Yanggang B2

Cities and Towns
Anju A3
Changjin B2
Changyŏn A3
Ch'ŏngjin C2
Chŏngju A3
Haeju A3
Hamhŭng B3
Hoeryŏng C1
Hŭich'ŏn B2
Hŭngnam B3
Hyesan C2
Ich'ŏn B3
Kaesŏng B4
Kanggye B2
Kilchu C2
Kimch'aek C2
Kosŏng C3
Kowŏn B3
Kusŏng A3
Manp'o B2
Musan C1
Najin D1
Namp'o A3
Ongjin A4
Onsŏng C1
P'anmunjŏm B4
Pukch'ŏng C2
P'ungsan C2
P'yŏnggang B3
P'yŏngsan B3
P'yŏngsŏng A3
P'yŏngyang, *capital* A3
Sariwŏn A3
Sinp'o C2
Sinŭiju A2
Songnim A3
Tanch'ŏn C2
Wŏnsan B3
Yangdŏk B3

Other Features
Chaeryŏng, *river* A3
Changjin, *river* B2
Ch'ongch'ŏn, *river* A3
Hamgyŏng, *mts.* C2
Imjin, *river* B3
Kanghwa, *bay* A4
Korea, *bay* A3
Musu-dan, *point* C2
Nangnim-sanmaek, *mts.* B3
Paektu-san, *mt.* C2
Sŏjosŏn, *bay* A3
Sup'ung, *reservoir* A2
Taedong, *river* B3
Tongjosŏn, *bay* B3
Tumen, *river* C1
Yalu, *river* B2

South Korea: Map Index

Provinces
Cheju .... Inset
Inch'ŏn B4
Kangwŏn B4
Kwangju B5
Kyŏnggi B4
North Chŏlla B5
North Ch'ungch'ŏng B4
North Kyŏngsang C4
Pusan C5
Seoul B4
South Chŏlla B5
South Ch'ungch'ŏng B4
South Kyŏngsang C5
Taegu C5
Taejŏn B4

Cities and Towns
Andong C4
Anyang B4
Chech'ŏn C4
Cheju .... Inset
Chinhae C5
Chinju C5
Chonju B5
Ch'ŏnan B4
Ch'ŏngju B4
Ch'unch'ŏn B4
Ch'ungju B4
Inch'ŏn B4
Iri B5
Kangnŭng C4
Kimch'ŏn C4
Kunsan B5
Kwangju B5
Kyŏngju C5
Masan C5
Mokp'o B5
Munsan B4
Nonsan B4
P'ohang C4
Pusan C5
Samch'ŏk C4
Seoul, *capital* B4
Sokch'o C3
Sŏngnam B4
Sunch'ŏn B5
Suwŏn B4
Taegu C5
Taejŏn B4
Ulchin C4
Ulsan C5
Wŏnju B4
Wando B5
Yŏngju C4
Yŏsu B5

Other Features
Cheju, *island* .... Inset
Cheju, *strait* .... Inset
Halla-san, *mt.* .... Inset
Han, *river* B4
Hŭksan Chedo, *islands* A5
Kanghwa, *bay* A4
Koje-do, *island* C5
Korea, *strait* C5
Kum, *river* B4
Naktong, *river* C5
Soan-kundo, *islands* B5
Sobaek, *mts.* B5
Taebaek-Sanmaek, *mts.* C3
Tŏkchŏk-kundo, *islands* A4
Ullŭng-do, *island* D4
Western, *channel* C5

North Korea

Capital: P'yŏngyang
Area: 47,399 sq. mi.
122,795 sq. km.
Population: 23,067,000
Largest City: P'yŏngyang
Language: Korean
Monetary Unit: Won

South Korea

Capital: Seoul
Area: 38,330 sq. mi.
99,301 sq. km.
Population: 45,083,000
Largest City: Seoul
Language: Korean
Monetary Unit: Won

© GeoSystems Global Corp.

Taiwan

Capital: Taipei
Area: 13,969 sq. mi.
36,189 sq. km.
Population: 21,299,000
Largest City: Taipei
Language: Mandarin Chinese
Monetary Unit: New Taiwan dollar

Taiwan: Map Index

Cities and Towns
Changhua B1
Chiai B2
Chilung B1
Chunan B1
Chungho B1
Chungli B1
Fangliao B2
Fengshan B2
Fengyüan B1
Hengch'un B2
Hsinchu B1
Hsinchuang B1
Hsintien B1
Hsinying B2
Hualien B2
Ilan B1
Kangshan B2
Kaohsiung B2
Makung A2
Miaoli B1
Nant'ou B2
Panch'iao B1
P'ingtung B2
Shanchung B1
T'aichung B1
T'ainan B2
Taipei, *capital* B1
T'aitung B2
Tanshui B1
T'aoyüan B1
Touliu B2
Yungho B1

Other Features
Choshui, *river* B2
Chungyang, *range* B2
East China, *sea* B1
Kaop'ing, *river* B2
Lan, *island* B2
Lü, *island* B2
Luzon, *strait* B3
P'enghu (Pescadores), *islands* A2
Pescadores, *channel* A2
Philippine, *sea* B2
South China, *sea* A2
Taiwan, *strait* A1
Tanshui, *river* B1
Tsengwen, *river* B2
Yü Shan, *mt.* B2

CHINA, HONG KONG

China

Capital: Beijing
Area: 3,696,500 sq. mi.
9,573,900 sq. km.
Population: 1,196,272,000
Largest City: Shanghai
Language: Mandarin Chinese
Monetary Unit: Yuan

China:
Map Index

Internal Divisions
Provinces
Anhui E2
Fujian E3
Gansu C1, D2
Guangdong....E3
Guizhou D3
Hainan....D4
Hebei E2
Heilongjiang....F1
Henan E2
Hubei E2
Hunan E3
Jiangsu E2
Jiangxi....E3
Jilin....F1
Liaoning F1
Qinghai C2
Shaanxi D2
Shandong E2
Shanxi....E2
Sichuan D2
Yunnan....C3
Zhejiang....E3

Autonomous Regions
Guangxi Zhuang D3
Inner Mongolia E1
Ningxia Hui....D2
Tibet (Xizang) B2
Xinjiang Uygur....B1

Independent Municipalities
Beijing....E1
Shanghai....F2
Tianjin....E2

Special Administrative Region (S.A.R.)
Hong Kong ....E3, Inset

Cities and Towns
Aksu....B1
Aberdeen ....Inset
Altay B1
Ankang....D2
Anqing....E2
Anshan....F1
Anyang E2
Baicheng F1
Baoding E2
Baoshan....C3
Baotou E1
Batang....C3
Bei'an....F1
Beihai D3
Beijing, *capital*....E2
Bengbu E2
Benxi....F1
Cangzhou E2
Changchun F1
Changde....E3
Changsha....E3
Changzhi E2
Changzhou F2
Chek Keng ....Inset
Chengde....E1
Chengdu....D2
Chifeng....E1
Chongqing....D3
Chung Hau ....Inset
Dachang D3
Dali D2
Dalian....F2
Dandong....F1
Danjiangkou....E2
Daqing....F1
Datong....E1
Erenhot E1
Fushun F1
Fuxin....F1
Fuzhou....E3
Ganzhou E3
Gejiu D3
Golmud....C2
Guangzhou E3
Guilin....E3
Guiyang D3
Haikou....E4
Hailar E1
Hami C1
Handan....E2
Hangzhou F2
Hanzhong D2
Harbin....F1
Hefei E2
Hegang G1
Hengyang E3
Hohhot E1
Hotan A2
Huainan E2
Jiamusi....G1
Ji'an....E3
Jilin....F1
Jinan....E2
Jingdezhen E3
Jining E2
Jinzhou....F1
Jiujiang....E3
Jixi....G1
Kaifeng....E2
Kashi....A2
Korla B1
Kowloon ....Inset
Kunming D3
Lanzhou D2
Lenghu....C2
Lhasa....C3
Lianyungang E2
Liaoyang F1
Liaoyuan....F1
Liuzhou D3
Lo Wu ....Inset
Luoyang....E2
Luzhou....D3
Mudanjiang....F1
Nanchang....E3
Nanchong....D2
Nanjing....E2
Nanning....D3
Nanyang....E2
Neijiang....D3
New Kowloon ....Inset
Ningbo....F3
Penzhihua D3
Pingxiang....E3
Qingdao....F2
Qinhuangdao....E2
Qiqihar....F1
Quanzhou E3
Sai Kung ....Inset
Sha Tin ....Inset
Shache....A2
Shanghai....F2
Shantou E3
Shanxi....F3
Shaoguan....E3
Shaoxing....F3
Shaoyang....E3
Shashi....E2
Shek Pik ....Inset
Shenyang....F1
Shijiazhuang....E2
Siping....F1
Suzhou....F2
Tai'an E2
Taiyuan E2
Tangshan E2
Tianjin....E2
Tonghua....F1
Tongliao....F1
Tsuen Wan....Inset
Tuen Mun ....Inset
Ürümqi B1
Weifang....E2
Wenshan D3
Wenzhou....F3
Wuhan E2
Wuhu E2
Wuwei....D2
Wuxi....F2
Wuzhong....D2
Wuzhou E3
Xiamen E3
Xi'an....D2
Xiangfan E2
Xiangtan E3
Xigaze....B3
Xining D2
Xinxiang....E2
Xinyang....E2
Xuzhou E2
Ya'an D2
Yangquan....E2
Yangzhou....E2
Yanji....F1
Yantai....F2
Yibin....D3
Yichang....E2
Yichun....F1
Yinchuan....D2
Yingkou....F1
Yining B1
Yuen Long ....Inset
Yueyang....E3
Yumen....C2
Yushu C2
Zhangjiakou....E1
Zhangye....D2
Zhanjiang....E3
Zhengzhou....E2
Zhenjiang....E2
Zhuzhou E3
Zibo E2
Zigong D3
Zunyi....D3

Other Features
Altai, *mts.*....B1
Altun, *range*....B2
Bayan Har, *range* C2
Bo Hai, *gulf* E2
Bosten, *lake*....B1
Brahmaputra, *river* B3
Chang (Yangtze), *river* .D2, E2
Deep, *bay* ....Inset
Dongting, *lake* E3
Dzungaria, *desert basin* B1
East China, *sea* F3
Fen, *river* E2
Gan, *river* E3
Gobi, *desert*....D1
Greater Hinggan, *range*....F1
Great Wall of China....D2
Han, *river*....E2
Heilong (Amur), *river*....F1
Himalayas, *mts.*....B3
Hong Kong, *island* ....Inset
Hongze, *lake* E2
Huai, *river*....E2
Huang (Yellow), *river* ...D2, E2
Hulun, *lake*....E1
Indus, *river*....A2
Jinsha (Yangtze), *river*....C2
Khanka, *lake*....G1
Kunlun, *mts.*....B2
K2 (Godwin Austen), *mt.* ...A2
Lantau, *island* ....Inset
Lesser Hinggan, *range*....F1
Liao, *river*....F1
Loess, *plateau*....D2
Lop, *lake*....C1
Manchurian, *plain* F1
Mekong, *river* C2
Nan Ling, *mts.*....E3
New Territories, *island* ....Inset
North China, *plain*....E2
Pamirs, *region* A2
Poyang, *lake*....E3
Qaidam, *basin* C2
Qilian, *range*....C2
Qinghai, *lake* C2
Qin Ling, *mts.*....D2
Salween, *river* C2
Songhua, *river* F1
South China, *sea* ....E4, Inset
StoneCutters (S.I.), *island* Inset

Tai, *lake*....F2
Taiwan, *strait*....E3
Takla Makan, *desert*....B2
Tanggula, *range*....C2
Tarim, *river*....B1
Tibet, *plateau*....B2
Tien Shan, *range*....A1
Tonkin, *gulf*....D4
Turfan, *depression* C1
Ulansuhai, *lake* D1
Wei, *river* D2
Xi, *river*....E3
Yalu, *river*....F1
Yangtze, *river* C2, D2
Yellow, *sea*....F2
Yin Shan, *mts.* E1
Yuan, *river* D3
Zhu, *river*....E3

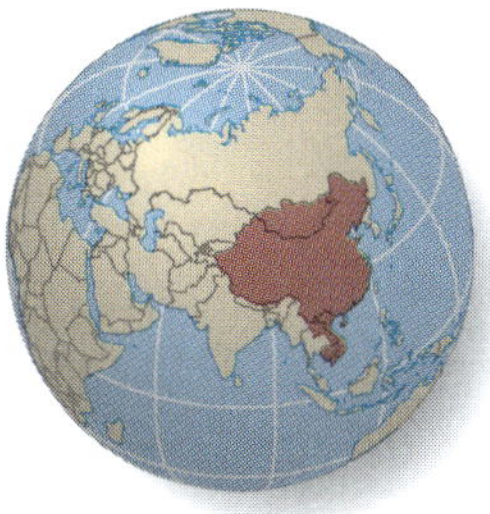

Vietnam

Capital: Hanoi
Area: 127,246 sq. mi.
329,653 sq. km.
Population: 73,104,000
Largest City: Ho Chi Minh City
Language: Vietnamese
Monetary Unit: Dong

Vietnam:
Map Index

Laos

Capital: Vientiane
Area: 91,429 sq. mi.
236,085 sq. km.
Population: 4,702,000
Largest City: Vientiane
Language: Lao
Monetary Unit: New kip

Laos:
Map Index

Mongolia

Capital: Ulan Bator
Area: 604,800 sq. mi.
1,566,839 sq. km.
Population: 2,430,000
Largest City: Ulan Bator
Language: Mongolian
Monetary Unit: Tughrik

Mongolia:
Map Index

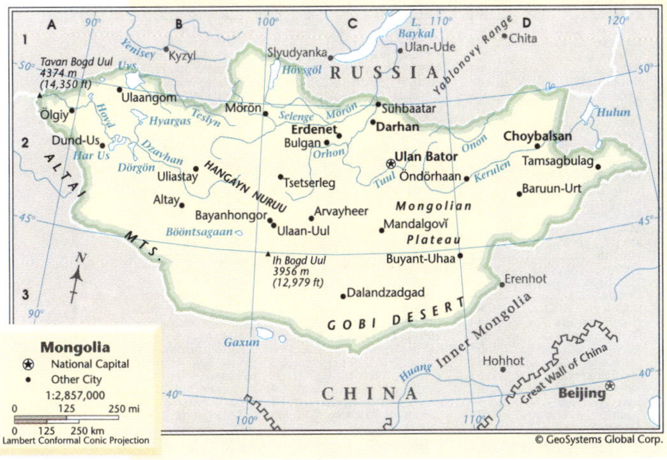

Cambodia

Capital: Phnom Penh
Area: 70,238 sq. mi.
181,964 sq. km.
Population: 10,265,000
Largest City: Phnom Penh
Language: Khmer
Monetary Unit: New riel

Cambodia:
Map Index

Thailand

Capital: Bangkok
Area: 198,115 sq. mi. 513,251 sq. km.
Population: 59,510,000
Largest City: Bangkok
Language: Thai
Monetary Unit: Baht

Thailand: Map Index

Cities and Towns

Aranyaprathet C3
Bangkok, *capital* B3
Ban Phai C2
Buriram C3
Chaiyaphum C3
Chiang Mai B2
Chiang Rai B2
Chon Buri B3
Chumphon B4
Hat Yai B5
Hua Hin B3
Khon Kaen C2
Lampang B2
Lamphun B2
Loei B2
Lop Buri B3
Nakhon Phanom C2
Nakhon Ratchasima C3
Nakhon Sawan B3
Nakhon Si Thammarat B4
Nam Tok B3
Nan B2
Narathiwat B5
Nong Khai C2
Nonthaburi B3
Pattani B5
Phatthalung B5
Phayao B2
Phetchabun B2
Phetchaburi B3
Phichit B2
Phitsanulok B2
Phrae B2
Phra Nakhon Si Ayutthaya B3
Phuket B5
Prachuap Khiri Khan B4
Ranong B4
Ratchaburi B3
Rayong B3
Roi Et C2
Sakon Nakhon C2
Sara Buri B3
Sattahip B3
Sisaket C3
Songkhla B5
Sukhothai B2
Surat Thani B4
Surin C3
Tak B2
Takua Pa B4
Trang B5
Trat C3
Ubon Ratchathani C3
Udon Thani C2
Uttaradit B2
Yala B5

Other Features

Bilauktaung, *range* B3
Chao Phraya, *river* B3
Chi, *river* C2
Dangrek, *mts.* C3
Dawna, *range* B2
Inthanon, *mt.* B2
Khorat, *plateau* C3
Ko Chang, *island* C3
Ko Kut, *island* C4
Ko Phangan, *island* B4
Ko Samui, *island* B4
Ko Tarutao, *island* B5
Kra, *isthmus* B4
Laem, *mt.* B3
Lam Pao, *reservoir* C2
Luang, *mt.* B4
Mae Klong, *river* B3
Malacca, *strait* B5
Malay, *peninsula* B4
Mekong, *river* C2
Mun, *river* C3
Nan, *river* B2
Pa Sak, *river* B3
Phetchabun, *range* B3
Ping, *river* B2
Salween, *river* A2
Sirinthorn, *reservoir* C3
Srinagarind, *reservoir* B3
Tanen, *range* B2
Thailand, *gulf* B4
Thale Luang, *lagoon* B5
Yom, *river* B2

Burma: Map Index

States and Divisions

Chin, *state* B2
Irrawaddy, *division* B3
Kachin, *state* C1
Karen, *state* C3
Kayah, *state* C2
Magwe, *division* B2
Mandalay, *division* B2
Mon, *state* C3
Pegu, *division* B3
Rakhine, *state* B2
Rangoon, *division* C3
Sagaing, *division* B2
Shan, *state* C2
Tenasserim, *division* C3

Cities and Towns

Bassein B3
Bhamo C1
Haka B2
Henzada B3
Kawthaung C4
Keng Tung C2
Kyaukpyu B2
Lashio C2
Loi-kaw C2
Mandalay C2
Maymyo C2
Meiktila B2
Mergui C3
Monywa B2
Moulmein C3
Myingyan B2
Myitkyina C1
Pa-an C3
Pegu C3
Prome B2
Putao C1
Rangoon, *capital* C3
Sagaing B2
Shwebo B2
Sittwe B2
Tamu B1
Taunggyi C2
Tavoy C3
Toungoo C2
Ye C3

Other Features

Andaman, *sea* B3
Arakan Yoma, *mts.* B2
Bengal, *bay* B3
Bilauktaung, *range* C3
Cheduba, *island* B2
Chin, *hills* B2
Chindwin, *river* B1
Coco, *islands* B3
Hkakabo Razi, *mt.* C1
Irrawaddy, *river* B2
Martaban, *gulf* C3
Mekong, *river* C2
Mergui, *archipelago* C4
Mouths of the Irrawaddy, *delta* B3
Preparis, *island* B3
Ramree, *island* B2
Salween, *river* C2
Shan, *plateau* C2
Sittang, *river* C2
Tavoy, *point* C3
Thailand, *gulf* C4

Burma (Myanmar)

Capital: Rangoon
Area: 261,228 sq. mi. 676,756 sq. km.
Population: 44,277,000
Largest City: Rangoon
Language: Burmese
Monetary Unit: Kyat

Philippines

Capital: Manila
Area: 115,860 sq. mi. 300,155 sq. km.
Population: 69,809,000
Largest City: Manila
Languages: Pilipino, English
Monetary Unit: Philippine peso

Philippines: Map Index

Regions

Bicol B3
Cagayan Valley B2
Central Luzon A3
Central Mindanao C5
Central Visayas B4
*Cordillera Autonomous Region B2
Eastern Visayas C4
Ilocos B2
*Moslem Mindanao Autonomous Region B5
National Capital Region B3
Northern Mindanao C4
Southern Mindanao C5
Southern Tagalog B3
Western Mindanao B5
Western Visayas B4

Cities and Towns

Angeles B3
Bacolod B4
Baguio B2
Basilan B5
Batangas B3
Bislig C4
Butuan C4
Cabanatuan B3
Cadiz B4
Cagayan de Oro C4
Calapan B3
Calbayog C3
Cebu B4
Cotabato C5
Dagupan B2
Davao C5
Dipolog B4
Dumaguete B4
General Santos C5
Iligan C4
Iloilo B4
Jolo B5
Laoag B2
Laoang C3
Legazpi B3
Lipa B3
Lucena B3
Mamburao B3
Mandaue B4
Manila, *capital* B3
Masbate B3
Naga B3
Olongapo B3
Ormoc C4
Pagadian B5
Puerto Princesa A4
Quezon City B3
Roxas B4
San Carlos B4
San Fernando B2
San Pablo B3
Silay B4
Surigao C4
Tacloban C4
Tuguegarao B2
Vigan B2
Zamboanga B5

Other Features

Agusan, *river* C4
Apo, *volcano* C5
Babuyan, *channel* B2
Babuyan, *islands* B2
Balabac, *island* A5
Balabac, *strait* A5
Bashi, *channel* B1
Basilan, *island* B5
Bataan, *peninsula* B3
Batan, *islands* B1
Bohol, *island* C4
Bohol, *sea* C4
Cagayan, *islands* B4
Cagayan, *river* B2
Cagayan Sulu, *island* A5
Calamian, *islands* A3
Caramoan, *peninsula* B3
Catanduanes, *island* C3
Cebu, *island* B4
Celebes, *sea* B5
Cordillera Central, *mts.* B2
Corregidor, *island* B3
Cuyo, *islands* B4
Davao, *gulf* C5
Dinagat, *island* C4
Diuata, *mts.* C4
Jolo, *island* B5
Laguna de Bay, *lake* B3
Lamon, *bay* B3
Leyte, *island* C4
Lingayen, *gulf* B2
Luzon, *island* B3
Luzon, *strait* B2
Manila, *bay* B3
Marinduque, *island* B3
Masbate, *island* B3
Mayon, *volcano* B3
Mindanao, *island* C5
Mindoro, *island* B3
Mindoro, *strait* B3
Moro, *gulf* B5
Negros, *island* B4
Palawan, *island* A4
Panay, *gulf* B4
Panay, *island* B4
Philippine, *sea* C3
Pulangi, *river* C4
Samar, *island* C4
Samar, *sea* C3
Siargao, *island* C4
Sibuyan, *island* B3
Sibuyan, *sea* B3
Sierra Madre, *mts.* B2
South China, *sea* A3
Sulu, *archipelago* B5
Sulu, *sea* A4
Tablas, *island* B3
Tawi Tawi, *island* A5
Visayan, *islands* B4
Visayan, *sea* B4
Zambales, *mts.* B3
Zamboanga, *peninsula* B5

*Not on map

Indonesia: Map Index

Cities and Towns
Amahai D2
Ambon D2
Balikpapan C2
Banda Aceh A1
Bandar Lampung B2
Bandung B2
Banjarmasin C2
Baubau D2
Bengkulu B2
Bogor B2
Cilacap B2
Cirebon B2
Denpasar C2
Dili D2
Ende D2
Fakfak E2
Gorontalo D1
Jakarta, *capital* B2
Jambi B2
Jayapura F2
Kediri C2
Kendari D2
Kupang D3
Madiun C2
Magelang C2
Malang C2
Manado D1
Manokwari E2
Mataram C2
Medan A1
Merauke F2
Padang B2
Palangkaraya C2
Palembang B2
Palu C2
Pangkalpinang B2
Parepare C2
Pekalongan B2
Pekanbaru B1
Pematangsiantar A1

© GeoSystems Global Corp.

Pontianak B2
Raba C2
Samarinda C2
Semarang C2
Sorong E2
Sukabumi B2
Surabaya C2
Surakarta C2
Tanjungpinang B1
Tarakan C1
Tasikmalaya B2
Tegal B2
Ternate D1
Ujung Pandang C2
Waingapu D2
Yogyakarta C2

Other Features
Agung, *mt.* C2
Alor, *island* D2
Arafura, *sea* E2
Aru, *islands* E2
Babar, *island* D2
Bali, *island* C2
Banda, *sea* D2
Bangka, *island* B2
Belitung, *island* B2
Biak, *island* E2
Borneo, *island* C1
Buru, *island* D2
Celebes (Sulawesi), *island* D2
Celebes, *sea* D1
Ceram, *island* D2
Ceram, *sea* D2
Digul, *river* E2
Enggano, *island* B2
Flores, *island* D2
Flores, *sea* C2
Greater Sunda, *islands* B2
Halmahera, *island* D1
Irian Jaya, *region* E2
Java, *island* C2
Java, *sea* C2
Jaya, *mt.* E2
Kahayan, *river* C2
Kai, *islands* E2
Kalimantan, *region* C2
Kerinci, *mt.* B2
Krakatau, *island* B2
Lesser Sunda, *islands* C2
Lingga, *island* B2
Lombok, *island* C2
Madura, *island* C2
Makassar, *strait* C2
Malacca, *strait* A1
Mentawai, *islands* A2
Misool, *island* E2
Moa, *island* D2
Molucca, *sea* D2
Moluccas, *islands* D2
Morotai, *island* D1
Muna, *island* D2
Natuna Besar, *island* B1
New Guinea, *island* E2
Nias, *island* A1
Obi, *island* D2
Peleng, *island* D2
Savu, *sea* D2
Semeru, *mt.* C2
Siberut, *island* A2
Simeulue, *island* A1
South China, *sea* C1
Sudirman, *range* E2
Sula, *islands* D2
Sulu, *sea* D1
Sumatra, *island* B2
Sumba, *island* D2
Sumbawa, *island* C2
Talaud, *islands* D1
Tanimbar, *islands* E2
Timor, *island* D2
Timor, *sea* D3
Waigeo, *island* E2
Wetar, *island* D2
Yapen, *island* E2

Indonesia

Capital: Jakarta
Area: 741,052 sq. mi.
1,919,824 sq. km.
Population: 200,410,000
Largest City: Jakarta
Language: Bahasa Indonesian
Monetary Unit: New rupiah

© GeoSystems Global Corp.

Brunei

Capital: Bandar Seri Begawan
Area: 2,226 sq. mi.
5,767 sq. km.
Population: 285,000
Largest City: Bandar Seri Begawan
Language: Malay
Monetary Unit: Brunei dollar

Brunei: Map Index

Cities and Towns
Badas A2
Bandar Seri Begawan, *capital* B2
Bangar C2
Batang Duri C2
Jerudong B2
Kerangan Nyatan B3
Kuala Abang B2
Kuala Belait A2
Labi A3
Labu C2
Lumut A2
Medit B2
Muara C1
Seria A2
Sukang B3
Tutong B2

Other Features
Belait, *river* B3
Brunei, *bay* C1
Brunei, *river* B2
Bukit Pagon, *mt.* C3
Pandaruan, *river* C2
South China, *sea* A2
Temburong, *river* C2
Tutong, *river* B2

Singapore: Map Index

Cities and Towns
Bedok B1
Bukit Panjang B1
Bukit Timah B1
Changi B1
Choa Chu Kang A1
Jurong A1
Kranji B1
Nee Soon B1
Punggol B1
Queenstown B1
Sembawang B1
Serangoon B1
Singapore, *capital* B1
Tampines B1
Thong Hoe A1
Toa Payoh B1
Tuas A1
Woodlands B1

Other Features
Ayer Chawan, *island* A1
Bukum, *island* B2
Johor, *strait* B1
Keppel, *harbor* B2
Pandan, *strait* A2
Semakau, *island* B2
Senang, *island* A2
Sentosa, *island* B2
Singapore, *island* B1
Singapore, *strait* B2
Tekong, *island* C1
Timah, *hill* B1
Ubin, *island* B1

Singapore

Capital: Singapore
Area: 247 sq. mi.
640 sq. km.
Population: 2,859,000
Largest City: Singapore
Languages: Mandarin Chinese, English, Malay, Tamil
Monetary Unit: Singapore dollar

© GeoSystems Global Corp.

© GeoSystems Global Corp.

Malaysia

Capital: Kuala Lumpur
Area: 127,584 sq. mi.
330,529 sq. km.
Population: 19,283,000
Largest City: Kuala Lumpur
Language: Bahasa Malaysia
Monetary Unit: Ringgit

Malaysia: Map Index

Cities and Towns
Alor Setar A1
Batu Pahat B2
George Town A2
Ipoh A2
Johor Baharu B2
Kelang A2
Keluang B2
Kota Baharu B1
Kota Kinabalu D2
Kuala Lumpur, *capital* A2
Kuala Terengganu B2
Kuantan B2
Kuching C2
Melaka B2
Miri D2
Muar B2
Sandakan D2
Seremban A2
Sibu C2
Tawau D2
Telok Anson A2

Other Features
Banggi, *island* D1
Baram, *river* D2
Crocker, *range* D2
Kinabalu, *mt.* D1
Kinabatangan, *river* D2
Labuan, *island* D2
Langkawi, *island* A1
Malacca, *strait* A2
Malay, *peninsula* A1
Pahang, *river* B2
Peninsular Malaysia, *region* B2
Perak, *river* A2
Pinang, *island* A2
Rajang, *river* C2
Sabah, *state* D2
Sarawak, *state* C2
Tahan, *mt.* B2

Australia:
Map Index

States and Territories
Australian Capital Territory.......D3
New South Wales D3
Northern Territory....................C2
Queensland. D2
South Australia.........................C2
Tasmania. D4
Victoria D3
Western Australia.....................B2

Aboriginal Lands
Alawa-Ngandji C1
Balwina B2
Central Australia B2
Central Desert..........................C2
Daly River................................B1
Haasts Bluff C2
Lake Mackay............................B2
Nganyatjara B2
Petermann B2
Pitjantjatjara............................C2
Waani/Garawa C1
Yandeyarra A2
Unnamed B2
Unnamed................................C1
Unnamed................................D1

Cities and Towns
Adelaide, S.A., *capital* ..C3, Inset II
Albany, W.A............................A3
Albury, N.S.W. D3
Alice Springs, N.T....................C2
Altona, Vic. ....Inset V
Armadale, W.A. ....Inset I
Armidale, N.S.W. E3
Asquith, N.S.W. ....Inset IV
Auburn, N.S.W. ....Inset IV
Balcatta, W.A. ....Inset I
Bald Hills, Qld. ....Inset III
Ballarat, Vic. D3
Bankstown, N.S.W............Inset IV
Bayswater, W.A. ....Inset I
Beenleigh, Qld. ....Inset III
Belmont, W.A......................Inset I
Bendigo, Vic. D3
Berwick, Vic. ....Inset V
Blacktown, N.S.W. ....Inset IV
Botany, N.S.W..................Inset IV
Bourke, N.S.W. D3
Bowen, Qld. D2
Box Hill, Vic. ....Inset V
Brighton, S.A. ....Inset II
Brighton, Qld. ....Inset III
Brighton, Vic. ....Inset V
Brisbane, Qld.,
capital ....E2, Inset III
Broadmeadows, Vic. ....Inset V
Broken Hill, N.S.W. D3
Broome, W.A. B1
Brown Plains, Qld.............Inset III
Bunbury, W.A. A3
Bundaberg, Qld.......................E2
Burnside, S.A. ....Inset II
Byford, W.A. ....Inset I
Cairns, Qld. D1
Campbelltown, S.A. ....Inset II
Campbelltown, N.S.W. ....Inset IV
Canberra, A.C.T.,
national capital D3
Cannington, W.A. ....Inset I
Canterbury, N.S.W. ....Inset IV
Carnarvon, W.A......................A2
Castle Hill, N.S.W. ....Inset IV
Caulfield, Vic. ....Inset V
Ceduna, S.A. C3
Charleville, Qld. D2
Charters Towers, Qld. D2
Chelsea, Vic. ....Inset V
Chermside, Qld. ....Inset III
City Beach, W.A. ....Inset I
Cleveland, Qld. ....Inset III
Cloncurry, Qld. D2
Coburg, Vic. ....Inset V
Coober Pedy, S.A. C2
Coopers Plains, Qld. ....Inset III
Cranbourne, Vic. ....Inset V
Cronulla, N.S.W. ....Inset IV
Dampier, W.A. A2
Dandenong, Vic. ....Inset V
Darwin, N.T., *capital* C1
Dee Why, N.S.W. ....Inset IV
Devonport, Tas. D4
Doncaster, Vic. ....Inset V
Dubbo, N.S.W. D3
Elizabeth, S.A. ....Inset II
Eltham, Vic. ....Inset V
Emerald, Qld. D2
Enfield, S.A. ....Inset II
Epping, N.S.W. ....Inset IV
Esperance, W.A.......................B3
Essendon, Vic. ....Inset V
Fairfield, N.S.W. ....Inset IV
Ferntree Gully, Vic. ....Inset V
Ferny Grove, Qld. .... Inset III
Frankston, Vic. .... Inset V
Fremantle, W.A. ....A3, Inset I
Geelong, Vic. D3
Geraldton, W.A. A2
Gladstone, Qld. E2
Glenelg, S.A. .... Inset II
Glen Forrest, W.A. .... Inset I
Gold Coast, Qld. E2
Goodna, Qld. .... Inset III
Gosford, N.S.W.......................E3
Gosnells, W.A. .... Inset I
Grafton, N.S.W. E2
Grange, S.A. .... Inset II
Greenslopes, Qld. .... Inset III
Griffith, N.S.W. D3
Gympie, Qld............................E2
Heidelberg, Vic. .... Inset V
Hobart, Tas., *capital* D4
Holland Park, Qld. .... Inset III
Holroyd, N.S.W. ....Inset IV
Hornsby, N.S.W. .... Inset IV
Hurstville, N.S.W. .... Inset IV
Inala, Qld. .... Inset III
Ipswich, Qld. .... Inset III
Kalamunda, W.A. .... Inset I
Kalgoorlie, W.A........................B3
Katherine, N.T.........................C1
Keilor, Vic. .... Inset V
Kelmscott, W.A. .... Inset I
Kersbrook, S.A. .... Inset II
Kwinana, W.A. .... Inset I
Kwinana Beach, W.A. .... Inset I
La Perouse, N.S.W. .... Inset IV
Launceston, Tas. D4
Leichhardt, N.S.W. .... Inset IV
Lilydale, Vic. .... Inset V
Lismore, N.S.W.......................E2
Liverpool, N.S.W. .... Inset IV
Lobethal, S.A. .... Inset II
Logan, Qld. .... Inset III
Longreach, Qld.......................D2
Mackay, Qld. D2
Mandurah, W.A.......................A3
Manly, Qld. .... Inset III
Manly, N.S.W. .... Inset IV
Marion, S.A. .... Inset II
Maryborough, Qld. E2
Melbourne, Vic.,
capital......................D3, Inset V
Melville, W.A. .... Inset I
Merredin, W.A. A3
Midland, W.A. .... Inset I
Mildura, Vic. D3
Mitcham, S.A. .... Inset II
Mona Vale, N.S.W........... Inset IV
Moorabbin, Vic. .... Inset V
Mordialloc, Vic. .... Inset V
Moree, N.S.W. D2
Morningside, Qld. .... Inset III
Mosman Park, W.A. .... Inset I
Mount Barker, S.A. .... Inset II
Mount Gambier, S.A. D3
Mount Gravatt, Qld. .... Inset III
Mount Isa, Qld........................C2
Mount Nebo, Qld. ....Inset III
Mullaloo, W.A. .... Inset I
Narrogin, W.A. A3
Nedlands, W.A. .... Inset I
Newcastle, N.S.W. E3
Newman, W.A. A2
Newmarket, Qld. .... Inset III
Noarlunga, S.A. .... Inset II
North Adelaide, S.A. .... Inset II
Northcote, Vic. .... Inset V
North Sydney, N.S.W. ..... Inset IV
Nunawading, Vic. .... Inset V
Oakleigh, Vic. .... Inset V
Orange, N.S.W. D3
Parramatta, N.S.W. .... Inset IV
Perth, W.A., *capital* ....A3, Inset I
Petrie, Qld. .... Inset III
Pickering Brook, W.A. .... Inset I
Port Adelaide, S.A. .... Inset II
Port Augusta, S.A. C3
Port Hedland, W.A...................A2
Port Lincoln, S.A. C3
Port Macquarie, N.S.W. E3
Port Pirie, S.A. C3
Prahran, Vic. .... Inset V
Preston, Vic. .... Inset V
Queenstown, Tas. D4
Randwick, N.S.W. .... Inset IV
Redcliffe, Qld. .... Inset III
Redland Bay, Qld. .... Inset III
Reynella, S.A. .... Inset II
Ringwood, Vic. .... Inset V
Rockdale, N.S.W. .... Inset IV
Rockhampton, Qld. E2
Roma, Qld. D2
Ryde, N.S.W. .... Inset IV
St. Ives, N.S.W. .... Inset IV
St. Kilda, S.A. .... Inset II
St. Kilda, Vic. .... Inset V
Salisbury, S.A. .... Inset II
Samford, Qld. .... Inset III
Sandgate, Qld. .... Inset III
Scarborough, W.A. .... Inset I
Spearwood, W.A. .... Inset I
Springvale, Vic. .... Inset V
Stirling, W.A. .... Inset I
Stirling, S.A. .... Inset II
Sunshine, Vic. .... Inset V
Sutherland, N.S.W. .... Inset IV
Sydney, N.S.W.,
capital, ...E3, Inset IV
Tamworth, N.S.W. E3
Taree, N.S.W...........................E3
Tea Tree Gully, S.A. .... Inset II
Tennant Creek, N.T. C1
Tom Price, W.A........................A2
Toowoomba, Qld. E2
Townsville, Qld. D1
Unley, S.A. .... Inset II
Victoria Park, W.A. .... Inset I
Victoria Point, Qld. .... Inset III
Wagga Wagga, N.S.W.............D3
Wanneroo, W.A. .... Inset I
Warrnambool, Vic. D3
Waverley, Vic. .... Inset V
Weipa, Qld. D1
Whyalla, S.A............................C3
Willoughby, N.S.W. .... Inset IV
Wollongong, N.S.W. E3
Woodside, S.A. .... Inset II
Woodville, S.A. .... Inset II
Woomera, S.A. C3
Wyndham, W.A. B1
Wynnum, Qld. .... Inset III

Other Features
Arafura, *sea*............................C1
Arnhem, *cape*..........................C1
Arnhem Land, *region* C1
Ashburton, *river*.......................A2
Ashmore and Cartier, *islands* B1
Australian Alps, *mts*.................D3
Barkly, *tableland*......................C1
Bass, *strait*...............................D3
Bate, *bay*.........................Inset IV
Blue, *mts*. E3
Botany, *bay*......................Inset IV
Brisbane, *river*..................Inset III
Burdekin, *river*.........................D1
Canning, *river* .... Inset I
Cape York, *peninsula*................D1
Carpentaria, *gulf* C1
Coral, *sea* E1
Daly, *river*...............................C1
Darling, *range* A3
Darling, *river*...........................D3
Drysdale River Natl. Park B1
Eyre, *lake* C2
Eyre, *peninsula* C3
Fitzroy, *river*............................B1
Flinders, *range*........................C3
Flinders, *river* D1
Frome, *lake*.............................D2
Gairdner, *lake*..........................C3
Garden, *island*.................... Inset I
Gascoyne *river*.........................A2
Gibson, *desert*..........................B2
Gilbert, *river*............................D1
Great Artesian, *basin*................D2
Great Australian, *bight*..............B3
Great Barrier, *reef*....................D1
Great Dividing, *range*........D1, D3
Great Sandy, *desert*..................B2
Great Victoria, *desert* B2
Gregory Natl. Park C1
Grey, *range* D2
Groote Eylandt, *island*..............C1
Hamersley, *range*.....................A2
Hobsons, *bay*................... Inset V
Jackson, *port* ....Inset IV
Kakadu Natl. Park C1
Kangaroo, *island* C3
Kimberley, *plateau*....................B1
King Leopold, *range* B1
Kosciusko, *mt*...........................D3
Lakefield Natl. Park D1
Leeuwin, *cape* A3
Leichhardt, *river* D1
Leveque, *cape*...........................B1
Logan, *river* ....Inset III
Macdonnell, *ranges*..................C2
Melville, *island* C1
Mitchell, *river*...........................D1
Moreton, *bay* ....Inset III
Murchison, *river* A2
Murray, *river* D3
Murrumbidgee, *river*................D3
Musgrave, *ranges*.....................C2
New England, *range* E3
North West, *cape* A2
Nullarbor, *plain* B3
Port Phillip, *bay*................ Inset V
Roper, *river*..............................C1
Rudall River Natl. Park B2
St. Vincent, *gulf*.................Inset II
Samsonvale, *lake* ....Inset III
Simpson, *desert*.......................C2
Simpson Desert Natl. Park........C2
Spencer, *gulf* C3
Swan, *river* .... Inset I
Tasman, *sea*.............................E3
Timor, *sea* B1
Torrens, *lake*............................C2
Torrens, *river* ....Inset II
Torres, *strait*.............................D1
Uluru (Ayers Rock) C2
Victoria, *river*...........................C1
Witjira Natl. Park.....................C2
Yampi, *sound*...........................B1
York, *cape* D1

Australia

Capital: Canberra
Area: 2,966,200 sq. mi.
7,684,456 sq. km.
Population: 18,077,000
Largest City: Sydney
Language: English
Monetary Unit: Australian dollar

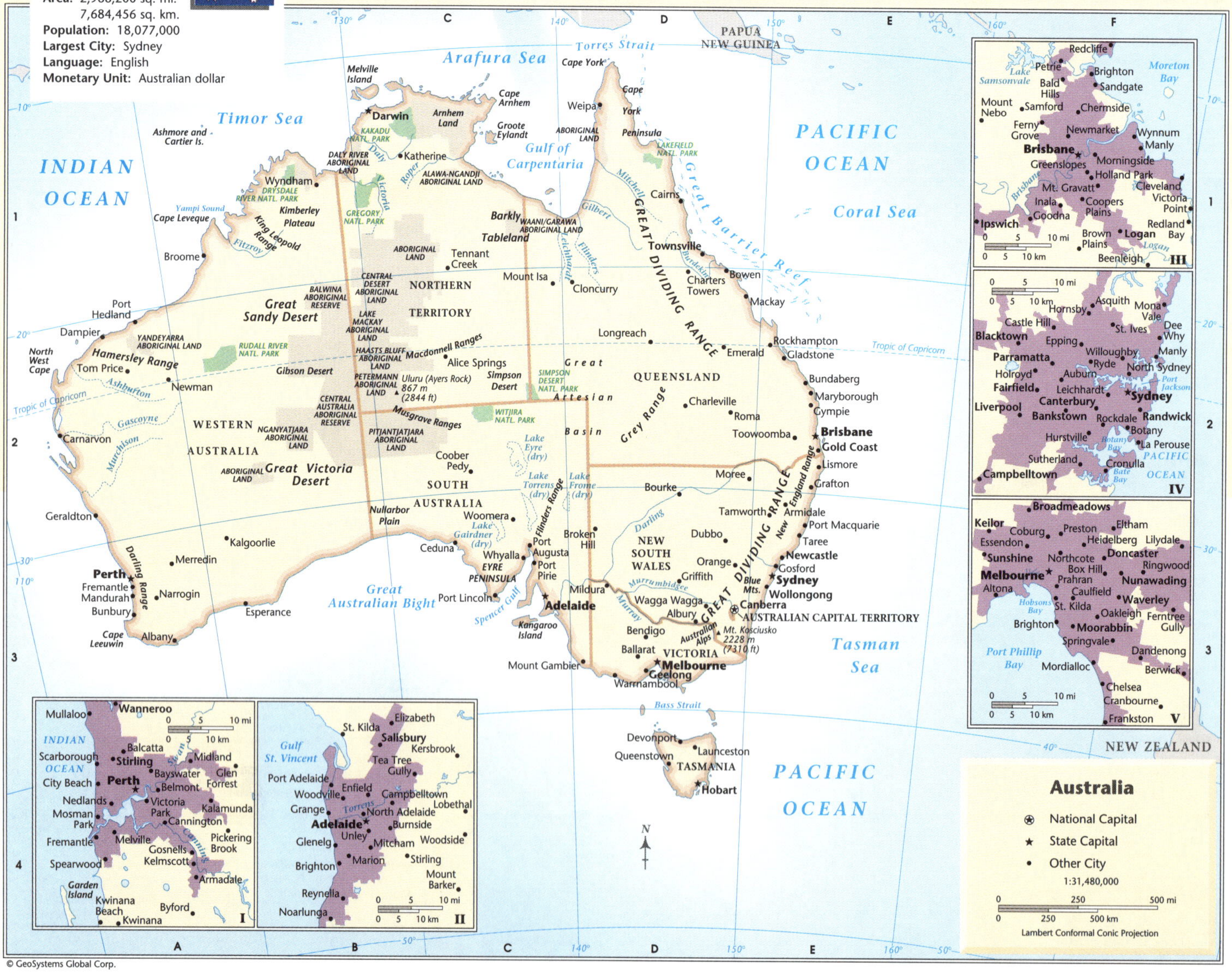

Papua New Guinea

Capital: Port Moresby
Area: 178,704 sq. mi.
462,964 sq. km.
Population: 4,197,000
Largest City: Port Moresby
Language: English
Monetary Unit: Kina

Papua New Guinea: Map Index

New Zealand

Capital: Wellington
Area: 104,454 sq. mi.
270,606 sq. km.
Population: 3,389,000
Largest City: Auckland
Language: English
Monetary Unit: New Zealand dollar

New Zealand: Map Index

Micronesia: Map Index

Micronesia

Capital: Palikir
Area: 271 sq. mi.
702 sq. km.
Population: 120,000
Largest City: Palikir
Language: English
Monetary Unit: U.S. dollar

© GeoSystems Global Corp.

Marshall Islands

Capital: Majuro
Area: 70 sq. mi.
181 sq. km.
Population: 54,000
Largest City: Majuro
Language: English
Monetary Unit: U.S. dollar

Marshall Islands: Map Index

City
Majuro, *capital* C2

Other Features
Ailinglapalap, *island* B2
Ailuk, *island* B1
Arno, *island* C2
Aur, *island* C2
Bikar, *island* C1
Bikini, *island* B1
Ebon, *island* B3
Enewetak, *island* A1
Jaluit, *island* B2
Kwajalein, *island* B2
Lae, *island* B2
Likiep, *island* B1
Majuro, *island* C2
Maloelap, *island* C2
Mili, *island* C2
Namu, *island* B2
Ralik, *island chain* A1
Ratak, *island chain* B1
Roi, *island* B2
Rongelap, *island* B1
Rongerik, *island* B1
Taka, *island* B1
Taongi, *island* B1
Ujae, *island* B2
Ujelang, *island* A2
Wotho, *island* B1
Wotje, *island* B2

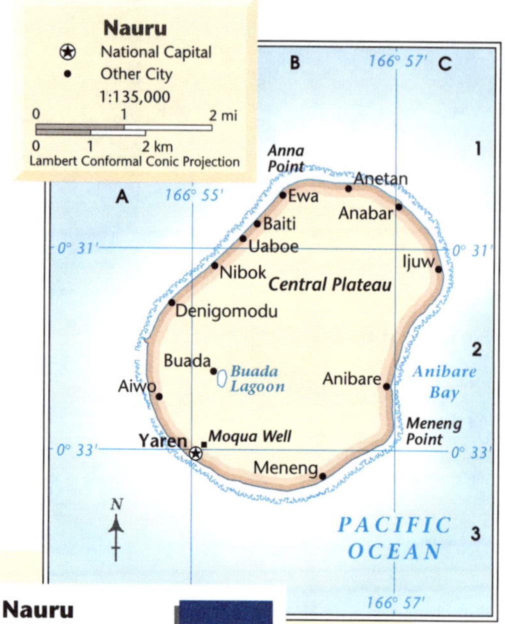

© GeoSystems Global Corp.

Nauru

Capital: Yaren
Area: 8.2 sq. mi.
21 sq. km.
Population: 10,000
Largest City: Yaren
Languages: Nauruan, English
Monetary Unit: Australian dollar

Nauru: Map Index

Cities and Towns
Aiwo A2
Anabar C1
Anetan B1
Anibare B2
Baiti B1
Buada B2
Denigomodu A2
Ewa B1
Ijuw C2
Meneng B3
Nibok B2
Uaboe B1
Yaren, *capital* B3

Other Features
Anibare, *bay* C2
Anna, *point* B1
Buada, *lagoon* B2
Central, *plateau* B2
Meneng, *point* C2
Moqua, *well* B2

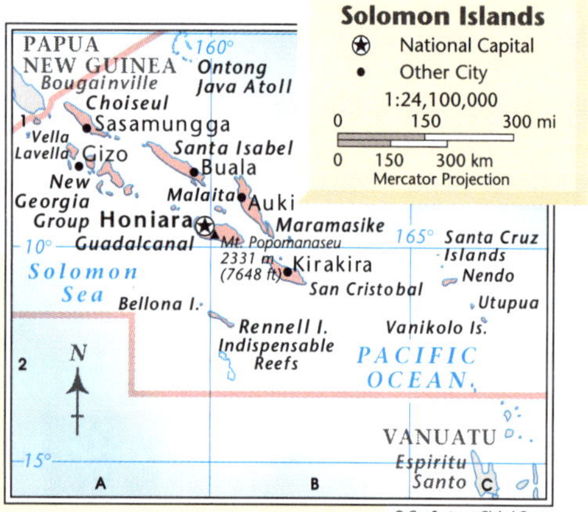

© GeoSystems Global Corp.

Solomon Islands: Map Index

Cities and Towns
Auki B1
Buala A1
Gizo A1
Honiara, *capital* A1
Kirakira B2
Sasamungga A1

Other Features
Bellona, *island* A2
Choiseul, *island* A1
Guadalcanal, *island* A1
Indispensable, *reefs* B2
Malaita, *island* B1
Maramasike, *island* B1
Nendo, *island* C2
New Georgia Group, *islands* A1
Ontong Java, *island* A1
Popomanaseu, *mt.* B1
Rennell, *island* B2
San Cristobal, *island* B2
Santa Cruz, *islands* C2
Santa Isabel, *island* A1
Solomon, *sea* A2
Utupua, *island* C2
Vanikolo, *islands* C2
Vella Lavella, *island* A1

Solomon Islands

Capital: Honiara
Area: 10,954 sq. mi.
28,378 sq. km.
Population: 386,000
Largest City: Honiara
Language: English
Monetary Unit: Dollar

Tuvalu

Capital: Funafuti
Area: 9.4 sq. mi.
24.4 sq. km.
Population: 10,000
Largest City: Funafuti
Languages: Tuvaluan, English
Monetary Unit: Tuvalu dollar, Australian dollar

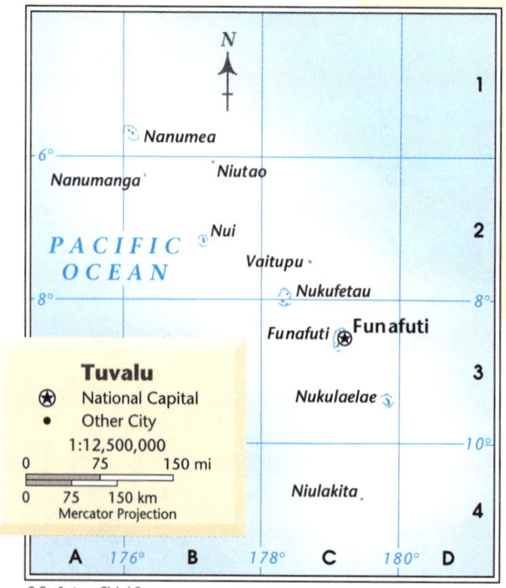

© GeoSystems Global Corp.

Tuvalu: Map Index

City
Funafuti, *capital* C3

Other Features
Funafuti, *island* C3
Nanumanga, *island* B2
Nanumea, *island* B1
Niulakita, *island* C4
Niutao, *island* B2
Nui, *island* B2
Nukufetau, *island* C2
Nukulaelae, *island* C3
Vaitupu, *island* C2

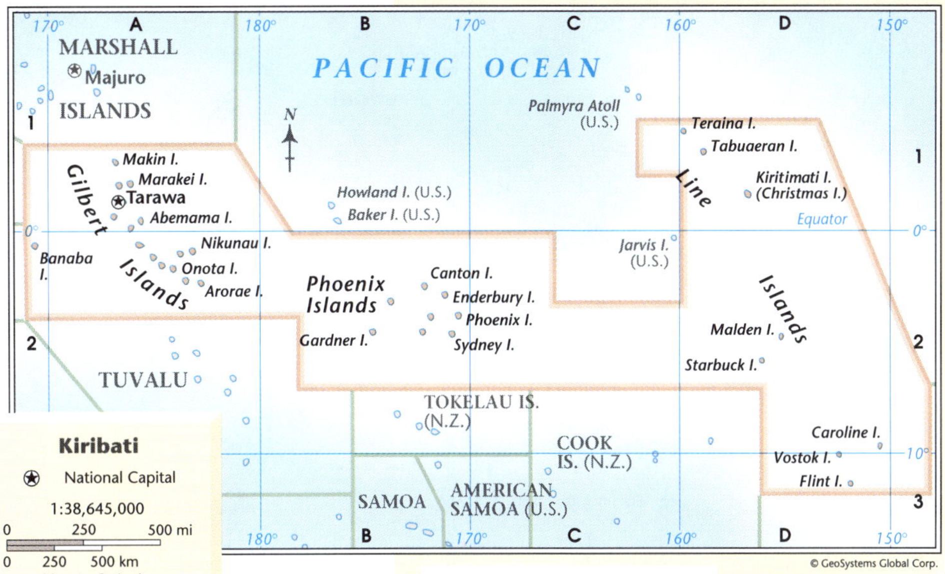

© GeoSystems Global Corp.

Kiribati

Capital: Tarawa
Area: 313 sq. mi.
811 sq. km.
Population: 78,000
Largest City: Tarawa
Languages: I-Kiribati (Gilbertese), English
Monetary Unit: Australian dollar

Kiribati: Map Index

Fiji: Map Index

Fiji

Capital: Suva
Area: 7,056 sq. mi.
18,280 sq. km.
Population: 764,000
Largest City: Suva
Languages: Fijian, Hindi, English
Monetary Unit: Fiji dollar

© GeoSystems Global Corp.

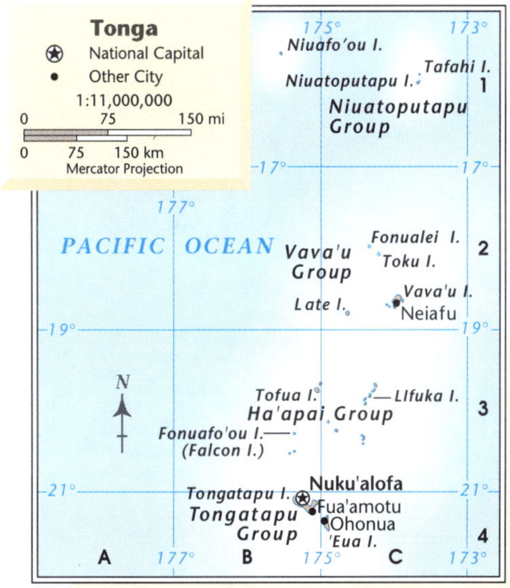

© GeoSystems Global Corp.

Palau: Map Index

© GeoSystems Global Corp.

Palau

Capital: Koror
Area: 177 sq. mi.
458 sq. km.
Population: 16,661
Largest City: Koror
Languages: English, Sonsorolese, Angaur, Japanese, Tobi, Palauan
Monetary Unit: U.S. dollar

Tonga

Capital: Nuku'alofa
Area: 301 sq. mi.
780 sq. km.
Population: 105,000
Largest City: Nuku'alofa
Languages: Tongan, English
Monetary Unit: Pa'anga

Tonga: Map Index

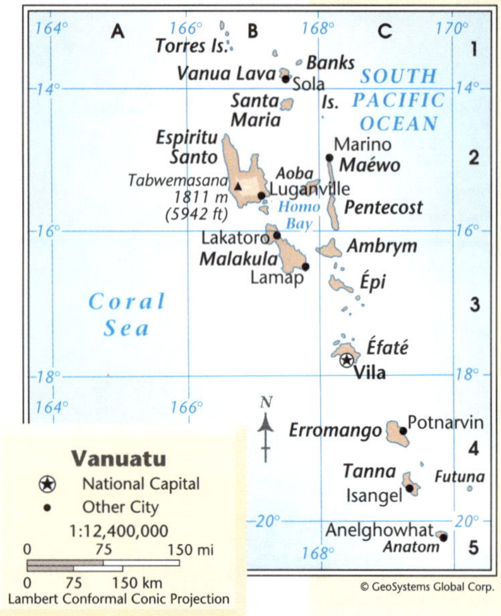

Vanuatu

Capital: Vila
Area: 4,707 sq. mi.
12,194 sq. km.
Population: 170,000
Largest City: Vila
Languages: French, English, Bislama
Monetary Unit: Vatu

Vanuatu:
Map Index

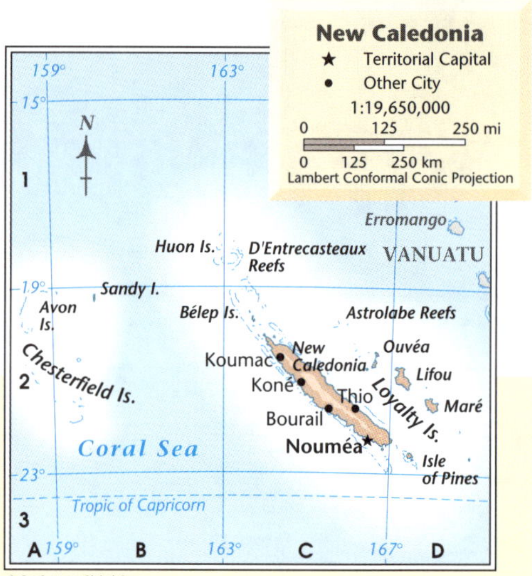

New Caledonia:
Map Index

New Caledonia

Capital: Nouméa
Area: 8,548 sq. mi.
21,912 sq. km.
Population: 172,000
Largest City: Nouméa
Language: French
Monetary Unit: CFA Franc

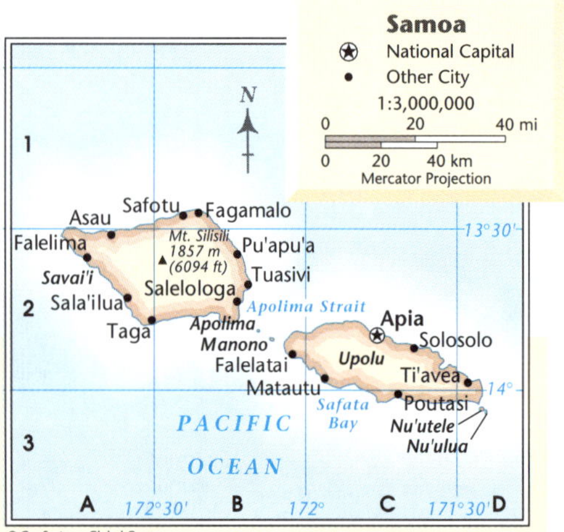

Samoa

Capital: Apia
Area: 1,093 sq. mi.
2,832 sq. km.
Population: 204,000
Largest City: Apia
Languages: Samoan, English
Monetary Unit: Tala

Samoa:
Map Index

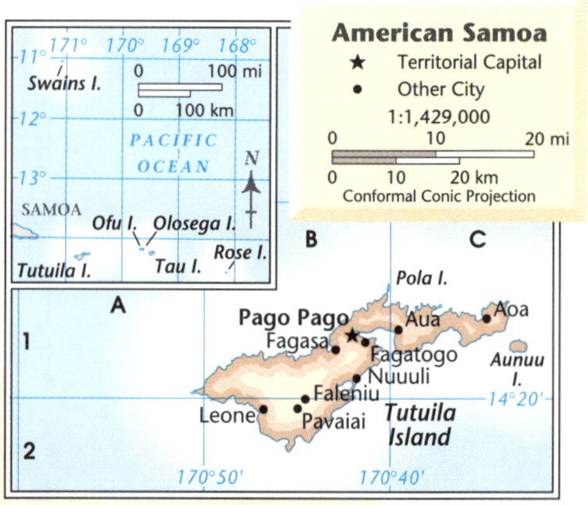

American Samoa:
Map Index

American Samoa

Capital: Pago Pago
Area: 77 sq. mi.
199 sq. km.
Population: 46,773
Largest City: Pago Pago
Language: English
Monetary Unit: U.S. dollar

Maldives

Capital: Male
Area: 115 sq. mi.
298 sq. km.
Population: 252,000
Largest City: Male
Language: Divehi
Monetary Unit: Rufiyaa

Nepal

Capital: Kathmandu
Area: 56,827 sq. mi.
147,220 sq. km.
Population: 21,042,000
Largest City: Kathmandu
Language: Nepali
Monetary Unit: Rupee

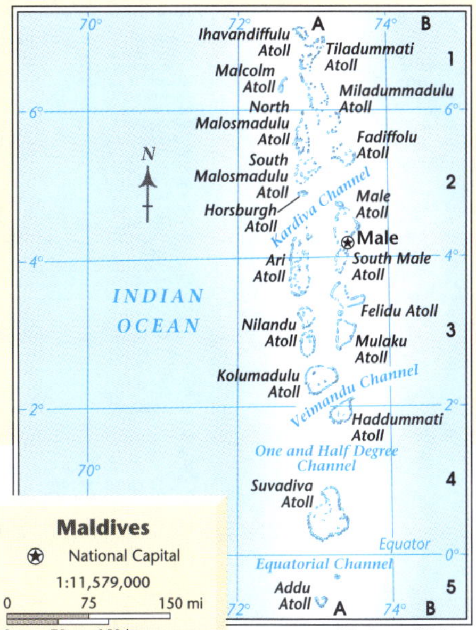

Sri Lanka

Capital: Colombo
Area: 25,332 sq. mi.
65,627 sq. km.
Population: 18,033,000
Largest City: Colombo
Language: Sinhalese
Monetary Unit: Rupee

Bhutan
National Capital
Other City
1:6,053,000
0 25 50 75 mi
0 25 50 75 km
Lambert Conformal Conic Projection

Bhutan

Capital: Thimphu
Area: 18,147 sq. mi.
47,013 sq. km.
Population: 1,739,000
Largest City: Thimphu
Language: Dzongkha
Monetary Unit: Ngultrum

India:
Map Index

Internal Divisions

Cities and Towns

Bangladesh

Capital: Dhaka
Area: 57,295 sq. mi.
148,433 sq. km.
Population: 125,149,000
Largest City: Dhaka
Language: Bengali
Monetary Unit: Taka

Bangladesh: Map Index

India: Map Index

Pakistan

Capital: Islamabad
Area: 339,697 sq. mi.
880,044 sq. km.
Population: 121,856,000
Largest City: Karachi
Languages: Urdu, English
Monetary Unit: Pakistani rupee

Pakistan: Map Index

Afghanistan:
Map Index

Cities and Towns
Asadabad C2
Baghlan B1
Balkh B1
Bamian B2
Baraki Barak B2
Chaghcharan B2
Charikar B1
Farah A2
Feyzabad C1
Gardez B2
Ghazni B2
Herat A2
Jalalabad C2
Kabul, *capital* B2
Khowst B2
Konduz B1
Kowt-e Ashrow B2
Lashkar Gah A2
Mazar-e Sharif B1
Meymaneh A1
Qalat B2
Qaleh-ye Now A2
Qaleh-ye Panjeh C1
Qandahar B2
Samangan B1
Sar-e Pol B1
Sheberghan B1
Shindand A2
Taloqan B1
Tarin Kowt B2
Zaranj A2
Zareh Sharan B2

Other Features
Amu Darya, *river* B1
Arghandab, *river* B2
Farah, *river* A2
Fuladi, *mt.* B2
Gowd-e Zereh, *lake* A3
Hamun-e Saberi, *lake* A2
Harirud, *river* A2
Helmand, *river* A2
Hindu Kush, *range* B1
Kabul, *river* B2
Khojak, *pass* B2
Khyber, *pass* C2
Konar, *river* C1
Konduz, *river* B1
Morghab, *river* A1
Nowshak, *mt.* C1
Panj, *river* C1
Paropamisus, *range* A2
Registan, *region* A2
Shibar, *pass* B2
Vakhan, *region* C1

Afghanistan

Capital: Kabul
Area: 251,825 sq. mi.
652,396 sq. km.
Population: 16,903,000
Largest City: Kabul
Languages: Pashto, Dari Persian
Monetary Unit: Afghani

Iran

Capital: Tehran
Area: 632,457 sq. mi.
1,638,490 sq. km.
Population: 65,612,000
Largest City: Tehran
Languages: Persian, Turkic, Luri, Kurdish
Monetary Unit: Rial

Iran:
Map Index

Cities and Towns
Abadan B3
Ahvaz B3
Arak B3
Ardabil B2
Bakhtaran B3
Bam D4
Bandar Beheshti E4
Bandar-e Abbas D4
Bandar-e Anzali B2
Bandar-e Bushehr C4
Bandar-e Khomeyni B3
Bandar-e Torkeman C2
Birjand D3
Dezful B3
Esfahan C3
Hamadan B3
Ilam B3
Iranshahr E4
Jask D4
Karaj C2
Kashan C3
Kerman D3
Khorramabad B3
Khorramshahr B3
Khvoy A2
Mashhad D2
Neyshabur D2
Orumiyeh (Urmia) A2
Qazvin B2
Qom C3
Rasht B2
Sabzevar D2
Sanandaj B2
Sari C2
Shahr-e Kord C3
Shiraz C4
Sirjan D4
Tabriz B2
Tehran, *capital* C2
Yasuj C3
Yazd C3
Zabol E3
Zahedan E4
Zanjan B2

Other Features
Aras, *river* B2
Atrak, *river* D2
Azerbaijan, *region* B2
Bakhtiari, *region* B3
Baluchistan, *region* E4
Caspian, *sea* C2
Damavand, *mt.* C2
Dasht-e Kavir, *desert* D3
Dasht-e Lut, *desert* D3
Elburz, *mts.* C2
Halil, *river* D4
Hamun-e Jaz Murian, *lake* D4
Hashtadan, *region* E3
Hormuz, *strait* D4
Karun, *river* B3
Kavir-e Namak, *desert* D3
Kerman, *region* D4
Kharg, *island* C4
Khorasan, *region* D2
Khuzestan, *region* B3
Kopet, *mts.* D2
Larestan, *region* C4
Mand, *river* C4
Mazandaran, *region* C2
Oman, *gulf* D5
Persian, *gulf* C4
Qareh, *river* B3
Qeshm, *island* D4
Shatt al-Arab, *river* B3
Urmia, *lake* B2
Yazd, *region* C3
Zagros, *mts.* B3

Turkmenistan:
Map Index

Cities and Towns
Ashgabat, *capital* C3
Bakhardok C2
Bayramaly D3
Büzmeyin C2
Chardzhou D2
Cheleken A2
Dashhowuz C2
Ensenguly A3
Gazanjyk B2
Gumdag B2
Gushgy D3
Gyzylarbat B2
Kerki D3
Krasnovodsk A2
Mary C3
Nebitdag B2
Tedzhen C3

Other Features
Amu Darya, *river* D2
Caspian, *sea* A2
Etrek, *river* B3
Garabil, *plateau* D3
Garabogazköl, *lake* A2
Gushgy, *river* D3
Kara-Kum, *canal* D3
Kara-Kum, *desert* C2
Kopet, *mts.* B2
Murgab, *river* D3
Sarygamysh Koli, *lake* B2
Sumbar, *river* B2
Tedzhen, *river* C3
Turan, *lowland* C2

Turkmenistan

Capital: Ashgabat
Area: 188,417 sq. mi.
488,127 sq. km.
Population: 3,995,000
Largest City: Ashgabat
Languages: Turkmen, Russian, Uzbek
Monetary Unit: Ruble

Kazakhstan

Capital: Almaty
Area: 1,049,200 sq. mi.
2,718,135 sq. km.
Population: 17,268,000
Largest City: Almaty
Language: Kazakh
Monetary Unit: Tenge

Uzbekistan

Capital: Tashkent
Area: 172,700 sq. mi.
447,409 sq. km.
Population: 22,609,000
Largest City: Tashkent
Languages: Uzbek, Russian
Monetary Unit: Ruble

Kyrgyzstan

Capital: Bishkek
Area: 76,642 sq. mi.
198,554 sq. km.
Population: 4,698,000
Largest City: Bishkek
Language: Kirghiz
Monetary Unit: Som

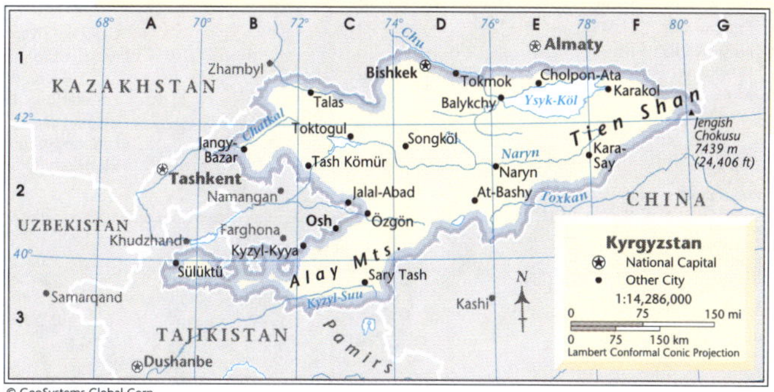

Tajikistan

Capital: Dushanbe
Area: 55,300 sq. mi.
143,264 sq. km.
Population: 5,995,000
Largest City: Dushanbe
Language: Tajik
Monetary Unit: Ruble

Iraq

Capital: Baghdad
Area: 167,975 sq. mi.
435,169 sq. km.
Population: 19,890,000
Largest City: Baghdad
Language: Arabic
Monetary Unit: Dinar

Kuwait

Capital: Kuwait
Area: 6,880 sq. mi.
17,924 sq. km.
Population: 1,819,000
Largest City: Kuwait
Language: Arabic
Monetary Unit: Dinar

Saudi Arabia

Capital: Riyadh
Area: 865,000 sq. mi.
2,240,933 sq. km.
Population: 18,197,000
Largest City: Riyadh
Language: Arabic
Monetary Unit: Riyal

Bahrain and Qatar: Map Index

Bahrain

Capital: Manama
Area: 268 sq. mi.
694 sq. km.
Population: 586,000
Largest City: Manama
Language: Arabic
Monetary Unit: Dinar

Qatar

Capital: Doha
Area: 4,412 sq. mi.
11,430 sq. km.
Population: 513,000
Largest City: Doha
Language: Arabic
Monetary Unit: Riyal

United Arab Emirates (U.A.E.)

Capital: Abu Dhabi
Area: 30,000 sq. mi.
77,720 sq. km.
Population: 2,791,000
Largest City: Abu Dhabi
Language: Arabic
Monetary Unit: Dirham

United Arab Emirates: Map Index

Yemen: Map Index

Yemen

Capital: Sana
Area: 205,356 sq. mi.
532,010 sq. km.
Population: 11,105,000
Largest City: Sana
Language: Arabic
Monetary Unit: Riyal

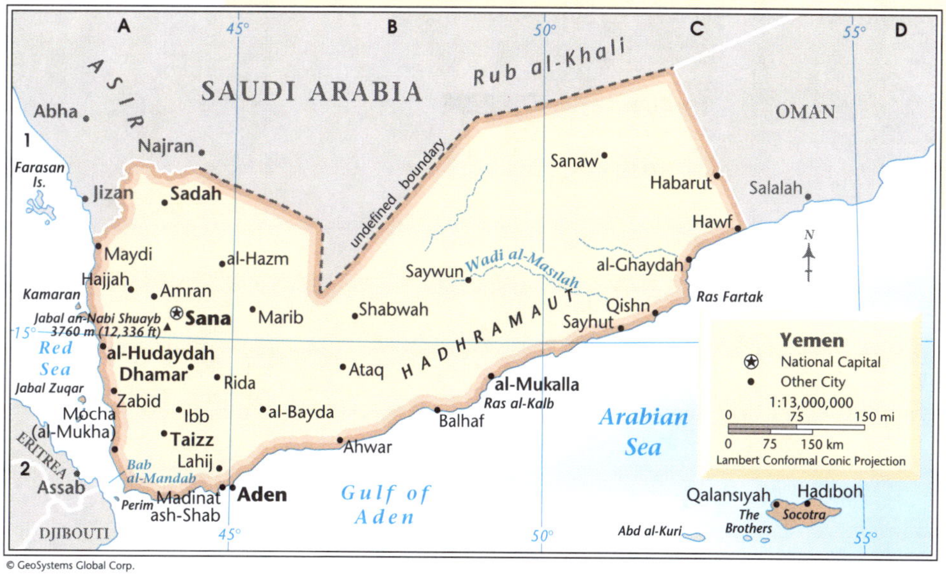

Oman: Map Index

Oman

Capital: Masqat
Area: 118,150 sq. mi.
305,829 sq. km.
Population: 1,701,000
Largest City: Masqat
Language: Arabic
Monetary Unit: Rial Omani

Lebanon

Capital: Beirut
Area: 3,950 sq. mi.
10,233 sq. km.
Population: 3,620,000
Largest City: Beirut
Languages: Arabic, French
Monetary Unit: Pound

Lebanon:
Map Index

Cities and Towns
Amyun A1
Baalbek B1
Babda A2
Batrun, al- A1
Beirut, *capital* A2
Bint Jubayl A2
Bsharri B1
Damur, ad- A2
Duma A1
Halba B1
Hirmil, al- B1
Jazzin A2
Jubayl A1
Juniyah A2
Marj Uyun A2
Nabatiyah at-Tahta, an- A2
Qubayyat, al- B1
Rashayya A2
Riyaq B2
Sidon (Sayda) A2
Sur (Tyre) A2
Tripoli (Tarabulus) A1
Zahlah A2

Other Features
Anti-Lebanon, *mts.* B1
Awwali, *river* A2
Bekaa, *valley* A2
Byblos, *ruins* A1
Hermon, *mt.* A2
Ibrahim, *river* A1
Kebir, *river* B1
Lebanon, *mts.* B1
Litani, *river* A2
Orontes, *river* B1
Qurnat as-Sawda, *mt.* B1

Israel

Israel

Capital: Jerusalem
Area: 7,992 sq. mi.
20,705 sq. km.
Population: 5,051,000
Largest City: Jerusalem
Languages: Hebrew, Arabic
Monetary Unit: New Shekel

Israel:
Map Index

Districts
Central B1
Haifa B1
Jerusalem B2
Northern B1
Southern B2
Tel Aviv B1

Cities and Towns
Acre (Akko) B1
Ashdod B2
Ashqelon B2
Beersheba B2
Dimona B2
Elat B3
Hadera B1
Haifa B1
Herzliyya B1
Holon B1
Jerusalem, *capital* B2
Lod (Lydda) B2
Mizpe Ramon B2
Nahariyya B1
Nazareth B1
Netanya B1
Petah Tiqwa B1
Qiryat Gat B2
Qiryat Shemona B1
Ramat Gan B1
Ramla B2
Rehovot B2
Tel Aviv-Jaffa B1
Tiberias B1
Yotvata B3
Zefat B1

Other Features
Aqaba, *gulf* B3
Arabah, al-, *river* B2
Besor, *river* B2
Dead, *sea* B2
Galilee, *region* B1
Haifa, *bay* B1
Jezreel (Esdraelon), *plain* B1
Jordan, *river* B1
Judea, *plain* B2
Masada, *ruins* B2
Meron, *mt.* B1
Negev, *region* B2
Ramon, *mt.* B2
Samarian, *hills* B1
Sharon, *plain* B1
Tiberias (Galilee), *lake* B1
Zevulun, *plain* B1

Jordan

Jordan:
Map Index

Cities and Towns
Amman, *capital* A2
Aqabah, al- A3
Azraq ash-Shishan B2
Bair B2
Irbid A1
Jafr, al- B2
Jarash A1
Karak, al- A2
Maan A2
Madaba A2
Mafraq, al- B1
Mudawwarah, al- B3
Qatranah, al- B2
Ramtha, ar- B1
Ras an-Naqb A2
Salt, as- A1
Tafilah, at- A2
Zarqa, az- B1

Other Features
Aqaba, *gulf* A3
Arabah, al-, *river* A2
Dead Sea, *lake* A2
Jabal Ramm, *mt.* A3
Jordan, *river* A2
Petra, *ruins* A2
Syrian, *desert* B1
Tiberias, *lake* A1
Wadi as-Sirhan, *depression* B2

Jordan

Capital: Amman
Area: 34,342 sq. mi.
88,969 sq. km.
Population: 3,961,000
Largest City: Amman
Language: Arabic
Monetary Unit: Dinar

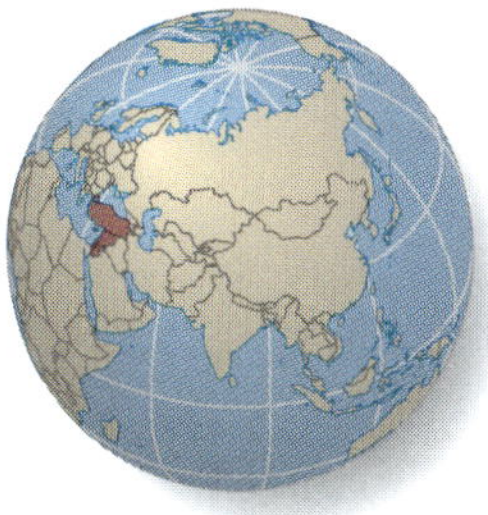

Turkey

- National Capital
- Other City

1:11,125,000

0 75 150 mi
0 75 150 km

Lambert Conformal Conic Projection

Turkey

Capital: Ankara
Area: 300,948 sq. mi.
779,658 sq. km.
Population: 62,154,000
Largest City: İstanbul
Language: Turkish
Monetary Unit: Lira

Turkey: Map Index

Cyprus

- National Capital
- Other City

1:5,091,000

0 25 50 mi
0 25 50 km

Lambert Conformal Conic Projection

Cyprus: Map Index

Cyprus

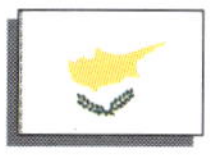

Capital: Nicosia
Area: 3,572 sq. mi.
9,254 sq. km.
Population: 730,000
Largest City: Nicosia
Languages: Greek, Turkish
Monetary Unit: Pound

Syria

- National Capital
- Other City

1:9,250,000

0 60 120 mi
0 60 120 km

Azimuthal Equal Area Projection

Syria: Map Index

Syria

Capital: Damascus
Area: 71,498 sq. mi.
185,228 sq. km.
Population: 14,887,000
Largest City: Damascus
Language: Arabic
Monetary Unit: Pound

MAJOR CITIES

Albania	
Tiranë	244,000
Andorra	
Andorra la Vella	16,000
Armenia	
Yerevan	1,254,000
Austria	
Vienna	1,539,000
Azerbaijan	
Baku	1,149,000
Belarus	
Minsk	1,613,000
Belgium	(metro)
Brussels	951,000
Antwerp	465,000
Bosnia and Hercegovina	
Sarajevo	416,000
Bulgaria	
Sofia	1,141,000
Croatia	
Zagreb	704,000
Czech Republic	
Prague	1,212,000
Denmark	
Copenhagen	617,000
Estonia	
Tallinn	478,000
Finland	
Helsinki	495,000
France	
Paris	2,152,000
Marseille	800,000
Lyon	416,000
Georgia	
Tbilisi	1,268,000
Germany	
Berlin	3,438,000
Hamburg	1,661,000
Munich	1,237,000
Cologne	956,000
Frankfurt	647,000
Essen	626,000
Dortmund	600,000
Stuttgart	584,000
Düsseldorf	577,000
Leipzig	508,000
Great Britain	
London	6,803,000
Birmingham	995,000
Leeds	706,000
Glasgow	688,000
Sheffield	520,000
Liverpool	475,000
Edinburgh	439,000
Manchester	433,000
Greece	
Athens	748,000
Hungary	
Budapest	2,017,000
Iceland	
Reykjavík	97,000
Ireland	
Dublin	478,000
Italy	
Rome	2,829,000
Milan	1,549,000
Naples	1,208,000
Turin	1,060,000
Genoa	742,000
Palermo	714,000
Latvia	
Riga	909,000
Liechtenstein	
Vaduz	5,000
Lithuania	
Vilnius	591,000
Luxembourg	
Luxembourg	75,000
F.Y.R. Macedonia	
Skopje	393,000
Malta	
Valletta	9,000
Moldova	
Chişinău	667,000
Monaco	
Monaco	27,000
Netherlands	
Amsterdam	713,000
Rotterdam	590,000
Norway	
Oslo	465,000
Poland	
Warsaw	1,654,000
Łódź	847,000
Kraków	751,000
Wrocław	643,000
Portugal	
Lisbon	678,000
Romania	
Bucharest	2,064,000
Russia (European)	
Moscow	8,747,000
St. Petersburg	4,437,000
Nizh. Novgorod	1,441,000
Samara	1,239,000
Kazan	1,104,000
Perm	1,099,000
Ufa	1,097,000
Rostov-na-Donu	1,027,000
Volgograd	1,006,000
San Marino	
San Marino	3,000
Slovakia	
Bratislava	441,000
Slovenia	
Ljubljana	277,000
Spain	
Madrid	2,991,000
Barcelona	1,668,000
Valencia	719,000
Seville	654,000
Sweden	
Stockholm	679,000
Switzerland	
Zürich	342,000
Bern	135,000
Turkey (European)	
İstanbul	6,620,000
Ukraine	
Kiev	2,643,000
Kharkov	1,622,000
Dnepropetrovsk	1,190,000
Donetsk	1,121,000
Odessa	1,096,000
Yugoslavia	
Belgrade	1,137,000

International comparability of city population data is limited by various data inconsistencies.

Gross National Product (GNP) per capita

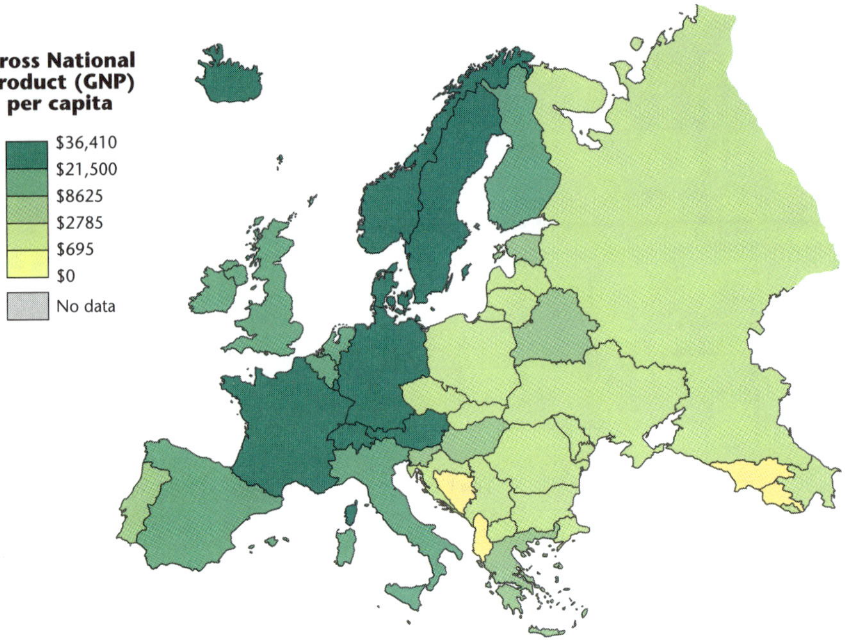

Vegetation

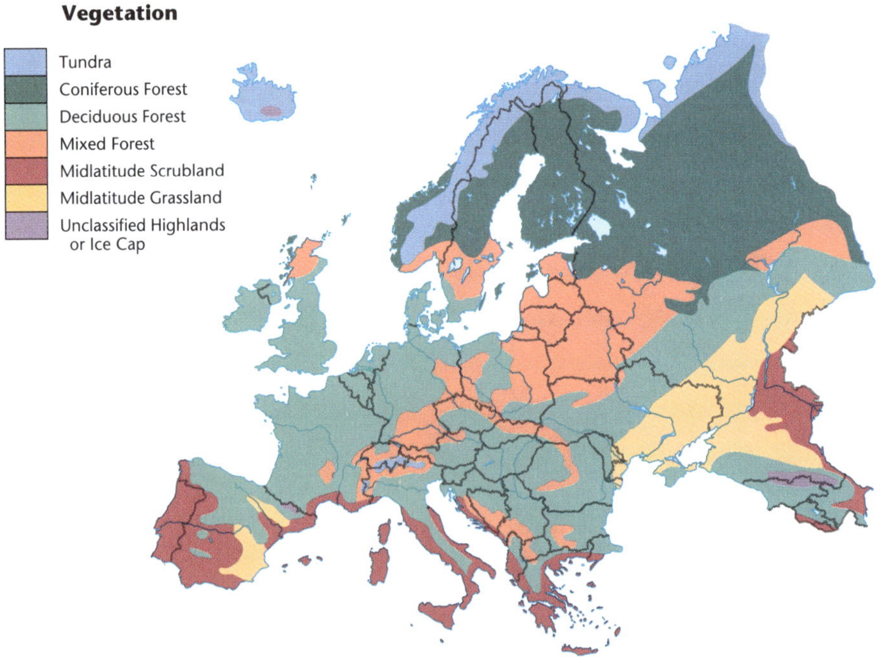

Europe: Population, by nation (in millions)

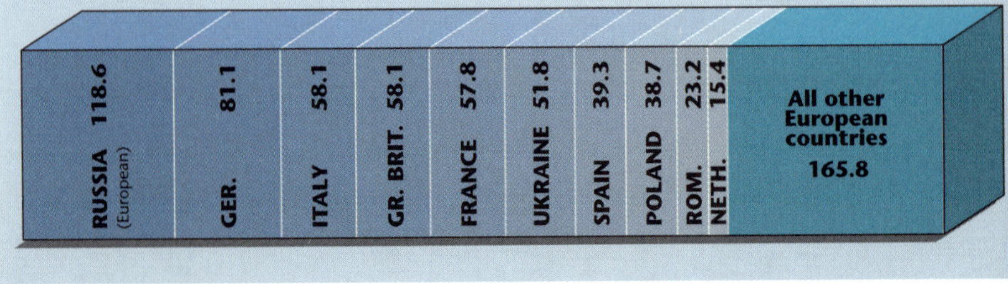

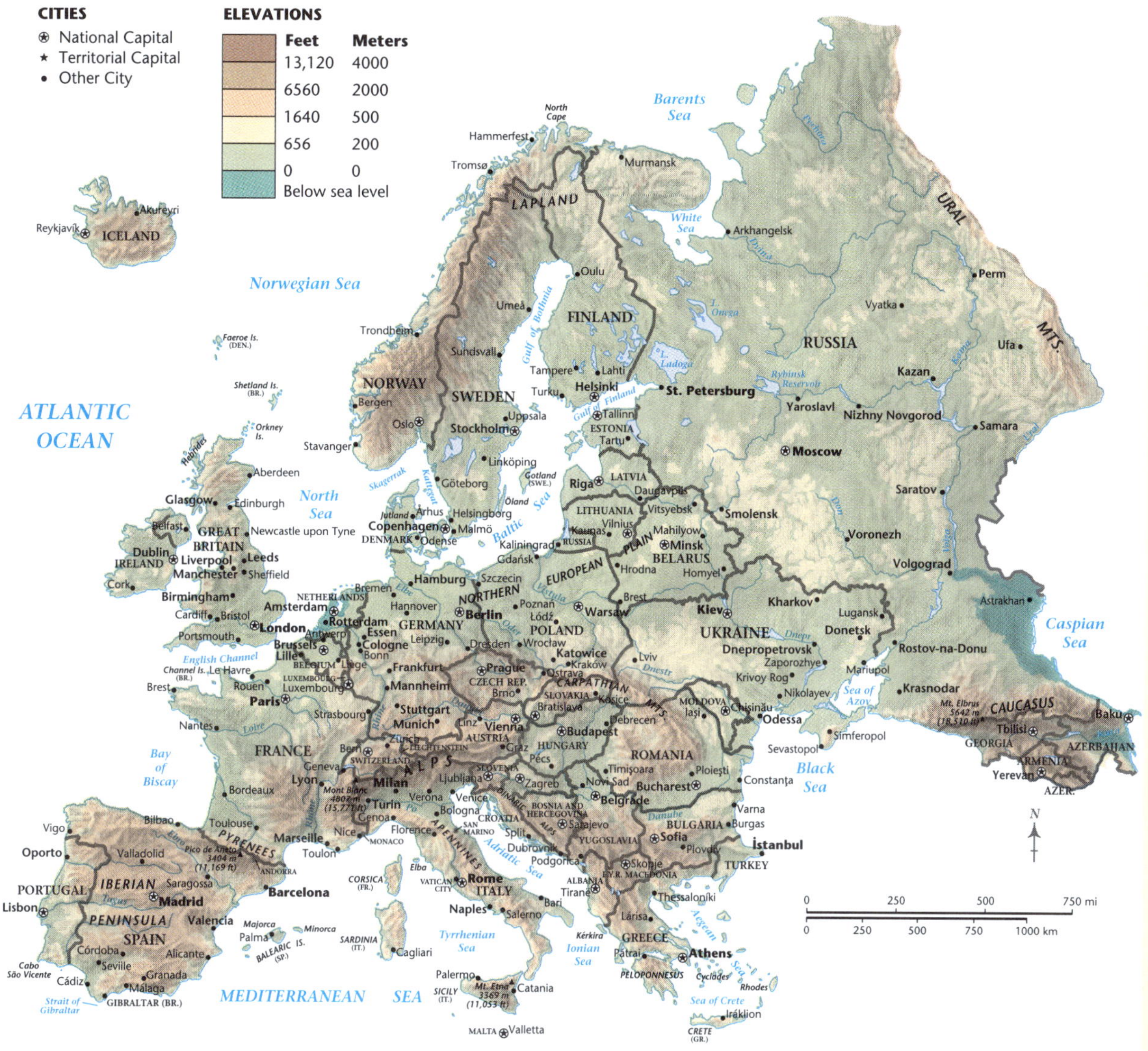
CITIES
National Capital
Territorial Capital
Other City
ELEVATIONS
Feet Meters
13,120 4000
6560 2000
1640 500
656 200
0 0
Below sea level
ATLANTIC OCEAN
Norwegian Sea
Barents Sea
White Sea
North Sea
Baltic Sea
Black Sea
Caspian Sea
MEDITERRANEAN SEA
Tyrrhenian Sea
Ionian Sea
Adriatic Sea
Aegean Sea
Bay of Biscay
English Channel
Reykjavík
Akureyri
ICELAND
NORWAY
SWEDEN
FINLAND
RUSSIA
ESTONIA
LATVIA
LITHUANIA
BELARUS
UKRAINE
POLAND
GERMANY
FRANCE
SPAIN
PORTUGAL
ITALY
AUSTRIA
HUNGARY
ROMANIA
BULGARIA
GREECE
TURKEY
YUGOSLAVIA
GREAT BRITAIN
IRELAND
DENMARK
NETHERLANDS
BELGIUM
LUXEMBOURG
SWITZERLAND
CZECH REP.
SLOVAKIA
CROATIA
MOLDOVA
GEORGIA
ARMENIA
AZERBAIJAN
LAPLAND
ALPS
PYRENEES
CARPATHIAN MTS.
URAL MTS.
CAUCASUS
NORTHERN EUROPEAN PLAIN
IBERIAN PENINSULA
Moscow
St. Petersburg
London
Paris
Berlin
Madrid
Rome
Vienna
Warsaw
Kiev
Athens
Budapest
Bucharest
Stockholm
Helsinki
Oslo
Copenhagen
Dublin
Lisbon
Prague
Minsk
Riga
Vilnius
Tallinn
Sofia
Belgrade
İstanbul
Mt. Elbrus 5642 m (18,510 ft)
Mont Blanc 4807 m (15,771 ft)
Mt. Etna 3369 m (11,053 ft)
N
0 250 500 750 mi
0 250 500 750 1000 km

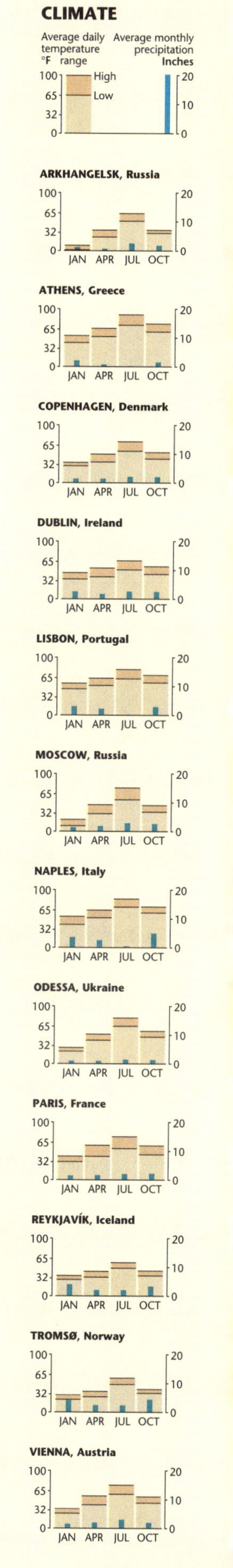
CLIMATE
Average daily temperature °F range
Average monthly precipitation Inches
High
Low
ARKHANGELSK, Russia
ATHENS, Greece
COPENHAGEN, Denmark
DUBLIN, Ireland
LISBON, Portugal
MOSCOW, Russia
NAPLES, Italy
ODESSA, Ukraine
PARIS, France
REYKJAVÍK, Iceland
TROMSØ, Norway
VIENNA, Austria
JAN APR JUL OCT

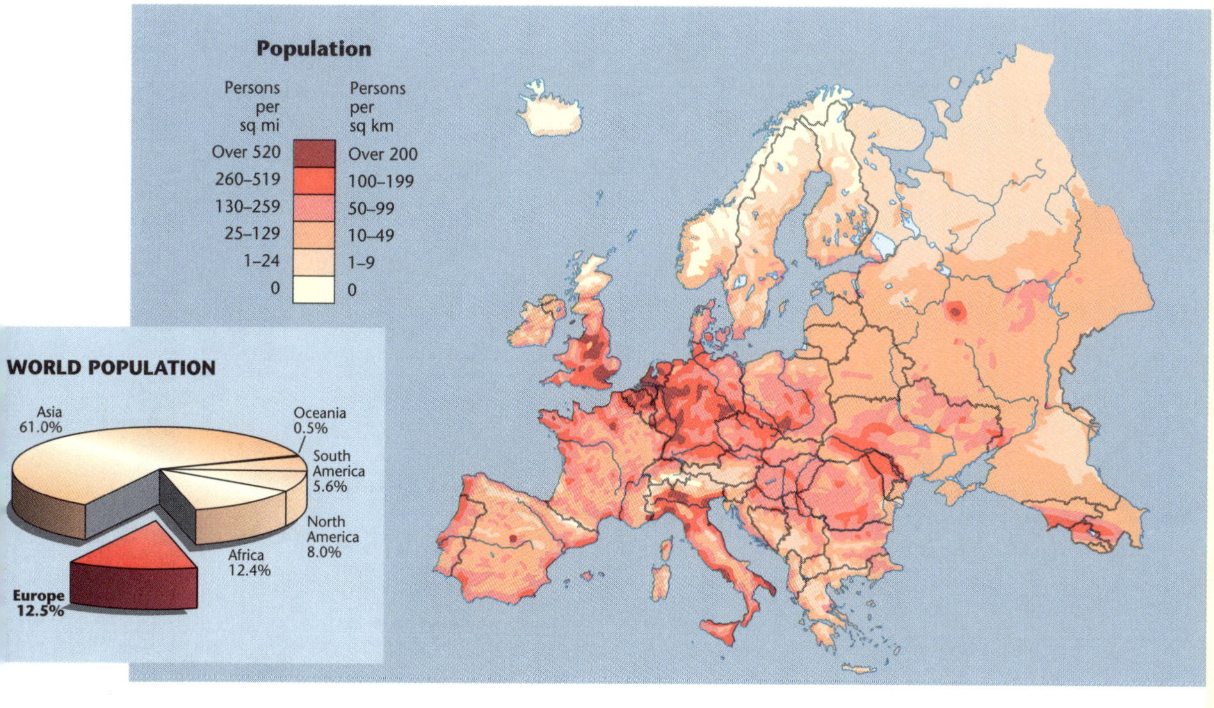
Population
Persons per sq mi
Persons per sq km
Over 520 Over 200
260–519 100–199
130–259 50–99
25–129 10–49
1–24 1–9
0 0
WORLD POPULATION
Asia 61.0%
Oceania 0.5%
South America 5.6%
North America 8.0%
Africa 12.4%
Europe 12.5%

Great Britain

Capital: London
Area: 94,251 sq. mi.
244,174 sq. km.
Population: 58,135,000
Largest City: London
Language: English
Monetary Unit: Pound

Great Britain: Map Index

CHANNEL ISLANDS
Features

ENGLAND
Cities and Towns

Republic of Ireland

Capital: Dublin
Area: 27,137 sq. mi.
70,303 sq. km.
Population: 3,539,000
Largest City: Dublin
Languages: English, Irish
Monetary Unit: Punt

Republic of Ireland: Map Index

Counties
Carlow ... C2
Cavan ... C2
Clare ... B2
Cork ... B3
Donegal ... B1
Dublin ... C2
Galway ... B2
Kerry ... B2
Kildare ... C2
Kilkenny ... C2
Laois ... C2
Leitrim ... B1
Limerick ... B2
Longford ... C2
Louth ... C2
Mayo ... B2
Meath ... C2
Monaghan ... C1
Offaly ... C2
Roscommon ... B2
Sligo ... B1
Tipperary North Riding ... B2
Tipperary South Riding ... B2
Waterford ... C2
Westmeath ... C2
Wexford ... C2
Wicklow ... C2

Cities and Towns
Ardara ... B1
Arklow ... C2
Athlone ... C2
Ballina ... B1
Bantry ... B3
Blarney ... B3
Carlingford ... C1
Carlow ... C2
Carrick-on-Shannon ... B2
Cashel ... C2
Castlebar ... B2
Cavan ... C2
Clara ... C2
Clifden ... A2
Clonmel ... C2
Cóbh ... B3
Cork ... B3
Dingle ... A2
Donegal ... B1
Drogheda ... C2
Dublin, *capital* ... C2
Dundalk ... C2
Dungarvan ... C2
Dún Laoghaire ... C2
Ennis ... B2
Ennistymon ... B2
Galway ... B2
Kildare ... C2
Kilkee ... B2
Kilkenny ... C2
Killarney ... B2
Letterkenny ... C1
Lifford ... C1
Limerick ... B2
Longford ... C2
Mallow ... B2
Maynooth ... C2
Monaghan ... C1
Mullingar ... C2
Naas ... C2
Nenagh ... B2
Port Laoise ... C2
Roscommon ... B2
Roscrea ... C2
Rosslare ... C2
Shannon ... B2
Sligo ... B1
Swords ... C2
Tipperary ... B2
Tralee ... B2
Trim ... C2
Tuam ... B2
Tullamore ... C2
Waterford ... C2
Westport ... B2
Wexford ... C2
Wicklow ... C2
Youghal ... C3

Other Features
Achill, *island* ... A2
Allen, *lake* ... B1
Aran, *islands* ... B2
Bantry, *bay* ... B3
Barrow, *river* ... C2
Benwee Head, *cape* ... B1
Blackwater, *river* ... B2
Blackwater, *river* ... C1
Boggeragh, *mts.* ... B2
Boyne, *river* ... C2
Caha, *mts.* ... B3
Carlingford, *lake* ... C1
Carnsore, *point* ... C2
Carrantuohill, *mt.* ... B3
Celtic, *sea* ... B3
Clear, *cape* ... B3
Conn, *lake* ... B1
Connaught, *province* ... B2
Connemara, *region* ... B2
Corrib, *lake* ... B2
Derg, *lake* ... B2
Dingle, *bay* ... A2
Donegal, *bay* ... B1
Erne, *river* ... B1
Errigal, *mt.* ... B1
Finn, *river* ... C1
Foyle, *inlet* ... C1
Galway, *bay* ... B2
Grand, *canal* ... C2
Irish, *sea* ... D2
Killala, *bay* ... B1
Knockboy, *mt.* ... B3
Lee, *river* ... B3
Leinster, *province* ... C2
Loop Head, *cape* ... B2
Malin Head, *cape* ... C1
Mask, *lake* ... B2
Maumturk, *mts.* ... B2
Mizen Head, *cape* ... B3
Moher, *cliffs* ... B2
Munster, *province* ... B2
Ree, *lake* ... B2
Royal, *canal* ... C2
Saint George's, *channel* ... C3
Shannon, *river* ... B2
Suir, *river* ... C2
Twelve Pins, *mt.* ... B2
Ulster, *province* ... C1
Wicklow, *mts.* ... C2
Wicklow Head, *cape* ... D2

Great Britain: Map Index

St. Austell ... B4
St. Helens ... C3
Salford ... C3
Salisbury ... C3
Scarborough ... C2
Scunthorpe ... C3
Sheffield ... C3
Shrewsbury ... C3
Slough ... Inset III
Solihull ... C3
Southampton ... C4
Southend-on-Sea ... D3
Southport ... C3
South Shields ... C2
Stafford ... C3
Stevenage ... Inset III
Stoke-on-Trent ... C3
Stratford-upon-Avon ... C3
Sunderland ... C2
Swindon ... C3
Taunton ... C3
Telford ... C3
Tewkesbury ... C3
Thetford ... D3
Tiverton ... B4
Tonbridge ... Inset III
Torbay ... B4
Trowbridge ... C3
Truro ... B4
Tunbridge Wells ... D3
Wakefield ... C3
Walsall ... C3
Warrington ... C3
Warwick ... C3
Watford ... Inset III
Westminster ... Inset III
Whitehaven ... B2
Wigan ... C3
Wimbledon ... Inset III
Winchester ... C3
Windsor ... Inset III
Wolverhampton ... C3
Worcester ... C3
Yeovil ... C4
York ... C3

Other Features
Avon, *river* ... C3
Black Country, *region* ... C3
Bristol, *channel* ... B3
Cheviot, *hills* ... C2
Cotswold, *hills* ... C3
Cumbrian, *mts.* ... B2
Dartmoor, *plateau* ... B4
Dee, *river* ... B3
Dover, *strait* ... D4
English, *channel* ... C4
Exmoor, *plateau* ... B3
Fens, *region* ... D3
Flodden Field, *plain* ... C2
Humber, *river* ... D3
Irish, *sea* ... B3
Lake, *district* ... B2
Land's End, *promontory* ... B4
Liverpool, *bay* ... B3
Lyme, *bay* ... C4
Mersey, *river* ... C3
Midlands, *region* ... C3
North, *sea* ... D2
North Downs, *hills* ... C3
North Foreland, *promontory* ... D3
Ouse, *river* ... C2, D3
Pennines, *mts.* ... C2
Scafell Pike, *mt.* ... B2
Scilly, *islands* ... A4
Severn, *river* ... C3
South Downs, *hills* ... C3
Spithead, *channel* ... C4
Start, *point* ... B4
Tees, *river* ... C2
Thames, *river* ... C3, Inset III
Trent, *river* ... C3
Tweed, *river* ... C2
Tyne, *river* ... C2
Wash, *bay* ... D3
Wight, *island* ... C4
Wye, *river* ... C3
Yare, *river* ... D3

ISLE OF MAN
City
Douglas ... B2

NORTHERN IRELAND
Cities and Towns
Armagh ... A2
Ballymena ... A2
Bangor ... B2
Belfast ... B2
Coleraine ... A2
Holywood ... B2
Larne ... B2
Londonderry ... A2
Newry ... A2
Omagh ... A2
Portadown ... A2
Strangford ... B2

Other Features
Antrim, *mts.* ... A2
Bann, *river* ... A2
Erne, *river* ... A2
Foyle, *lake* ... A2
Foyle, *river* ... A2
Giant's Causeway, *headland* ... A2
Irish, *sea* ... B3
Lough Erne, *lake* ... A2
Mourne, *mts.* ... A2
Neagh, *lake* ... A2
North, *channel* ... A2
Rathlin, *island* ... A2
Slieve Donard, *mt.* ... B2
Sperrin, *mts.* ... A2
Upper Lough Erne, *lake* ... A2

SCOTLAND
Cities and Towns
Aberdeen ... C1
Aviemore ... B1
Ayr ... B2
Campbeltown ... B2
Clydebank ... B2
Cupar ... B2
Dornoch ... B1
Dumfries ... B2
Dundee ... C2
Dunfermline ... B2
Edinburgh ... B2
Elgin ... B1
Fort William ... B2
Fraserburgh ... C1
Glasgow ... B2
Greenock ... B2
Hamilton ... B2
Hawick ... C2
Inverness ... B1
Kilmarnock ... B2
Kirkcaldy ... B2
Kirkwall ... Inset I
Kyle of Lochalsh ... B1
Lairg ... B1
Lerwick ... Inset I
Mallaig ... B1
Montrose ... C2
Motherwell ... B2
Newtown St. Boswells ... C2
Oban ... B2
Paisley ... B2
Perth ... B2
Peterhead ... C1
Pitlochry ... B2
Portree ... A1
St. Andrews ... C2
Scone ... B2
Sconser ... A1
Stirling ... B2
Stornoway ... A1
Stranraer ... B2
Thurso ... B1
Ullapool ... B1
Wick ... B1

Other Features
Arran, *island* ... B2
Barra, *island* ... A2
Bass Rock, *islet* ... C2
Bell Rock (Inchcape), *reef* ... C2
Ben Nevis, *mt.* ... B2
Bute, *island* ... B2
Cheviot, *hills* ... C2
Clyde, *estuary* ... B2
Clyde, *river* ... B2
Coll, *island* ... A2
Colonsay, *island* ... A2
Dee, *river* ... C1
Dornoch, *estuary* ... B1
Duncansby, *cape* ... B1
Dunsinane, *mt.* ... B2
Eigg, *island* ... A2
Fair, *island* ... Inset I
Forth, *estuary* ... C2
Forth, *river* ... B2
Grampian, *mts.* ... B2
Hebrides, *sea* ... A1
Hoy, *island* ... Inset I
Inner Hebrides, *islands* ... A2
Islay, *island* ... A2
Jura, *island* ... B2
Katrine, *lake* ... B2
Kinnairds, *cape* ... C1
Lammermuir, *hills* ... C2
Lewis, *island* ... A1
Linnhe, *lake* ... B2
Lomond, *lake* ... B2
Lorne, *estuary* ... A2
Mainland, *island* ... Inset I
Merrick, *mt.* ... B2
Minch, *strait* ... B1
Moray, *estuary* ... B1
Mull, *island* ... A2
Ness, *lake* ... B1
North Uist, *island* ... A1
Ochil, *hills* ... B2
Orkney, *islands* ... Inset I
Outer Hebrides, *islands* ... A1
Rhum, *island* ... A1
Sanday, *island* ... Inset I
Shetland, *islands* ... Inset I
Sidlaw, *hills* ... B2
Skye, *island* ... A1
Solway, *estuary* ... B2
Southern Uplands, *mts.* ... B2
South Ronaldsay, *island* ... Inset I
South Uist, *island* ... A1
Spey, *river* ... B1
Stronsay, *island* ... Inset I
Tay, *estuary* ... C2
Tay, *lake* ... B2
Tay, *river* ... B2
Tiree, *island* ... A2
Tweed, *river* ... C2
Unst, *island* ... Inset I
Westray, *island* ... Inset I
Wrath, *cape* ... B1
Yell, *island* ... Inset I

WALES
Cities and Towns
Aberystwyth ... B3
Bangor ... B3
Caerleon ... C3
Caernarfon ... B3
Cardiff ... B3
Carmarthen ... B3
Conwy ... B3
Fishguard ... B3
Holyhead ... B3
Lampeter ... B3
Llandrindod Wells ... B3
Merthyr Tydfil ... B3
Milford Haven ... B3
Mold ... B3
Newport ... C3
Pembroke ... B3
Port Talbot ... B3
Rhondda ... B3
St. David's ... B3
Swansea ... B3
Welshpool ... B3

Other Features
Anglesey, *island* ... B3
Bala, *lake* ... B3
Brecon Beacons, *mts.* ... B3
Bristol, *channel* ... B3
Cambrian, *mts.* ... B3
Cardigan, *bay* ... B3
Dee, *river* ... B3
Lleyn, *peninsula* ... B3
Menai, *strait* ... B3
Snowdon, *mt.* ... B3
Teifi, *river* ... B3
Tywi, *river* ... B3
Usk, *river* ... C3
Wye, *river* ... C3

Denmark

Capital: Copenhagen
Area: 16,639 sq. mi.
43,080 sq. km.
Population: 5,188,000
Largest City: Copenhagen
Language: Danish
Monetary Unit: Krone

Denmark: Map Index

Netherlands: Map Index

Netherlands

Capital: Amsterdam
Area: 16,033 sq. mi.
41,536 sq. km.
Population: 15,368,000
Largest City: Amsterdam
Language: Dutch
Monetary Unit: Guilder

Belgium:
Map Index

Provinces
- Antwerp C1
- Brabant C2
- East Flanders B2
- Hainaut B2
- Liège D2
- Limburg D1
- Luxembourg D3
- Namur C2
- West Flanders B1

Cities and Towns
- Aalst C2
- Anderlecht C2
- Antwerp C1
- Arlon D3
- Ath B2
- Bastogne D2
- Binche C2
- Brugge B1
- Brussels, *capital* C2
- Charleroi C2
- Chimay C2
- Dinant C2
- Gembloux C2
- Genk D2
- Ghent B1
- Halle C2
- Hasselt D2
- Ixelles C2
- Knokke B1
- Kortrijk B2
- La Louvière C2
- Liège D2
- Limbourg D2
- Louvain C2
- Malmédy E2
- Mechelen C1
- Mons B2
- Mouscron B2
- Namur C2
- Neufchâteau D3
- Oostende A1
- Poperinge A2
- Roeselare B2
- Schaerbeek C2
- Sint-Niklaas C1
- Sint-Truiden D2
- Spa D2
- Tournai B2
- Turnhout C1
- Uccle C2
- Verviers D2
- Ypres A2
- Zeebrugge B1

Other Features
- Albert, *canal* C1
- Ardennes, *plateau* D2
- Botrange, *mt.* E2
- Brugge-Ghent, *canal* B1
- Dender, *river* B2
- Kempenland, *region* D1
- Leie, *river* B2
- Maas, *river* D2
- Meuse, *river* D2
- Oostende-Brugge, *canal* B1
- Ourthe, *river* D2
- Rupel, *river* C1
- Sambre, *river* C2
- Schelde, *river* B2
- Semois, *river* D3
- Senne, *river* C2

Belgium

Capital: Brussels
Area: 11,787 sq. mi.
30,536 sq. km.
Population: 10,063,000
Largest City: Brussels
Languages: Flemish, French, German
Monetary Unit: Belgian franc

Liechtenstein

Capital: Vaduz
Area: 62 sq. mi.
161 sq. km.
Population: 30,000
Largest City: Vaduz
Language: German
Monetary Unit: Swiss franc

Liechtenstein:
Map Index

Cities and Towns
- Balzers B2
- Eschen B1
- Gamprin B1
- Malbun B2
- Mauren B1
- Planken B1
- Ruggell B1
- Schaan B2
- Schellenberg B1
- Triesen B2
- Triesenberg B2
- Vaduz, *capital* B2

Other Features
- Alps, *range* A2
- Grauspitz, *mt.* B2
- Rhine, *canal* B1, B2
- Rhine, *river* A1, A2
- Samina, *river* B2

Luxembourg

Capital: Luxembourg
Area: 999 sq. mi.
2,588 sq. km.
Population: 402,000
Largest City: Luxembourg
Languages: French, German
Monetary Unit: Luxembourg franc

Luxembourg:
Map Index

Cities and Towns
- Clervaux B1
- Diekirch B2
- Differdange A2
- Dudelange B2
- Echternach B2
- Esch-sur-Alzette A2
- Ettelbruck B2
- Grevenmacher B2
- Larochette B2
- Luxembourg, *capital* B2
- Mersch B2
- Redange A2
- Remich B2
- Troisvierges B1
- Vianden B2
- Wiltz A2

Other Features
- Alzette, *river* B2
- Ardennes, *plateau* A1
- Bon Pays, *region* B2
- Buurgplaatz, *mt.* B1
- Clerve, *river* B1
- Mosel, *river* B2
- Our, *river* B1
- Sûre, *river* A2, B2

France
National Capital
Other City
1:5,625,000
0 50 100 mi
0 50 100 km
Lambert Conformal Conic Projection
GREAT BRITAIN
ENGLAND
London
Bristol
Exeter
Plymouth
Portsmouth
Brighton
Dover
Thames
Bristol Channel
English Channel
Strait of Dover
Channel Islands (Br.)
Guernsey
Sark
Jersey
Golfe de Saint-Malo
Cap de la Hague
Utah Beach
Omaha Beach
Cotentin
NETHERLANDS
Eindhoven
BELGIUM
Brussels
Antwerp
Brugge
Ghent
Liège
Namur
Ardennes
LUXEMBOURG
Luxembourg
GERMANY
Essen
Düsseldorf
Cologne
Bonn
Koblenz
Wiesbaden
Trier
Mannheim
Saarbrücken
Karlsruhe
Freiburg
Rhine
Meuse
Sambre
Saar
NORD-PAS-DE-CALAIS
Dunkirk (Dunkerque)
Calais
Boulogne-sur-Mer
Lille
Tourcoing
Roubaix
Lens
Douai
Arras
Cambrai
Valenciennes
PICARDIE
Abbeville
Amiens
Beauvais
Compiègne
Soissons
Laon
Chantilly
Somme
Oise
Aisne
HAUTE-NORMANDIE
Dieppe
Le Havre
Rouen
Trouville
Deauville
Évreux
Seine
BASSE-NORMANDIE
Cherbourg
Bayeux
Caen
Saint-Lô
Alençon
Mont-Saint-Michel
Orne
BRETAGNE
Brest
Morlaix
Saint-Brieuc
Saint-Malo
Quimper
Rennes
Lorient
Vannes
Carnac
Belle-Île
Pointe du Raz
Rance
Vilaine
ÎLE-DE-FRANCE
Paris
Versailles
Dreux
Chartres
Fontainebleau
CHAMPAGNE-ARDENNE
Reims
Charleville Mézières
Sedan
Châlons-sur-Marne
Saint-Dizier
Troyes
Chaumont
Marne
Argonne
Aube
LORRAINE
Verdun
Metz
Nancy
Bar-le-Duc
Épinal
Moselle
ALSACE
Strasbourg
Colmar
Mulhouse
VOSGES
PAYS DE LA LOIRE
Le Mans
Laval
Angers
Saumur
Nantes
Saint-Nazaire
Cholet
La-Roche-sur-Yon
Loire
Île d'Yeu
CENTRE
Orléans
Montargis
Blois
Tours
Vierzon
Bourges
Châteauroux
Vienne
BOURGOGNE
Auxerre
Dijon
Nevers
Le Creusot
Cluny
Mâcon
Yonne
FRANCHE-COMTÉ
Besançon
Dôle
Vesoul
Belfort
Belfort Gap
JURA
SWITZERLAND
Bern
Basel
Lausanne
L. Geneva
Geneva
Aare
Rhône
POITOU-CHARENTES
Châtellerault
Poitiers
Niort
La Rochelle
Rochefort
Saintes
Cognac
Angoulême
Île de Ré
Île d'Oléron
Charente
LIMOUSIN
Limoges
Guéret
Brive-la-Gallarde
AUVERGNE
Montluçon
Vichy
Clermont-Ferrand
Aurillac
Le Puy
Allier
MASSIF CENTRAL
RHÔNE-ALPES
Roanne
Bourg-en-Bresse
Lyon
Saint-Étienne
Annecy
Aix-les-Bains
Chambéry
Grenoble
Valence
Privas
Montélimar
Saône
Isère
Mont Blanc 4807 m (15,771 ft)
Chamonix-Mont-Blanc
Great St. Bernard Pass
Little St. Bernard Pass
ALPS
ITALY
Turin
Cuneo
Po
Maritime Alps
Bay of Biscay
AQUITAINE
Bordeaux
Arcachon
Bergerac
Périgueux
Agen
Biarritz
Bayonne
Pau
LANDES
Gironde
Dordogne
Garonne
Adour
MIDI-PYRÉNÉES
Cahors
Rodez
Montauban
Albi
Auch
Toulouse
Tarbes
Lourdes
Carcassonne
Foix
Lot
LANGUEDOC-ROUSSILLON
Mende
Alès
Nîmes
Montpellier
Béziers
Narbonne
Perpignan
CÉVENNES
PROVENCE-ALPES-CÔTE-D'AZUR
Briançon
Gap
Digne
Avignon
Arles
Draguignan
Aix-en-Provence
Marseille
Toulon
Nice
Cannes
Fréjus
St.-Tropez
Durance
MONACO
Golfe du Lion
Mediterranean Sea
PYRENEES
Pic de Vignemale 3298 m (10,820 ft)
ANDORRA
SPAIN
Santander
Pamplona
Burgos
Soria
Saragossa
Lérida
Tarragona
Gerona
Castellón de la Plana
Duero
Ebro
N
I
Same scale as main map
Mediterranean Sea
CORSICA
CORSE
Calvi
Bastia
Ajaccio
Porto-Vecchio
II
L'Isle-Adam
Luzarches
Louvres
Dammartin-en-Goële
Pontoise
Meulan
Taverny
Domont
Conflans-Sainte-Honorine
Sarcelles
Maisons-Laffitte
Argenteuil
Saint-Denis
Sevran
Poissy
Levallois-Perret
Clichy
Bondy
Chelles
Saint-Germain-en-Laye
Nanterre
Paris
Montreuil
Saint-Cloud
Boulogne-Billancourt
Sèvres
Vincennes
Pontchartrain
Versailles
Gentilly
Créteil
Maurepas
Choisy-le Roi
Ozoir-la-Ferrière
Massy
Villeneuve-Saint-Georges
Chevreuse
Palaiseau
Coubert
Les Ulis
Savigny-sur-Orge
Limours
Évry
Arpajon
Corbeil-Essonnes
Mennecy
Etrechy
Ballancourt-sur-Essonne
Melun
0 5 10 mi
0 5 10 km

Switzerland

Capital: Bern
Area: 15,943 sq. mi.
41,303 sq. km.
Population: 7,040,000
Largest City: Zürich
Languages: German, French, Italian
Monetary Unit: Swiss franc

© GeoSystems Global Corp.

© GeoSystems Global Corp.

Monaco: Map Index

Districts
Fontvieille A2
La Condamine B1
Monaco, *capital* B1
Monte Carlo B1

Other Features
Casino B1
Fontvieille, *port* B2
Monaco, *port* B1
Palace B2
Sporting Club C1

Monaco

Capital: Monaco
Area: 0.75 sq. mi.
1.94 sq. km.
Population: 31,000
Language: French
Monetary Unit: French franc or Monégasque franc

Switzerland: Map Index

Cantons
Aargau C1
Appenzell Ausser-Rhoden D1
Appenzell Inner-Rhoden D1
Basel-Land B1
Basel-Stadt B1
Bern B2
Fribourg B2
Geneva A2
Glarus D2
Graubünden D2
Jura B1
Lucerne C1
Neuchâtel A2
Nidwalden C2
Obwalden C2
Sankt Gallen D1
Schaffhausen C1
Schwyz C1
Solothurn B1
Thurgau C1
Ticino C2
Uri C2
Valais B2
Vaud A2
Zug C1
Zürich C1

Cities and Towns
Aarau C1
Altdorf C2
Baden C1
Basel B1
Bellinzona D2
Bern, *capital* B2
Biel B1
Bolligen B2
Bulle B2
Chur D2
Davos D2
Einsiedeln C1
Fribourg B2
Frutigen B2
Geneva A2
Horgèn C1
Interlaken B2
La Chaux-de-Fonds A1
Lausanne A2
Locarno C2
Lucerne C1
Lugano C3
Montreux A2
Morges A2
Neuchâtel A2
St. Moritz D2
Sankt Gallen D1
Schaffhausen C1
Schwyz C1
Sempach C1
Sion B2
Thun B2
Uster C1
Winterthur C1
Yverdon A2
Zermatt B2
Zug C1
Zürich C1

Other Features
Aare, *river* B1, B2
Alps, *mts.* B2
Bernese Alps, *mts.* B2
Biel, *lake* B1
Brienzersee, *lake* B2
Constance (Bodensee), *lake* D1
Doubs, *river* A1
Dufourspitze, *mt.* B3
Engadine, *valley* D2
Geneva, *lake* A2
Inn, *river* D2
Jungfrau, *mt.* B2
Jura, *mts.* A2
Lepontine Alps, *mts.* C2
Lucerne, *lake* C2
Lugano, *lake* C3
Maggiore, *lake* C2
Matterhorn, *mt.* B3
Neuchâtel, *lake* A2
Pennine Alps, *mts.* B2
Reuss, *river* C2
Rhaetian Alps, *mts.* D2
Rhine, *river* C1, D2
Rhône, *river* B2
St. Gotthard, *pass* C2
St. Gotthard, *tunnel* C2
Splügen, *pass* D2
Staubbach, *falls* B2
Thunersee, *lake* B2
Ticino, *river* C2
Walensee, *lake* D1
Zürichsee, *lake* C1

France

Capital: Paris
Area: 210,026 sq. mi.
544,109 sq. km.
Population: 57,840,000
Largest City: Paris
Language: French
Monetary Unit: Franc

France: Map Index

Regions
Alsace D2
Aquitaine B4
Auvergne C4
Basse-Normandie B2
Bourgogne C3
Bretagne B2
Centre C3
Champagne-Ardenne D2
Corse ....Inset I
Franche-Comté D3
Haute-Normandie C2
Île-de-France C2
Languedoc-Roussillon C5
Limousin C4
Lorraine D2
Midi-Pyrénées C5
Nord-Pas-de-Calais C1
Pays De La Loire B3
Picardie C2
Poitou-Charentes C3
Provence-Alpes-Côte-d'Azur D4
Rhône-Alpes D4

Cities and Towns
Abbeville C1
Agen C4
Aix-en-Provence D5
Aix-les-Bains D4
Ajaccio ....Inset I
Albi C5
Alençon C2
Alès D4
Amiens C2
Angers B3
Angoulême C4
Annecy D4
Arachon B4
Argenteuil ....Inset II
Arles D5
Arpajon ....Inset II
Arras C1
Auch C5
Aurillac C4
Auxerre C3
Avignon D5
Ballancourt-sur-Essonne ....Inset II
Bar-le-Duc D2
Bastia ....Inset I
Bayeux B2
Bayonne B5
Beauvais C2
Belfort D3
Bergerac C4
Besançon D3
Béziers C5
Biarritz B5
Blois C3
Bondy ....Inset II
Bordeaux B4
Boulogne-Billancourt ....Inset II
Boulogne-sur-Mer C1
Bourg-en-Bresse D3
Bourges C3
Brest A2
Briançon D4
Brive-la-Gallarde C4
Caen B2
Cahors C4
Calais C1
Calvi ....Inset I
Cambrai C1
Cannes D5
Carcassonne C5
Carnac B3
Châlons-sur-Marne D2
Chambéry D4
Chamonix-Mont-Blanc D4
Chantilly C2
Charleville Mézières D2
Chartres C2
Châteauroux C3
Châtellerault C3
Chaumont D2
Chelles ....Inset II
Cherbourg B2
Chevreuse ....Inset II
Choisy-le Roi ....Inset II
Cholet B3
Clermont-Ferrand C4
Clichy ....Inset II
Cluny D3
Cognac B4
Colmar D2
Compiègne C2
Conflans-Sainte-Honorine ....Inset II
Corbeil-Essonnes ....Inset II
Coubert ....Inset II
Créteil ....Inset II
Dammartin-en-Goële ....Inset II
Deauville C2
Dieppe C2
Digne D4
Dijon D3
Dôle D3
Domont ....Inset II
Douai C1
Draguignan D5
Dreux C2
Dunkirk (Dunkerque) C1
Épinal D2
Etrechy ....Inset II
Évreux C2
Évry ....Inset II
Foix C5
Fontainebleau C2
Fréjus D5
Gap D4
Gentilly ....Inset II
Grenoble D4
Guéret C3
Laon C2
La Rochelle B3
La-Roche-sur-Yon B3
Laval B2
Le Creusot D3
Le Havre C2
Le Mans C2
Lens C1
Le Puy C4
Les Ulis ....Inset II
Levallois-Perret ....Inset II
Lille C1
Limoges C4
Limours ....Inset II
L'Isle-Adam ....Inset II
Lorient B3
Lourdes B5
Louvres ....Inset II
Luzarches ....Inset II
Lyon D4
Mâcon D3
Maisons-Laffitte ....Inset II
Marseille D5
Massy ....Inset II
Maurepas ....Inset II
Melun ....Inset II
Mende C4
Mennecy ....Inset II
Metz D2
Meulan ....Inset II
Montargis C2
Montauban C4
Montélimar D4
Montluçon C3
Montpellier C5
Montreuil ....Inset II
Mont-Saint-Michel B2
Morlaix B2
Mulhouse D3
Nancy D2
Nanterre ....Inset II
Nantes B3
Narbonne C5
Nevers C3
Nice D5
Nîmes D5
Niort B3
Orléans C3
Ozoir-la-Ferrière ....Inset II
Palaiseau ....Inset II
Paris, *capital* ....C2, Inset II
Pau B5
Périgueux C4
Perpignan C5
Poissy ....Inset II
Poitiers C3
Pontchartrain ....Inset II
Pontoise ....Inset II
Porto-Vecchio ....Inset I
Privas D4
Quimper A2
Reims D2
Rennes B2
Roanne D3
Rochefort B4
Rodez C4
Roubaix C1
Rouen C2
Saint-Brieuc B2
Saint-Cloud ....Inset II
Saint-Denis ....Inset II
Saint-Dizier D2
Saintes B4
Saint-Étienne D4
Saint-Germain-en-Laye ....Inset II
Saint-Lô B2
Saint-Malo B2
Saint-Nazaire B3
Saint-Tropez D5
Sarcelles ....Inset II
Saumur B3
Savigny-sur-Orge ....Inset II
Sedan D2
Sevran ....Inset II
Sèvres ....Inset II
Soissons C2
Strasbourg D2
Tarbes C5
Taverny ....Inset II
Toulon D5
Toulouse C5
Tourcoing C1
Tours C3
Trouville C2
Troyes D2
Valence D4
Valenciennes C1
Vannes B3
Verdun D2
Versailles ....C2, Inset II
Vesoul D3
Vichy C3
Vierzon C3
Villeneuve-Saint-Georges ....Inset II
Vincennes ....Inset II

Other Features
Adour, *river* B5
Aisne, *river* D2
Allier, *river* C3
Alps, *range* D4
Ardennes, *region* D1
Argonne, *forest* D2
Aube, *river* D3
Belfort, *gap* D3
Belle, *island* B3
Biscay, *bay* B4
Blanc, *mt.* D4
Cévennes, *mts.* C4
Charente, *river* B4
Corsica, *island* ....Inset I
Cotentin, *peninsula* B2
Dordogne, *river* C4
Dover, *strait* C1
Durance, *river* D5
English, *channel* B2
Garonne, *river* C4
Geneva, *lake* D3
Gironde, *river* B4
Hague, *cape* B2
Isère, *river* D4
Jura, *mts.* D3
Landes, *region* B5
Lion, *gulf* D5
Little St. Bernard, *pass* D4
Loire, *river* C3
Lot, *river* C4
Maritime Alps, *range* D4
Marne, *river* ....C2, Inset II
Massif Central, *plateau* C4
Meuse, *river* D2
Moselle, *river* D2
Oise, *river* ....C2, Inset II
Oléron, *island* B4
Omaha, *beach* B2
Orne, *river* B2
Pyrenees, *range* C5
Rance, *river* B2
Raz, *point* A3
Ré, *island* B3
Rhine, *river* D2
Rhône, *river* D4
Saint-Malo, *gulf* B2
Sambre, *river* C1
Saône, *river* D3
Seine, *river* ....C2, Inset II
Somme, *river* C2
Utah, *beach* B2
Vienne, *river* C3
Vignemale, *mt.* B5
Vilaine, *river* B3
Vosges, *mts.* D2
Yeu, *island* B3
Yonne, *river* C2

Portugal

Capital: Lisbon
Area: 35,672 sq. mi.
92,415 sq. km.
Population: 10,524,000
Largest City: Lisbon
Language: Portuguese
Monetary Unit: Escudo

Malta

Capital: Valletta
Area: 122 sq. mi.
316 sq. km.
Population: 367,000
Largest City: Valletta
Languages: Maltese, English
Monetary Unit: Maltese lira

Gibraltar

Area: 2.25 sq. mi.
5.83 sq. km.
Population: 30,000
Language: English
Monetary Unit: British Pound

Andorra

Capital: Andorra la Vella
Area: 181 sq. mi.
469 sq. km.
Population: 64,000
Largest City: Andorra la Vella
Language: Catalan
Monetary Unit: French franc

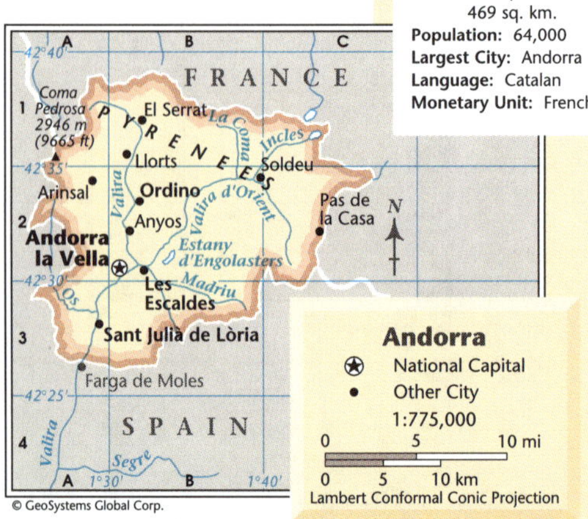

Spain

Capital: Madrid
Area: 194,898 sq. mi.
504,917 sq. km.
Population: 39,303,000
Largest City: Madrid
Language: Spanish
Monetary Unit: Peseta

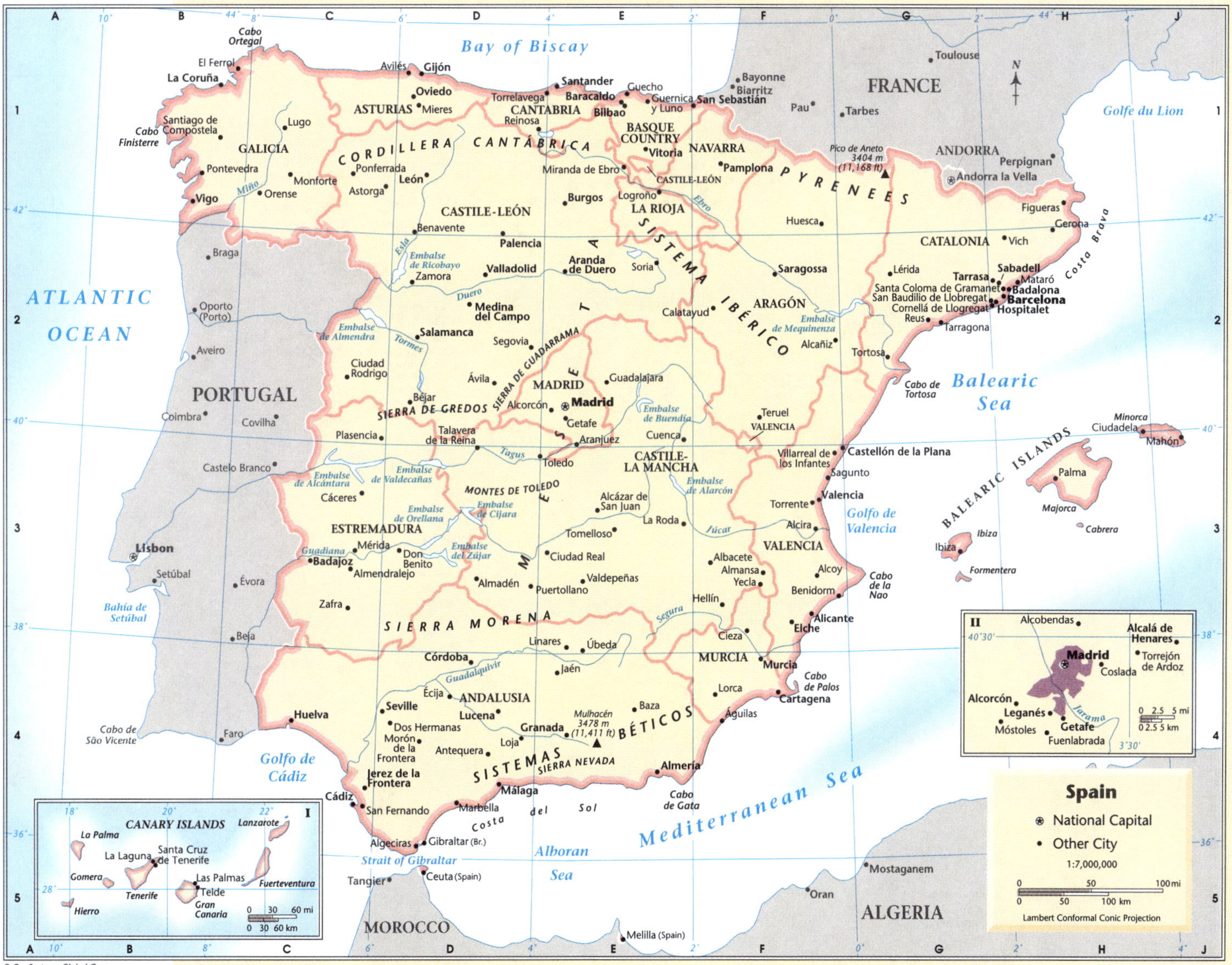

Italy

Capital: Rome
Area: 116,333 sq. mi.
301,381 sq. km.
Population: 58,138,000
Largest City: Rome
Language: Italian
Monetary Unit: Lira

Austria: Map Index

Provinces
Burgenland E3
Carinthia C4
Lower Austria D2
Salzburg C3
Styria D3
Tirol B3, C4
Upper Austria C2
Vienna E2
Vorarlberg A3

Cities and Towns
Amstetten D2
Baden E2
Bad Ischl C3
Braunau C2
Feldkirch A3
Fürstenfeld E3
Gmünd D2
Graz D3
Hieflau D3
Innsbruck B3
Kapfenberg D3
Klagenfurt D4
Köflach D3
Kufstein C3
Lech B3
Leoben D3
Lienz C4
Linz D2
Mistelbach E2
Salzburg C3
Sankt Pölten D2
Steyr D2
Stockerau E2
Vienna, *capital* E2
Villach C4
Vöcklabruck C2
Wels C2
Wiener Neustadt E3
Wolfsberg D4

Other Features
Alps, *range* B3
Bavarian Alps, *range* B3
Brenner, *pass* B3
Carnic Alps, *range* C4
Constance, *lake* A3
Danube, *river* D2
Drava, *river* C4
Enns, *river* D3
Grossglockner, *mt.* C3
Hohe Tauern, *mts.* C3
Inn, *river* B3, C2
Karawanken, *range* D4
Mur, *river* D3
Mürz, *river* D3
Neusiedler, *lake* E3
Niedere Tauern, *range* D3
Ötztal Alps, *range* B4
Salzach, *river* C3
Salzburg Alps, *range* C3
Semmering, *pass* D3
Traun, *river* D2
Ybbs, *river* D2
Zillertal Alps, *range* B3

Austria

Capital: Vienna
Area: 32,378 sq. mi.
83,881 sq. km.
Population: 7,955,000
Largest City: Vienna
Language: German
Monetary Unit: Schilling

Vatican City

Area: 108.7 acres
Population: 811
Languages: Italian, Latin
Monetary Unit: Lira

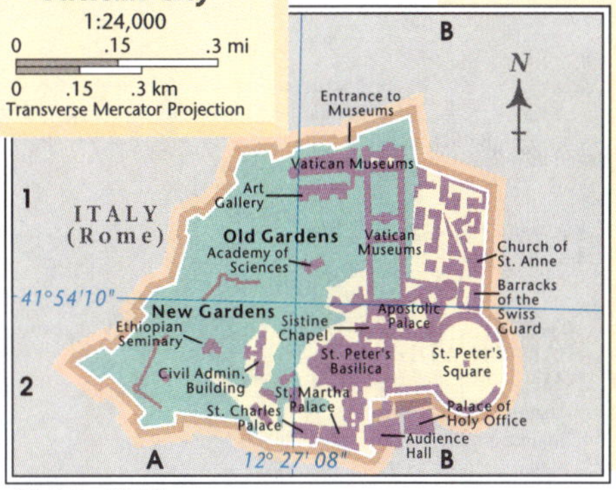

Vatican City: Map Index

Features
Academy of Sciences B1
Apostolic Palace B2
Art Gallery B1
Audience Hall B2
Barracks of the Swiss Guard B1
Church of St. Anne B1
Civil Administration Building A2
Entrance to Museums B1
Ethiopian Seminary A2
New Gardens A2
Old Gardens A1
Palace of Holy Office B2
St. Charles Palace B2
St. Martha Palace B2
St. Peter's Basilica B2
St. Peter's Square B2
Sistine Chapel B2
Vatican Museums B1

Italy: Map Index

Regions
Abruzzi C2
Apulia C2
Basilicata C2
Calabria D3
Campania C2
Emilia-Romagna B1
Friuli-Venezia Giulia C1
Latium C2
Liguria B1
Lombardy B1
Marche C2
Molise C2
Piedmont A1
Puglia C2
Sardinia B3
Sicily C3
Trentino-Alto Adige B1
Tuscany B2
Umbria C2
Valle d'Aosta A1
Veneto B1

Cities and Towns
Agrigento C3
Alessandria B1
Alghero B2
Ancona C2
Aosta A1
Aquileia C1
Arezzo B2
Ascoli Piceno C2
Asti B1
Avellino C2
Bari D2
Barletta D2
Belluno C1
Benevento C2
Bergamo B1
Bologna B1
Bolzano B1
Brescia B1
Brindisi D2
Cagliari B3
Caltanissetta C3
Campobasso C2
Canossa B1
Capua C2
Carbonia B3
Caserta C2
Castel Gandolfo C2
Catania C3
Catanzaro D3
Cefalù C3
Chieti C2
Chioggia C1
Civitavecchia B2
Como B1
Cortina d'Ampezzo C1
Cortona B2
Cosenza D3
Cremona B1
Crotone D3
Cuneo A1
Enna C3
Faenza B1
Ferrara B1
Florence B2
Foggia C2
Forlì C1
Frosinone C2
Gaeta C2
Gela C3
Genoa B1
Gorizia C1
Grosseto B2
Isernia C2
L'Aquila C2
La Spezia B1
Latina C2
Lecce D2
Livorno B2
Lucca B2
Macerata C2
Manfredonia C2
Mantova B1
Mantua (Mantova) B1
Marsala C3
Matera D2
Merano B1
Messina C3
Milan B1
Modena B1
Monopoli D2
Montepulciano B2
Monza B1
Naples C2
Novara B1
Nuoro B2
Olbia B2
Oristano B3
Otranto D2
Padova B1
Padua (Padova) B1
Palermo C3
Parma B1
Pavia B1
Perugia C2
Pesaro C2
Pescara C2
Pisa B2
Pistoia B2
Placenza B1
Potenza C2
Prato B2
Ragusa C3
Ravenna C1
Reggio di Calabria C3
Reggio nell'Emilia B1
Rieti C2
Rimini C1
Rome, *capital* C2
Rovigo B1
Salerno C2
San Gimignano B2
San Remo A2
San Severo C2
Sassari B2
Savona B1
Siena B2
Siracusa C3
Sondrio B1
Sorrento C2
Spoleto C2
Syracuse (Siracusa) C3
Taranto D2
Teramo C2
Termoli C2
Terni C2
Torre del Greco C2
Trapani C3
Trento B1
Treviso C1
Trieste C1
Turin A1
Udine C1
Venice C1
Ventimiglia A2
Vercelli B1
Verona B1
Vicenza B1
Viterbo C2

Other Features
Adige, *river* B1
Adriatic, *sea* C2
Alps, *mts.* A1, B1
Apennines, *range* B1
Arno, *river* B2
Asinara, *island* B2
Blanc, *mt.* A1
Bolsena, *lake* B2
Botte Donato, *mt.* D3
Bracciano, *lake* C2
Brenner, *pass* B1
Cagliari, *gulf* B3
Campagna di Roma, *region* C2
Caprara, *point* B2
Capri, *island* C2
Carbonara, *cape* B3
Cervati, *mt.* C2
Cimone, *mt.* B1
Como, *lake* B1
Corno, *mt.* C2
Dolomites, *range* B1
Egadi, *islands* C3
Elba, *island* B2
Etna, *mt.* C3
Garda, *lake* B1
Gennargentu, *mts.* B2
Genoa, *gulf* B1
Giglio, *island* B2
Ionian, *sea* D3
Ischia, *island* C2
Ligurian, *sea* B2
Lipari, *islands* C3
Lombardy, *plain* B1
Lugano, *lake* B1
Maggiore, *lake* B1
Maremma, *region* B2
Mediterranean, *sea* C3
Messina, *strait* C3
Montalto, *mt.* C3
Montecristo, *island* B2
Naples, *bay* C2
Oglio, *river* B1
Pantelleria, *island* C3
Passero, *cape* C3
Pianosa, *island* B2
Piave, *river* C1
Po, *river* A1, B1
Pontine, *islands* C2
Pontine, *marshes* C2
Rosa, *mt.* A1
Salerno, *gulf* C2
Sangro, *river* C2
San Pietro, *island* B3
Santa Maria di Leuca, *cape* D3
Sant'Antioco, *island* B3
San Vito, *cape* C3
Sardinia, *island* B2
Sicily, *island* C3
Sicily, *strait* B3
Spartivento, *cape* D3
Stromboli, *island* C3
Taranto, *gulf* D2
Testa del Gargano, *point* D2
Teulada, *cape* B3
Tiber, *river* C2
Tirso, *river* B2
Trasimeno, *lake* C2
Tyrrhenian, *sea* B2
Ustica, *island* C3
Venice, *gulf* C1
Vesuvius, *volcano* C2

San Marino

Capital: San Marino
Area: 24 sq. mi.
62 sq. km.
Population: 24,000
Largest City: San Marino
Language: Italian
Monetary Unit: Italian lira

San Marino: Map Index

Cities and Towns
Acquaviva A1
Borgo Maggiore B1
Chiesanuova B2
Domagnano B1
Falciano C1
Montegiardino B2
San Marino, *capital* B1
Serravalle B1

Other Features
Ausa, *river* C1
Marano, *river* C1
San Marino, *river* A1
Titano, *mt.* B1

DENMARK
Baltic Sea
North Sea
Bornholm (Den.)
North Frisian Is.
East Frisian Is.
Helgoland
Kiel Bay
Mecklenburg Bay
Pomeranian Bay
Sønderborg
Flensburg
Schleswig
Rødby Havn
Puttgarden
Fehmarn
Rügen
Sassnitz
Stralsund
Greifswald
Rostock
Kiel
Neumünster
Nord-Ostsee Canal
SCHLESWIG-HOLSTEIN
Lübeck
Wismar
Güstrow
Świnoujście
Cuxhaven
Wilhelmshaven
Bremerhaven
Emden
Nordenham
Groningen
HAMBURG
Hamburg
Schwerin
Schweriner See
MECKLENBURG-WESTERN POMERANIA
Neubrandenburg
Oderhaff
Szczecin
Neustrelitz
Müritz
BREMEN
Bremen
Oldenburg
Lüneburger Heide
Lüneburg
Uelzen
Elbe
NORTHERN EUROPEAN PLAIN
Havel
Wittenberge
Schwedt
POLAND
Gorzów Wielkopolski
LOWER SAXONY
BRANDENBURG
Eberswalde
Oder
Ems
Nienburg
Stendal
BERLIN
Berlin
Spandau
Potsdam
Brandenburg
Frankfurt an der Oder
Warta
Nordhorn
NETHERLANDS
Mittelland Canal
Osnabrück
Hannover
Wolfsburg
Brunswick
Hildesheim
Salzgitter
Weser
Hameln
Bielefeld
Magdeburg
Luckenwalde
Eisenhüttenstadt
Odra
Arnhem
Münster
Detmold
Goslar
Halberstadt
Bernburg
Guben
Zielona Góra
Neisse
Bocholt
NORTH RHINE-WESTPHALIA
Wittenberg
Dessau
Spree
Cottbus
Kleve
Recklinghausen
Paderborn
Harz
SAXONY-ANHALT
Gelsenkirchen
Marl
Hamm
Lippstadt
Northeim
Bottrop
Herne
Lünen
Oberhausen
Dortmund
Büren
Göttingen
Eisleben
Saale
Mulde
Duisburg
Bochum
Moers
Essen
Witten
Arnsberg
Nordhausen
Halle
Mülheim an der Ruhr
Ratingen
Hagen
Krefeld
Wuppertal
Ruhr
Kassel
Leipzig
Riesa
Bautzen
Düsseldorf
Neuss
Remscheid
Mönchengladbach
Solingen
Werra
Mühlhausen
Meissen
Görlitz
Dresden
Maas
Leverkusen
Fulda
Naumburg
SAXONY
Maastricht
Cologne
Bergisch Gladbach
Eisenach
Weimar
Zittau
Aachen
Siegen
HESSE
Gotha
Erfurt
Jena
Freiberg
Gera
Chemnitz
Liberec
Liège
Bonn
Marburg
THURINGIA
Zwickau
Thuringian Forest
Suhl
Lahn
Giessen
ERZGEBIRGE
Remagen
Rhine
Wetzlar
Fulda
Plauen
BELGIUM
Fichtelberg 1214 m (3983 ft)
Bad Ems
Frankenwald
Koblenz
Taunus
Frankfurt am Main
Coburg
Hof
Karlovy Vary
Eifel
Hanau
Offenbach
Spessart
Kulmbach
Labe
Prague
Wiesbaden
Schweinfurt
Mosel
Mainz
Bingen
Bayreuth
Fichtelgebirge
Hunsrück
Bad Kreuznach
Darmstadt
Main
Bamberg
CZECH REPUBLIC
LUXEMBOURG
Trier
Odenwald
Würzburg
Oberpfälzer Wald
Plzeň
Luxembourg
RHINELAND-PALATINATE
Worms
Main-Danube Canal
Jura
Weiden
SAARLAND
Ludwigshafen am Rhein
Mannheim
Erlangen
Saar
Kaiserslautern
Fürth
Bohemian Forest
Neunkirchen
Heidelberg
Nuremberg
Amberg
Vltava
Saarbrücken
Speyer
Ansbach
Pirmasens
Franconian Jura
Moselle
Metz
Heilbronn
Bayerischer Wald
Karlsruhe
Regensburg
Ludwigsburg
Straubing
Nancy
Pforzheim
Baden-Baden
Schwäbisch Gmünd
Stuttgart
Esslingen
Ingolstadt
Strasbourg
Göppingen
Heidenheim
FRANCE
BAVARIA
Isar
Passau
Tübingen
Landshut
Reutlingen
Swabian Jura
Meuse
Vosges
Black Forest
Neckar
Ulm
Augsburg
Danube
Dachau
Inn
Lech
Munich
BADEN-WÜRTTEMBERG
Ammersee
Salzach
Freiburg
Memmingen
Kaufbeuren
Starnberg See
Rosenheim
Chiem See
Salzburg
Mulhouse
Singen
Ravensburg
Kempten
AUSTRIA
Saône
Constance
Friedrichshafen
BAVARIAN ALPS
Bad Reichenhall
Basel
Lake Constance
Lindau
Oberammergau
Aare
Zürich
Hindelang
Garmisch-Partenkirchen
Zugspitze 2962 m (9718 ft)
Vaduz
Innsbruck
Lucerne
LIECHTENSTEIN
SWITZERLAND
Chur
ITALY
ALPS
Bolzano
Germany
Capital: Berlin
Area: 137,735 sq. mi. 356,826 sq. km.
Population: 81,088,000
Largest City: Berlin
Language: German
Monetary Unit: Mark
Germany
National Capital
Other City
1:4,066,000
0 25 50 75 mi
0 25 50 75 km
Lambert Conformal Conic Projection
N

Poland

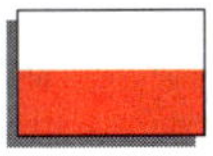

Capital: Warsaw
Area: 120,727 sq. mi.
312,764 sq. km.
Population: 38,655,000
Largest City: Warsaw
Language: Polish
Monetary Unit: Zloty

Poland:
Map Index

Cities and Towns
Biała Podlaska F2
Białystok F2
Bielsko-Biała D4
Bydgoszcz C2
Bytom D3
Chełm F3
Chojnice C2
Chorzów D3
Ciechánow E2
Częstochowa D3
Darłowo C1
Elbląg D1
Ełk F2
Gdańsk D1
Gdynia D1
Gliwice D3
Głogów C3
Gorzów Wielkopolski B2
Grudziądz D2
Hel D1
Jelenia Góra B3
Katowice D3
Kielce E3
Kołobrzeg B1
Konin D2
Koszalin C1
Kraków D3
Krosnow E4
Kutno D2
Legnica C3
Leszno C3
Łódź D3
Łomża F2
Lublin F3
Nowy Sącz E4
Nysa C3
Olsztyn E2
Opole C3
Ostrołęka E2
Piła C2
Piotrków Trybunalski D3
Płock D2
Poznań C2
Przemyśl F4
Puck D1
Puławy E3
Radom E3
Ruda Śląka D3
Rybnik D3
Rzeszów F3
Sczcecinek C2
Siedlce F2
Sieradz D3
Skierniewice E3
Słupsk C1
Sosnowiec D3
Suwałki F1
Świnoujście B2
Szczecin B2
Tarnobrzeg E3
Tarnów E3
Toruń D2
Tychy D3
Ustka C1
Wałbrzych C3
Warsaw, *capital* E2
Władysławowo D1
Włocławek D2
Wodzisław Śląski D3
Wrocław C3
Zabrze D3
Zakopane D4
Zamość F3
Zielona Góra B3

Other Features
Baltic, *sea* B1
Beskid, *mts.* D4
Bug, *river* E2, F3
Carpathian, *mts.* E4
Frisches Haff, *bay* D1
Gdańsk, *gulf* D1
High Tatra, *mts.* D4
Mamry, *lake* E1
Narew, *river* E2
Neisse, *river* B3
Noteć, *river* C2, D2
Oder, *river* B2, C3
Pilica, *river* E3
Pomeranian, *bay* B1
Rysy, *mt.* E4
San, *river* F3
Silesia, *region* C3
Śniardwy, *lake* E2
Sudeten, *mts.* B3
Vistula, *river* D2, E3
Warta, *river* B2, C2
Wieprz, *river* F3

Germany:
Map Index

States
Baden-Württemberg B4
Bavaria B4
Berlin C2
Brandenburg C2
Bremen B2
Hamburg B2
Hesse B3
Lower Saxony B2
Mecklenburg-Western Pomerania C2
North Rhine-Westphalia A3
Rhineland-Palatinate A4
Saarland A4
Saxony C3
Saxony-Anhalt B3
Schleswig-Holstein B2
Thuringia B3

Cities and Towns
Aachen A3
Amberg B4
Ansbach B4
Arnsberg B3
Augsburg B4
Bad Ems A3
Baden-Baden B4
Bad Kreuznach A4
Bad Reichenhall C5
Bamberg B4
Bautzen C3
Bayreuth B4
Bergisch Gladbach A3
Berlin, *capital* C2
Bernburg B3
Bielefeld B2
Bingen A4
Bocholt A3
Bochum A3
Bonn A3
Bottrop A3
Brandenburg C2
Bremen B2
Bremerhaven B2
Brunswick B2
Büren B3
Chemnitz C3
Coburg B3
Cologne A3
Constance B5
Cottbus C3
Cuxhaven B2
Dachau B4
Darmstadt B4
Dessau C3
Detmold B3
Dortmund A3
Dresden C3
Duisburg A3
Düsseldorf A3
Eberswalde C2
Eisenach B3
Eisenhüttenstadt C2
Eisleben B3
Emden A2
Erfurt B3
Erlangen B4
Essen A3
Esslingen B4
Flensburg B1
Frankfurt am Main B3
Frankfurt an der Oder C2
Freiberg C3
Freiburg A5
Friedrichshafen B5
Fulda B3
Fürth B4
Garmisch-Partenkirchen B5
Gelsenkirchen A3
Gera C3
Giessen B3
Göppingen B4
Görlitz C3
Goslar B3
Gotha B3
Göttingen B3
Greifswald C1
Guben C3
Güstrow C2
Hagen A3
Halberstadt B3
Halle B3
Hamburg B2
Hameln B2
Hamm A3
Hanau B3
Hannover B2
Heidelberg B4
Heidenheim B4
Heilbronn B4
Herne A3
Hildesheim B2
Hindelang B5
Hof B3
Ingolstadt B4
Jena B3
Kaiserslautern A4
Karlsruhe B4
Kassel B3
Kaufbeuren B5
Kempten B5
Kiel B1
Kleve A3
Koblenz A3
Krefeld A3
Kulmbach B3
Landshut C4
Leipzig C3
Leverkusen A3
Lindau B5
Lippstadt B3
Lübeck B2
Luckenwalde C2
Ludwigsburg B4
Ludwigshafen am Rhein B4
Lüneburg B2
Lünen A3
Magdeburg B2
Mainz B4
Mannheim B4
Marburg B3
Marl A3
Meissen C3
Memmingen B5
Moers A3
Mönchengladbach A3
Mühlhausen B3
Mülheim an der Ruhr A3
Munich B4
Münster A3
Naumburg B3
Neubrandenburg C2
Neumünster B1
Neunkirchen A4
Neuss A3
Neustrelitz C2
Nienburg B2
Nordenham B2
Nordhausen B3
Nordhorn A2
Northeim B3
Nuremberg B4
Oberammergau B5
Oberhausen A3
Offenbach B3
Oldenburg B2
Osnabrück B2
Paderborn B3
Passau C4
Pforzheim B4
Pirmasens A4
Plauen C3
Potsdam C2
Puttgarden B1
Ratingen A3
Ravensburg B5
Recklinghausen A3
Regensburg C4
Remagen A3
Remscheid A3
Reutlingen B4
Riesa C3
Rosenheim C5
Rostock C1
Saarbrücken A4
Salzgitter B2
Sassnitz C1
Schleswig B1
Schwäbisch Gmünd B4
Schwedt C2
Schweinfurt B3
Schwerin B2
Siegen B3
Singen B5
Solingen A3
Spandau C2
Speyer B4
Stendal B2
Stralsund C1
Straubing C4
Stuttgart B4
Suhl B3
Trier A4
Tübingen B4
Uelzen B2
Ulm B4
Weiden C4
Weimar B3
Wetzlar B3
Wiesbaden B3
Wilhelmshaven B2
Wismar B2
Witten A3
Wittenberg C3
Wittenberge B2
Wolfsburg B2
Worms B4
Wuppertal A3
Würzburg B4
Zittau C3
Zwickau C3

Other Features
Ammersee, *lake* B4
Baltic, *sea* C1
Bavarian Alps, *mts.* B5
Bayerischer Wald, *mts.* C4
Black, *forest* A4
Bohemian, *forest* C4
Chiem, *lake* C5
Constance, *lake* B5
Danube, *river* B4
East Frisian, *islands* A2
Eifel, *plateau* A3
Elbe, *river* B2, C3
Ems, *river* A2
Erzgebirge, *mts.* C3
Fehmarn, *island* B1
Fichtelberg, *mt.* C3
Fichtelgebirge, *mts.* B4
Franconian Jura, *mts* B4
Frankenwald, *mts.* B3
Fulda, *river* B3
Harz, *mts.* B3
Havel, *river* C2
Helgoland, *island* A1
Hünsruck, *mts.* A4
Inn, *river* C4
Isar, *river* C4
Kiel, *bay* B1
Lahn, *river* B3
Lech, *river* B4
Lüneburger Heide, *region* B2
Main, *river* B4
Main-Danube, *canal* B4
Mecklenburg, *bay* B1
Mittelland, *canal* B2
Mosel, *river* A4
Mulde, *river* C3
Müritz, *lake* C2
Neckar, *river* B4
Neisse, *river* C3
Nord-Ostsee, *canal* B1
North, *sea* A1
Northern European, *plain* B2
North Frisian, *islands* B1
Oberpfälzer Wald, *mts.* C4
Odenwald, *forest* B4
Oder, *river* C2
Oderhaff, *lake* C2
Pomeranian, *bay* C1
Rhine, *river* A3, A4
Rügen, *island* C1
Ruhr, *river* B3
Saale, *river* B3
Saar, *river* A4
Salzach, *river* C4
Schweriner, *lake* B2
Spessart, *mts.* B4
Spree, *river* C3
Starnberg, *lake* B5
Swabian Jura, *mts.* B4
Taunus, *mts.* B3
Thuringian, *forest* B3
Werra, *river* B3
Weser, *river* B2
Zugspitze, *mt.* B5

Czech Republic

Capital: Prague
Area: 30,449 sq. mi.
78,883 sq. km.
Population: 10,408,000
Largest City: Prague
Language: Czech
Monetary Unit: Koruna

Czech Republic: Map Index

Slovakia

Capital: Bratislava
Area: 18,933 sq. mi.
49,049 sq. km.
Population: 5,404,000
Largest City: Bratislava
Language: Slovak
Monetary Unit: New Koruna

Slovakia: Map Index

Romania: Map Index

Hungary

Capital: Budapest
Area: 35,919 sq. mi.
93,054 sq. km.
Population: 10,319,000
Largest City: Budapest
Language: Hungarian
Monetary Unit: Forint

Hungary: Map Index

Romania

Capital: Bucharest
Area: 91,699 sq. mi.
267,174 sq. km.
Population: 23,181,000
Largest City: Bucharest
Language: Romanian
Monetary Unit: Leu

44 RUSSIA

Part of Russia extends onto the continent of Asia.

© GeoSystems Global Corp.

Russia

Capital: Moscow
Area: 6,592,800 sq. mi.
17,079,793 sq. km.
Population: 149,609,000
Largest City: Moscow
Language: Russian
Monetary Unit: Ruble

Russia:
Map Index

Internal Divisions

Cities and Towns

Other Features

© GeoSystems Global Corp.

Armenia

Capital: Yerevan
Area: 11,500 sq. mi.
29,793 sq. km.
Population: 3,522,000
Largest City: Yerevan
Language: Armenian
Monetary Unit: Dram

Armenia: Map Index

© GeoSystems Global Corp.

Georgia: Map Index

Georgia

Capital: Tbilisi
Area: 26,900 sq. mi.
69,689 sq. km.
Population: 5,681,000
Largest City: Tbilisi
Language: Georgian
Monetary Unit: Lari

© GeoSystems Global Corp.

Azerbaijan

Capital: Baku
Area: 33,400 sq. mi.
86,528 sq. km.
Population: 7,684,000
Largest City: Baku
Language: Azerbaijani
Monetary Unit: Manat

Azerbaijan: Map Index

ESTONIA, LATVIA, LITHUANIA

Estonia:
Map Index

Cities and Towns

Haapsalu	B2
Kärdla	B1
Keila	C1
Kohtla-Järve	D1
Kunda	D1
Kuressaare	B2
Mustvee	D2
Narva	E1
Paldiski	C1
Pärnu	C2
Rapla	C1
Tallinn, *capital*	C1
Tapa	C1
Tartu	D2
Tõrva	C2
Türi	C2
Valga	D3
Viljandi	C2
Virtsu	B2
Võru	D3

Other Features

Baltic, *sea*	A1
Finland, *gulf*	C1
Hiiumaa, *island*	B2
Irbe, *strait*	A3
Munamägi, *mt.*	D3
Narva, *river*	D1
Pärnu, *river*	C2
Pedja, *river*	D2
Peipus, *lake*	D2
Pskov, *lake*	D3
Riga, *gulf*	B3
Saaremaa, *island*	B2
Võrts Järv, *lake*	D2

Estonia

Capital: Tallinn
Area: 17,413 sq. mi.
45,111 sq. km.
Population: 1,617,000
Largest City: Tallinn
Language: Estonian
Monetary Unit: Kroon

Latvia:
Map Index

Cities and Towns

Aluksne	D2
Bauska	C2
Cesis	C2
Daugavpils	D3
Gulbene	D2
Jekabpils	C2
Jelgava	B2
Jurmala	B2
Kuldiga	A2
Liepāja	A2
Limbaži	C2
Ogre	C2
Pavilosta	A2
Rezekne	D2
Riga, *capital*	C2
Salacgriva	C2
Saldus	B2
Smiltene	C2
Talsi	B2
Tukums	B2
Valka	C2
Valmiera	C2
Ventspils	A2

Other Features

Baltic, *sea*	A2
Burtnieku, *lake*	C2
Gaizina, *mt.*	C2
Reznas, *lake*	D2
Riga, *gulf*	B2
Usmas, *lake*	B2
Western Dvina, *river*	C2

Latvia

Capital: Riga
Area: 24,900 sq. mi.
64,508 sq. km.
Population: 2,749,000
Largest City: Riga
Language: Latvian
Monetary Unit: Lat

Lithuania

Capital: Vilnius
Area: 25,213 sq. mi.
65,319 sq. km.
Population: 3,848,000
Largest City: Vilnius
Language: Lithuanian
Monetary Unit: Lit

Lithuania:
Map Index

Cities and Towns

Alytus	C2
Biržai	C1
Druskininkai	B2
Jonava	C2
Jurbarkas	B2
Kaunas	B2
Kėdainiai	B2
Klaipėda	A2
Kretinga	A2
Kuršėnai	B1
Marijampolė	B2
Mažeikiai	B1
Naujoji Akmenė	B1
Palanga	A2
Panevėžys	C2
Radviliškis	B2
Šiauliai	B2
Šilalė	B2
Šilutė	A2
Tauragė	B2
Telšiai	B2
Ukmergė	C2
Utena	C2
Vilkaviškis	B2
Vilnius, *capital*	C2

Other Features

Baltic, *sea*	A2
Courland, *lagoon*	A2
Dubysa, *river*	B2
Juozapines, *mt.*	C2
Jura, *river*	A2
Merkys, *river*	C2
Minija, *river*	A2
Mūša, *river*	B1
Nemunas, *river*	A2, C2
Neris, *river*	C2
Nevėžis, *river*	B2
Šventoji, *river*	C2
Venta, *river*	B1

Belarus

Capital: Minsk
Area: 80,134 sq. mi.
207,601 sq. km.
Population: 10,405,000
Largest City: Minsk
Languages: Belarussian, Russian
Monetary Unit: Belarus ruble

© GeoSystems Global Corp.

Belarus: Map Index

Cities and Towns

Asipovichy D3
Babruysk D3
Baranavichy C3
Brest A3
Homyel E3
Hrodna A3
Krychaw E3
Lida B3
Mahilyow E3
Maladzyechna C2
Mazyr D3
Minsk, *capital* C3
Orsha E2
Pastavy C2
Pinsk C3
Polotsk D2
Rechytsa E3
Salihorsk C3
Smilovichi D3
Smolevichi D2
Vawkavysk B3
Vitsyebsk E2
Zhlobin D3

Other Features

Bug, *river* A3
Byarezina, *river* D3
Byelaruskaya Hrada, *range* C3
Dnepr, *river* E3
Dnepr-Bug, *canal* B3
Dzyarzhynskaya Hara, *mt.* C3
Nyoman, *river* B3
Pripyats, *marshes* C4
Pripyats, *river* C3
Ptsich, *river* D3
Sozh, *river* E3
Western Dvina, *river* D2

Ukraine: Map Index

Cities and Towns

Balaklava C4
Belaya Tserkov C2
Berdyansk D3
Cherkassy C2
Chernigov C1
Chernobyl C1
Chernovtsi B2
Dneprodzerzhinsk C2
Dnepropetrovsk D2
Donetsk D2
Feodosiya D3
Gorlovka D2
Ivano-Frankovsk A2
Izmail B3
Kachovka C3
Kerch D3
Kharkov D1
Kherson C3
Khmelnytskyy B2
Khust A2
Kiev, *capital* C1
Kirovograd C2
Konotop C1
Korosten B1
Kotovsk B2
Kovel A1
Kramatorsk D2
Kremenchug C2
Krivoy Rog C2
Lisichansk D2
Lugansk D2
Lutsk B1
Lviv A2
Makeyevka D2
Mariupol D3
Melitopol D3
Mogilev Podolskiy B2
Nikolayev C3
Nikopol C2
Odessa C3
Pervomaysk C2
Poltava C2
Priluki C1
Rovno B1
Sevastopol C4
Shostka C1
Simferopol C4
Sumy C1
Ternopol B1
Uman C2
Uzhgorod A2
Vinnitsa B2
Yalta C4
Yevpatoriya C3
Zaporozhye D2
Zhitomir B1

Other Features

Azov, *sea* D3
Black, *sea* C3
Bug, *river* A1
Carpathian, *mts.* A2
Crimean, *mts.* C4
Crimean, *peninsula* C3
Desna, *river* C1
Dnepr, *river* C1,C3
Dneprodzerzhinsk, *reservoir* C2
Dnestr, *river* B2
Donets, *basin* D2
Donets, *river* D2
Hoverla, *mt.* A2
Kakhovka, *reservoir* C3
Karkinit, *bay* C3
Kerch, *strait* D3
Kiev, *reservoir* C1
Kremenchug, *reservoir* C2
Pripyat, *river* A1
Prut, *river* B2
Psel, *river* C1
Sluch, *river* B1
Southern Bug, *river* B2
Taganrog, *gulf* D3
Tisza, *river* A2
Volyno-Podol'skaya Vozvyshennost, *uplands* B2
Vorskla, *river* C1

Ukraine

Capital: Kiev
Area: 233,100 sq. mi.
603,886 sq. km.
Population: 51,847,000
Largest City: Kiev
Languages: Ukrainian, Russian
Monetary Unit: Karbovanets

© GeoSystems Global Corp.

Slovenia

Capital: Ljubljana
Area: 7,821 sq. mi.
20,262 sq. km.
Population: 1,972,000
Largest City: Ljubljana
Languages: Slovenian, Serbo-Croatian
Monetary Unit: Tolar

Slovenia: Map Index

Cities and Towns

Other Features

Croatia

Capital: Zagreb
Area: 21,829 sq. mi.
56,552 sq. km.
Population: 4,698,000
Largest City: Zagreb
Language: Serbo-Croatian
Monetary Unit: Croatian dinar

Croatia: Map Index

Cities and Towns

Other Features

Bosnia and Hercegovina: Map Index

Cities and Towns

Other Features

Bosnia and Hercegovina

Capital: Sarajevo
Area: 19,741 sq. mi.
51,142 sq. km.
Population: 4,651,000
Largest City: Sarajevo
Language: Serbo-Croatian
Monetary Unit: New Yugoslav dinar

F.Y.R. Macedonia

Capital: Skopje
Area: 9,928 sq. mi.
25,720 sq. km.
Population: 2,214,000
Largest City: Skopje
Languages: Macedonian, Albanian, Serbo-Croatian, Turkish
Monetary Unit: Denar

F.Y.R. Macedonia: Map Index

Cities and Towns

Other Features

Albania

Capital: Tiranë
Area: 11,100 sq. mi.
28,756 sq. km.
Population: 3,374,000
Largest City: Tiranë
Languages: Albanian, Greek
Monetary Unit: Lek

Yugoslavia

Capital: Belgrade
Area: 39,449 sq. mi.
102,199 sq. km.
Population: 10,760,000
Largest City: Belgrade
Language: Serbo-Croatian
Monetary Unit: New Yugoslav dinar

© GeoSystems Global Corp.

Moldova

Capital: Chişinău
Area: 13,012 sq. mi.
33,710 sq. km.
Population: 4,473,000
Largest City: Chişinău
Languages: Romanian, Russian
Monetary Unit: Moldovan leu

Moldova: Map Index

Bulgaria: Map Index

Bulgaria

Capital: Sofia
Area: 42,855 sq. mi.
111,023 sq. km.
Population: 8,800,000
Largest City: Sofia
Language: Bulgarian
Monetary Unit: Lev

Greece:
Map Index

Greece

Capital: Athens
Area: 50,949 sq. mi.
131,992 sq. km.
Population: 10,565,000
Largest City: Athens
Language: Greek
Monetary Unit: Drachma

© GeoSystems Global Corp.

Iceland

National Capital

Other City

1:10,240,000

0 50 100 mi

0 50 100 km

Lambert Conformal Conic Projection

Iceland

Capital: Reykjavík
Area: 36,699 sq. mi.
95,075 sq. km.
Population: 264,000
Largest City: Reykjavík
Language: Icelandic
Monetary Unit: New Icelandic króna

Iceland:
Map Index

Cities and Towns
- Akranes A2
- Akureyri B2
- Dalvík B2
- Eskifjördhur C2
- Hafnarfjördhur A3
- Höfn C2
- Ísafjördhur A1
- Keflavík A3
- Kópavogur A2
- Ólafsvík A2
- Reykjavík, *capital* A2
- Saudhárkrókur B2
- Siglufjördhur B1
- Thingvellir A2
- Vestmannaeyjar A3

Other Features
- Blanda, *river* B2
- Breidhafjördhur, *fjord* A2
- Faxaflói, *bay* A2
- Greenland, *sea* B1
- Grimsey, *island* B1
- Heimaey, *island* A3
- Hekla, *volcano* B3
- Horn, *cape* A1
- Húnaflói, *bay* A2
- Hvannadalshnúkur, *mt.* B3
- Hvítá, *river* A2
- Laki, *volcano* B2
- Surtsey, *island* A3
- Vatnajökull, *ice cap* B2

Norway

National Capital

Other City

1:12,075,000

0 50 100 150 200 mi

0 100 200 300 km

Lambert Conformal Conic Projection

Norway

Capital: Oslo
Area: 125,050 sq. mi.
323,964 sq. km.
Population: 4,315,000
Largest City: Oslo
Language: Norwegian
Monetary Unit: Norwegian krone

Norway:
Map Index

Cities and Towns
- Ålesund B3
- Alta E1
- Arendal B4
- Bergen B3
- Bodø C2
- Drammen C4
- Dumbås B3
- Egersund B4
- Florø A3
- Fredrikstad C4
- Gjøvik C3
- Hamar C3
- Hammerfest E1
- Harstad D2
- Haugesund B4
- Kinsarvik B3
- Kirkenes F2
- Kristiansand B4
- Kristiansund B3
- Lakselv F1
- Leikanger B3
- Lillehammer C3
- Mo C2
- Molde B3
- Mosjøen C2
- Moss C4
- Namsos C3
- Narvik D2
- Oslo, *capital* C3
- Skien B4
- Stavanger B4
- Steinkjer C3
- Tromsø D2
- Trondheim C3
- Vadsø F1

Other Features
- Barents, *sea* E1
- Boknafjord, *fjord* B4
- Dovrefjell, *mts.* B3
- Finnmark, *plateau* E2
- Glåma, *river* C3
- Glittertinden, *mt.* B3
- Hallingdal, *valley* B3
- Hardangerfjord, *fjord* B4
- Hardangervidda, *plateau* B3
- Jotunheimen, *mts.* B3
- Lofoten, *islands* C2
- Mjøsa, *lake* C3
- North, *cape* F1
- North, *sea* A3
- Norwegian, *sea* A2
- Oslofjord, *fjord* C4
- Skagerrak, *strait* B4
- Sognafjord, *fjord* B3
- Tana, *river* F1
- Trondheimsfjord, *fjord* B3
- Vesterålen, *islands* C2

Finland: Map Index

Finland

Capital: Helsinki
Area: 130,559 sq. mi.
338,236 sq. km.
Population: 5,069,000
Largest City: Helsinki
Languages: Finnish, Swedish
Monetary Unit: Markka

Sweden

Capital: Stockholm
Area: 173,732 sq. mi.
450,083 sq. km.
Population: 8,778,000
Largest City: Stockholm
Language: Swedish
Monetary Unit: Krona

Sweden: Map Index

MAJOR CITIES

Country	City	Population
Algeria	Algiers	1,483,000
	Oran	590,000
	Constantine	483,000
Angola	Luanda	1,100,000
Benin	Cotonou	402,000
	Porto-Novo	144,000
Botswana	Gaborone	137,000
Burkina Faso	Ouagadougou	442,000
Burundi	Bujumbura	235,440
Cameroon	Douala	852,000
	Yaoundé	700,000
Cape Verde	Praia	61,000
Central African Republic	Bangui	474,000
Chad	N'Djamena	687,000
Comoros		(metro)
	Moroni	30,000
Congo, Democratic Republic of the	Kinshasa	3,800,000
	Lubumbashi	739,000
Congo, Republic of the	Brazzaville	596,000
Côte d'Ivoire	Abidjan	2,700,000
	Yamoussoukro	107,000
Djibouti		(metro)
	Djibouti	450,000
Egypt	Cairo	6,800,000
	Alexandria	3,380,000
	Port Said	460,000
	Suez	388,000
Equatorial Guinea	Malabo	38,000
Eritrea	Asmara	358,000
Ethiopia	Addis Ababa	1,913,000
Gabon	Libreville	275,000
The Gambia	Banjul	40,000
Ghana	Accra	949,000
Guinea	Conakry	705,000
Guinea-Bissau	Bissau	138,000
Kenya	Nairobi	959,000
	Mombasa	401,000
Lesotho	Maseru	109,000
Liberia	Monrovia	400,000
Libya	Tripoli	591,000
Madagascar	Antananarivo	802,000
Malawi	Blantyre	332,000
	Lilongwe	234,000
Mali	Bamako	658,000
Mauritania	Nouakchott	550,000
Mauritius	Port Louis	142,000
Morocco	Casablanca	2,600,000
	Fez	852,000
	Rabat	556,000
Mozambique	Maputo	931,000
Namibia	Windhoek	114,000
Niger	Niamey	392,000
Nigeria	Lagos	1,300,000
	Ibadan	1,300,000
	Abuja	250,000
Rwanda	Kigali	237,000
São Tomé & Príncipe	São Tomé	43,000
Senegal	Dakar	1,700,000
Seychelles		(metro)
	Victoria	24,000
Sierra Leone	Freetown	470,000
Somalia	Mogadishu	700,000
South Africa		(metro)
	Johannesburg	1,900,000
	Cape Town	1,900,000
	Durban	1,100,000
	Pretoria	1,000,000
	Bloemfontein	270,000
Sudan	Khartoum	476,000
Swaziland	Mbabane	38,000
Tanzania	Dar es-Salaam	1,096,000
Togo	Lomé	600,000
Tunisia	Tunis	620,000
Uganda	Kampala	773,000
Western Sahara	el-Aaiún	90,000
Zambia	Lusaka	982,000
Zimbabwe		(metro)
	Harare	1,200,000

International comparability of city population data is limited by various data inconsistencies.

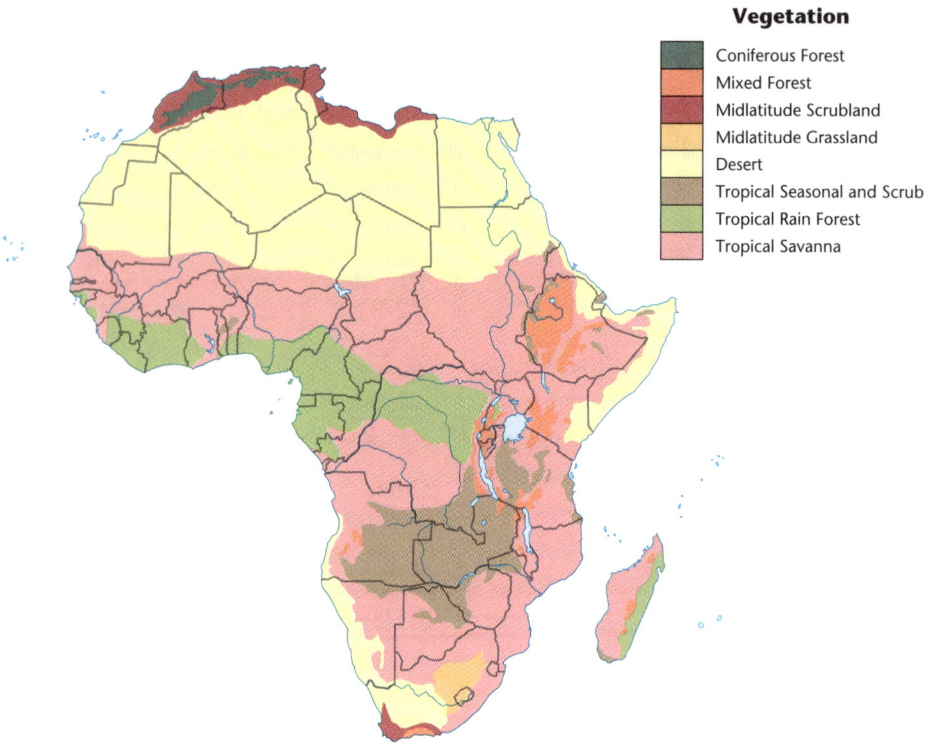

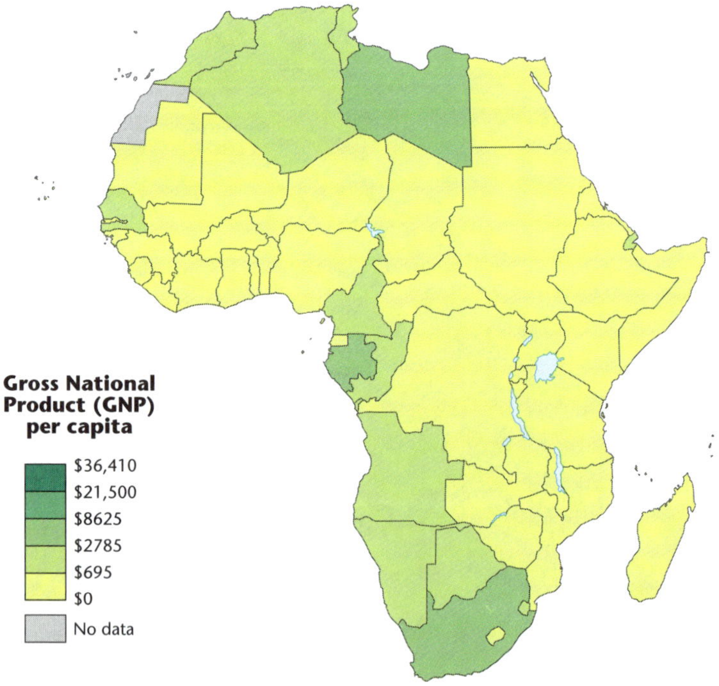

Africa: Population, by nation (in millions)

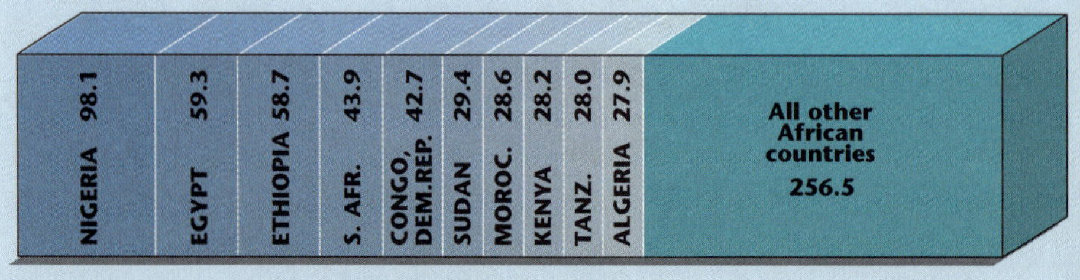

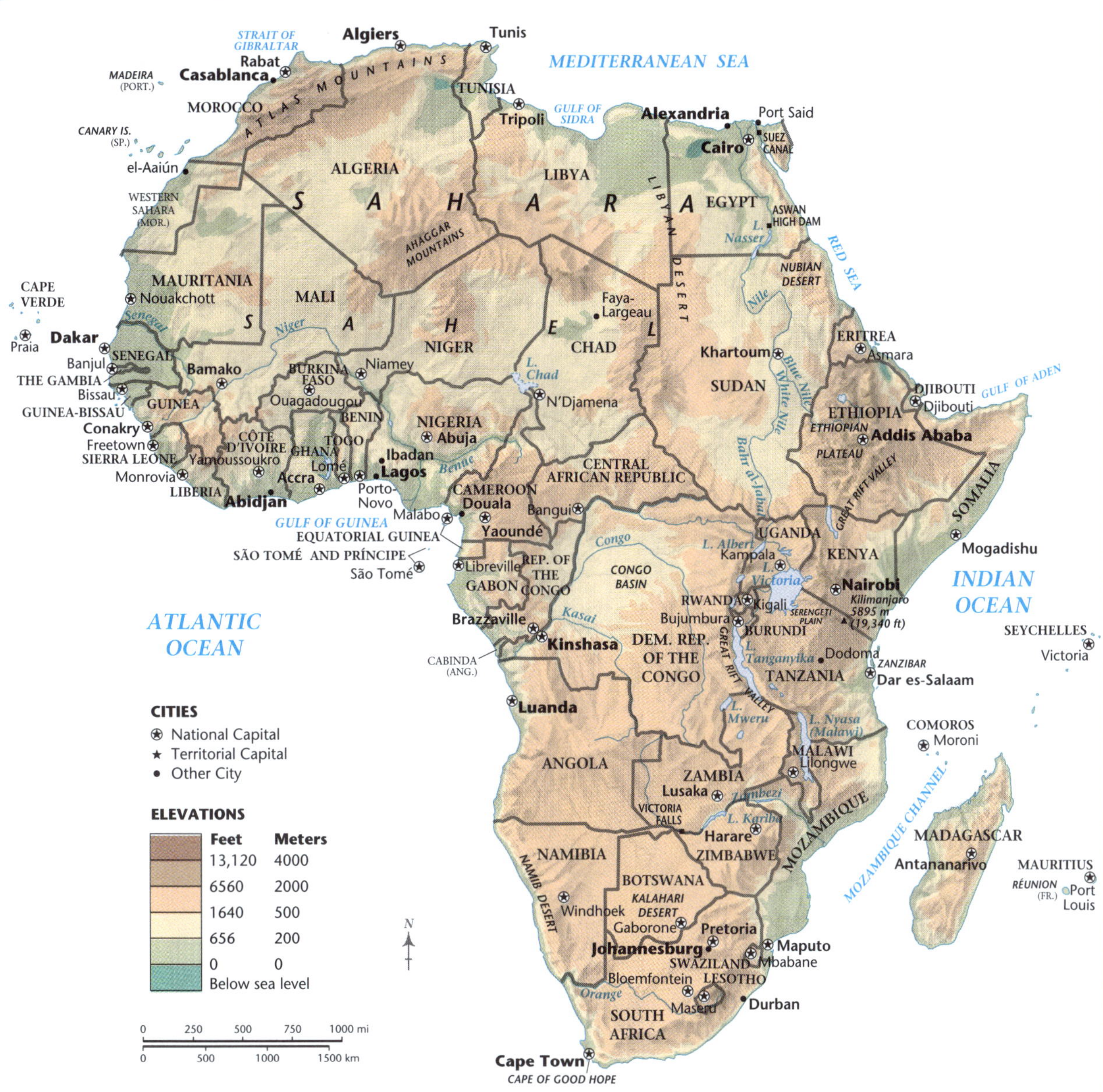
STRAIT OF GIBRALTAR
MADEIRA (PORT.)
CANARY IS. (SP.)
Rabat
Casablanca
Algiers
Tunis
ATLAS MOUNTAINS
MOROCCO
TUNISIA
MEDITERRANEAN SEA
GULF OF SIDRA
Tripoli
Alexandria
Port Said
Cairo
SUEZ CANAL
el-Aaiún
WESTERN SAHARA (MOR.)
ALGERIA
LIBYA
EGYPT
S A H A R A
LIBYAN DESERT
ASWAN HIGH DAM
L. Nasser
RED SEA
NUBIAN DESERT
AHAGGAR MOUNTAINS
CAPE VERDE
Praia
MAURITANIA
Nouakchott
MALI
Senegal
Niger
Nile
Faya-Largeau
S A H E L
Dakar
SENEGAL
Banjul
THE GAMBIA
Bissau
GUINEA-BISSAU
GUINEA
Conakry
Freetown
SIERRA LEONE
Monrovia
LIBERIA
Bamako
BURKINA FASO
Ouagadougou
Niamey
NIGER
CHAD
L. Chad
N'Djamena
CÔTE D'IVOIRE
Yamoussoukro
Abidjan
GHANA
Accra
TOGO
Lomé
BENIN
Porto-Novo
NIGERIA
Abuja
Ibadan
Lagos
Benue
GULF OF GUINEA
Malabo
EQUATORIAL GUINEA
SÃO TOMÉ AND PRÍNCIPE
São Tomé
CAMEROON
Douala
Yaoundé
CENTRAL AFRICAN REPUBLIC
Bangui
SUDAN
Khartoum
Blue Nile
White Nile
Bahr al-Jabal
ERITREA
Asmara
DJIBOUTI
Djibouti
GULF OF ADEN
ETHIOPIA
ETHIOPIAN PLATEAU
Addis Ababa
GREAT RIFT VALLEY
SOMALIA
Mogadishu
UGANDA
L. Albert
Kampala
L. Victoria
KENYA
Nairobi
Kilimanjaro 5895 m (19,340 ft)
SERENGETI PLAIN
INDIAN OCEAN
Congo
CONGO BASIN
Libreville
GABON
REP. OF THE CONGO
Brazzaville
Kinshasa
Kasai
ATLANTIC OCEAN
CABINDA (ANG.)
DEM. REP. OF THE CONGO
RWANDA
Kigali
Bujumbura
BURUNDI
GREAT RIFT VALLEY
L. Tanganyika
Dodoma
TANZANIA
ZANZIBAR
Dar es-Salaam
SEYCHELLES
Victoria
Luanda
L. Mweru
L. Nyasa (Malawi)
COMOROS
Moroni
ANGOLA
ZAMBIA
Lusaka
Zambezi
MALAWI
Lilongwe
VICTORIA FALLS
L. Kariba
Harare
ZIMBABWE
MOZAMBIQUE
MOZAMBIQUE CHANNEL
MADAGASCAR
Antananarivo
MAURITIUS
RÉUNION (FR.)
Port Louis
NAMIBIA
NAMIB DESERT
Windhoek
BOTSWANA
KALAHARI DESERT
Gaborone
Pretoria
Johannesburg
Maputo
SWAZILAND
Mbabane
Bloemfontein
LESOTHO
Maseru
Orange
Durban
SOUTH AFRICA
Cape Town
CAPE OF GOOD HOPE
N
CITIES
National Capital
Territorial Capital
Other City
ELEVATIONS
Feet Meters
13,120 4000
6560 2000
1640 500
656 200
0 0
Below sea level
0 250 500 750 1000 mi
0 500 1000 1500 km

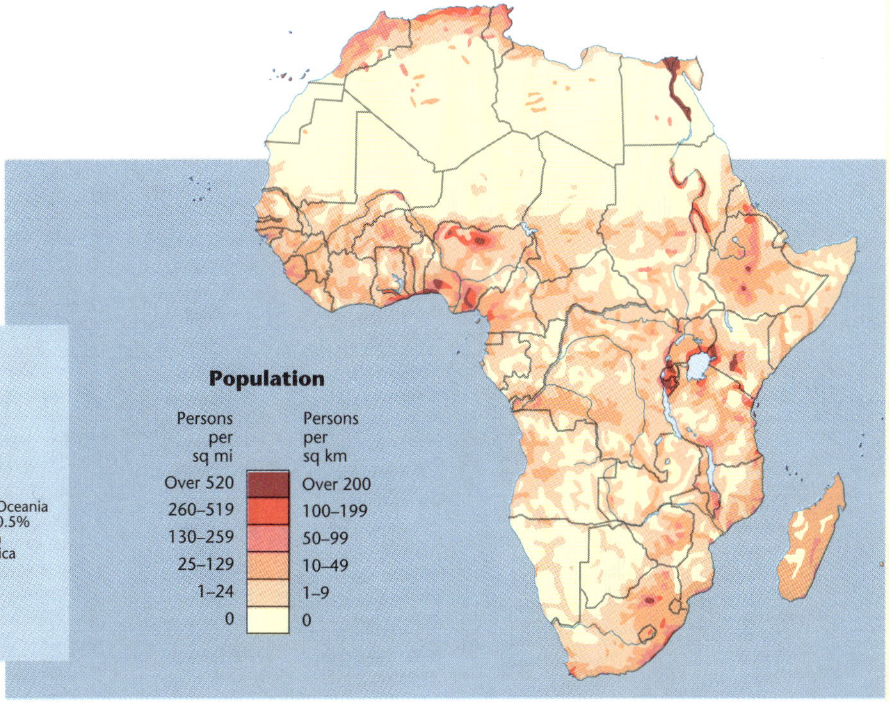
Population
Persons per sq mi
Persons per sq km
Over 520 Over 200
260–519 100–199
130–259 50–99
25–129 10–49
1–24 1–9
0 0

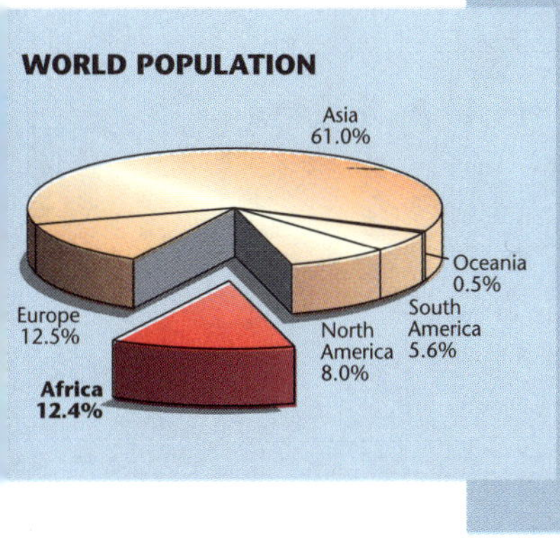
WORLD POPULATION
Asia 61.0%
Oceania 0.5%
South America 5.6%
North America 8.0%
Europe 12.5%
Africa 12.4%

CLIMATE

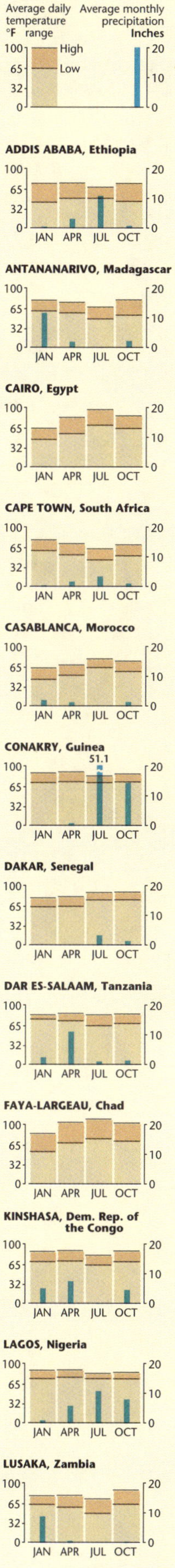
Average daily temperature °F range
Average monthly precipitation Inches
High
Low
ADDIS ABABA, Ethiopia
ANTANANARIVO, Madagascar
CAIRO, Egypt
CAPE TOWN, South Africa
CASABLANCA, Morocco
CONAKRY, Guinea
51.1
DAKAR, Senegal
DAR ES-SALAAM, Tanzania
FAYA-LARGEAU, Chad
KINSHASA, Dem. Rep. of the Congo
LAGOS, Nigeria
LUSAKA, Zambia
JAN APR JUL OCT
100 65 32 0
20 10 0

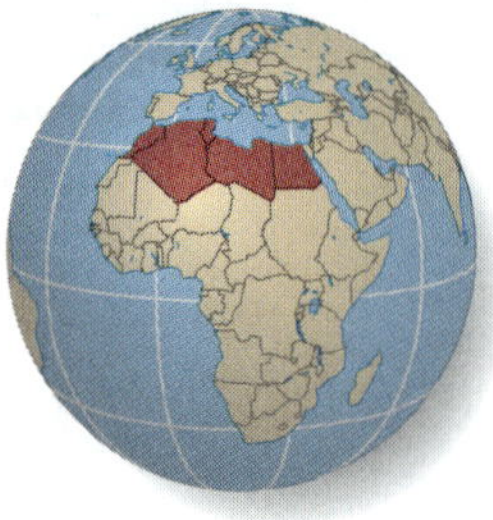

Egypt

Capital: Cairo
Area: 385,229 sq. mi.
998,003 sq. km.
Population: 59,325,000
Largest City: Cairo
Language: Arabic
Monetary Unit: Pound

Egypt:
Map Index

Cities and Towns

Other Features

Libya

Capital: Tripoli
Area: 679,359 sq. mi.
1,759,997 sq. km.
Population: 5,057,000
Largest City: Tripoli
Language: Arabic
Monetary Unit: Dinar

Libya:
Map Index

Cities and Towns

Other Features

Algeria

Capital: Algiers
Area: 919,595 sq. mi.
2,382,371 sq. km.
Population: 27,895,000
Largest City: Algiers
Language: Arabic
Monetary Unit: Dinar

Algeria: Map Index

Cities and Towns

Adrar	B2
Algiers, *capital*	B1
Annaba	B1
Asnam, el-	B1
Batna	B1
Béchar	A1
Bejaïa	B1
Biskra	B1
Blida	B1
Chenachane	A2
Constantine	B1
Djanet	B2
Djelfa	B1
Ghardaia	B1
Golea, el-	B2
I-n-Amenas	B2
I-n-Amguel	B2
I-n-Salah	B2
Laghouat	B1
Mostaganem	B1
Oran	A1
Ouargla	B1
Sétif	B1
Sidi bel Abbès	A1
Silet	B2
Skikda	B1
Tabelbala	A2
Tamanrasset	B2
Tarat	B2
Tindouf	A2
Ti-n-Zaouâtene	B2
Tlemcen	A1
Touggourt	B1

Other Features

Ahaggar, *mts.*	B2
Atlas, *mts.*	A1
Bejaïa, *gulf*	B1
Chelif, *river*	B1
Daoura, *river*	A2
Drâa, *river*	A1
Erg Chech, *desert*	A2
Erg Iguidi, *desert*	A2
Grand Erg Occidental, *desert*	B1
Grand Erg Oriental, *desert*	B2
Hauts Plateaux, *plateau*	B1
Sahara, *desert*	B2
Tademait, *plateau*	B2
Tahat, *mt.*	B2
Tanezrouft, *mts.*	A2
Tell Region	B1
Timgad, *ruins*	B1

Tunisia

Capital: Tunis
Area: 63,378 sq. mi.
164,192 sq. km.
Population: 8,727,000
Largest City: Tunis
Language: Arabic
Monetary Unit: Dinar

Tunisia: Map Index

Cities and Towns

Ariana	C1
Béja	B1
Bizerte	B1
Gabès	C3
Gafsa	B2
Hammamat, al-	C1
Houmt Souk	C3
Kasserine	B2
Kebili	B3
Kef, el-	B1
La Goulette	C1
Mahdia	C2
Menzel Bourguiba	B1
Monastir	C2
Nabeul	C1
Nefta	A3
Qayrawan, al-	C2
Sfax	C2
Sidi Bou Zid	B2
Siliana	B1
Sousse	C2
Sukhayrah, as-	B2
Tataouine	C3
Tozeur	B3
Tunis, *capital*	C1
Zaghouan	C1
Zarzis	C3

Other Features

Atlas, *mts.*	A1
Bon, *cape*	C1
Carthage, *ruin*	C1
Djerba, *island*	C3
Djerid, *salt marsh*	B3
Gabès, *gulf*	C2
Galite, *island*	B1
Grand Erg Oriental, *dune*	B3
Hammamet, *gulf*	C1
Kerkennah, *islands*	C2
Majardah, *river*	B1
Mediterranean, *sea*	A1
Rharsa, *salt marsh*	A2
Sahara, *desert*	B4
Tabassah, *mts.*	A1
Tunis, *gulf*	C1

Morocco

Capital: Rabat
Area: 177,117 sq. mi.
458,852 sq. km.
Population: 28,559,000
Largest City: Casablanca
Language: Arabic
Monetary Unit: Dirham

Morocco: Map Index

Cities and Towns

Agadir	B2
Beni Mellal	C1
Casablanca	C1
Essaouira	B2
Fez	C1
Figuig	D1
Hoceima, al-	D1
Jadida, el-	B1
Kenitra	C1
Khouribga	C1
Larache	C1
Marrakech	B2
Meknès	C1
Mohammedia	C1
Ouarzazate	C2
Ouezzane	C1
Oujda	D1
Rabat, *capital*	C1
Rachidia, er-	C2
Safi	B1
Salé	C1
Settat	C1
Tangier	C1
Tan-Tan	B2
Taroudant	B2
Tata	C2
Taza	C1
Tétouan	C1
Tiznit	B2

Other Features

Anti-Atlas, *ranges*	B2
Atlas, *mts.*	B2
Dades, *river*	C2
Drâa, *river*	B2, C2
Er Rif, *range*	C1
Gibraltar, *strait*	C1
High Atlas, *ranges*	B2
Jebel Toubkal, *mt.*	C2
Mediterranean, *sea*	D1
Middle Atlas, *ranges*	C1
Moulouya, *river*	D1
Oum er-Rbia, *river*	C1
Sahara, *desert*	B2
Sebou, *river*	C1
Sous, *plain*	B2
Sous, *river*	B2

© GeoSystems Global Corp.

Western Sahara

Area: 103,000 sq. mi.
266,000 sq. km.
Population: 217,000
Largest City: el-Aaiún
Language: Arabic
Monetary Unit: Moroccan Dirham

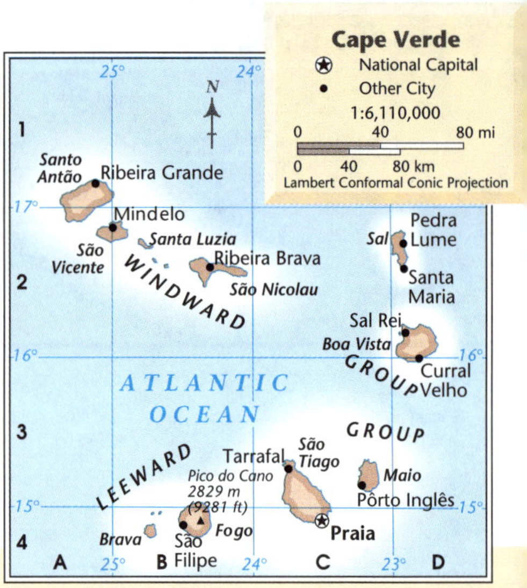

© GeoSystems Global Corp.

Cape Verde

Capital: Praia
Area: 1,557 sq. mi.
4,034 sq. km.
Population: 423,000
Largest City: Praia
Language: Portuguese
Monetary Unit: Escudo

Mali

Capital: Bamako
Area: 482,077 sq. mi.
1,248,904 sq. km.
Population: 9,113,000
Largest City: Bamako
Language: French
Monetary Unit: Franc

© GeoSystems Global Corp.

Mauritania

Capital: Nouakchott
Area: 398,000 sq. mi.
1,031,088 sq. km.
Population: 2,193,000
Largest City: Nouakchott
Languages: Arabic, Wolof
Monetary Unit: Ouguiya

© GeoSystems Global Corp.

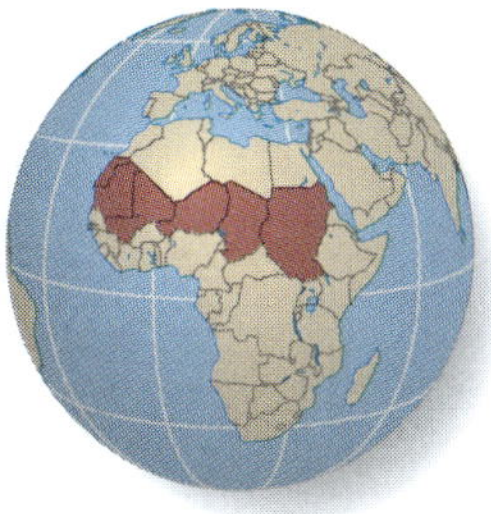

Niger

Capital: Niamey
Area: 497,000 sq. mi.
1,287,565 sq. km.
Population: 8,635,000
Largest City: Niamey
Language: French
Monetary Unit: CFA franc

Niger:
Map Index

Cities and Towns
Agadès B2
Arlit B2
Bilma C2
Birni Nkonni B3
Diffa C3
Djado C1
Dogondoutchi A3
Dosso A3
Gaya A3
Gouré C3
Maradi B3
Nguigmi C3
Niamey, *capital* A3
Tahoua B3
Téra A3
Tessaoua B3
Tillabéry A3
Zinder B3

Other Features
Air, *mts.* B2
Bagzane, *mt.* B2
Chad, *lake* C3
Dallol Bosso, *river* A3
Dillia, *river* C2
Djado, *plateau* C1
Erg du Ténéré, *desert* B2
Grand Erg de Bilma, *desert* C2
Gréboun, *mt.* B1
Komadugu Yobe, *river* C3
Manga, *region* C2
Niger, *river* A3
Sahara, *desert* A1
Sahel, *region* A3
Talak, *region* B2
Ténéré, *desert* C1

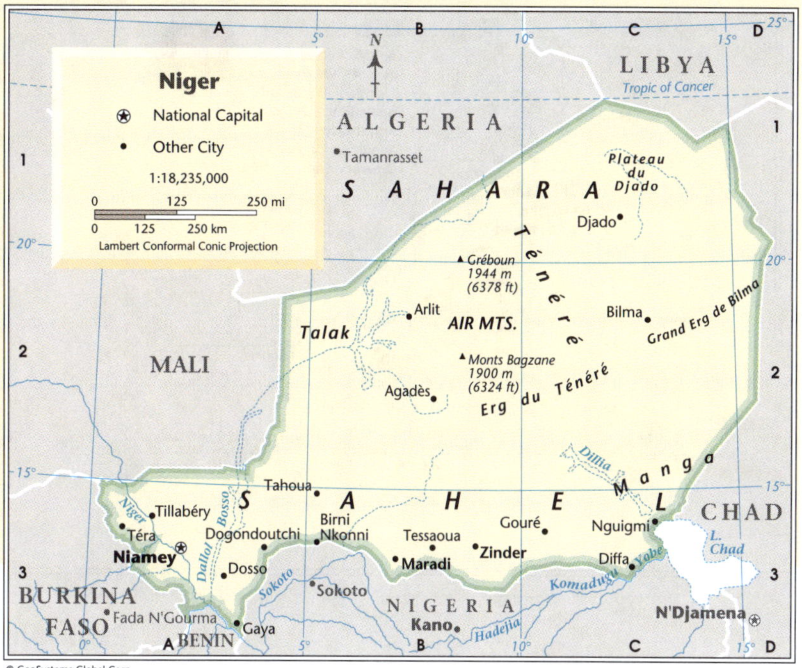

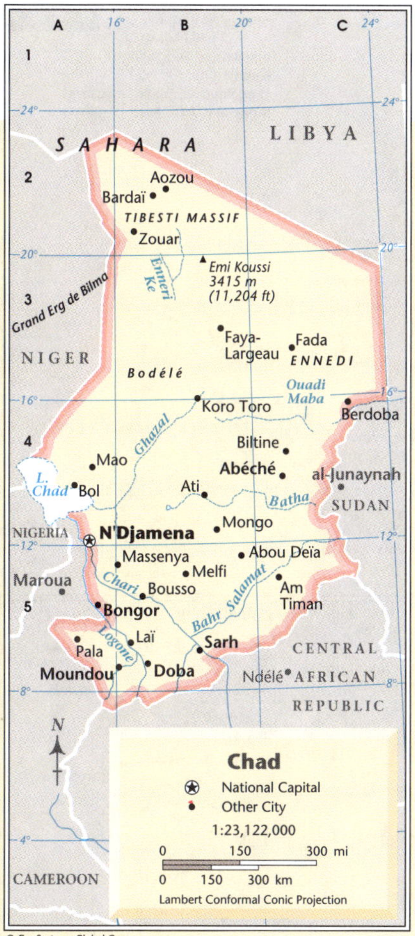

Chad:
Map Index

Cities and Towns
Abéché C4
Abou Deïa B5
Am Timan C5
Aozou B2
Ati B4
Bardaï B2
Berdoba C4
Biltine C4
Bol A4
Bongor A5
Bousso B5
Doba B5
Fada C3
Faya-Largeau B3
Koro Toro B4
Laï B5
Mao A4
Massenya B5
Melfi B5
Mongo B4
Moundou B5
N'Djamena, *capital* A4
Pala A5
Sarh B5
Zouar B2

Chad

Capital: N'Djamena
Area: 495,755 sq. mi.
1,248,339 sq. km.
Population: 5,467,000
Largest City: N'Djamena
Languages: French, Arabic
Monetary Unit: CFA franc

Other Features
Bahr Salamat, *river* B5
Batha, *river* C4
Bodélé, *depression* B3
Chad, *lake* A4
Chari, *river* A5
Emi Koussi, *mt.* B3
Ennedi, *plateau* C3
Enneri Ke, *river* B3
Ghazal, *river* B4
Grand Erg de Bilma, *desert* A3
Logone, *river* A5
Ouadi Maba, *river* C4
Sahara, *desert* A2
Tibesti, *massif* B2

Sudan:
Map Index

Cities and Towns
Atbarah C2
Babanusah B3
Damazin, ad- C3
Dunqulah C1
Fashir, al- B2
Halaib D1
Juba C4
Junaynah, al- A2
Kaduqli B3
Kassala D2
Khartoum, *capital* C2
Khartoum North C2
Khashm al-Qirbah C2
Kuraymah C1
Kusti C2
Malakal C3
Nuhud, an- B2
Nyala B2
Omdurman C2
Pibor Post C3
Port Sudan D1
Qadarif, al- C2
Rumbek B3
Sannar C2
Ubayyid, al- C2
Wadi Halfa C1
Wad Madani C2
Waw B3
Yambio B4

Other Features
Akobo, *river* C3
Atbarah, *river* C2
Bahr al-Arab, *river* B3
Bahr al-Ghazal, *river* C3
Bahr al-Jabal, *river* C3
Blue Nile, *river* C2
Kangen, *river* C3
Kinyeti, *mt.* C4
Libyan, *desert* B1
Lol, *river* B3
Nasser, *lake* C1
Nile, *river* C1, C2
Nuba, *mts.* C3
Nubian, *desert* C1
Red, *sea* D1
Red Sea, *hills* D1
Sobat, *river* C3
Sudd, *region* B3
Sue, *river* B3
Wadi al-Malik, *river* B2
Wadi Howar, *river* B2
White Nile, *river* C3

Sudan

Capital: Khartoum
Area: 966,757 sq. mi.
2,530,459 sq. km.
Population: 29,420,000
Largest City: Khartoum
Language: Arabic
Monetary Unit: Pound

© GeoSystems Global Corp.

Eritrea

Capital: Asmara
Area: 45,300 sq. mi.
117,358 sq. km.
Population: 3,200,000
Largest City: Asmara
Language: Tigrinya
Monetary Unit: Ethiopian birr

Eritrea: Map Index

Cities and Towns
- Adi Keyih B2
- Adi Ugri B2
- Akordat A2
- Asmara, *capital* B2
- Assab D3
- Ed C3
- Keren B2
- Massawa B2
- Nakfa B1
- Teseney A2
- Tio C2

Other Features
- Bab al-Mandab, *strait* D3
- Dahlak, *archipelago* C2
- Danakil, *desert* C2
- Gash, *river* B2
- Red, *sea* C1

Djibouti

National Capital
Other City
1:5,500,000
0 25 50 mi
0 25 50 km
Transverse Mercator Proj.

© GeoSystems Global Corp.

Djibouti: Map Index

Cities and Towns
- Alayli Dadda B1
- Ali Adde B2
- Ali-Sabieh B2
- Arta B2
- As Ela B2
- Balho B1
- Dikhil B2
- Djibouti, *capital* C2
- Dorra B1
- Holhol B2
- Khor Angar C1
- Loyada C2
- Obock C2
- Randa B2
- Tadjoura B2
- Yoboki B2

Other Features
- Abhé, *lake* A2
- Aden, *gulf* C2
- Assal, *lake* B2
- Bab al-Mandab, *strait* C1
- Gaggade, *plain* B2
- Mabla, *mts.* B2
- Moussa Ali, *mt.* B1
- Red, *sea* C1
- Tadjoura, *gulf* B2

Djibouti

Capital: Djibouti
Area: 8,950 sq. mi.
23,187 sq. km.
Population: 413,000
Largest City: Djibouti
Languages: Cushitic languages
Monetary Unit: Franc

Ethiopia

National Capital
Other City
1:15,053,000
0 100 200 mi
0 100 200 km
Lambert Conformal Conic Projection

© GeoSystems Global Corp.

Ethiopia

Capital: Addis Ababa
Area: 437,794 sq. mi.
1,134,181 sq. km.
Population: 58,710,000
Largest City: Addis Ababa
Language: Amharic
Monetary Unit: Birr

Ethiopia: Map Index

Cities and Towns
- Addis Ababa, *capital* C2
- Adwa C1
- Arba Minch B3
- Asela C3
- Asosa B2
- Awasa C3
- Bahir Dar B2
- Debre Birhan C2
- Debre Markos B2
- Degeh Bur D2
- Dese C2
- Dire Dawa D2
- Goba C3
- Gonder B1
- Gore B2
- Harer D2
- Imi D3
- Jima B3
- Mekele C1
- Nazret C2
- Negele C3
- Nekemte B2
- Shewa Gimira B3
- Weldiya C2
- Werder D3

Other Features
- Abaya, *lake* B3
- Abhe, *lake* C2
- Akobo, *river* A3
- Atbara, *river* B1
- Awash, *river* C2
- Baro, *river* B2
- Blue Nile, *river* B2
- Choke, *mts.* B2
- Dawa, *river* C3
- Denakil, *desert* C1
- Dinder, *river* B1
- Ethiopian, *plateau* C2
- Genale, *river* C3
- Great Rift, *valley* C3
- Ogaden, *region* D3
- Omo, *river* B3
- Provisional Administrative Line D3
- Ras Dashen, *mt.* C1
- Tana, *lake* B1
- Tekeze, *river* B1
- Turkana, *lake* B3
- Wabe Gestro, *river* C3
- Wabe Shebele, *river* D3
- Ziway, *lake* C3

Somalia: Map Index

Cities and Towns
- Baraawe A3
- Baydhabo A3
- Beledweyne B3
- Benderbeyla C2
- Berbera B1
- Boosaaso B1
- Burco B2
- Ceerigaabo B1
- Dhuusamareeb B2
- Eyl B2
- Gaalkacyo B2
- Garoowe B2
- Hargeysa A2
- Hobyo B2
- Jamaame A3
- Jawhar B3
- Jilib A3
- Kismayu A4
- Luuq A3
- Marka A3
- Mogadishu, *capital* B3
- Qardho B2
- Xuddur A3

Other Features
- Aden, *gulf* B1
- Gees Gwardafuy, *cape* C1
- Juba, *river* A3
- Nugaal, *valley* B2
- Raas Xaafun, *cape* C1
- Surud Ad, *mt.* B1
- Webi Shabeelle, *river* B3

Somalia

Capital: Mogadishu
Area: 246,300 sq. mi.
638,083 sq. km.
Population: 6,667,000
Largest City: Mogadishu
Language: Somali, Arabic
Monetary Unit: Shilling

© GeoSystems Global Corp.

Kenya

Capital: Nairobi
Area: 224,961 sq. mi.
582,801 sq. km.
Population: 28,241,000
Largest City: Nairobi
Language: Swahili
Monetary Unit: Shilling

Kenya

National Capital
Other City
1:12,105,000
0 100 200 mi
0 100 200 km
Mercator Projection

Kenya: Map Index

Provinces
Central D4
Coast E5
Eastern E3
Nairobi Area D4
North-Eastern F3
Nyanza C4
Rift Valley D3
Western C3

Cities and Towns
Eldoret C3
Embu D4
Garissa E4
Kakamega C3
Kericho C4
Kisumu C4
Kitale C3
Lamu F5
Lodwar C2
Machakos D4
Malindi F5
Marsabit E2
Meru D3
Mombasa E5
Moyale E2
Nairobi, *capital* D4
Nakuru D4
Nyeri D4
Ramu F2
Thika D4
Tsavo E5
Wajir F3

Other Features
Aberdare, *range* D4
Athi, *river* E5
Baringo, *lake* D3
Chalbi, *desert* D2
Daua, *river* F1
Galana, *river* E5
Great Rift, *valley* C3
Kenya, *mt.* D4
Laga Bor, *river* E2
Lorian, *swamp* E3
Lotikipi, *plain* C1
Magadi, *lake* D4
Mara, *river* C4
Ngiro, *river* D3
Nzoia, *river* C3
Tana, *river* F4
Turkana (Rudolf), *lake* D2
Turkwel, *river* C2
Victoria, *lake* B4
Yatta, *plateau* E5

Uganda

Capital: Kampala
Area: 93,070 sq. mi.
241,114 sq. km.
Population: 19,859,000
Largest City: Kampala
Language: English
Monetary Unit: Shilling

Uganda

National Capital
Other City
1:11,600,000
0 75 150 mi
0 75 150 km
Mercator Projection

Uganda: Map Index

Cities and Towns
Arua B2
Atiak C2
Entebbe C3
Fort Portal B3
Gulu C2
Jinja C3
Kabale A4
Kampala, *capital* C3
Kitgum C2
Lira C2
Loyoro D2
Masaka B4
Masindi B3
Mbale D3
Mbarara B4
Moroto D2
Mubende B3
Soroti C3
Tororo D3

Other Features
Achwa, *river* C2
Albert, *lake* B3
Albert Nile, *river* B2
Bahr al-Jabal, *river* B2
Edward, *lake* A4
Elgon, *mt.* D3
George, *lake* B4
Kafu, *river* B3
Kagera, *river* B4
Kyoga, *lake* C3
Margherita, *peak* A3
Ruwenzori, *range* B3
Sese, *islands* C4
Victoria, *lake* C4
Victoria Nile, *river* B2,C3

Rwanda

National Capital
Other City
1:4,624,000
0 25 50 mi
0 25 50 km
Gauss-Krüger Projection

Rwanda

Capital: Kigali
Area: 10,169 sq. mi.
26,345 sq. km.
Population: 8,374,000
Largest City: Kigali
Languages: French, Kinyarwanda
Monetary Unit: Franc

Rwanda: Map Index

Cities and Towns
Butare B2
Byumba C1
Cyangugu A2
Gikongoro B2
Gisenyi B1
Gitarama B2
Kagitumba C1
Kibungo C2
Kibuye B2
Kigali, *capital* B1
Nyanza B2
Ruhengeri B1

Other Features
Akanyaru, *river* B2
Bulera, *lake* B1
Cyohoha Sud, *lake* C2
Ihema, *lake* C1
Kagera National Park C1
Kagera, *river* C1, C2
Karisimbi, *mt.* B1
Kivu, *lake* B1
Muhazi, *lake* C1
Nyaba, *river* B2
Nyabarongo, *river* C2
Ruhondo, *lake* B1
Ruhwa, *river* B2
Ruzizi, *river* A2
Rwayakizinga, *lake* C1
Rweru, *lake* C2
Virunga, *mts.* B1

Burundi

National Capital
Other City
1:6,548,000
0 50 100 mi
0 50 100 km
Conic Equidistant Projection

Burundi

Capital: Bujumbura
Area: 10,740 sq. mi.
27,824 sq. km.
Population: 6,125,000
Largest City: Bujumbura
Languages: French, Kirundi
Monetary Unit: Franc

Burundi: Map Index

Cities and Towns
Bubanza B2
Bujumbura, *capital* B2
Bururi B2
Cankuzo C2
Gitega B2
Karuzi C2
Makamba B3
Muramvya B2
Muyinga C1
Ngozi B1
Rutana B2
Ruyigi C2

Other Features
Heha, *mt.* B2
Kagera, *river* C1
Malagarasi, *river* C2
Ruvubu, *river* C2
Ruzizi, *river* A1
Tanganyika, *lake* B2

SENEGAL, THE GAMBIA, GUINEA, GUINEA-BISSAU

Senegal

Capital: Dakar
Area: 75,951 sq. mi.
196,764 sq. km.
Population: 8,731,000
Largest City: Dakar
Language: French
Monetary Unit: CFA franc

Senegal: Map Index

Cities and Towns

Bakel C2
Bignona A3
Dakar, *capital* A2
Dara B2
Dialakoto C3
Diourbel A2
Fatick A2
Goudiri C2
Haïré Lao B1
Kaffrine B2
Kaolack A2
Kédougou C3
Kolda B3
Koungheul B2
Linguère B2
Louga A2
Mamâri C2
Matam C2
Mbaké A2
Mbour A2
Nioro du Rip B3
Payar B2
Richard-Toll B1
Rufisque A2
Saint-Louis A1
Saraya D3
Sédhiou B3
Tambacounda C3
Thiès A2
Tivaouane A2
Vélingara B2
Vélingara B3
Ziguinchor A3

Other Features

Casamance, *region* B3
Casamance, *river* B3
Falémé, *river* C3
Ferlo, *river* B2
Gambia, *river* C3
Guiers, *lake* B1
Koulountou, *river* C3
Mboune, *river* B2
Niéri Ko, *river* C2
Sahel, *region* C2
Saloum, *river* B2
Sandougou, *river* B3
Senegal, *river* B1, C2
Siné, *river* B2
Soungrougrou, *river* B3
Vert, *cape* A2

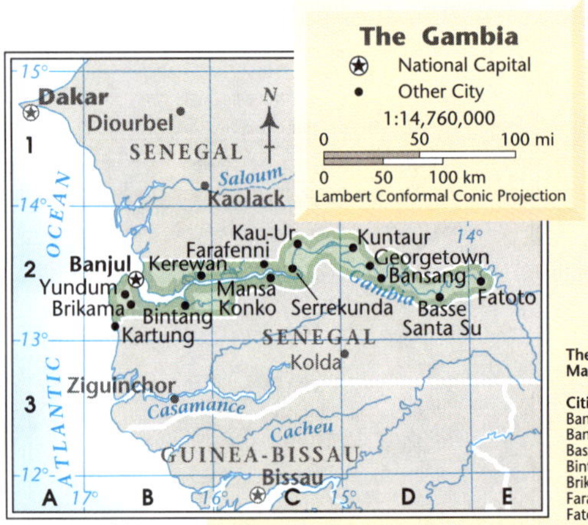

The Gambia

Capital: Banjul
Area: 4,127 sq. mi.
10,692 sq. km.
Population: 959,000
Largest City: Banjul
Language: English
Monetary Unit: Dalasi

The Gambia: Map Index

Cities and Towns

Banjul, *capital* B2
Bansang D2
Basse Santa Su D2
Bintang B2
Brikama B2
Farafenni C2
Fatoto E2
Georgetown D2
Kartung B2
Kau-Ur C2
Kerewan B2
Kuntaur D2
Mansa Konko C2
Serrekunda C2
Yundum B2

Other Feature

Gambia, *river* D2

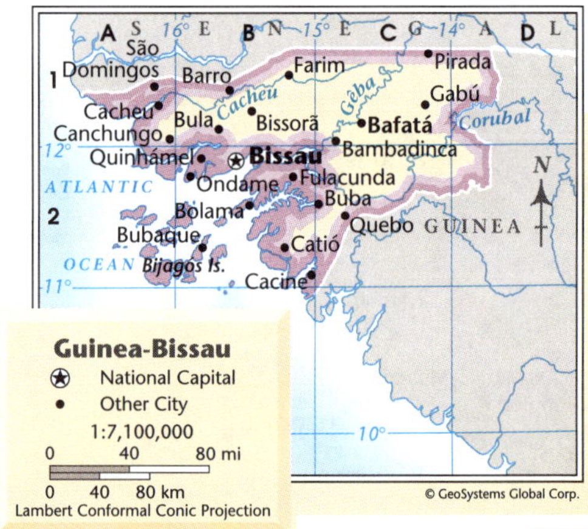

Guinea-Bissau

Capital: Bissau
Area: 13,948 sq. mi.
36,135 sq. km.
Population: 1,098,000
Largest City: Bissau
Language: Portuguese
Monetary Unit: Peso

Guinea-Bissau: Map Index

Cities and Towns

Bafatá C1
Bambadinca C1
Barro B1
Bissau, *capital* B2
Bissorã B1
Bolama B2
Buba C2
Bubaque B2
Bula B1
Cacheu A1
Cacine B2
Canchungo A1
Catió B2
Farim B1
Fulacunda B2
Gabú C1
Ondame B2
Pirada C1
Quebo C2
Quinhámel B2
São Domingos A1

Other Features

Bijagós, *islands* A2
Cacheu, *river* B1
Corubal, *river* D1
Gêba, *river* C1

Guinea: Map Index

Cities and Towns

Beyla D3
Conakry, *capital* B3
Coyah B3
Dabola C2
Fria B2
Guéckédou C3
Kailahun C3
Kali C1
Kamsar A2
Kankan D2
Kérouané D3
Kindia B2
Kissidougou C3
Kouroussa D2
Labé B2
Lélouma B2
Macenta D3
Mamou B2
Niagassola D1
Nzérékoré D4
Siguiri D2
Tougué C2
Yomou D4

Other Features

Bafing, *river* C2
Futa Jallon, *plateau* B1
Gambia, *river* B2
Los, *islands* A3
Milo, *river* D3
Niger, *river* C2
Nimba, *mts.* D4
Tinkissa, *river* C2

Guinea

Capital: Conakry
Area: 94,926 sq. mi.
245,922 sq. km.
Population: 6,392,000
Largest City: Conakry
Language: French
Monetary Unit: Guinea franc

Sierra Leone

National Capital
Other City
1:8,250,000
0 50 100 mi
0 50 100 km
Lambert Conformal Conic Projection

Sierra Leone

Capital: Freetown
Area: 27,699 sq. mi.
71,759 sq. km.
Population: 4,630,000
Largest City: Freetown
Language: English
Monetary Unit: Leone

Côte d'Ivoire (Ivory Coast)

National Capital
Other City
1:9,789,000
0 75 150 mi
0 75 150 km
Lambert Conformal Conic Projection

Côte d'Ivoire

Capital: Yamoussoukro
Area: 124,504 sq. mi.
322,549 sq. km.
Population: 14,296,000
Largest City: Abidjan
Language: French
Monetary Unit: CFA franc

Liberia

Capital: Monrovia
Area: 38,250 sq. mi.
99,093 sq. km.
Population: 2,973,000
Largest City: Monrovia
Language: English
Monetary Unit: U.S. dollar

Liberia

National Capital
Other City
1:11,221,000
0 60 120 mi
0 60 120 km
Lambert Conformal Conic Projection

São Tomé & Príncipe

Capital: São Tomé
Area: 386 sq. mi.
1,000 sq. km.
Population: 137,000
Largest City: São Tomé
Language: Portuguese
Monetary Unit: Dobra

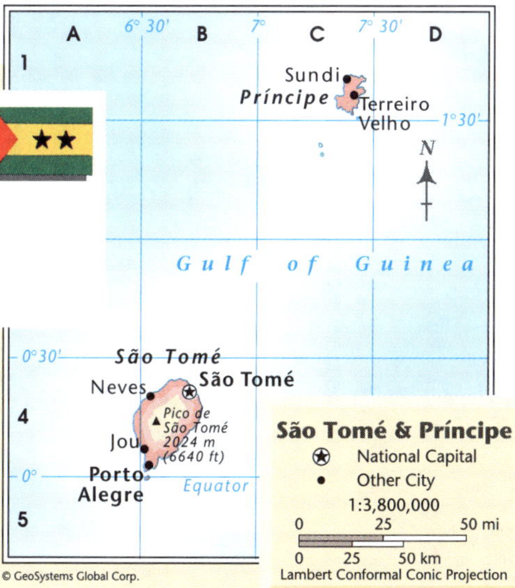

São Tomé & Príncipe

National Capital
Other City
1:3,800,000
0 25 50 mi
0 25 50 km
Lambert Conformal Conic Projection

Ghana
- ⊛ National Capital
- • Other City

1:9,560,000

0 50 100 mi
0 50 100 km

Lambert Conformal Conic Projection

Ghana

Capital: Accra
Area: 92,098 sq. mi.
238,596 sq. km.
Population: 17,225,000
Largest City: Accra
Language: English
Monetary Unit: Cedi

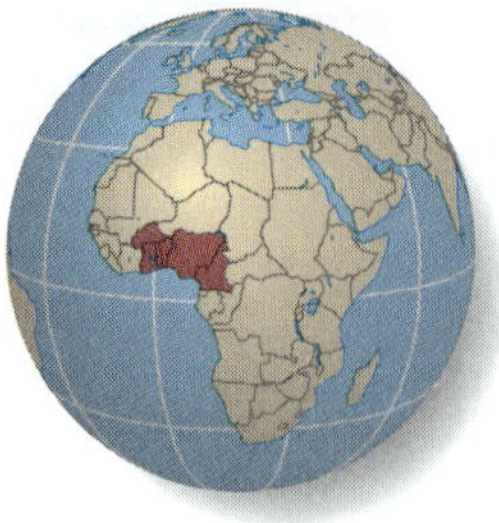

Ghana:
Map Index

Burkina Faso

Capital: Ouagadougou
Area: 105,946 sq. mi.
274,472 sq. km.
Population: 10,135,000
Largest City: Ouagadougou
Language: French
Monetary Unit: CFA franc

Burkina Faso
- ⊛ National Capital
- • Other City

1:14,785,000

0 100 200 mi
0 100 200 km

Lambert Conformal Conic Projection

Burkina Faso:
Map Index

Benin
- ⊛ National Capital
- • Other City

1:14,800,000

0 100 200 mi
0 100 200 km

Lambert Conformal Conic Projection

Benin

Capital: Porto-Novo
Area: 43,500 sq. mi.
112,694 sq. km.
Population: 5,342,000
Largest City: Cotonou
Language: French
Monetary Unit: CFA franc

Benin:
Map Index

Togo

Capital: Lomé
Area: 21,925 sq. mi.
56,801 sq. km.
Population: 4,255,000
Largest City: Lomé
Language: French
Monetary Unit: CFA franc

Togo:
Map Index

Togo
- ⊛ National Capital
- • Other City

1:8,600,000

0 50 100 mi
0 50 100 km

Lambert Conformal Conic Projection

Nigeria

Capital: Abuja
Area: 356,669 sq. mi.
924,013 sq. km.
Population: 98,091,000
Largest City: Lagos
Language: English
Monetary Unit: Naira

Nigeria: Map Index

Cities and Towns

Other Features

Cameroon

Capital: Yaoundé
Area: 183,569 sq. mi.
475,567 sq. km.
Population: 13,132,000
Largest City: Douala
Languages: English, French
Monetary Unit: CFA franc

Cameroon: Map Index

Cities and Towns

Other Features

Equatorial Guinea

Capital: Malabo
Area: 10,831 sq. mi.
28,060 sq. km.
Population: 410,000
Largest City: Malabo
Language: Spanish
Monetary Unit: CFA franc

Equatorial Guinea: Map Index

Gabon

Capital: Libreville
Area: 103,347 sq. mi.
267,738 sq. km.
Population: 1,139,000
Largest City: Libreville
Language: French
Monetary Unit: CFA franc

Gabon: Map Index

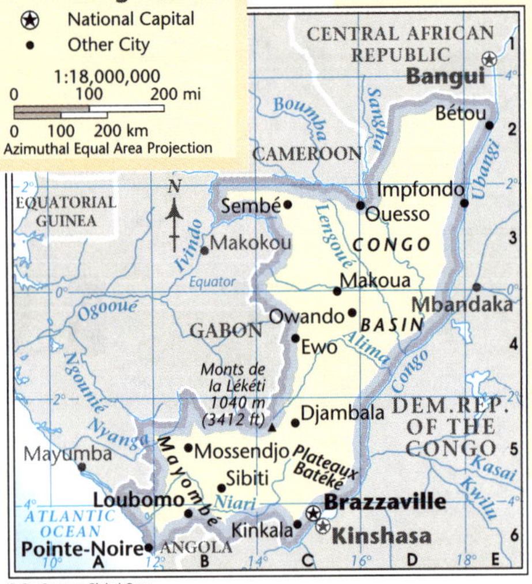

Republic of the Congo

Capital: Brazzaville
Area: 132,047 sq. mi.
342,091 sq. km.
Population: 2,447,000
Largest City: Brazzaville
Language: French
Monetary Unit: CFA franc

Republic of the Congo: Map Index

Central African Republic (C.A.R.)

Capital: Bangui
Area: 240,324 sq. mi.
622,601 sq. km.
Population: 3,142,000
Largest City: Bangui
Language: French
Monetary Unit: CFA franc

Central African Republic: Map Index

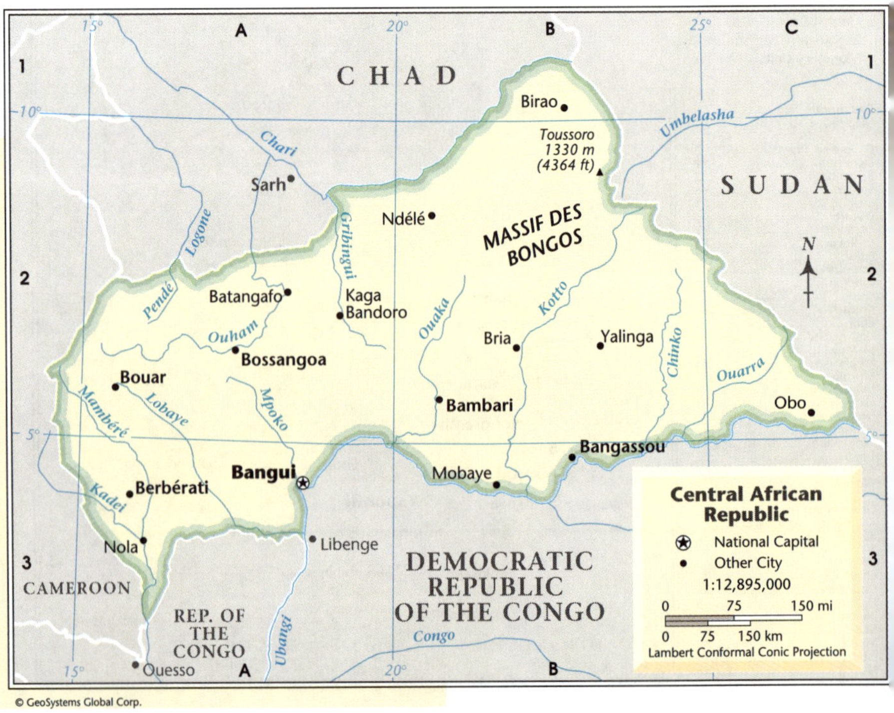

Democratic Republic of the Congo

Capital: Kinshasa
Area: 905,446 sq. mi.
2,345,715 sq. km.
Population: 42,684,000
Largest City: Kinshasa
Language: French
Monetary Unit: New Zaire

Democratic Republic of the Congo: Map Index

Regions

Bandundu	B2
Bas-Congo	A2
Équateur	B1
Kasai-Occidental	B2
Kasai-Oriental	B2
Katanga	C3
Kinshasa	B2
Maniema	C2
Nord-Kivu	C2
Orientale	C1
Sud-Kivu	C2

Cities and Towns

Banana	A2
Bandundu	B2
Boende	B2
Bolobo	B2
Boma	A2
Bondo	B1
Bukavu	C2
Bumba	B1
Bunia	C1
Buta	C1
Dilolo	B3
Gemena	B1
Goma	C2
Ikela	B2
Ilebo	B2
Inga	A2
Isiro	C1
Kabalo	C2
Kahemba	B2
Kalemie	C2
Kamina	C3
Kananga	B2
Kikwit	B2
Kindu	C2
Kinshasa, *capital*	A2
Kisangani	C1
Kolwezi	C3
Likasi	C3
Lisala	B1
Lodja	B2
Lubumbashi	C3
Lusambo	B2
Manono	C2
Matadi	A2
Mbandaka	B2
Mbanza-Ngungu	A2
Mbuji-Mayi	B2
Moba	C2
Mwene-Ditu	B2
Tshikapa	B2
Uvira	C2
Watsa	C1
Yangambi	C1

Other Features

Albert, *lake*	C1
Aruwimi, *river*	C1
Bomu, *river*	C1
Congo, *river*	B1
Congo Basin, *region*	B1
Edward, *lake*	C2
Kasai, *river*	B2
Katanga, *plateau*	B3
Kivu, *lake*	C2
Kwa, *river*	B2
Kwango, *river*	B2
Lomami, *river*	C2
Lualaba, *river*	C2
Luapula, *river*	C3
Lukuga, *river*	C2
Luvua, *river*	C2
Mai-Ndombe, *lake*	B2
Margherita, *peak*	C1
Mitumba, *mts.*	C2
Mweru, *lake*	C3
Sankuru, *river*	B2
Tanganyika, *lake*	C2
Tshuapa, *river*	B2
Tumba, *lake*	B2
Ubangi, *river*	B1
Uele, *river*	C1
Upemba, *lake*	C3

Zambia

Capital: Lusaka
Area: 290,586 sq. mi.
752,813 sq. km.
Population: 9,188,000
Largest City: Lusaka
Language: English
Monetary Unit: Kwach

Zambia: Map Index

Cities and Towns

Chililabombwe	B2
Chingola	B2
Chipata	C2
Choma	B3
Isoka	C2
Kabwe	B2
Kafue	B3
Kaoma	A2
Kasama	C2
Kitwe	B2
Livingstone	B3
Luangwa	C3
Luanshya	B2
Lundazi	C2
Lusaka, *capital*	B3
Mansa	B2
Mazabuka	B3
Mbala	C1
Mongu	A3
Mpika	C2
Mporokoso	C1
Mufulira	B2
Mumbwa	B3
Mwinilunga	A2
Namwala	B3
Nchelenge	B1
Ndola	B2
Petauke	C2
Serenje	C2
Sesheke	A3
Solwezi	B2
Zambezi	A2

Other Features

Bangweulu, *lake*	B2
Chambeshi, *river*	C2
Cuando, *river*	A3
Dongwe, *river*	A2
Kabompo, *river*	A2
Kafue, *river*	B2
Kariba, *lake*	B3
Luangwa, *river*	C2
Luapula, *river*	B2
Lunga, *river*	B2
Lungwebungu, *river*	A2
Luvua, *river*	B1
Muchinga, *mts.*	C2
Mweru, *lake*	B1
Tanganyika, *lake*	C1
Victoria, *falls*	B3
Zambezi, *river*	A3, B3

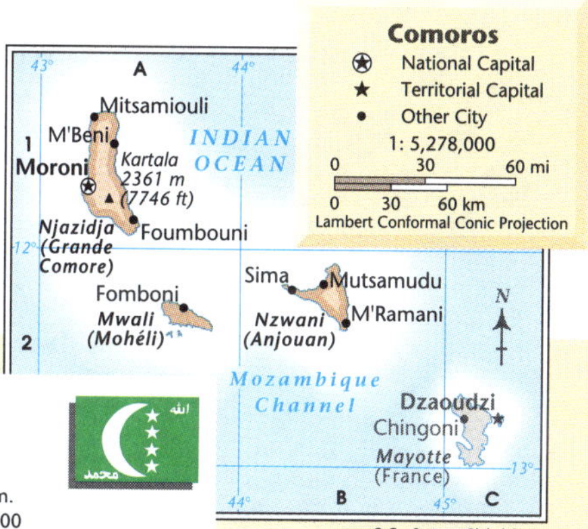

Comoros

Capital: Moroni
Area: 719 sq. mi.
1,863 sq. km.
Population: 530,000
Largest City: Moroni
Languages: Arabic, French
Monetary Unit: CFA franc

Comoros: Map Index

Cities and Towns

Chingoni	C2
Dzaoudzi, *territorial capital*	C2
Fomboni	A2
Foumbouni	A1
M'Beni	A1
Mitsamiouli	A1
Moroni, *national capital*	A1
M'Ramani	B2
Mutsamudu	B2
Sima	B2

Other Features

Kartala, *mt.*	A1
Mayotte, *island*	C2
Mozambique, *channel*	B2
Mwali (Mohéli), *island*	A2
Njazidja (Grande Comore), *island*	A1
Nzwani (Anjouan), *island*	B2

TANZANIA, MALAWI, MOZAMBIQUE

Tanzania

Capital: Dar es-Salaam
Area: 364,017 sq. mi.
943,049 sq. km.
Population: 27,986,000
Largest City: Dar es-Salaam
Languages: Swahili, English
Monetary Unit: Shilling

Tanzania:
Map Index

Cities and Towns
Arusha C1
Bukoba B1
Dar es-Salaam, *capital* C2
Dodoma C2
Iringa C2
Kigoma A1
Kilwa Kivinje C2
Lindi C2
Mbeya B2
Morogoro C2
Moshi C1
Mpanda B2
Mtwara D3
Musoma B1
Mwanza B1
Ngara B1
Shinyanga B1
Singida B1
Songea C3
Sumbawanga B2
Tabora B2
Tanga C2
Wete C1
Zanzibar C2

Other Features
Eyasi, *lake* B1
Great Rift, *valley* B2, C1
Great Ruaha, *river* C2
Igombe, *river* B1
Kagera, *river* B1
Kilimanjaro, *mt.* C1
Kilombero, *river* C2
Kipengere, *range* B2
Luwegu, *river* C2
Mafia, *island* C2
Malagarasi, *river* B1
Manyara, *lake* C1
Mara, *river* B1
Masai, *steppe* C1
Mbemkuru, *river* C3
Moyowosi, *river* B1
Natron, *lake* C1
Ngorongoro, *crater* C1
Njombe, *river* B2
Nyasa (Malawi), *lake* B3
Pangani, *river* C1
Pemba, *island* C2
Ruaha Natl. Park B2
Rufiji, *river* C2
Rukwa, *lake* B2
Rungwa, *river* B2
Ruvuma, *river* C3
Serengeti Natl. Park B1
Tanganyika, *lake* A2
Tarangire Natl. Park C1
Ugalla, *river* B2
Victoria, *lake* B1
Wami, *river* C2
Wembere, *river* B1
Zanzibar, *island* C2

Malawi

Capital: Lilongwe
Area: 45,747 sq. mi.
118,516 sq. km.
Population: 9,732,000
Largest City: Blantyre
Languages: English, Chichewa
Monetary Unit: Kwacha

Malawi:
Map Index

Cities and Towns
Blantyre B3
Chitipa B1
Dedza B2
Karonga B1
Kasungu B2
Lilongwe, *capital* B2
Mchinji A2
Monkey Bay B2
Mzimba B2
Mzuzu B2
Nkhata Bay B2
Nkhotakota B2
Nsanje C3
Salima B2
Zomba C3

Other Features
Bua, *river* B2
Chilwa, *lake* C3
Great Rift, *valley* B1
Malawi (Nyasa), *lake* B2
Malombe, *lake* C2
Nyika, *plateau* B2
Sapitwa, *mt.* C3
Shire, *river* B3
Songwe, *river* B1

Mozambique

Capital: Maputo
Area: 313,661 sq. mi.
812,593 sq. km.
Population: 17,346,000
Largest City: Maputo
Language: Portuguese
Monetary Unit: Metical

Mozambique:
Map Index

Cities and Towns
Angoche C3
Beira B3
Chimoio B3
Chinde C3
Cuamba C2
Inhambane B5
Lichinga B2
Maputo, *capital* B5
Moçambique D2
Mocímboa da Praia D1
Nacala D2
Nampula C2
Pebane C3
Pemba D2
Quelimane C3
Tete B3
Vilanculos B4
Xai-Xai B5

Other Features
Binga, *mt.* B3
Búzi, *river* B4
Cabora Bassa, *dam* B2
Cabora Bassa, *lake* A2
Changane, *river* B4
Chilwa, *lake* B2
Chire, *river* B3
Lebombo, *mts.* A4
Limpopo, *river* B4
Lugenda, *river* C2
Lúrio, *river* C2
Mozambique, *channel* C3
Namuli, *highlands* C2
Nyasa (Malawi), *lake* B2
Rovuma, *river* C1
Save, *river* B4
Zambezi, *river* B3

Mauritius:
Map Index

Cities and Towns

Other Features

Mauritius

Capital: Port Louis
Area: 788 sq. mi.
2,041 sq. km.
Population: 1,117,000
Largest City: Port Louis
Language: English
Monetary Unit: Rupee

Zimbabwe

National Capital
Other City
1:13,730,000
0 75 150 mi
0 75 150 km
Lambert Conformal Conic Projection

Zimbabwe

Capital: Harare
Area: 150,872 sq. mi.
390,860 sq. km.
Population: 10,975,000
Largest City: Harare
Language: English
Monetary Unit: Dollar

Zimbabwe:
Map Index

Cities and Towns

Other Features

Botswana

National Capital
Other City
1:16,700,000
0 75 150 mi
0 75 150 km
Lambert Conformal Conic Proj.

Botswana

Capital: Gaborone
Area: 224,607 sq. mi.
581,883 sq. km.
Population: 1,359,000
Largest City: Gaborone
Language: English
Monetary Unit: Pula

Botswana:
Map Index

Cities and Towns

Other Features

Madagascar

National Capital
Other City
1:17,474,000
0 100 200 mi
0 100 200 km
Lambert Conformal Conic Projection

Madagascar

Capital: Antananarivo
Area: 226,658 sq. mi.
587,197 sq. km.
Population: 13,428,000
Largest City: Antananarivo
Languages: Malagasy, French
Monetary Unit: Malagasy franc

Madagascar:
Map Index

Cities and Towns

Other Features

Angola

National Capital
Other City
1:17,333,000
0 100 200 mi
0 100 200 km
Lambert Conformal Conic Projection

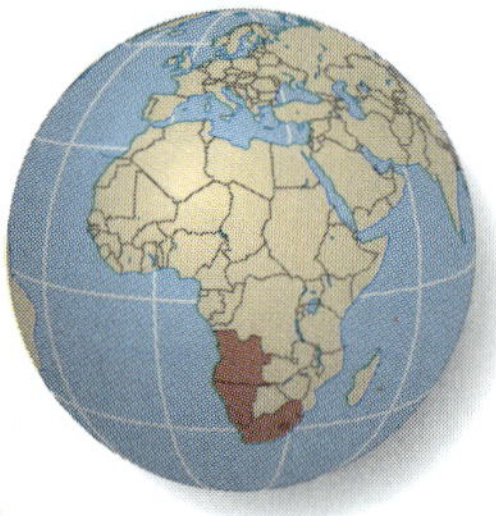

Angola

Capital: Luanda
Area: 481,354 sq. mi.
1,247,031 sq. km.
Population: 9,804,000
Largest City: Luanda
Language: Portuguese
Monetary Unit: Kwanza

Seychelles

National Capital
Other City
1:18,500,000
0 100 200 mi
0 100 200 km
Lambert Conformal Conic Projection

Seychelles

Capital: Victoria
Area: 176 sq. mi.
456 sq. km.
Population: 72,000
Largest City: Victoria
Languages: English, French
Monetary Unit: Rupee

Namibia

Capital: Windhoek
Area: 318,146 sq. mi.
824,212 sq. km.
Population: 1,596,000
Largest City: Windhoek
Language: English
Monetary Unit: Dollar

Namibia

National Capital
Other City
1:16,153,000
0 100 200 mi
0 100 200 km
Lambert Conformal Conic Projection

South Africa

Capital: Cape Town, Pretoria, Bloemfontein
Area: 473,290 sq. mi. 1,226,140 sq. km.
Population: 43,931,000
Largest City: Johannesburg
Languages: Afrikaans, English
Monetary Unit: Rand

South Africa: Map Index

Provinces
Eastern Cape....C3
Free State....C2
Gauteng....C2
Kwazulu Natal....C2
Northern Province....C1
North-West....B2
Mpumalanga....C2
Northern Cape....B3
Western Cape....A3

Cities and Towns
Alice....C3
Aliwal North....C3
Beaufort West....B3
Bellville....A3
Benoni....C2
Bethlehem....C2
Bloemfontein, *judicial apital*....C2
Boksburg....C2
Brakpan....C2
Calvinia....A3
Cape Town, *legislative capital*....A3
Carnarvon....B3
Cradock....C3
De Aar....B3
Durban....D2
East London....C3
Ellisras....C1
Ermelo....C2
George....B3
Germiston....C2
Graaf-Reinet....B3
Grahamstown....C3
Griquatown....B2
Johannesburg....C2
Kimberley....B2
Kroonstad....C2
Krugersdorp....C2
Kuruman....B2
Ladysmith....C2
Mafeking....C2
Messina....D1
Middelburg....C3
Mmabatho....C2
Mossel Bay....B3
Nelspruit....D2
Newcastle....C2
Oudtshoorn....B3
Pietermaritzburg....D2
Pietersburg....C1
Port Edward....D3
Port Elizabeth....C3
Port Nolloth....A2
Pretoria, *administrative capital*....C2
Queenstown....C3
Richards Bay....D2
Roodepoort....C2
Saldanha....A3
Soweto....C2
Springbok....A2
Springs....C2
Stellenbosch....A3
Sun City....C2
Uitenhage....C3
Umtata....C3
Upington....B2
Vanrhynsdorp....A3
Vereeniging....C2
Vryburg....B2
Welkom....C2
Worcester....A3

Other Features
Agulhas, *cape*....B3
Auob, *river*....B2
Bloemhof, *reservoir*....C2
Bushmanland, *plain*....A2
Caledon, *river*....C2
Drakensberg, *mts.*....C3
Good Hope, *cape*....A3
Great Fish, *river*....C3
Great Karroo, *plateau*....B3
Griqualand East, *region*....C3
Griqualand West, *region*....B2
Grootvloer, *pan*....B2
Hendrik Verwoerd, *reservoir*....C3
Kalahari, *desert*....B2
Kruger Natl. Park....D1
Langeberg, *mts.*....B3
Lebombo, *mts.*....D1
Limpopo, *river*....C1
Molopo, *river*....B2
Namib, *desert*....A2
Nossob, *river*....B2
Olifants, *river*....A3
Olifants, *river*....C1
Orange, *river*....B2
St. Lucia, *lake*....D2
Sak, *river*....B3
Swartberg, *mts.*....B3
Tugela, *river*....D2
Vaal, *reservoir*....C2
Vaal, *river*....B2
Wilge, *river*....C2
Zululand, *region*....D2

Swaziland

Capital: Mbabane
Area: 6,704 sq. mi. 17,368 sq. km.
Population: 936,000
Largest City: Mbabane
Languages: Siswati, English
Monetary Unit: Lilangeni

Swaziland: Map Index

Cities and Towns
Bhunya....B2
Big Bend....B2
Bulembu....B1
Gege....B2
Hiatikulu....B2
Ka Dake....B2
Lavumisa....B3
Lobamba....B2
Mankayane....B2
Manzini....B2
Mbabane, *capital*....B2
Mhlume....B2
Mliba....B2
Ngonini....B1
Nhlangano....B3
Nsoko....B3
Piggs Peak....B1
Sidvokodvo....B2
Siteki....B2
Tshaneni....B1

Other Features
Emlembe, *mt.*....B1
Komati, *river*....B2
Lebombo, *mts.*....C2
Lusutfu, *river*....B2
Mbuluzane, *river*....B2
Mbuluzi, *river*....B2
Mgwavuma, *river*....B3
Mkondvo, *river*....B2
Ngwempisi, *river*....A2
Nyetane, *river*....B2
Umbeluzi, *river*....B2

Lesotho

Capital: Maseru
Area: 11,716 sq. mi. 30,352 sq. km.
Population: 1,944,000
Largest City: Maseru
Language: English
Monetary Unit: Loti

Lesotho: Map Index

Cities and Towns
Butha-Buthe....B1
Leribe....B1
Libono....B1
Mafeteng....A2
Maseru, *capital*....A2
Mohales Hoek....A3
Mokhotlong....C2
Morija....A2
Pitseng....B2
Qachas Nek....B3
Quthing....A3
Roma....A2
Sekake....B2
Teyateyaneng....A2
Thaba-Tseka....B2

Other Features
Caledon, *river*....A1
Central, *range*....B2
Drakensberg, *mts.*....B3
Makhaleng, *river*....A2
Maloti, *mts.*....B2
Matsoku, *river*....B2
Orange, *river*....A3, B2
Sources, *mt.*....B1
Thabana Ntlenyana, *mt.*....C2
Tsedike, *river*....B3

MAJOR CITIES

City	Population
Argentina	
Buenos Aires	2,961,000
Córdoba	1,148,000
Rosario	895,000
Bolivia	
La Paz	711,000
Santa Cruz	695,000
Sucre	131,000
Brazil	
São Paulo	9,480,000
Rio de Janeiro	5,336,000
Salvador	2,056,000
Belo Horizonte	2,049,000
Fortaleza	1,758,000
Brasília	1,596,000
Recife	1,290,000
Curitiba	1,290,000
Pôrto Alegre	1,263,000
Belém	1,246,000
Manaus	1,011,000
Chile	
Santiago	4,385,000
Concepción	306,000
Colombia	(metro)
Bogotá	3,975,000
Medellín	1,452,000
Cali	1,369,000
Barranquilla	917,000
Ecuador	
Guayaquil	1,508,000
Quito	1,101,000
Falkland Islands	
Stanley	1,200
French Guiana	
Cayenne	41,000
Guyana	
Georgetown	195,000
Paraguay	
Asunción	502,000
Peru	(metro)
Lima	6,415,000
Arequipa	635,000
Trujillo	532,000
Suriname	
Paramaribo	192,000
Uruguay	
Montevideo	1,360,000
Venezuela	
Caracas	1,825,000
Maracaibo	1,208,000
Valencia	903,000
Barquisimeto	603,000

International comparability of city population data is limited by various data inconsistencies.

South America: Population, by nation (in millions)

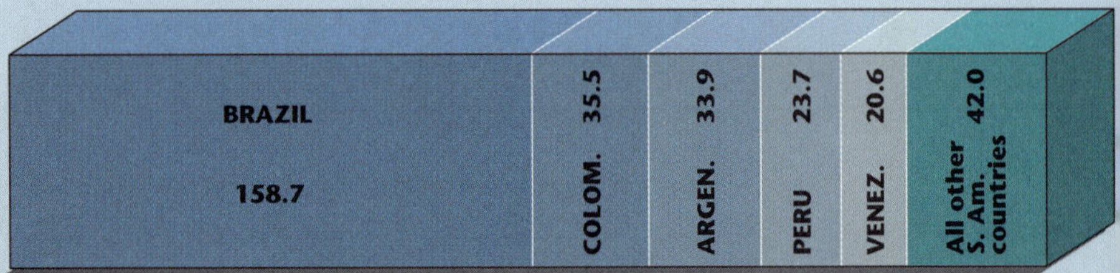

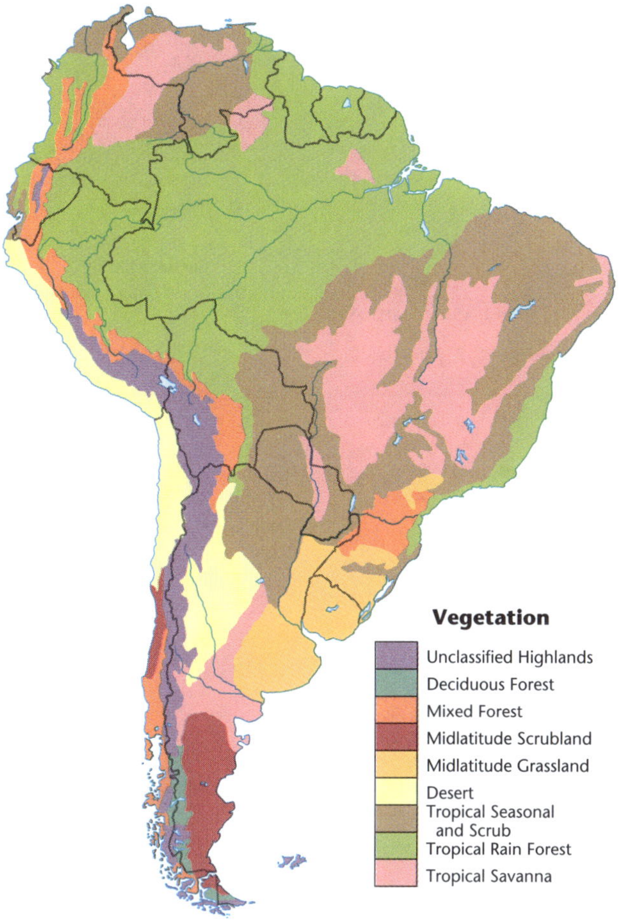
Vegetation
Unclassified Highlands
Deciduous Forest
Mixed Forest
Midlatitude Scrubland
Midlatitude Grassland
Desert
Tropical Seasonal and Scrub
Tropical Rain Forest
Tropical Savanna

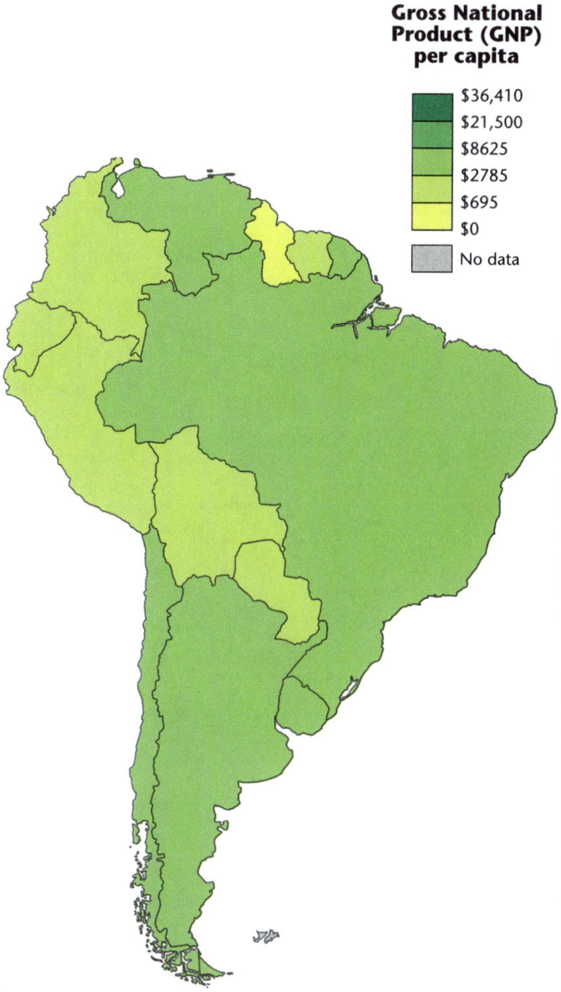
Gross National Product (GNP) per capita
$36,410
$21,500
$8625
$2785
$695
$0
No data

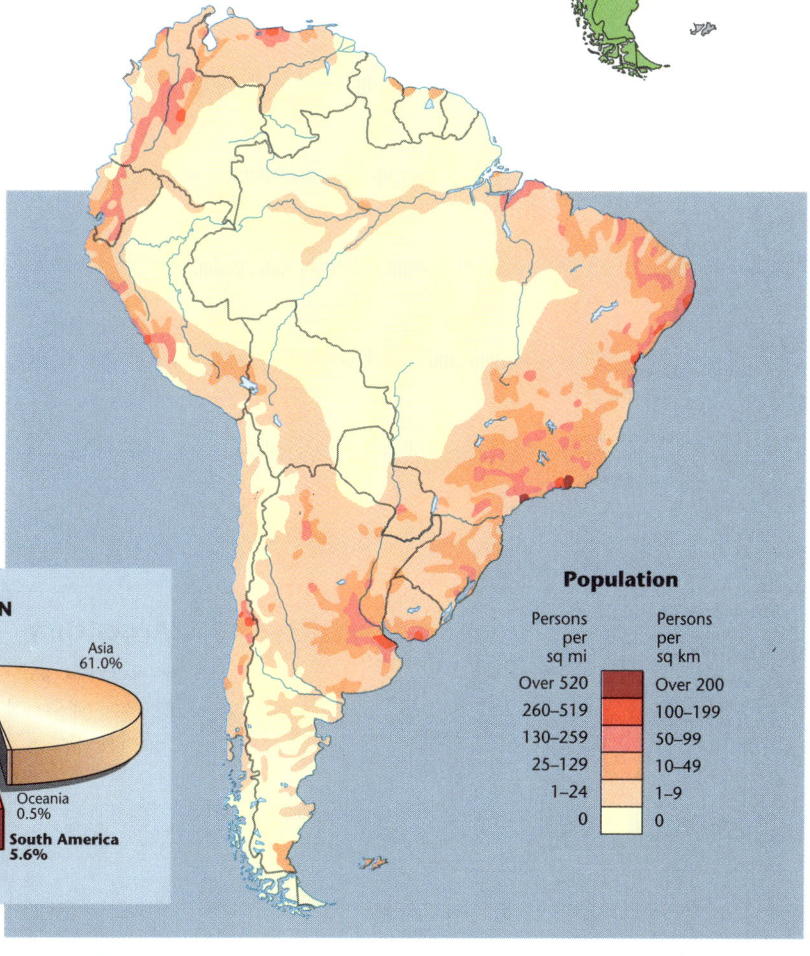
Population
Persons per sq mi
Persons per sq km
Over 520
Over 200
260–519
100–199
130–259
50–99
25–129
10–49
1–24
1–9
0
0

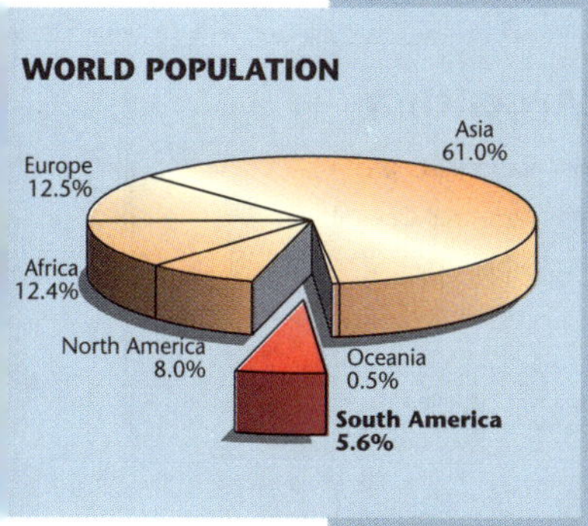
WORLD POPULATION
Asia 61.0%
Europe 12.5%
Africa 12.4%
North America 8.0%
Oceania 0.5%
South America 5.6%

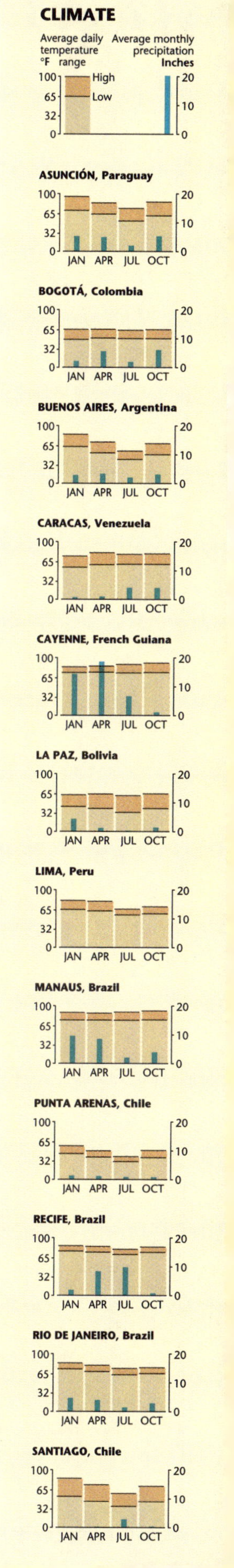
CLIMATE
Average daily temperature °F range
Average monthly precipitation Inches
High
Low
ASUNCIÓN, Paraguay
BOGOTÁ, Colombia
BUENOS AIRES, Argentina
CARACAS, Venezuela
CAYENNE, French Guiana
LA PAZ, Bolivia
LIMA, Peru
MANAUS, Brazil
PUNTA ARENAS, Chile
RECIFE, Brazil
RIO DE JANEIRO, Brazil
SANTIAGO, Chile
JAN APR JUL OCT

BOLIVIA
PARAGUAY
BRAZIL
CHILE
URUGUAY
PACIFIC OCEAN
ATLANTIC OCEAN
ATACAMA DESERT
ANDES
GRAN CHACO
PAMPAS
PATAGONIA
Tropic of Capricorn
Chuquicamata
Antofagasta
Llullaillaco 6723 m (22,057 ft)
JUJUY
Embarcación
San Salvador de Jujuy
Salta
SALTA
FORMOSA
Formosa
Concepción
Asunción
Foz do Iguaçu
Iguaçu Falls
Curitiba
MISIONES
Posadas
CHACO
Presidencia Roque Sáenz Peña
Resistencia
Corrientes
CORRIENTES
San Miguel de Tucumán
TUCUMÁN
SANTIAGO DEL ESTERO
Santiago del Estero
Ojos del Salado 6880 m (22,572 ft)
CATAMARCA
Catamarca
La Rioja
LA RIOJA
Reconquista
SANTA FE
Curuzú Cuatiá
Santa Maria
La Serena
Desaguadero
Córdoba
Salado
Pilcomayo
Bermejo
Paraná
Uruguay
Iguaçu
L. Mar Chiquita
CÓRDOBA
Córdoba
San Francisco
Santa Fe
ENTRE RÍOS
Paraná
Concordia
Pôrto Alegre
L. dos Patos
Pelotas
SAN JUAN
San Juan
Mercedario 6770 m (22,211 ft)
Champaquí 2850 m (9350 ft)
Villa María
Sierras de Córdoba
Aconcagua 6960 m (22,834 ft)
Mendoza
Godoy Cruz
San Luis
Río Cuarto
Rosario
San Nicolás
Negro
Santiago
Tupungato 6800 m (22,310 ft)
SAN LUIS
San Rafael
DISTRITO FEDERAL
Buenos Aires
Avellaneda
Montevideo
Lanús
Lomas de Zamora
La Plata
Río de la Plata
MENDOZA
Atuel
Domuyo 4709 m (15,450 ft)
LA PAMPA
Santa Rosa
BUENOS AIRES
Olavarría
Tandil
Cabo San Antonio
Concepción
Colorado
NEUQUÉN
Mar del Plata
Neuquén
Bahía Blanca
Necochea
Bahía Blanca
Lanín 3776 m (12,389 ft)
RÍO NEGRO
San Antonio Oeste
San Carlos de Bariloche
Viedma
Punta Rasa
Puerto Montt
Golfo San Matías
Península Valdés
Chubut
Chiloé
Esquel
Rawson
CHUBUT
Chico
Comodoro Rivadavia
Golfo San Jorge
Coihaique
Península Taitao
Deseado
L. Buenos Aires
Cabo Tres Puntas
Puerto Deseado
SANTA CRUZ
L. San Martín
L. Cardiel
Fitzroy 3375 m (11,073 ft)
L. Viedma
Santa Cruz
Calafate
Puerto Santa Cruz
L. Argentino
Bahía Grande
West Falkland I.
East Falkland I.
Stanley
Gallegos
Río Gallegos
Punta Dungeness
Strait of Magellan
Falkland Islands (Islas Malvinas) (Br.) (claimed by Argentina)
Punta Arenas
TIERRA DEL FUEGO
Ushuaia
Isla de los Estados
Beagle Channel
Cape Horn
N
Argentina
National Capital
Territorial Capital
Other City
1:17,760,000
0 200 400 mi
0 200 400 km
Modified Chamberlain Trimetric Projection

Argentina

Capital: Buenos Aires
Area: 1,073,518 sq. mi.
2,781,134 sq. km.
Population: 33,913,000
Largest City: Buenos Aires
Language: Spanish
Monetary Unit: Peso

Argentina: Map Index

Provinces
Buenos Aires C4
Catamarca B2
Chaco C2
Chubut B5
Córdoba C3
Corrientes D2
Distrito Federal D3
Entre Ríos D3
Formosa D1
Jujuy B1
La Pampa B4
La Rioja B2
Mendoza B3
Misiones E2
Neuquén B4
Río Negro B5
Salta B2
San Juan B3
San Luis B3
Santa Cruz A6
Santa Fe C2
Santiago del Estero C2
Tierra del Fuego B7
Tucumán B2

Cities and Towns
Avellaneda D3
Bahía Blanca C4
Buenos Aires, *capital* D3
Calafate A7
Catamarca B2
Comodoro Rivadavia B6
Concordia D3
Córdoba C3
Corrientes D2
Curuzú Cuatiá D2
Embarcación C1
Esquel A5
Formosa D2
Godoy Cruz B3
Lanús D3
La Plata D4
La Rioja B2
Lomas de Zamora D4
Mar del Plata D4
Mendoza B3
Necochea D4
Neuquén B4
Olavarría C4
Paraná C3
Posadas D2
Presidencia Roque Sáenz Peña C2
Puerto Deseado B6
Puerto Santa Cruz B7
Rawson B5
Reconquista D2
Resistencia D2
Río Cuarto C3
Río Gallegos B7
Rosario C3
Salta B1
San Antonio Oeste B5
San Carlos de Bariloche A5
San Francisco C3
San Juan B3
San Luis B3
San Miguel de Tucumán B2
San Nicolás C3
San Rafael B3
San Salvador de Jujuy B1
Santa Fe C3
Santa Rosa C4
Santiago del Estero C2
Tandil D4
Ushuaia B7
Viedma C5
Villa María C3

Other Features
Aconcagua, *mt.* A3
Andes, *mts.* A6–B1
Argentino, *lake* A7
Atuel, *river* B4
Beagle, *channel* B7
Bermejo, *river* C2
Blanca, *bay* C4
Buenos Aires, *lake* A6
Cardiel, *lake* A6
Champaquí, *mt.* C3
Chico, *river* B6
Chubut, *river* A5
Colorado, *river* B4
Córdoba, *range* B3
Desaguadero, *river* B2
Deseado, *river* B6
Domuyo, *volcano* A4
Dungeness, *point* B7
Estados, *island* C7
Fitzroy, *mt.* A6
Gallegos, *river* A7
Gran Chaco, *region* C1
Grande, *bay* B7
Iguaçu, *falls* E2
Iguaçu, *river* E2
Lanín, *volcano* A4
Llullaillaco, *volcano* B1
Magellan, *strait* B7
Mar Chiquita, *lake* C3
Mercedario, *mt* B3
Negro, *river* B4
Ojos del Salado, *mt.* B2
Pampas, *plain* C4
Paraguay, *river* D2
Paraná, *river* D2
Patagonia, *region* A6
Pilcomayo, *river* C1
Plata, Río de la, *estuary* D3
Rasa, *point* C5
Salado, *river* B3
Salado, *river* C2
San Antonio, *cape* D4
San Jorge, *gulf* B6
San Martín, *lake* A6
San Matías, *gulf* C5
Santa Cruz, *river* A7
Tres Puntas, *cape* B6
Tupungato, *mt.* B3
Uruguay, *river* D3
Valdés, *peninsula* C5
Viedma, *lake* A6

Paraguay

Capital: Asunción
Area: 157,048 sq. mi.
406,752 sq. km.
Population: 4,007,000
Largest City: Asunción
Language: Spanish
Monetary Unit: Guarani

Paraguay: Map Index

Departments
Alto Paraguay C2
Alto Paraná E4
Amambay E3
Asunción D4
Boquerón B3
Caaguazú D4
Caazapá D5
Canendiyú E4
Central D4
Chaco C2
Concepción D3
Cordillera D4
Guairá D4
Itapúa E5
Misiones D5
Ñeembucú C5
Nueva Asunción B2
Paraguarí D5
Presidente Hayes C4
San Pedro D4

Cities and Towns
Abaí E4
Asunción, *capital* D4
Caacupé D4
Caaguazú E4
Caazapá D5
Capitán Pablo Lagerenza B1
Ciudad del Este E4
Concepción D3
Coronel Oviedo D4
Doctor Pedro P. Peña A3
Encarnación E5
Filadelfia B3
Fuerte Olimpo D2
General Eugenio A. Garay A2
Mariscal Estigarribia B3
Paraguarí D4
Pedro Juan Caballero E3
Pilar C5
Pozo Colorado C3
Puerto Bahía C2
Puerto Pinasco D3
Salto del Guairá E4
San Juan Bautista D5
San Lorenzo D4
San Pedro D4
Villa Hayes D4
Villarrica D4

Other Features
Acaray, *river* E4
Amambay, *mts.* E3
Apa, *river* D3
Chaco Boreal, *region* B2
Gran Chaco, *region* B3
Iguazú, *falls* E4
Itaipú, *reservoir* E4
Jejuí-Guazú, *river* D4
Montelindo, *river* C3
Paraguay, *river* C2, C5
Paraná, *river* C5, E5
Pilcomayo, *river* B3, C4
Tebicuary, *river* D5
Verde, *river* C3
Ypané, *river* D3
Ypoá, *lake* D4

Uruguay

Capital: Montevideo
Area: 68,037 sq. mi.
176,215 sq. km.
Population: 2,921,798
Largest City: Montevideo
Language: Spanish
Monetary Unit: New peso

Uruguay: Map Index

Cities and Towns
Artigas B1
Bella Unión B1
Canelones B3
Carmelo A2
Colonia B3
Durazno B2
Florida B3
Fray Bentos A2
Las Piedras B3
Melo C2
Mercedes A2
Minas C3
Montevideo, *capital* B3
Nueva Palmira A2
Pando C3
Paso de los Toros B2
Paysandú A2
Piedra Sola B2
Punta del Este C3
Rivera C1
Rocha C3
Salto B1
San Carlos C3
San José B3
Tacuarembó C1
Treinta y Tres C2
Trinidad B2

Other Features
Arapey Grande, *river* B1
Baygorria, *lake* B2
Cebollatí, *river* C2
Cuareim, *river* B1
Daymán, *river* B1
Grande, *range* C2
Haedo, *range* B2
Merín, *lagoon* D2
Mirador Nacional, *mt.* C3
Negra, *lagoon* D2
Negro, *river* C2
Paso de Palmar, *lake* B2
Plata, *river* B3
Queguay Grande, *river* B2
Rincón del Bonete, *lake* B2
Salto Grande, *reservoir* B1
San José, *river* B2
San Salvador, *river* A2
Santa Ana, *range* C1
Santa Lucía, *river* B3
Tacuarembó, *river* C1
Tacuarí, *river* D2
Uruguay, *river* A1
Yaguarí, *river* C1
Yaguarón, *river* D2
Yi, *river* C2

Chile

Capital: Santiago
Area: 292,135 sq. mi.
756,826 sq. km.
Population: 12,951,000
Largest City: Santiago
Language: Spanish
Monetary Unit: Peso

Chile:
Map Index

Peru

Capital: Lima
Area: 496,225 sq. mi.
1,285,216 sq. km.
Population: 21,256,000
Largest City: Lima
Languages: Spanish, Quechua
Monetary Unit: Nuevo Sol

Bolivia

Capital: La Paz, Sucre
Area: 424,164 sq. mi.
1,098,871 sq. km.
Population: 7,719,000
Largest City: La Paz
Languages: Spanish, Quechua, Aymara
Monetary Unit: Boliviano

Colombia

Capital: Bogotá
Area: 440,831 sq. mi.
1,142,049 sq. km.
Population: 35,578,000
Largest City: Bogotá
Language: Spanish
Monetary Unit: Peso

Colombia: Map Index

Internal Divisions
Amazonas (commissary)...........B5
Antioquia (dept.).......................B3
Arauca (intendency).................C3
Atlántico (dept.).......................B2
Bolívar (dept.) B2
Boyacá (dept.)...........................B3
Caldas (dept.) B3
Capital District B4
Caquetá (dept.)......................... B4
Casanare (intendency) C3
Cauca (dept.)............................A4
César (dept.) B2
Chocó (dept.) A3
Córdoba (dept.) B2
Cundinamarca (dept.) B3
Guainía (commissary) C4
Guaviare (commissary) B4
Huila (dept.)...............................A4
La Guajira (dept.) B2
Magdalena (dept.) B2
Meta (dept.)...............................B4
Nariño (dept.).............................A4
Norte de Santander (dept.) B2
Putumayo (intendency).............A4
Quindío (dept.) B3
Risaralda (dept.) B3
San Andrés y Providencia (intendency) ....Inset
Santander (dept.) B3
Sucre (dept.) B2
Tolima (dept.) B4
Valle del Cauca (dept.)..............A4
Vaupés (commissary) C4
Vichada (commissary)...............C3

Cities and Towns
Arauca C3
Armenia B3
Barrancabermeja B3
Barranquilla B2
Bogotá, *capital* B3
Bucaramanga B3
Buenaventura.............................A4
Cali A4
Cartagena B2
Cravo Norte...............................C3
Cúcuta B3
El Encanto B5
Florencia B4
Ibagué..B3
Leticia C6
Manizales B3
Medellín.....................................B3
Miraflores B4
Mitú..C4
Mocoa A4
Montería B2
Neiva B4
Orocué C3
Palmira.......................................A4
Pasto A4
Pereira..B3
Popayán A4
Puerto Carreño D3
Puerto Inírida D4
Puerto Leguízamo B5
Quibdó A3
Ríohacha B2
San Felipe D4
San José del Guaviare B4
Santa Marta B2
Sincelejo.....................................B2
Tumaco A4
Tunja B3
Turbo A2
Valledupar B2
Villavicencio...............................B3
Vista Hermosa B4
Yopal B3

Other Features
Albuquerque, *cays*...................Inset
Amazon, *river*............................C5
Andes, *range*.............................A4
Apaporis, *river*...........................C4
Atrato, *river*...............................A3
Caquetá, *river*............................B5
Cauca, *river*...............................B3
Cordillera Central, *range* A4
Cordillera Occidental, *range*...................................A4
Cordillera Oriental, *range* B4
Cristóbal Colón, *peak* B2
Gallinas, *point* C1
Guainía, *river*.............................C4
Guajira, peninsula C1
Guaviare, *river*...........................C4
Huila, *mt.*....................................A4
Llanos, *prairie*.............................C3
Magdalena, *river*.........................B3
Meta, *river* C3
Orinoco, *river*.............................D3
Patía, *river* A4
Providencia, *island*.................Inset
Putumayo, *river* B5
Roncador, *cay* ....Inset
San Andrés, *island*...................Inset
San Juan, *river* A3
Serranilla, *bank*........................Inset
Sierra Nevada de Santa Marta, *mts.* B2
Tolima, *mt.*.................................B3
Vaupés, *river*..............................B4
Vichada, *river* C3

Venezuela: Map Index

Internal Divisions
Amazonas (territory)................C3
Anzoátegui (state) D2
Apure (state).............................C2
Aragua (state)...........................C2
Barinas (state)...........................C2
Bolívar (state) D2
Carabobo (state) C2
Cojedes (state)..........................C2
Delta Amacuro (territory) D2
Dependencias Federales...........C1
Distrito Federal C1
Falcón (state) B1
Guárico (state)..........................C2
Lara (state)................................B1
Mérida (state) B2
Miranda (state)..........................C1
Monagas (state) D2
Nueva Esparta (state) D1
Portuguesa (state).....................C2
Sucre (state) D1
Táchira (state) B2
Trujillo (state) B2
Yaracuy (state)..........................C1
Zulia (state)...............................B2

Cities and Towns
Acarigua C2
Anaco...D2
Barcelona D1
Barinas B2
Barquisimeto C1
Baruta...C1
Cabimas......................................B1
Calabozo C2
Canaima.....................................D2
Caracas, *capital*..........................C1
Carora C1
Carúpano D1
Ciudad Bolívar..........................D2
Ciudad Guayana.......................D2
Coro C1
Cumaná D1
El Tigre......................................D2
Guanare C2
Güiria D1
La Asunción...............................D1
La Guaira Maiquetía C1
Los Teques.................................C1
Maiquetía C1
Maracaibo..................................B1
Maracay C1
Maturin D2
Mérida B2
Petare C1
Puerto Ayacucho C2
Puerto Cabello..........................C1
Puerto La Cruz..........................D1
Punto Fijo B1
San Cristóbal.............................B2
San Felipe C1
San Fernando de Apure C2
San Juan de Los Morros C2
Santa Elena de Uairén..............D3
Trujillo.......................................B2
Tucupita D2
Valencia C1
Valera..B2

Other Features
Angel, *falls*.................................D2
Apure, *river*................................C2
Arauca, *river*..............................C2
Bolívar, *mt.*.................................B2
Caroni, *river*...............................D2
Casiquiare, *river*.........................C3
Caura, *river*................................D2
Cojedes, *river*.............................C2
Guri, *reservoir* D2
Guiana, *highlands*.......................D2
La Tortuga, *island* C1
Llanos, *plain*...............................B2
Maracaibo, *lake*.........................B2
Margarita, *island*........................D1
Mérida, *mts.*...............................B2
Meta, *river* C2
Neblina, *mt.* C3
Negro, *river*................................B3
Orinoco, *river*....................C3, D2
Pacaraima, *mts.* D3
Paria, *gulf* D1
Parima, *mts.* D3
Roraima, *mt.*...............................D2
Venezuela, *gulf*..........................B1

Venezuela

Capital: Caracas
Area: 352,144 sq. mi.
912,050 sq. km.
Population: 10,677,000
Largest City: Caracas
Language: Spanish
Monetary Unit: Bolivar

Ecuador

Capital: Quito
Area: 105,037 sq. mi.
272,117 sq. km.
Population: 10,677,000
Largest City: Guayaquil
Language: Spanish
Monetary Unit: Sucre

Ecuador: Map Index

Guyana

Capital: Georgetown
Area: 83,000 sq. mi.
214,969 sq. km.
Population: 754,000
Largest City: Georgetown
Language: English
Monetary Unit: Guyana dollar

Guyana: Map Index

Cities and Towns
Anna Regina B2
Apoteri B4
Bartica B2
Biloku B5
Charity B2
Georgetown, *capital* B2
Isherton B4
Lethem B4
Linden B3
Mabaruma B1
Mahdia B3
Matthews Ridge A2
New Amsterdam C2
Suddie B2

Other Features
Acarai, *mts.* B5
Barama, *river* B2
Berbice, *river* B3
Courantyne, *river* B3
Cuyuni, *river* A2
Demerara, *river* B3
Essequibo, *river* B3, B5
Kaieteur, *falls* B3
Kanuku, *mts.* B4
Mazaruni, *river* A2
Merume, *mts.* A2
New, *river* C4
Pakaraima, *mts.* A3
Potaro, *river* B3
Rawa, *river* B4
Roraima, *mt.* A3
Takutu, *river* B4

Suriname

Capital: Paramaribo
Area: 63,037 sq. mi.
163,265 sq. km.
Population: 423,000
Largest City: Paramaribo
Language: Dutch
Monetary Unit: Suriname guilder

Suriname: Map Index

Cities and Towns
Albina B2
Apetina B3
Apoera A2
Benzdorp B3
Brokopondo B2
Groningen B2
Moengo B2
Nieuw Amsterdam B2
Nieuw Nickerie A2
Paramaribo, *capital* B2
Paranam B2
Sipaliwini A3
Totness A2
Zanderij B2

Other Features
Coeroeni, *river* A3
Coppename, *river* A2
Corantijn, *river* A2
Eilerts de Haan, *mts.* A3
Juliana Top, *mt.* A3
Kabelebo, *river* A2
Kayser, *mts.* A3
Lawa, *river* B2
Litani, *river* B3
Lucie, *river* A3
Marowijne, *river* B2
Nickerie, *river* A2
Oelemari, *river* B3
Oranje, *mts.* B3
Saramacca, *river* B2
Suriname, *river* B3
Tapanahoni, *river* B3
Tumuc-Humac, *mts.* B3
Wilhelmina, *mts.* A2
W.J. van Blommestein, *lake* B2

French Guiana: Map Index

Cities and Towns
Apatou A1
Cacao B1
Camopi B2
Cayenne, *capital* B1
Grand Santi A1
Iracoubo B1
Kaw B1
Kourou B1
Mana B1
Maripasoula A2
Ouanary C1
Régina B1
Rémire B1
Saint-Élie B1
Saint-Georges C2
Saint-Laurent du Maroni A1
Saül B2

Other Features
Camopi, *river* B2
Devil's, *island* B1
Lawa, *river* A2
Litani, *river* A2
Mana, *river* B1
Maroni, *river* A1
Oyapock, *river* B2
Salut, *islands* B1
Tampok, *river* B2
Tumuc-Humac, *mts.* A2

French Guiana

Capital: Cayenne
Area: 35,135 sq. mi.
91,000 sq. km.
Population: 94,700
Largest City: Cayenne
Language: French
Monetary Unit: French franc

Brazil:
Map Index

States and Federal District
Acre A2
Alagoas E2
Amapá C1
Amazonas B2
Bahia D3
Ceará E2
Espírito Santo D3
Federal District D3
Goiás D3
Maranhão D2
Mato Grosso C3
Mato Grosso do Sul C4
Minas Gerais D3
Pará C2
Paraíba E2
Paraná C4
Pernambuco E2
Piauí D2
Rio de Janeiro D4, Inset I
Rio Grande do Norte E2
Rio Grande do Sul C4
Rondônia B3
Roraima B1
Santa Catarina C4
São Paulo C4, Inset II
Sergipe E3
Tocantins D3

Cities and Towns
Alagoinhas E3
Altamira C2
Anápolis D3
Aracaju E3
Bacabal D2
Bauru D4
Belém D2
Belford Roxo Inset I
Belo Horizonte D3
Boa Vista B1
Bom Jesus da Lapa D3
Brasília, *capital* D3
Cáceres C3
Cachimbo C2
Campina Grande E2
Campinas D4
Campo Grande C4
Campos D4
Campos Elísios Inset I
Carapicuíba Inset II
Corumbá C3
Cotia Inset II
Cruzeiro do Sul A2
Cubatão Inset II
Cuiabá C3
Curitiba D4
Diadema Inset II
Dourados C4
Duque de Caxias Inset I
Feira de Santana E3
Floriano D2
Florianópolis D4
Fortaleza E2
Foz do Iguaçu C4
Goiânia D3
Governador Valadares D3
Guajara Mirim B3
Guarujá Inset II
Guarulhos Inset II
Ilhéus E3
Imbariê Inset I
Imperatriz D2
Inhomirim Inset I
Ipíba Inset I
Itabira D3
Itabuna E3
Itaipu Inset I
Itajaí D4
Itapecerica da Serra Inset II
Itapeva Inset II
Itaquaquecetuba Inset II
Jaboatão E2
Jacare-Acanga C2
Japeri Inset I
Jir Paraná B3
João Pessoa E2
Joinville D4
Juàzeiro D2
Juàzeiro do Norte E2
Juiz de Fora D4
Jundiai D4
Lajes C4
Londrina C4
Macapá C1
Maceió E2
Majé Inset I
Manaus C2
Maraba D2
Mariana D3
Mauá Inset II
Mogi das Cruzes Inset II
Monjolo Inset I
Montes Claros D3
Mozzoro E2
Natal E2
Neves Inset I
Nilópolis Inset I
Niterói D4, Inset I
Nova Iguaçu Inset I
Olinda E2
Osasco Inset II
Palmas D3
Paranaguá D4
Parnaiba D2
Passo Fundo C4
Paulo Afonso E2
Pelotas C5
Petrólina D2
Petrópolis D4, Inset I
Piracicaba D4
Poá Inset II
Pôrto Alegre C5
Pôrto Velho B2
Queimados Inset I
Randonopolis C3
Recife E2
Ribeirão Pires Inset II
Ribeirão Prêto D4
Rio Branco B2
Rio de Janeiro D4, Inset I
Rio Grande C5
Rio Verde C3
Salvador E3
Santa Maria C4
Santana do Livramento C5
Santarém C2
Santo André Inset II
Santos D4, Inset II
São Bernardo do Campo Inset II
São Caetano do Sul Inset II
São Gonçalo Inset I
São João de Meriti Inset I
São José do Rio Prêto D4
São Luís D2
São Paulo D4, Inset II
São Vincente Inset II
Sobral D2
Sorocaba D4
Suzano Inset II
Taboão da Serra Inset II
Tefé B2
Teresina D2
Tubarão D4
Uberaba D3
Uberlândia D3
Vincente de Carvalho Inset II
Vitória D4
Vitória da Conquista D3
Volta Redonda D4

Other Features
Acaraí, *range* C1
Açúcar, *mt.* Inset I
Amazon, *basin* B2
Amazon, *river* B2
Araguaia, *river* C3
Aripuanã, *river* C2
Baleia, *point* E3
Bandeira, *mt.* D4
Billings, *reservoir* Inset II
Branco, *river* B1
Brazilian, *highlands* D3
Caviana, *island* D1
Chapada dos Parecis, *range* C3
Corcovado, *mt.* Inset I
Corumbau, *point* E3
Furnas, *reservoir* D4
Geral, *range* C4
Grande, *river* D3
Guandu, *river* Inset I
Guaporé, *river* B3
Guiana, *highlands* B1
Içá, *river* B2
Iguaçu, *falls* C4
Itaipu, *reservoir* C4
Japurá, *river* B2
Jari, *river* C1
Javari, *river* A2
Juruá, *river* B2
Juruena, *river* C3
Madeira, *river* B2
Mantiqueira, *range* D4
Mar, *range* D4
Marajó, *island* D2
Mato Grosso, *plateau* C3
Mexiana, *island* D1
Neblina, *mt.* B1
Negro, *river* B2
Órgãos, *range* Inset I
Pantanal, *lowland* C4
Pará, *river* C2
Paraguai, *river* C3
Paraná, *river* C4
Parima, *range* B1
Parnaíba, *river* D2
Patos, *lagoon* C5
Paulo Afonso, *falls* E2
Pedra Açú, *mt.* Inset I
Purus, *river* B2
Roncador, *range* C3
São Francisco, *river* D3
Selvas, *region* B2
Sobradinho, *reservoir* D3
Tapajós, *river* C2
Taquari, *river* C3
Teles Pires, *river* C2
Tietê, *river* Inset II
Tocantins, *river* D2
Tucuruí, *reservoir* D2
Tumucumaque, *range* C1
Uruguai, *river* C4
Xingu, *river* C3

Brazil

Capital: Brasília
Area: 3,286,470 sq. mi.
8,514,171 sq. km.
Population: 158,739,000
Largest City: São Paulo
Language: Portuguese
Monetary Unit: Cruzeiro real

MAJOR CITIES

Antigua & Barbuda	
St. Johns	27,000
Bahamas	
Nassau	172,000
Barbados	
Bridgetown	6,000
Belize	
Belize City	45,000
Belmopan	4,000
Canada	(metro)
Toronto	3,893,000
Montréal	3,127,000
Vancouver	1,603,000
Ottawa	921,000
Costa Rica	(metro)
San José	1,000,000
Cuba	
Havana	2,119,000
Dominica	
Roseau	16,000
Dominican Republic	
Santo Domingo	2,400,000
El Salvador	
San Salvador	423,000
Grenada	
St. George's	30,000
Guatemala	
Guatemala	1,676,000
Haiti	
Port-au-Prince	690,000
Honduras	
Tegucigalpa	608,000
Jamaica	(metro)
Kingston	587,000
Mexico	(metro)
Mexico City	20,000,000
Guadalajara	3,000,000
Monterrey	2,700,000
Nicaragua	
Managua	1,000,000
Panama	
Panamá	447,000
St. Kitts & Nevis	
Basseterre	15,000
St. Lucia	
Castries	45,000
St. Vincent & Grenadines	
Kingstown	15,000
Trinidad & Tobago	
Port of Spain	51,000
United States	
New York	7,323,000
Los Angeles	3,485,000
Chicago	2,784,000
Houston	1,631,000
Philadelphia	1,586,000
San Diego	1,111,000
Detroit	1,028,000
Washington, D.C.	607,000

International comparability of city population data is limited by various data inconsistencies.

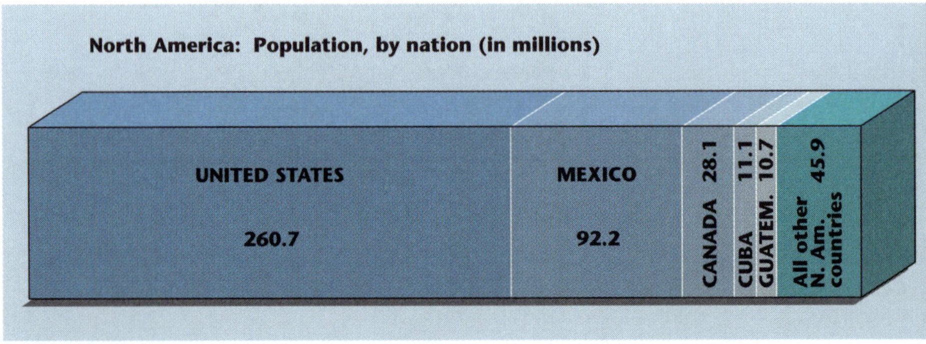

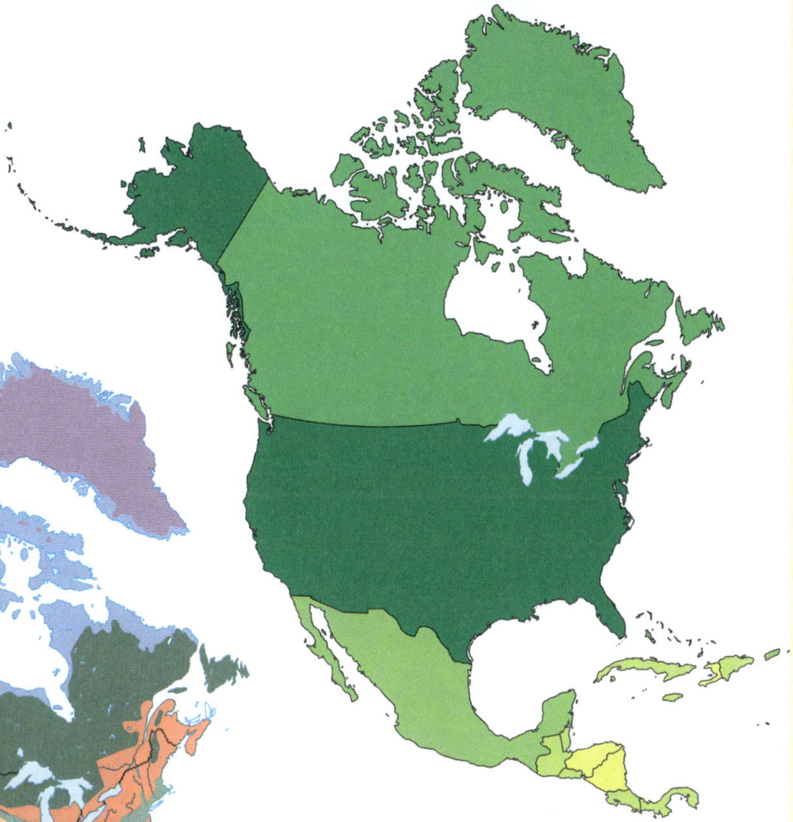
Gross National Product (GNP) per capita
$36,410
$21,500
$8625
$2785
$695
$0
No data

Vegetation
Ice Cap
Tundra
Coniferous Forest
Deciduous Forest
Broadleaf Evergreen Forest
Mixed Forest
Midlatitude Scrubland
Midlatitude Grassland
Desert
Tropical Seasonal and Scrub
Tropical Rain Forest

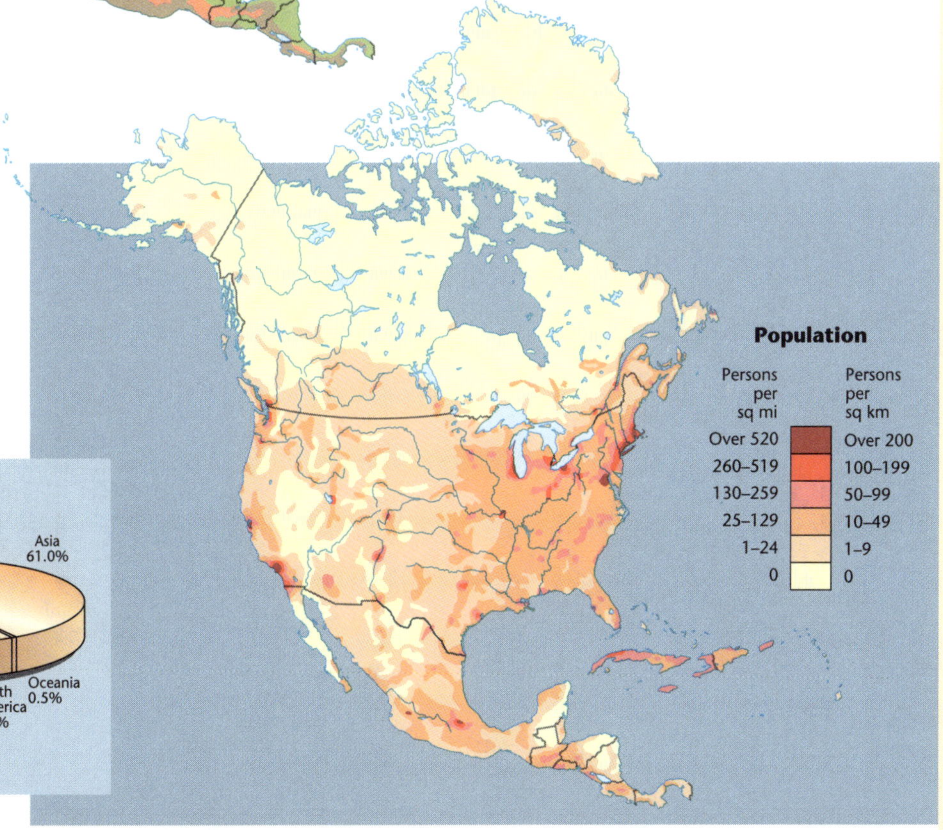
Population
Persons per sq mi
Persons per sq km
Over 520
Over 200
260–519
100–199
130–259
50–99
25–129
10–49
1–24
1–9
0
0

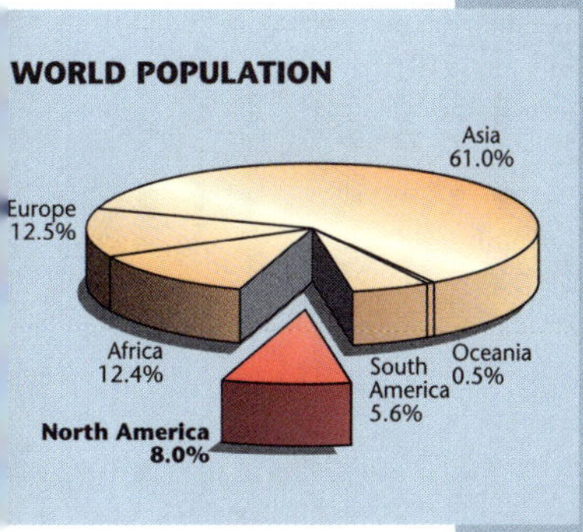
WORLD POPULATION
Asia 61.0%
Europe 12.5%
Africa 12.4%
South America 5.6%
Oceania 0.5%
North America 8.0%

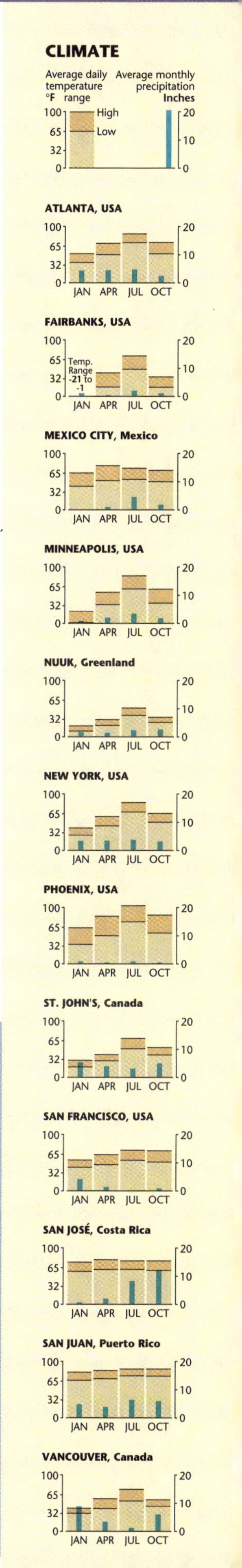
CLIMATE
Average daily temperature °F range
Average monthly precipitation Inches
High
Low
ATLANTA, USA
FAIRBANKS, USA
Temp. Range -21 to -1
MEXICO CITY, Mexico
MINNEAPOLIS, USA
NUUK, Greenland
NEW YORK, USA
PHOENIX, USA
ST. JOHN'S, Canada
SAN FRANCISCO, USA
SAN JOSÉ, Costa Rica
SAN JUAN, Puerto Rico
VANCOUVER, Canada
JAN APR JUL OCT

UNITED STATES
Gulf of Mexico
PACIFIC OCEAN
Gulf of California
Bay of Campeche
Gulf of Tehuantepec
Gulf of Honduras
Sierra Madre Occidental
Sierra Madre Oriental
Sierra Madre del Sur
Yucatán Peninsula
Isthmus of Tehuantepec
Bolsón de Mapimí
Desierto de Vizcaíno
Tropic of Cancer
BAJA CALIFORNIA
BAJA CALIFORNIA SUR
SONORA
CHIHUAHUA
COAHUILA
NUEVO LEÓN
TAMAULIPAS
DURANGO
SINALOA
ZACATECAS
SAN LUIS POTOSÍ
NAYARIT
AGUASCALIENTES
JALISCO
GUANAJUATO
QUERÉTARO
HIDALGO
MÉXICO
DISTRITO FEDERAL
TLAXCALA
PUEBLA
VERACRUZ
MICHOACÁN
COLIMA
MORELOS
GUERRERO
OAXACA
CHIAPAS
TABASCO
CAMPECHE
YUCATÁN
QUINTANA ROO
BELIZE
GUATEMALA
HONDURAS
EL SALVADOR
CALIFORNIA
ARIZONA
NEW MEXICO
TEXAS
OKLAHOMA
ARKANSAS
MISSISSIPPI
ALABAMA
GEORGIA
Mexico City
Tijuana
Mexicali
Ensenada
Hermosillo
Chihuahua
Ciudad Juárez
Monterrey
Saltillo
Torreón
Durango
Culiacán
Mazatlán
Zacatecas
Guadalajara
León
Aguascalientes
San Luis Potosí
Querétaro
Morelia
Toluca
Puebla
Veracruz
Oaxaca
Acapulco
Tampico
Matamoros
Mérida
Campeche
Chetumal
Cancún
Villahermosa
Tuxtla Gutiérrez
La Paz
Tepic
Colima
Pico de Orizaba / Citlaltépetl 5747 m (18,855 ft)
Mexico
National Capital
State Capital
Other City
Ruins
1:12,584,000
0 125 250 mi
0 125 250 km
Lambert Conformal Conic Projection
México
Distrito Federal
Netzahualcóyotl
Tlalnepantla
Naucalpan de Juárez
Ecatepec
Coyoacán
Xochimilco
Iztapalapa
Tlalpan
0 4 8 mi
0 4 8 km
© GeoSystems Global Corp.

Mexico

Capital: Mexico City
Area: 756,066 sq. mi.
1,958,720 sq. km.
Population: 92,202,000
Largest City: Mexico City
Language: Spanish
Monetary Unit: New peso

Guatemala

Capital: Guatemala City
Area: 42,042 sq. mi.
108,917 sq. km.
Population: 10,721,000
Largest City: Guatemala City
Language: Spanish
Monetary Unit: Quetzal

Belize

Capital: Belmopan
Area: 8,867 sq. mi.
22,972 sq. km.
Population: 209,000
Largest City: Belize City
Language: English
Monetary Unit: Belize dollar

Honduras

Capital: Tegucigalpa
Area: 43,277 sq. mi.
112,117 sq. km.
Population: 5,315,000
Largest City: Tegucigalpa
Language: Spanish
Monetary Unit: Lempira

Honduras: Map Index

El Salvador

Capital: San Salvador
Area: 8,124 sq. mi.
21,047 sq. km.
Population: 5,753,000
Largest City: San Salvador
Language: Spanish
Monetary Unit: Colón

El Salvador: Map Index

Costa Rica

Capital: San José
Area: 19,730 sq. mi.
51,114 sq. km.
Population: 3,342,000
Largest City: San José
Language: Spanish
Monetary Unit: Colón

Costa Rica: Map Index

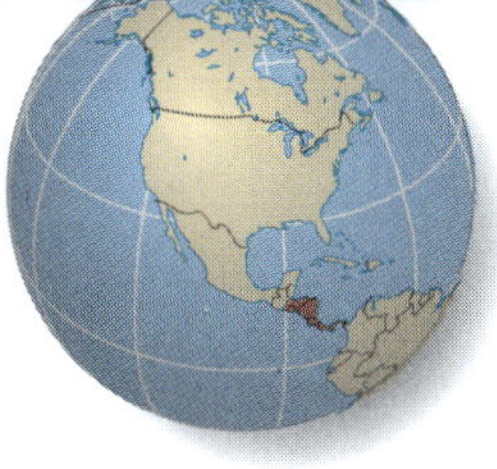

Nicaragua

Capital: Managua
Area: 50,880 sq. mi.
131,813 sq. km.
Population: 4,097,000
Largest City: Managua
Language: Spanish
Monetary Unit: Córdoba

Panama

Capital: Panamá
Area: 29,157 sq. mi.
75,536 sq. km.
Population: 2,630,000
Largest City: Panamá
Language: Spanish
Monetary Unit: Balboa

Cuba

Capital: Havana
Area: 42,804 sq. mi.
110,890 sq. km.
Population: 11,064,000
Largest City: Havana
Language: Spanish
Monetary Unit: Peso

Cuba:
Map Index

Jamaica

Capital: Kingston
Area: 4,244 sq. mi.
10,995 sq. km.
Population: 2,555,000
Largest City: Kingston
Language: English
Monetary Unit: Dollar

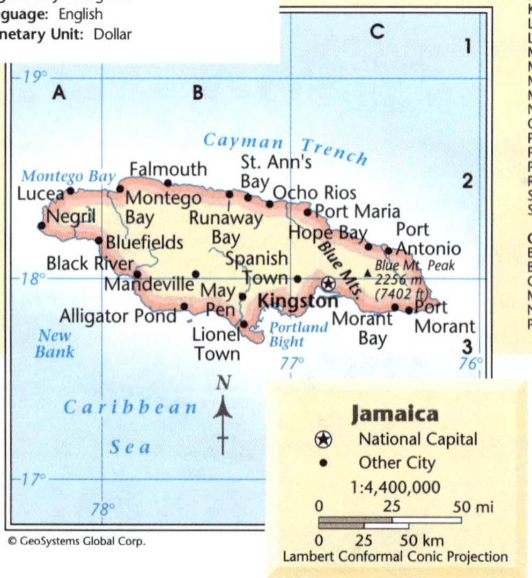

Jamaica:
Map Index

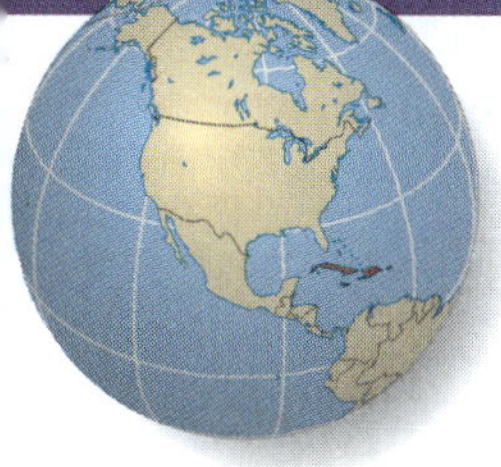

Dominican Republic: Map Index

Dominican Republic

Capital: Santo Domingo
Area: 18,704 sq. mi.
48,456 sq. km.
Population: 88,000
Largest City: Santo Domingo
Language: Spanish
Monetary Unit: Peso

Haiti: Map Index

Haiti

Capital: Port-au-Prince
Area: 10,695 sq. mi.
27,614 sq. km.
Population: 6,491,000
Largest City: Port-au-Prince
Language: French
Monetary Unit: Gourde

The Bahamas

Capital: Nassau
Area: 5,382 sq. mi.
13,943 sq. km.
Population: 273,000
Largest City: Nassau
Languages: English, Creole
Monetary Unit: Dollar

Turks and Caicos Is.

Capital: Grand Turk
Area: 193 sq. mi.
500 sq. km.
Population: 11,700
Largest City: Grand Turk
Language: English
Monetary Unit: U.S. Dollar

Bahamas and Turks & Caicos Islands: Map Index

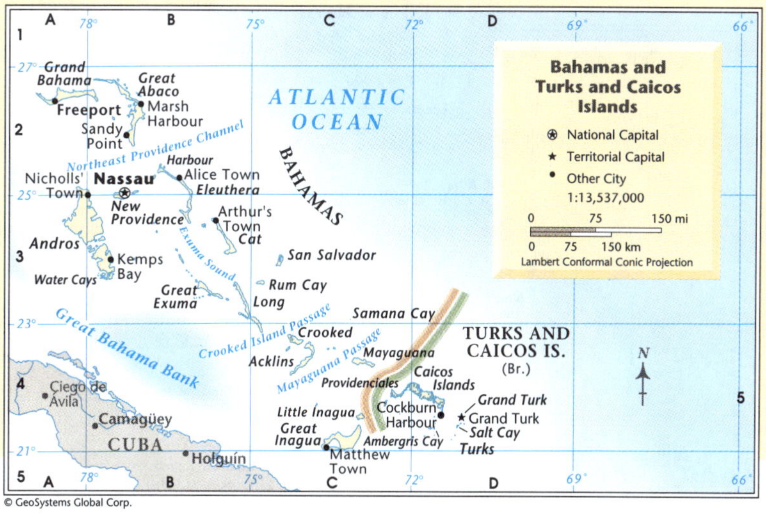

© GeoSystems Global Corp.

Puerto Rico

Capital: San Juan
Area: 3,492 sq. mi.
9,047 sq. km.
Population: 3,522,037
Largest City: San Juan
Languages: Spanish, English
Monetary Unit: U.S. dollar

© GeoSystems Global Corp.

Antigua and Barbuda

Capital: St. John's
Area: 171 sq. mi.
443 sq. km.
Population: 65,000
Largest City: St. John's
Language: English
Monetary Unit: East Caribbean dollar

Dominica

Capital: Roseau
Area: 290 sq. mi.
751 sq. km.
Population: 88,000
Largest City: Roseau
Language: English
Monetary Unit: East Caribbean dollar

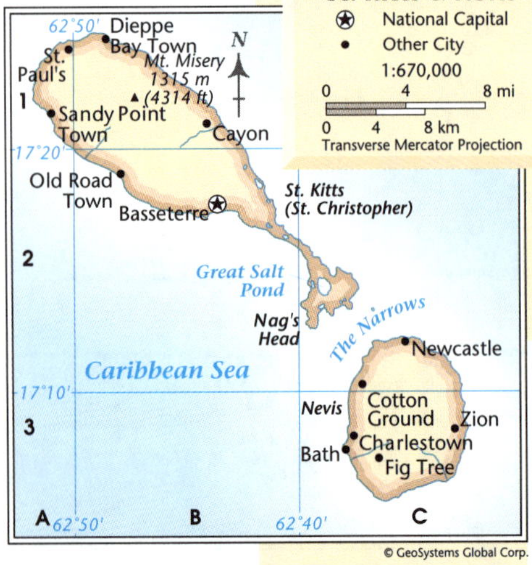

© GeoSystems Global Corp.

St. Kitts & Nevis

Capital: Basseterre
Area: 104 sq. mi.
269 sq. km.
Population: 41,000
Largest City: Basseterre
Language: English
Monetary Unit: East Caribbean dollar

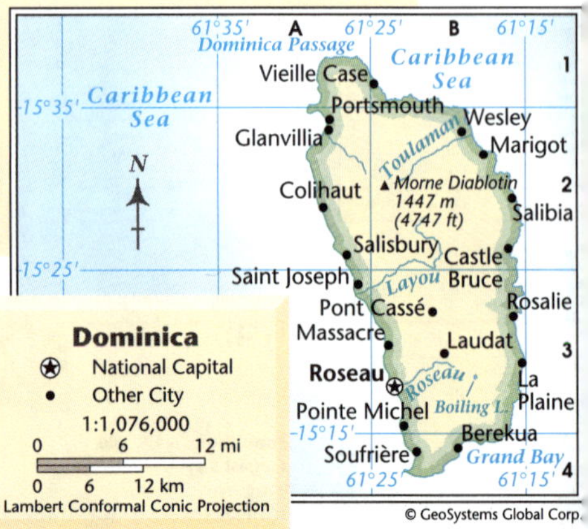

© GeoSystems Global Corp.

St. Lucia

Capital: Castries
Area: 238 sq. mi.
617 sq. km.
Population: 145,000
Largest City: Castries
Language: English
Monetary Unit: East Caribbean dollar

St. Lucia
National Capital
Other City
1:1,000,000
0 5 10 mi
0 5 10 km
Miller Cylindrical Projection

St. Lucia: Map Index

Barbados
National Capital
Other City
1:809,000
0 5 10 mi
0 5 10 km
Azimuthal Equal Area Projection

Barbados

Capital: Bridgetown
Area: 166 sq. mi.
430 sq. km.
Population: 256,000
Largest City: Bridgetown
Language: English
Monetary Unit: Dollar

Barbados: Map Index

St. Vincent and the Grenadines: Map Index

St. Vincent and the Grenadines
National Capital
Other City
1:1,900,000
0 10 20 mi
0 10 20 km
Miller Cylindrical Projection

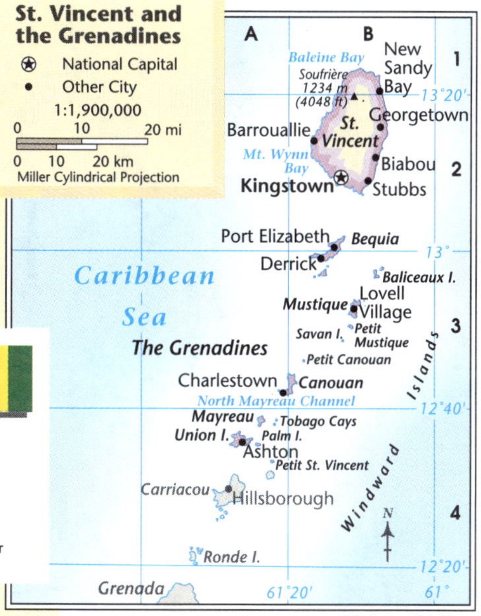

St. Vincent and The Grenadines

Capital: Kingstown
Area: 150 sq. mi.
389 sq. km.
Population: 115,000
Largest City: Kingstown
Language: French patois
Monetary Unit: East Caribbean dollar

Trinidad & Tobago

Capital: Port of Spain
Area: 1,980 sq. mi.
5,130 sq. km.
Population: 1,328,000
Largest City: Port of Spain
Language: English
Monetary Unit: Dollar

Trinidad & Tobago: Map Index

Trinidad & Tobago
National Capital
Other City
1:2,700,000
0 15 30 mi
0 15 30 km
Azimuthal Equal Area Projection

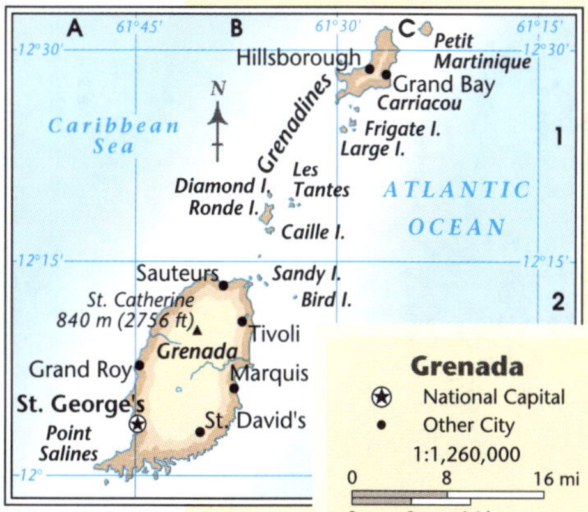

Grenada
National Capital
Other City
1:1,260,000
0 8 16 mi
0 8 16 km
Transverse Mercator Projection

Grenada: Map Index

Grenada

Capital: St. George's
Area: 133 sq. mi.
345 sq. km.
Population: 94,000
Largest City: St. George's
Language: English
Monetary Unit: East Caribbean dollar

Canada
National Capital
Provincial/Territorial Capital
Other City
1:30,244,000
0 250 500 750 mi
0 250 500 750 km
Azimuthal Equal Area Projection
ARCTIC OCEAN
ATLANTIC OCEAN
PACIFIC OCEAN
Hudson Bay
Baffin Bay
Labrador Sea
Beaufort Sea
Chukchi Sea
Davis Strait
Denmark Strait
Hudson Strait
Foxe Basin
James Bay
Gulf of St. Lawrence
Bay of Fundy
Cabot Strait
GREENLAND (KALAALLIT NUNAAT) (Denmark)
ICELAND
Reykjavík
Alaska (United States)
UNITED STATES
YUKON TERRITORY
NORTHWEST TERRITORIES
BRITISH COLUMBIA
ALBERTA
SASKATCHEWAN
MANITOBA
ONTARIO
QUÉBEC
NEWFOUNDLAND
LABRADOR
NEW BRUNSWICK
NOVA SCOTIA
PRINCE EDWARD ISLAND
ST. PIERRE AND MIQUELON (France)
INUVIK REGION
FORT SMITH REGION
KITIKMEOT REGION
KEEWATIN REGION
BAFFIN REGION
QUEEN ELIZABETH ISLANDS
ELLESMERE ISLAND
BAFFIN ISLAND
Victoria Island
Banks Island
Devon Island
Southampton Island
ROCKY MOUNTAINS
COAST MOUNTAINS
MACKENZIE MTS.
GREAT PLAINS
BROOKS RANGE
APPALACHIAN MTS.
CASCADE RANGE
Ottawa
Whitehorse
Yellowknife
Victoria
Edmonton
Regina
Winnipeg
Toronto
Québec
Fredericton
Halifax
Charlottetown
St. John's
Iqaluit
Vancouver
Calgary
Montréal
Mt. Logan 5951 m (19,524 ft)
Mt. St. Elias 5489 m (18,008 ft)
Mt. McKinley 6194 m (20,320 ft)
Mt. Robson 3954 m (12,972 ft)
Mt. Waddington 3994 m (13,104 ft)
Arctic Circle
© GeoSystems Global Corp.

Canada

Capital: Ottawa
Area: 3,849,674 sq. mi.
9,973,249 sq. km.
Population: 28,114,000
Largest City: Toronto
Languages: English, French
Monetary Unit: Canadian dollar

Alberta

Capital: Edmonton
Area: 255,287 sq. mi.
661,265 sq. km.
Population: 2,545,553
Largest City: Edmonton

British Columbia

Capital: Victoria
Area: 365,947 sq. mi.
948,049 sq. km.
Population: 3,282,061
Largest City: Vancouver

Manitoba

Capital: Winnipeg
Area: 250,947 sq. mi.
650,122 sq. km.
Population: 1,091,942
Largest City: Winnipeg

New Brunswick

Capital: Fredericton
Area: 28,355 sq. mi.
73,459 sq. km.
Population: 723,900
Largest City: Saint John

Newfoundland

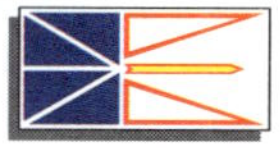

Capital: St. John's
Area: 156,949 sq. mi.
406,604 sq. km.
Population: 568,474
Largest City: St. John's

Northwest Territories

Capital: Yellowknife
Area: 1,322,909 sq. mi.
3,427,225 sq. km.
Population: 57,649
Largest City: Yellowknife

Nova Scotia

Capital: Halifax
Area: 21,425 sq. mi.
55,505 sq. km.
Population: 899,942
Largest City: Halifax

Ontario

Capital: Toronto
Area: 412,581 sq. mi.
1,068,863 sq. km.
Population: 10,084,885
Largest City: Toronto

Prince Edward Island

Capital: Charlottetown
Area: 2,185 sq. mi.
5,661 sq. km.
Population: 10,084,885
Largest City: Charlottetown

Québec

Capital: Québec
Area: 594,860 sq. mi.
1,541,088 sq. km.
Population: 6,895,963
Largest City: Montréal

Saskatchewan

Capital: Regina
Area: 251,866 sq. mi.
652,503 sq. km.
Population: 988,928
Largest City: Saskatoon

Yukon Territory

Capital: Whitehorse
Area: 186,661 sq. mi.
483,578 sq. km.
Population: 27,797
Largest City: Whitehorse

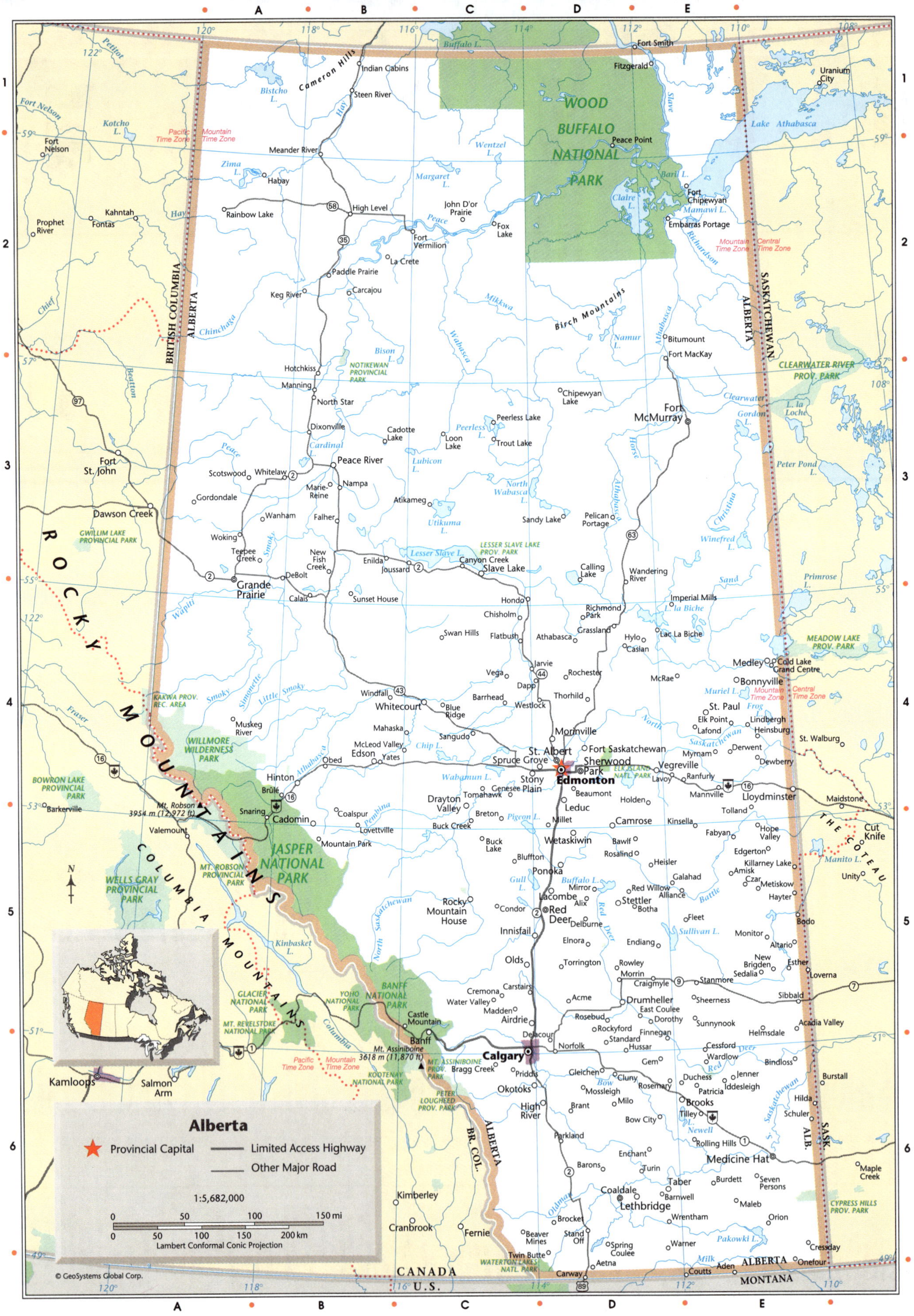
A
B
C
D
E
1
2
3
4
5
6
120°
118°
116°
114°
112°
110°
108°
122°
59°
57°
55°
53°
51°
49°
Fort Smith
Fitzgerald
Uranium City
Indian Cabins
Cameron Hills
Steen River
Bistcho L.
Buffalo L.
WOOD BUFFALO NATIONAL PARK
Lake Athabasca
Slave
Fort Nelson
Kotcho L.
Pacific Time Zone
Mountain Time Zone
Meander River
Peace Point
Zima L.
Habay
Wentzel L.
Margaret L.
Barr L.
Fort Chipewyan
Claire L.
Mamawi L.
Embarras Portage
Rainbow Lake
High Level
John D'or Prairie
Peace
Fox Lake
Hay
Kahntah
Fontas
Prophet River
Fort Vermilion
La Crete
Mountain Time Zone
Central Time Zone
Richardson
Paddle Prairie
Keg River
Carcajou
Mikkwa
Birch Mountains
Chief
Chinchaga
BRITISH COLUMBIA
ALBERTA
SASKATCHEWAN
Wabasca
Namur L.
Athabasca
Bitumount
Fort MacKay
Bison L.
NOTIKEWAN PROVINCIAL PARK
Hotchkiss
Manning
North Star
CLEARWATER RIVER PROV. PARK
Beatton
Chipewyan Lake
Clearwater
L. la Loche
Gordon L.
Fort McMurray
Dixonville
Cadotte Lake
Peerless Lake
Peerless L.
Loon Lake
Trout Lake
Cardinal L.
Peace
Peace River
Lubicon L.
Horse
Peter Pond L.
Fort St. John
Scotswood
Whitelaw
Nampa
Marie-Reine
Gordondale
North Wabasca L.
Atikameg
Wanham
Dawson Creek
Falher
Utikuma L.
Sandy Lake
Pelican Portage
Christina
GWILLIM LAKE PROVINCIAL PARK
Woking
Winefred L.
ROCKY MOUNTAINS
Teepee Creek
Smoky
New Fish Creek
Lesser Slave L.
LESSER SLAVE LAKE PROV. PARK
Canyon Creek
Enilda
Joussard
Slave Lake
Calling Lake
Wandering River
Primrose L.
Grande Prairie
DeBolt
Calais
Sunset House
Hondo
Sand
Wapiti
Imperial Mills
Richmond Park
la Biche
Chisholm
Swan Hills
Flatbush
Athabasca
Grassland
Hylo
Caslan
Lac La Biche
MEADOW LAKE PROV. PARK
Jarvie
Rochester
Vega
Medley
Cold Lake
Grand Centre
McRae
Windfall
Dapp
Thorhild
Bonnyville
KAKWA PROV. REC. AREA
Smoky
Simonette
Little Smoky
Whitecourt
Blue Ridge
Barrhead
Westlock
Muriel L.
Mountain Time Zone
Central Time Zone
St. Paul
Frog
Fraser
Muskeg River
Mahaska
Sangudo
Morinville
Elk Point
Lafond
Lindbergh
Heinsburg
North
WILLMORE WILDERNESS PARK
McLeod Valley
Edson
Yates
Chip L.
St. Albert
Fort Saskatchewan
Saskatchewan
Myrnam
Derwent
St. Walburg
Obed
Spruce Grove
Sherwood Park
Vegreville
Dewberry
Hinton
Athabasca
Wabamun L.
Stony Plain
Edmonton
ELK ISLAND NATL. PARK
Lavoy
Ranfurly
BOWRON LAKE PROVINCIAL PARK
Brulé
Genesee
Tomahawk
Beaumont
Mannville
Lloydminster
Maidstone
Barkerville
Mt. Robson 3954 m (12,972 ft)
Snaring
Drayton Valley
Holden
Cadomin
Coalspur
Pembina
Breton
Pigeon L.
Leduc
Tolland
Valemount
Millet
Camrose
Kinsella
Lovettville
Buck Creek
Hope Valley
Fabyan
Cut Knife
JASPER NATIONAL PARK
Mountain Park
Buck Lake
Wetaskiwin
Bawlf
THE COTEAU
COLUMBIA
Edgerton
Rosalind
Blufton
Heisler
Killarney Lake
Manito L.
MT. ROBSON PROVINCIAL PARK
Ponoka
Amisk
Unity
Galahad
Czar
N
WELLS GRAY PROVINCIAL PARK
Gull L.
Buffalo L.
Mirror
Red Willow
Metiskow
Alliance
Battle
Hayter
Rocky Mountain House
Lacombe
Alix
Stettler
Botha
Condor
Red Deer
Delburne
Fleet
Bodo
Sullivan L.
Innisfail
Monitor
Kinbasket L.
North Saskatchewan
Red Deer
Elnora
Endiang
Altario
Olds
Torrington
Rowley
New Brigden
Esther
Morrin
Sedalia
Loverna
Craigmyle
Stanmore
BANFF NATIONAL PARK
Carstairs
Cremona
Sibbald
GLACIER NATIONAL PARK
YOHO NATIONAL PARK
Water Valley
Acme
Drumheller
Sheerness
East Coulee
Madden
Dorothy
Rosebud
Airdrie
Sunnynook
Acadia Valley
MT. REVELSTOKE NATIONAL PARK
Castle Mountain
Rockyford
Finnegan
Helmsdale
Standard
Banff
Delacour
Norfolk
Hussar
Cessford
Mt. Assiniboine 3618 m (11,870 ft)
Calgary
Wardlow
Deer
Bindloss
Columbia
MT. ASSINIBOINE PROV. PARK
Bragg Creek
Priddis
Gem
Gleichen
Cluny
Duchess
Jenner
Burstall
Pacific Time Zone
Mountain Time Zone
Bow
Red
Patricia
Iddesleigh
Kamloops
Salmon Arm
KOOTENAY NATIONAL PARK
Okotoks
Mossleigh
Rosemary
Hilda
PETER LOUGHEED PROV. PARK
High River
Milo
Brooks
Brant
Tilley
Schuler
Bow City
Newell L.
BR. COL.
ALBERTA
Parkland
Rolling Hills
South Saskatchewan
ALB.
SASK.
Enchant
Medicine Hat
Barons
Turin
Maple Creek
Taber
Burdett
Seven Persons
Coaldale
Barnwell
Kimberley
Lethbridge
Oldman
Maleb
CYPRESS HILLS PROV. PARK
Wrentham
Orion
Cranbrook
Brocket
Fernie
Beaver Mines
Stand Off
Pakowki L.
Spring Coulee
Warner
Cressday
Twin Butte
WATERTON LAKES NATL. PARK
Aetna
Milk
Aden
ALBERTA
Onefour
CANADA
U.S.
Carway
Coutts
MONTANA
Alberta
Provincial Capital
Limited Access Highway
Other Major Road
1:5,682,000
0
50
100
150 mi
0
50
100
150
200 km
Lambert Conformal Conic Projection
© GeoSystems Global Corp.

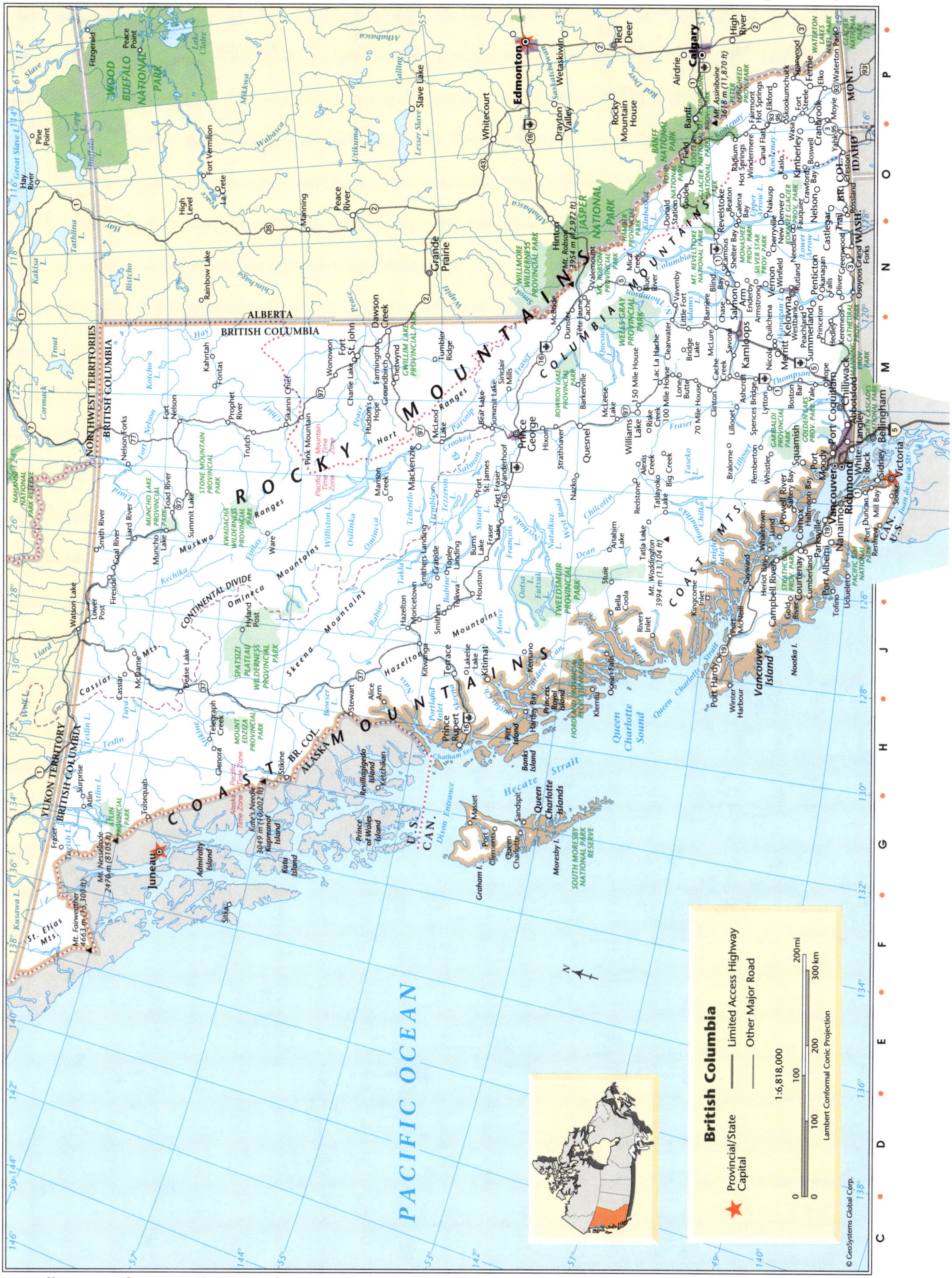
British Columbia
Provincial/State Capital
Limited Access Highway
Other Major Road
1:6,818,000
Lambert Conformal Conic Projection
© GeoSystems Global Corp.
PACIFIC OCEAN
ROCKY MOUNTAINS
COAST MOUNTAINS
COLUMBIA MOUNTAINS
ALASKA
ALBERTA
BRITISH COLUMBIA
NORTHWEST TERRITORIES
YUKON TERRITORY
Edmonton
Calgary
Victoria
Vancouver
Juneau
Prince George
Prince Rupert
Kamloops
Kelowna
Queen Charlotte Islands
Vancouver Island
Queen Charlotte Sound
Hecate Strait
WOOD BUFFALO NATIONAL PARK
JASPER NATIONAL PARK
BANFF NATIONAL PARK
Mt. Robson 3954 m (12,972 ft)
Mt. Waddington 3994 m (13,104 ft)
Mt. Fairweather 4663 m (15,300 ft)
Mt. Assiniboine 3618 m (11,870 ft)

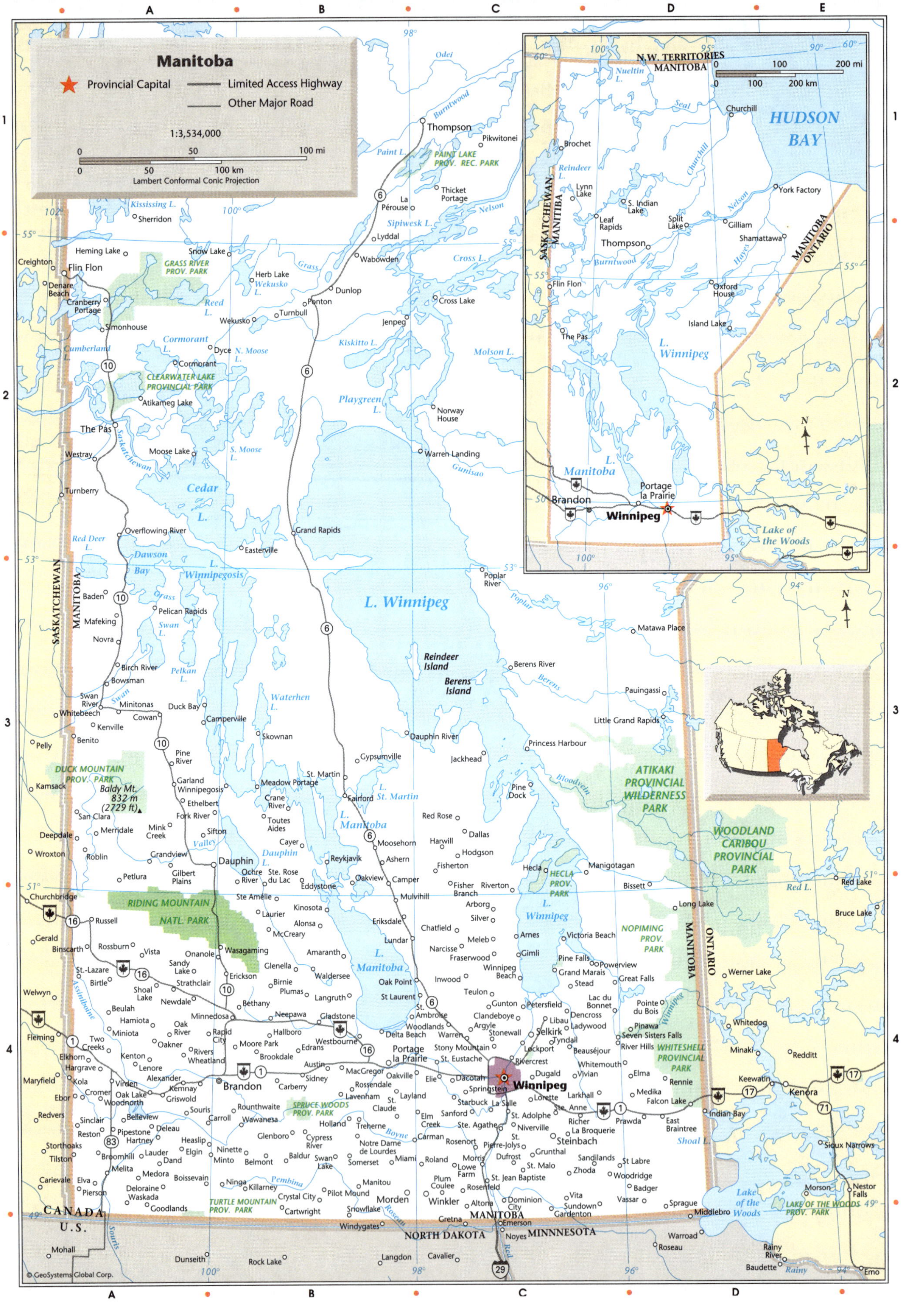
Manitoba
Provincial Capital
Limited Access Highway
Other Major Road
1:3,534,000
0 50 100 mi
0 50 100 km
Lambert Conformal Conic Projection
A
B
C
D
E
1
2
3
4
Thompson
Pikwitonei
Paint L.
PAINT LAKE PROV. REC. PARK
Burntwood
Odei
Thicket Portage
La Pérouse
Nelson
Sipiwesk L.
Lyddal
Wabowden
Kississing L.
Sherridon
Heming Lake
Snow Lake
Creighton
Flin Flon
Denare Beach
Cranberry Portage
GRASS RIVER PROV. PARK
Herb Lake
Wekusko L.
Grass
Dunlop
Ponton
Reed L.
Wekusko
Turnbull
Cross L.
Cross Lake
Jenpeg
Simonhouse
Cormorant L.
Dyce
N. Moose L.
Cormorant
Cumberland L.
CLEARWATER LAKE PROVINCIAL PARK
Atikameg Lake
Kiskitto L.
Molson L.
Playgreen L.
Norway House
The Pas
Westray
Moose Lake
S. Moose L.
Saskatchewan
Warren Landing
Gunisao
Cedar L.
Turnberry
Overflowing River
Red Deer L.
Grand Rapids
Easterville
Dawson Bay
L. Winnipegosis
Poplar River
Poplar
L. Winnipeg
Baden
Grass
Pelican Rapids
Mafeking
Swan L.
Novra
Matawa Place
SASKATCHEWAN
MANITOBA
Birch River
Pelkan L.
Reindeer Island
Berens Island
Berens River
Berens
Bowsman
Swan River
Swan
Minitonas
Whitebeech
Duck Bay
Waterhen L.
Pauingassi
Cowan
Camperville
Little Grand Rapids
Kenville
Benito
Skownan
Dauphin River
Pelly
Pine River
Princess Harbour
Gypsumville
Jackhead
DUCK MOUNTAIN PROV. PARK
Baldy Mt. 832 m (2729 ft)
Kamsack
Garland
Winnipegosis
Meadow Portage
St. Martin
Fairford
L. St. Martin
Bloodvein
Pine Dock
ATIKAKI PROVINCIAL WILDERNESS PARK
Ethelbert
Crane River
San Clara
Fork River
Toutes Aides
L. Manitoba
Red Rose
WOODLAND CARIBOU PROVINCIAL PARK
Deepdale
Merridale
Mink Creek
Sifton
Valley
Cayer
Moosehorn
Harwill
Dallas
Wroxton
Roblin
Grandview
Dauphin
Dauphin L.
Reykjavik
Ashern
Hodgson
Fisherton
Hecla
Manigotagan
Petlura
Gilbert Plains
Ochre River
Ste. Rose du Lac
Eddystone
Oakview
Camper
Fisher Branch
Riverton
HECLA PROV. PARK
Bissett
Red L.
Red Lake
Churchbridge
Ste Amélie
Mulvihill
Arborg
L. Winnipeg
Long Lake
Kinosota
RIDING MOUNTAIN NATL. PARK
Laurier
Silver
Bruce Lake
Russell
Alonsa
Eriksdale
Chatfield
Gerald
Binscarth
Rossburn
Vista
McCreary
Lundar
Meleb
Arnes
Victoria Beach
NOPIMING PROV. PARK
Onanole
Wasagaming
Amaranth
Narcisse
Gimli
Sandy Lake
Fraserwood
Pine Falls
Powerview
St.-Lazare
Glenella
L. Manitoba
Winnipeg Beach
Grand Marais
Werner Lake
Birtle
Strathclair
Erickson
Waldersee
Inwood
Great Falls
Welwyn
Shoal Lake
Birnie
Plumas
Oak Point
Stead
Assiniboine
Newdale
Langruth
St Laurent
Teulon
Lac du Bonnet
Beulah
Bethany
Gunton
Petersfield
Pointe du Bois
Hamiota
Minnedosa
Neepawa
Gladstone
St. Ambroise
Clandeboye
Libau
Dencross
Winnipeg
Whitedog
Fleming
Miniota
Oak River
Rapid City
Hallboro
Woodlands
Argyle
Selkirk
Ladywood
Pinawa
Seven Sisters Falls
Two Creeks
Oakner
Westbourne
Delta Beach
Warren
Stonewall
Tyndall
River Hills
WHITESHELL PROVINCIAL PARK
Minaki
Reddit
Elkhorn
Kenton
Rivers
Moore Park
Edrans
Portage la Prairie
Stony Mountain
Lockport
Beauséjour
Hargrave
Lenore
Wheatland
Brookdale
Austin
St. Eustache
Rivercrest
Whitemouth
Maryfield
Kola
Virden
Alexander
Kemnay
Brandon
Carberry
Sidney
MacGregor
Oakville
Elie
Dacotah
Dugald
Vivian
Elma
Keewatin
Kenora
Rennie
Ebor
Cromer
Oak Lake
Woodnorth
Griswold
Rossendale
Lavenham
Layland
Springstein
Winnipeg
Lorette
Larkhall
Medika
Falcon Lake
Redvers
Bellevue
Souris
Rounthwaite
SPRUCE WOODS PROV. PARK
St. Claude
Starbuck
La Salle
Ste. Anne
Indian Bay
Sinclair
Carroll
Wawanesa
Holland
Treherne
Elm Creek
Sanford
St. Adolphe
Richer
Prawda
East Braintree
Reston
Pipestone
Deleau
Boyne
Carman
Ste. Agathe
Niverville
La Broquerie
Storthoaks
Hartney
Heaslip
Glenboro
Cypress River
Rosenort
St. Pierre-Jolys
Steinbach
Shoal L.
Sioux Narrows
Tilston
Broomhill
Lauder
Elgin
Ninette
Baldur
Swan Lake
Notre Dame de Lourdes
Miami
Roland
Morris
Dufrost
Grunthal
Sandilands
St Labre
Melita
Dand
Minto
Belmont
Somerset
Lowe Farm
St. Malo
Zhoda
Woodridge
Carievale
Elva
Medora
Boissevain
Ninga
Pembina
Manitou
Plum Coulee
Rosenfeld
St. Jean Baptiste
Badger
Morson
Nestor Falls
Pierson
Deloraine
Waskada
Killarney
Crystal City
Pilot Mound
Morden
Winkler
Altona
Dominion City
Vita
Sundown
Vassar
Sprague
Lake of the Woods
LAKE OF THE WOODS PROV. PARK
CANADA
U.S.
Goodlands
TURTLE MOUNTAIN PROV. PARK
Cartwright
Snowflake
Rosea
Gretna
MANITOBA
Emerson
Gardenton
Middlebro
Windygates
NORTH DAKOTA
Noyes
MINNESOTA
Warroad
Roseau
Mohall
Souris
Dunseith
Rock Lake
Langdon
Cavalier
Red
Rainy River
Baudette
Rainy
Emo
102°
100°
98°
96°
94°
55°
53°
51°
49°
© GeoSystems Global Corp.
N.W. TERRITORIES
MANITOBA
0 100 200 mi
0 100 200 km
Nueltin L.
Seal
Churchill
HUDSON BAY
Brochet
Reindeer L.
Lynn Lake
S. Indian Lake
Churchill
Nelson
York Factory
Leaf Rapids
Split Lake
Gilliam
Shamattawa
MANITOBA ONTARIO
Thompson
Burntwood
Hayes
Flin Flon
Oxford House
Island Lake
The Pas
L. Winnipeg
L. Manitoba
Portage la Prairie
Brandon
Winnipeg
Lake of the Woods
ONTARIO

QUÉBEC
RIMOUSKI PROVINCIAL RESERVE
PORT-DANIEL PROVINCIAL RESERVE
Lac-des-Aigles
Cabano
Notre-Dame-du-Lac
Rivière-Bleue
Nouvelle
New Richmond
Bonaventure
Campbellton
Matapédia
Tide Head
Dalhousie
Balmoral
Charlo
Robinsonville
Jacquet River
Chaleur Bay
New Carlisle
Miscou I.
Miscou Centre
Belledune
Pointe-Verte
Grande-Anse
Bas-Caraquet
Lamèque
Ile Lamèque
Caraquet
Shippagan
RESTIGOUCHE
Kedgwick
St.-Quentin
Restigouche R.
Petit-Rocher
Nigadoo
Beresford
Bathurst
Janeville
Paquetville
Pokemouche
GLOUCESTER
St.-Isidore
Tracadie-Sheila
Val Comeau
Rivière-du-Portage
Tabusintac
MADAWASKA
St.-Jacques
St.-Basile
Edmundston
Baker Brook
Rivière-Verte
Clair
St.-Milaire
Fort Kent
Ste.-Anne-de-Madawaska
Nictau
Nepisiguit R.
MT. CARLETON PROVINCIAL PARK
Heath Steele
Allardville
Neguac
Miramichi Bay
Van Buren
St.-Léonard
St.-André
VICTORIA
Eagle Lake
Grand Falls
Drummond
Lake Edward
Plaster Rock
Four Falls
Aroostook
Perth-Andover
NORTHUMBERLAND
Miramichi
NEW BRUNSWICK
Baie-Ste.-Anne
Pointe Sapin
St. Margarets
KOUCHIBOUGUAC N. P.
Caribou
Fort Fairfield
Presque Isle
Ashland
MAINE
Mars Hill
Renous
Blackville
Rogersville
Kouchibouguac
St.-Louis-de-Kent
P.E.I.
O'Leary
Richibucto
Bath
Bristol
SW Miramichi R.
Juniper
Florenceville
Napadogan
Doaktown
Boiestown
KENT
Rexton
Harcourt
Bouctouche
Northumberland Str.
CARLETON
Hartland
U.S.
CAN.
Stanley
Nashwaak Bridge
Smyrna Mills
Houlton
Patten
Woodstock
YORK
Millville
Nackawic
Taymouth
Gaspereau Forks
Chipman
Minto
QUEENS
Grand L.
Notre-Dame
Cocagne
Summerside
Shediac
Cap-Pelé
Borden
WESTMORLAND
Moncton
Dieppe
Riverview
St. Joseph
Cape Tormentine
Port Elgin
Meductic
St. John R.
Fredericton
Canterbury
Youngs Cove
Coles Island
Petitcodiac
Hillsborough
Sackville
Aulac
Amherst
Millinocket
Fosterville
King's Landing
Oromocto
Harvey
Jemseg
Gagetown
Waterborough
Cambridge-Narrows
Elgin
ALBERT
Hopewell Cape
Riverside-Albert
Thomaston Corner
Tracy
Fredericton Jct.
Sussex
Vanceboro
McAdam
St. Croix
SUNBURY
Evandale
Norton
KINGS
FUNDY N.P.
Alma
Joggins
Lincoln
Topsfield
Lawrence Station
Oak Point
Hampton
Hammondvale
Quispamsis
Welsford
Rothesay
Chignecto Bay
CHARLOTTE
Westfield
Grand Bay
ST. JOHN
St. Martins
Parrsboro
St. Stephen
Calais
St. George
Saint John
St. Andrews
Lepreau
Minas Channel
BAY OF FUNDY
Blacks Harbour
Kentville
Wolfville
Berwick
Campobello Island
Lubec
Greenwood
North Head
Grand Harbour
Grand Manan Island
Seal Cove
Bridgetown
Windsor
PORT ROYAL N.H.P.
Victoria Beach
Annapolis Royal
New Ross
Digby
NOVA SCOTIA
Sandy Cove
Chester
Mahone Bay
Weymouth
KEJIMKUJIK NATIONAL PARK
South Brookfield
Bridgewater
Lunenburg
L. Rossignol
Liverpool
Port Mouton
Shelburne
Sable River
Lockeport
Clyde River
ATLANTIC OCEAN
New Brunswick
Provincial Capital
Limited Access Highway
Other Major Road
1:2,398,000
0 25 50 75 100 mi
0 25 50 75 100 km
Lambert Conformal Conic Projection
© GeoSystems Global Corp.

Newfoundland
Provincial Capital
Major Road
1:3,984,000
0 50 100 mi
0 50 100 150 km
Lambert Conformal Conic Projection
A B C D E
1 2 3 4 5
Hopedale
Deep Inlet
Aillik
Makkovik
Kikkertavak I.
Postville
Big R.
Holton
Rigolet
Inlet
Hamilton
North West River
Lake Melville
North R.
Cartwright
Sandwich Bay
MEALY MOUNTAINS
Happy Valley-Goose Bay
Eagle R.
Paradise River
Black Tickle
Batteau
Hawke Harbour
Snug Harbour
Square Islands
Charlottetown
LABRADOR
Paradise R.
Alexis R.
Williams Harbour
Port Hope Simpson
St. Lewis
Mary's Harbour
St. Lewis R.
Cape Charles
St. Paul R.
NEWFOUNDLAND
QUÉBEC
Belle Isle
Henley Harbour
Red Bay
West St. Modeste
Cook's Harbour
Ship Cove
L'Anse-au-Loup
Forteau
L'ANSE AUX MEADOWS N.H.S.
Strait of Belle Isle
Eddies Cove
St. Anthony
Main Brook
Pond Cove
St. Barbe
New Ferolle
Conche
Roddickton
Port au Choix
Port Saunders
Englee
Hawke's Bay
430
Williamsport
Bellburns
Harbour Deep
White Bay
Fleur de Lys
Daniel's Harbour
Portland Creek
Baie Verte
La Scie
Parson's Pond
LONG RANGE MTS.
Seal Cove
Notre Dame Bay
Cow Head
Jackson's Arm
Middle Arm
Twillingate
Fogo
Joe Batt's Arm
Little Seldom
Purbeck's Cove
Beachside
Sally's Cove
GROS MORNE N.P.
King's Point
Leading Tickles
Summerford
Musgrave Harbour
Rocky Harbour
Springdale
Triton
Boyd's Cove
Carmanville
Lumsden
Woody Point
Norris Point
Hampden
South Brook
Point Leamington
Birchy Bay
Lewisporte
Gander Bay
Wesleyville
Trout River
Wiltondale
Cormack
Botwood
Notre Dame Junction
Gulf of St. Lawrence
Deer Lake
Sandy L.
Bishop's Falls
Norris Arm
Glenwood
Centreville
Cox's Cove
Deer L.
Howley
Grand L.
Badger
Hare Bay
Bonavista Bay
St. Brendan's
Lark Harbour
Pasadena
Grand Falls-Windsor
Gander
Gambo
Salvage
Bonavista
Benoit's Cove
Buchans
Glovertown
King's Cove
Atlantic Time Zone
Newfoundland Time Zone
Corner Brook
Red Indian L.
NEWFOUNDLAND
Gander R.
TERRA NOVA NATIONAL PARK
Eastport
Catalina
Summerville
Musgravetown
Trinity East
Port au Port
Stephenville
Port Blandford
Lethbridge
Old Perlican
Meelpaeg L.
Lloyds R.
Northwest
Britannia
Trinity Bay
Bay de Verde
Cape St. George
St. George's
360
Jeddore L.
Jubilee L.
Clarenville
Heart's Content
Goobies
Pouch Cove
St. George's Bay
Round Pond
Swift Current
Carbonear
Torbay
1
Millertown
Wabana
Bay Roberts
St. John's
South Branch
LONG RANGE
Grey R.
St. Alban's
Rencontre East
210
Arnold's Cove
Holyrood
Bay Bulls
Little Bay
Grand Bruit
McCallum
Gaultois
Terrenceville
Whitbourne
Avalon Pen.
Witless Bay
Cape Ray
Francois
Hermitage-Sandyville
St. Bernard's
Argentia
Channel-Port aux Basques
Isle aux Morts
Rose Blanche
Burgeo
Ramea
Grey River
Harbour Breton
Wreck Cove
Placentia Bay
Placentia
St. Catherine's
Garnish
Marystown
Ferryland
Cabot Strait
Miquelon
Grand Bank
Fortune Bay
Burin Pen.
Burin
St. Mary's
Great Miquelon
Fortune
Lawn
St. Bride's
Branch
Trepassey
Cape Breton Island
St. Pierre and Miquelon (Fr.)
220
Lamaline
St. Lawrence
St. Shotts
Cape Race
Little Miquelon
© GeoSystems Global Corp.
60° 58° 56° 54° 52° 55° 53° 51° 49° 47°
Port Burwell
Ungava Bay
TORNGAT MTS.
0 100 200 mi
0 100 200 300 km
Kangiqsualujjuaq
Hebron
LABRADOR SEA
R. George
Nutak
S. Aulatsivik I.
Nain
Davis Inlet
Hopedale
MAIN MAP
Schefferville
Menihek
LABRADOR
Esker
Smallwood Res.
Labrador City
Churchill Falls
500
Wabush
Happy Valley-Goose Bay
NFLD.
QUÉ.
65° 60° 55° 52°
ATLANTIC OCEAN
N

Northwest Territories
Territorial Capital
Road
1:14,778,000
Lambert Conformal Conic Projection
Nunavut Settlement Area
ARCTIC OCEAN
Beaufort Sea
Baffin Bay
Davis Strait
Hudson Bay
Hudson Strait
Foxe Basin
Foxe Channel
Parry Channel
Amundsen Gulf
M'Clure Strait
Viscount Melville Sound
M'Clintock Channel
Queen Maud Gulf
Coronation Gulf
Gulf of Boothia
Prince Regent Inlet
Franklin Strait
Lancaster Sound
Jones Sound
Cumberland Sound
Frobisher Bay
Ungava Bay
ELLESMERE ISLAND
AXEL HEIBERG ISLAND
QUEEN ELIZABETH ISLANDS
DEVON ISLAND
BAFFIN ISLAND
BAFFIN REGION
SOMERSET ISLAND
PRINCE OF WALES ISLAND
VICTORIA ISLAND
BANKS ISLAND
MELVILLE ISLAND
PRINCE PATRICK ISLAND
SOUTHAMPTON ISLAND
KITIKMEOT REGION
KEEWATIN REGION
INUVIK REGION
FORT SMITH REGION
GREENLAND (KALAALLIT NUNAAT) (Denmark)
QUÉBEC
MANITOBA
SASKATCHEWAN
BRITISH COLUMBIA
YUKON TERR.
N.W. TERR.
UNITED STATES
CANADA
ALASKA
NORTHWEST TERRITORIES
MACKENZIE MTS.
ELLESMERE ISLAND NATIONAL PARK RESERVE
AUYUITTUQ NATIONAL PARK
WOOD BUFFALO NATIONAL PARK
NAHANNI NATIONAL PARK
Yellowknife
Iqaluit (Frobisher Bay)
Resolute
Alert
Inuvik
Tuktoyaktuk
Aklavik
Coppermine
Cambridge Bay
Baker Lake
Chesterfield Inlet
Whale Cove
Eskimo Point
Rankin Inlet
Hay River
Fort Smith
Fort Simpson
Fort Providence
Fort Resolution
Fort Good Hope
Fort Norman
Fort Franklin
Norman Wells
Holman
Paulatuk
Pangnirtung
Clyde River
Pond Inlet
Arctic Bay
Hall Beach
Igloolik
Spence Bay
Gjoa Haven
Pelly Bay
Great Bear L.
Great Slave L.
Pacific Time Zone
Mountain Time Zone
Central Time Zone
Eastern Time Zone
Atlantic Time Zone
Arctic Circle
© GeoSystems Global Corp.

100 NOVA SCOTIA, PRINCE EDWARD ISLAND

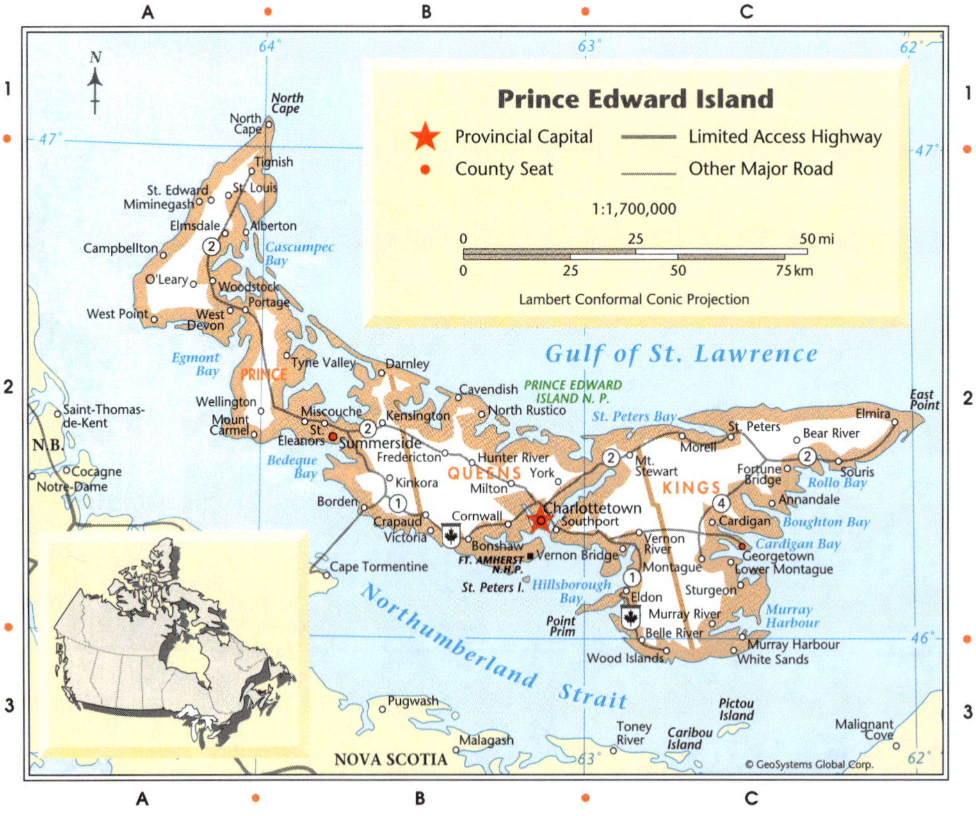

Hudson Bay
James Bay
Akimiski I.
Charlton I.
Thompson
Gillam
Shamattawa
Fort Severn
Winisk
Gods L.
Sachigo R.
Severn R.
Big Trout Lake
Sandy Lake
Sandy L.
Asheweig R.
Ekwan R.
Little Grand Rapids
Weagamow Lake
Winisk R.
Webequie
Winisk R.
Attawapiskat
Attawapiskat R.
Pikangikum
Lansdowne House
Kapiskau R.
Fort Albany
Trout L.
Pickle Lake
Balmertown
Albany R.
Moosonee
Ear Falls
Ogoki R.
Moose R.
Moose Factory
MANITOBA
ONTARIO
Kenora
Sioux Lookout
Armstrong
Nakina
Dryden
L. of the Woods
L. Nipigon
Geraldton
Longlac
Hearst
Fraserdale
Kapuskasing
Fort Frances
Atikokan
Nipigon
Schreiber
Manitouwadge
Hornepayne
Cochrane
Marathon
Thunder Bay
PUKASKWA NAT'L PARK
Iroquois Falls
Timmins
Kirkland Lake
MINN.
CANADA
U.S.
Central Time Zone
Eastern Time Zone
L. Superior
Wawa
Chapleau
Gogama
Rouyn-Noranda
New Liskeard
Duluth
Sault Ste. Marie
Sudbury
Sturgeon Falls
North Bay
Minneapolis
St. Paul
Georgian Bay
ONT.
MICH.
L. Huron
L. Simcoe
Ottawa
Peterborough
Belleville
Brampton
Toronto
Kitchener
Hamilton
L. Ontario
Sarnia
London
Buffalo
Windsor
Erie
L. Erie
Binghamton
Jamestown
Cleveland
Scranton
N.Y.
ONTARIO
QUÉBEC
Rivière de Rupert
R. Nottaway
Chibougamau
Matagami
Réservoir Gouin
Amos
Maniwaki
Mont-Laurier
GATINEAU PARK
Ontario
National Capital
Provincial/State Capital
Limited Access Highway
Other Major Road
1:15,610,000
0 200 400 mi
0 200 400 600 km
Lambert Conformal Conic Projection
© GeoSystems Global Corp.

Ivujivik
Salluit
Kangiqsujuaq
Quaqtaq
Akpatok Island
Eastern Time Zone
Atlantic Time Zone
Mansel Island
Akulivik
Kangirsuk
Povungnituk
Ungava Bay
Lac Payne
R. Arnaud
Kangiqsualujjuaq
Kuujjuaq
Inukjuak
R. aux Feuilles
R. George
Hudson Bay
Lac Minto
R. aux Mélèzes
R. à la Baleine
Caniapiscau
Labrador Sea
Belcher Islands
Lac à l'Eau Claire
LABRADOR
Kuujjuarapik
Schefferville
Cartwright
Grande R. de la Baleine
Lac Bienville
Smallwood Res.
Lac Caniapiscau
Happy Valley-Goose Bay
Chisasibi
La Grande Rivière
Keyano
NEWFOUNDLAND
QUÉBEC
Blanc-Sablon
Labrador City
St-Augustin
Newfoundland Time Zone
James Bay
Gagnon
Eastmain
Rivière Eastmain
Rés. Manicouagan
Rivière Péribonca
Natashquan
Havre-St-Pierre
Grand Falls
Gander
Waskaganish
Sept-Îles
MINGAN ARCHIPELAGO NATL. PARK RESERVE
NEWFOUNDLAND
Port-Cartier
Anticosti Island
Corner Brook
Lac Mistassini
Mistassini
Matagami
Chibougamau
Gaspé
FORILLON N.P.
Gulf of St. Lawrence
St. Lawrence River
Baie-Comeau
Percé
Matane
Îles de la Madeleine
ONTARIO
QUÉBEC
Amos
Rés. Gouin
Alma
Rimouski
Senneterre
Val-d'Or
Chicoutimi
N.B.
Rivière-du-Loup
Rouyn-Noranda
Ville-Marie
LA MAURICIE NATIONAL PARK
Québec
Mont-Laurier
Trois-Rivières
North Bay
CAN.
U.S.
GATINEAU PARK
Maniwaki
Drummondville
Pembroke
Hull
Ottawa
Montréal
© GeoSystems Global Corp.
Québec
National Capital
Provincial Capital
Limited Access Highway
Other Major Road
1:18,171,000
0 200 400 mi
0 200 400 600 km
Lambert Conformal Conic Projection

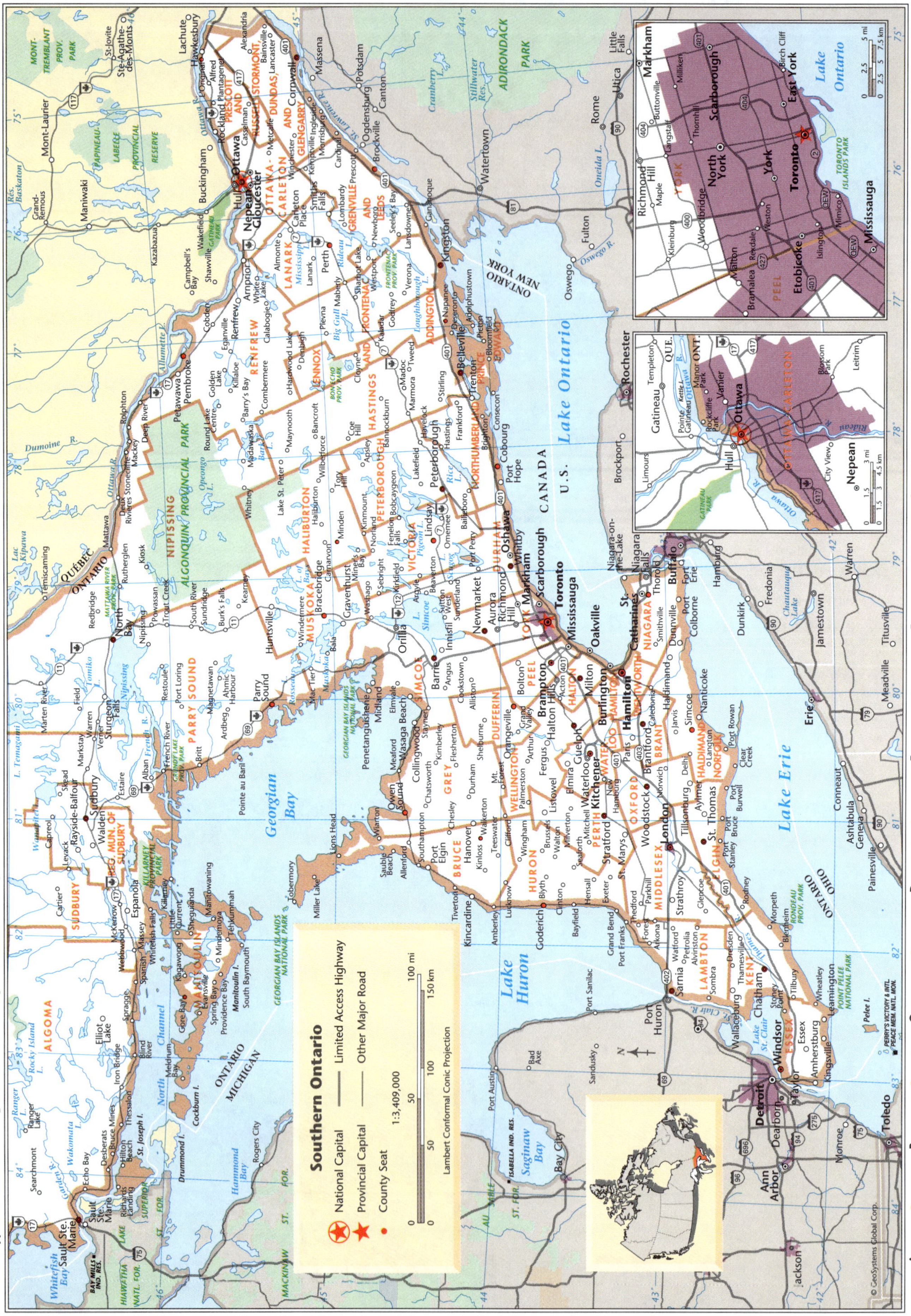

Southern Ontario
National Capital
Provincial Capital
County Seat
Limited Access Highway
Other Major Road
1:3,409,000
0 50 100 mi
0 50 100 150 km
Lambert Conformal Conic Projection
© GeoSystems Global Corp.
Lake Ontario
Lake Erie
Lake Huron
Georgian Bay
ONTARIO
QUÉBEC
NEW YORK
MICHIGAN
OHIO
CANADA
U.S.
Ottawa
Toronto
Hamilton
London
Kingston
Windsor
Detroit
Buffalo
Rochester
Sudbury
North Bay
ALGONQUIN PROVINCIAL PARK
ADIRONDACK PARK
Markham
Scarborough
North York
York
East York
Etobicoke
Mississauga
Nepean
Gatineau
Hull
Vanier

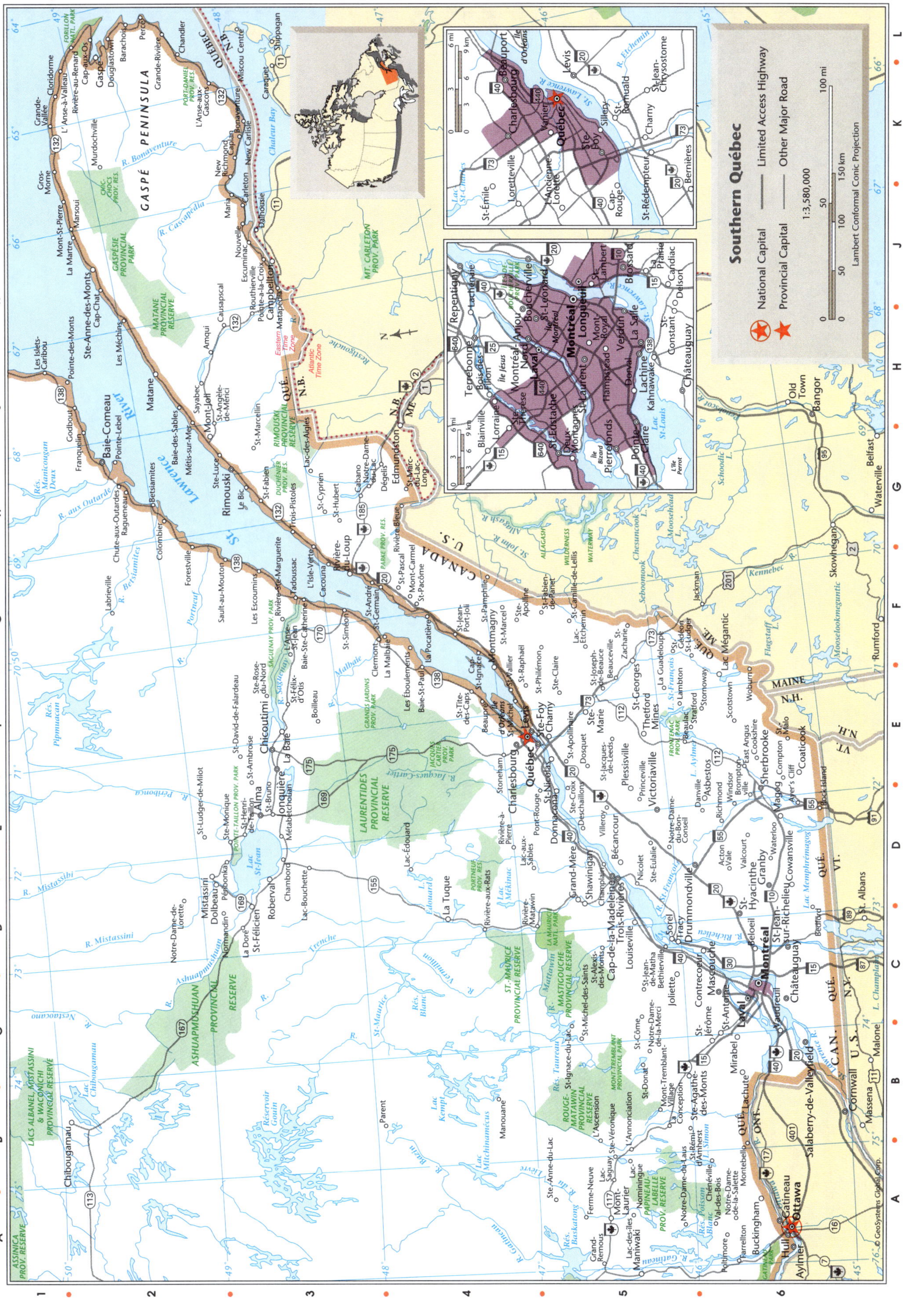
Southern Québec
National Capital
Provincial Capital
Limited Access Highway
Other Major Road
1:3,580,000
Lambert Conformal Conic Projection
GASPÉ PENINSULA
St. Lawrence River
Chaleur Bay
Québec
Montréal
Ottawa
Lévis
Trois-Rivières
Sherbrooke
Chicoutimi
Rimouski
Baie-Comeau
Laval
Longueuil
LAURENTIDES PROVINCIAL RESERVE
ASHUAPMUSHUAN PROVINCIAL RESERVE
ST. MAURICE PROVINCIAL RESERVE
MASTIGOUCHE PROVINCIAL RESERVE
GASPÉSIE PROVINCIAL PARK
MATANE PROVINCIAL RESERVE
LA MAURICIE NATL. PARK
FORILLON NATL. PARK
MT. CARLETON PROV. PARK
CANADA
U.S.
MAINE
N.B.
N.H.
VT.
N.Y.
ONT.
QUÉ.
Eastern Time Zone
Atlantic Time Zone
© GeoSystems Global Corp.

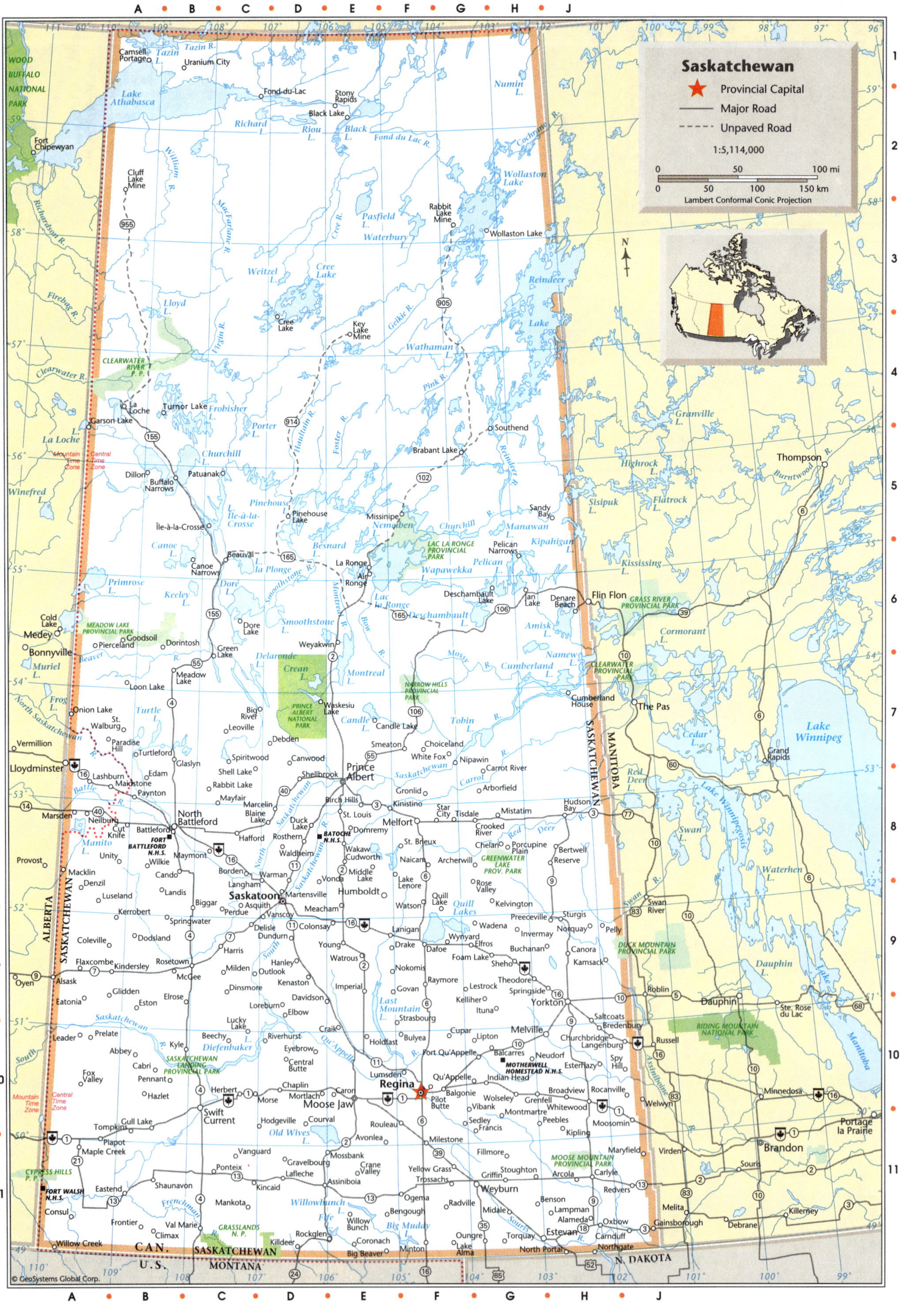

Saskatchewan
Provincial Capital
Major Road
Unpaved Road
1:5,114,000
0 50 100 mi
0 50 100 150 km
Lambert Conformal Conic Projection
SASKATCHEWAN
MANITOBA
ALBERTA
CAN.
U.S.
MONTANA
N. DAKOTA
Mountain Time Zone
Central Time Zone
WOOD BUFFALO NATIONAL PARK
CLEARWATER RIVER P.P.
MEADOW LAKE PROVINCIAL PARK
PRINCE ALBERT NATIONAL PARK
LAC LA RONGE PROVINCIAL PARK
NARROW HILLS PROVINCIAL PARK
GRASS RIVER PROVINCIAL PARK
CLEARWATER PROVINCIAL PARK
GREENWATER LAKE PROV. PARK
DUCK MOUNTAIN PROVINCIAL PARK
RIDING MOUNTAIN NATIONAL PARK
MOOSE MOUNTAIN PROVINCIAL PARK
SASKATCHEWAN LANDING PROVINCIAL PARK
CYPRESS HILLS P.P.
GRASSLANDS N.P.
FORT WALSH N.H.S.
FORT BATTLEFORD N.H.S.
BATOCHE N.H.S.
MOTHERWELL HOMESTEAD N.H.S.
Lake Athabasca
Tazin L.
Wollaston Lake
Reindeer Lake
Lake Winnipeg
Cedar L.
Churchill L.
Lac la Ronge
Cumberland L.
Last Mountain L.
Lake Diefenbaker
Old Wives L.
Quill Lakes
Uranium City
Camsell Portage
Fond-du-Lac
Stony Rapids
Black Lake
Fort Chipewyan
Cluff Lake Mine
Rabbit Lake Mine
Wollaston Lake
Key Lake Mine
Cree Lake
La Loche
Turnor Lake
Garson Lake
Southend
Brabant Lake
Dillon
Buffalo Narrows
Patuanak
Pinehouse Lake
Île-à-la-Crosse
Missinipe
Beauval
La Ronge
Air Ronge
Sandy Bay
Pelican Narrows
Flin Flon
Denare Beach
Jan Lake
Deschambault Lake
Thompson
The Pas
Cumberland House
Grand Rapids
Cold Lake
Medley
Bonnyville
Goodsoil
Pierceland
Dorintosh
Green Lake
Meadow Lake
Loon Lake
Waskesiu Lake
Big River
Candle Lake
Onion Lake
St. Walburg
Paradise Hill
Turtleford
Glaslyn
Vermillion
Lloydminster
Lashburn
Maidstone
Edam
Paynton
Marsden
Neilburg
Cut Knife
North Battleford
Battleford
Spiritwood
Canwood
Shellbrook
Prince Albert
Smeaton
Choiceland
White Fox
Nipawin
Carrot River
Arborfield
Melfort
Tisdale
Kinistino
Birch Hills
St. Louis
Hudson Bay
Rosthern
Wakaw
Cudworth
Humboldt
Warman
Saskatoon
Martensville
Biggar
Kindersley
Rosetown
Outlook
Davidson
Watrous
Lanigan
Wynyard
Foam Lake
Kamsack
Canora
Yorkton
Melville
Dauphin
Swan River
Russell
Esterhazy
Fort Qu'Appelle
Balcarres
Indian Head
Regina
Moose Jaw
Lumsden
Pilot Butte
Balgonie
Weyburn
Estevan
Carlyle
Redvers
Moosomin
Kipling
Grenfell
Broadview
Virden
Brandon
Minnedosa
Portage la Prairie
Swift Current
Herbert
Maple Creek
Gull Lake
Shaunavon
Eastend
Consul
Assiniboia
Gravelbourg
Rockglen
Coronach
Bengough
Radville
Oxbow
Carnduff
North Portal
Leader
Kyle
Eston
Oyen
Provost
Unity
Macklin
Wilkie
Kerrobert
Luseland
Willow Creek

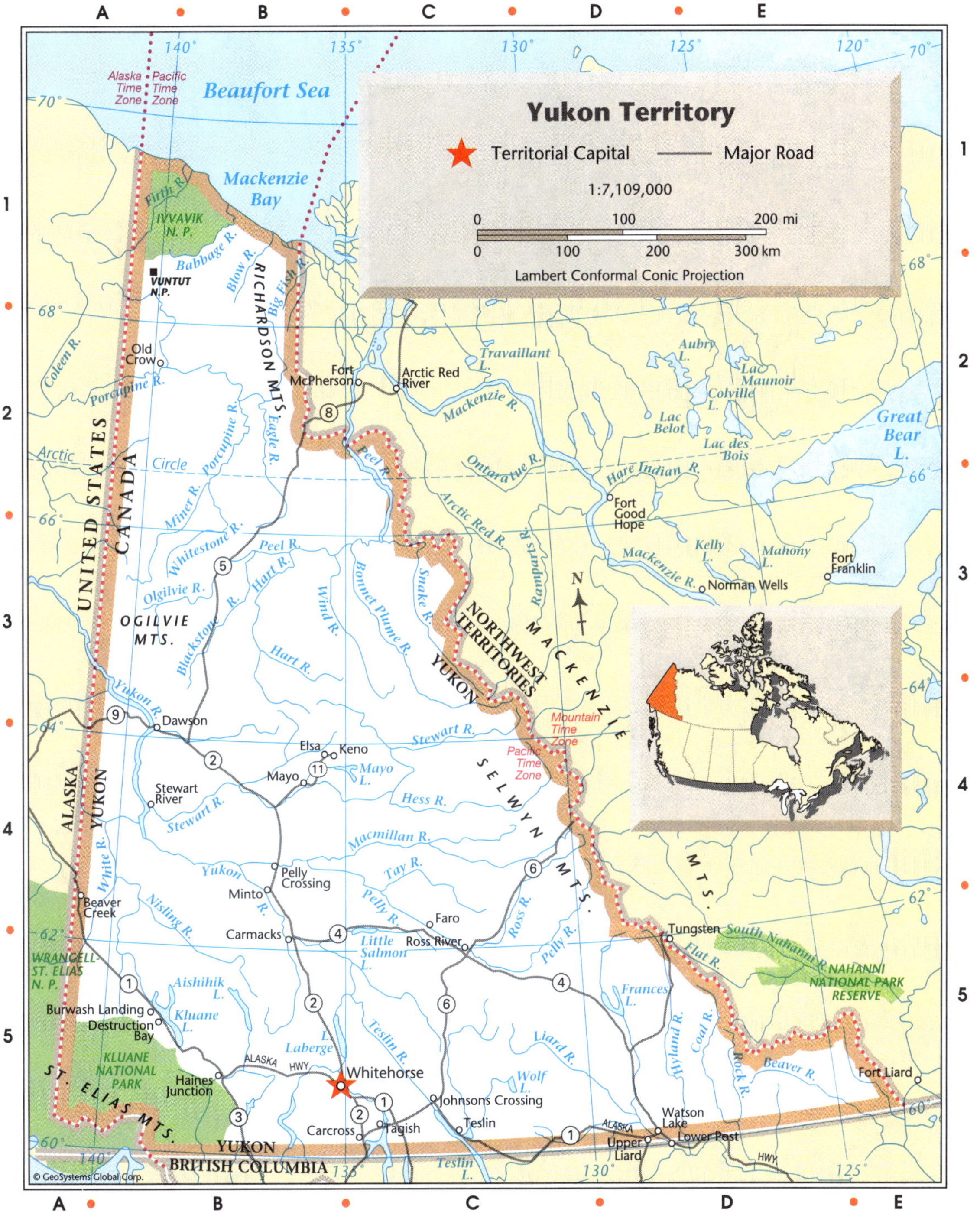
Yukon Territory
Territorial Capital
Major Road
1:7,109,000
0 100 200 mi
0 100 200 300 km
Lambert Conformal Conic Projection
A B C D E
1 2 3 4 5
140° 135° 130° 125° 120°
70° 68° 66° 64° 62° 60°
Beaufort Sea
Alaska Time Zone
Pacific Time Zone
Mackenzie Bay
Firth R.
IVVAVIK N. P.
Babbage R.
VUNTUT N.P.
Blow R.
RICHARDSON MTS.
Big Fish R.
Old Crow
Porcupine R.
Coleen R.
Fort McPherson
Arctic Red River
Travaillant L.
Aubry L.
Lac Maunoir
Colville L.
Lac Belot
Lac des Bois
Great Bear L.
Mackenzie R.
Eagle R.
Peel R.
Ontaratue R.
Hare Indian R.
Arctic Circle
UNITED STATES
CANADA
Miner R.
Fort Good Hope
Arctic Red R.
Ramparts R.
Whitestone R.
Peel R.
Hart R.
Bonnet Plume R.
Snake R.
Kelly L.
Mahony L.
Fort Franklin
Norman Wells
Ogilvie R.
OGILVIE MTS.
Blackstone R.
Wind R.
NORTHWEST TERRITORIES
YUKON
MACKENZIE MTS.
Hart R.
Yukon R.
Dawson
Mountain Time Zone
Pacific Time Zone
Stewart R.
Elsa
Keno
Mayo
Mayo L.
SELWYN MTS.
Stewart River
Stewart R.
Hess R.
ALASKA
YUKON
White R.
Macmillan R.
Yukon R.
Pelly Crossing
Tay R.
Minto
Beaver Creek
Nisling R.
Pelly R.
Faro
Ross R.
Carmacks
Ross River
Pelly R.
Tungsten
South Nahanni R.
Little Salmon L.
Flat R.
WRANGELL-ST. ELIAS N. P.
NAHANNI NATIONAL PARK RESERVE
Aishihik L.
Frances L.
Burwash Landing
Kluane L.
Destruction Bay
Teslin R.
Liard R.
Hyland R.
Coal R.
Rock R.
Beaver R.
Laberge L.
KLUANE NATIONAL PARK
ALASKA HWY.
Wolf L.
Fort Liard
Haines Junction
Whitehorse
Johnsons Crossing
ST. ELIAS MTS.
Tagish
Teslin
Watson Lake
Carcross
ALASKA HWY.
Upper Liard
Lower Post
YUKON
BRITISH COLUMBIA
Teslin L.
© GeoSystems Global Corp.

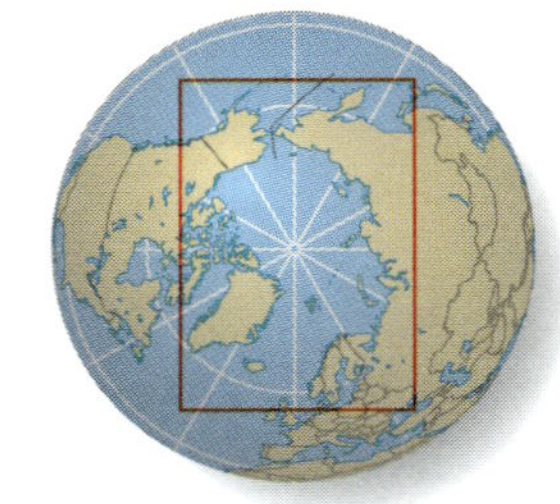

Greenland

Capital: Nuuk (Godthåb)
Area: 840,000 sq. mi.
2,176,000 sq. km.
Population: 57,000
Largest City: Nuuk (Godthåb)
Languages: Inuit dialect, Danish
Monetary Unit: Danish Krone

Greenland: Map Index

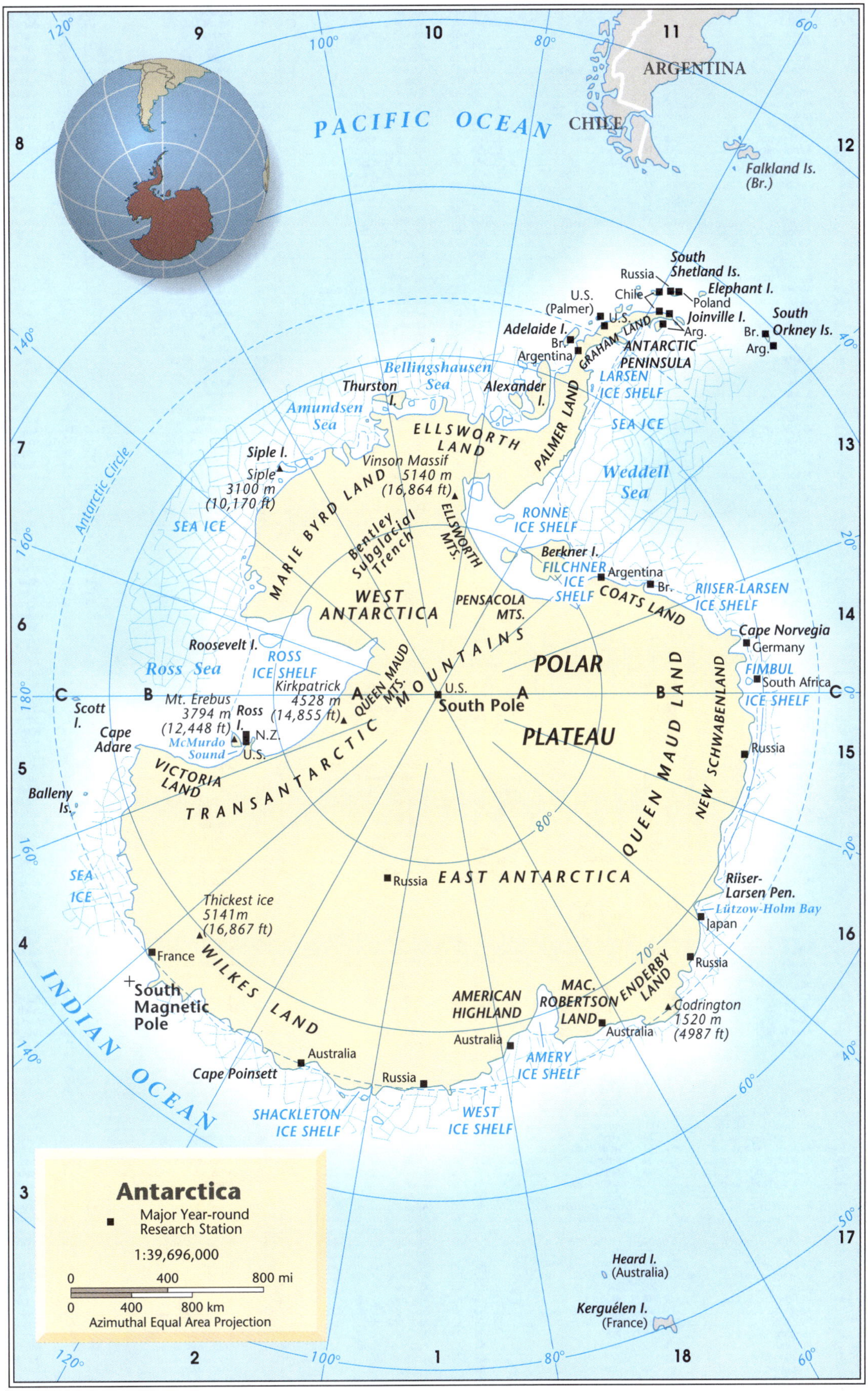
PACIFIC OCEAN
ARGENTINA
CHILE
Falkland Is. (Br.)
South Shetland Is.
Elephant I.
Joinville I.
South Orkney Is.
ANTARCTIC PENINSULA
GRAHAM LAND
PALMER LAND
Adelaide I.
Alexander I.
Thurston I.
Bellingshausen Sea
Amundsen Sea
LARSEN ICE SHELF
SEA ICE
Weddell Sea
ELLSWORTH LAND
Siple I.
Siple 3100 m (10,170 ft)
Vinson Massif 5140 m (16,864 ft)
MARIE BYRD LAND
Bentley Subglacial Trench
ELLSWORTH MTS.
RONNE ICE SHELF
Berkner I.
FILCHNER ICE SHELF
COATS LAND
RIISER-LARSEN ICE SHELF
Cape Norvegia
FIMBUL ICE SHELF
WEST ANTARCTICA
PENSACOLA MTS.
Roosevelt I.
ROSS ICE SHELF
Ross Sea
Kirkpatrick 4528 m (14,855 ft)
QUEEN MAUD MTS.
TRANSANTARCTIC MOUNTAINS
South Pole
POLAR PLATEAU
QUEEN MAUD LAND
NEW SCHWABENLAND
Scott I.
Mt. Erebus 3794 m (12,448 ft)
Ross I.
McMurdo Sound
Cape Adare
VICTORIA LAND
Balleny Is.
EAST ANTARCTICA
Thickest ice 5141m (16,867 ft)
WILKES LAND
South Magnetic Pole
Cape Poinsett
INDIAN OCEAN
AMERICAN HIGHLAND
MAC. ROBERTSON LAND
ENDERBY LAND
Codrington 1520 m (4987 ft)
Riiser-Larsen Pen.
Lützow-Holm Bay
AMERY ICE SHELF
WEST ICE SHELF
SHACKLETON ICE SHELF
Heard I. (Australia)
Kerguélen I. (France)
Antarctic Circle
Antarctica
Major Year-round Research Station
1:39,696,000
0 400 800 mi
0 400 800 km
Azimuthal Equal Area Projection

A

C

D

E

F

K

L

N

O

P

S

T

U

V

Capital: Washington, D.C. **Population:** 260,714,000
Area: 3,787,300 sq. mi. 9,809,200 sq. km. **Largest City:** New York
Monetary Unit: U.S. dollar

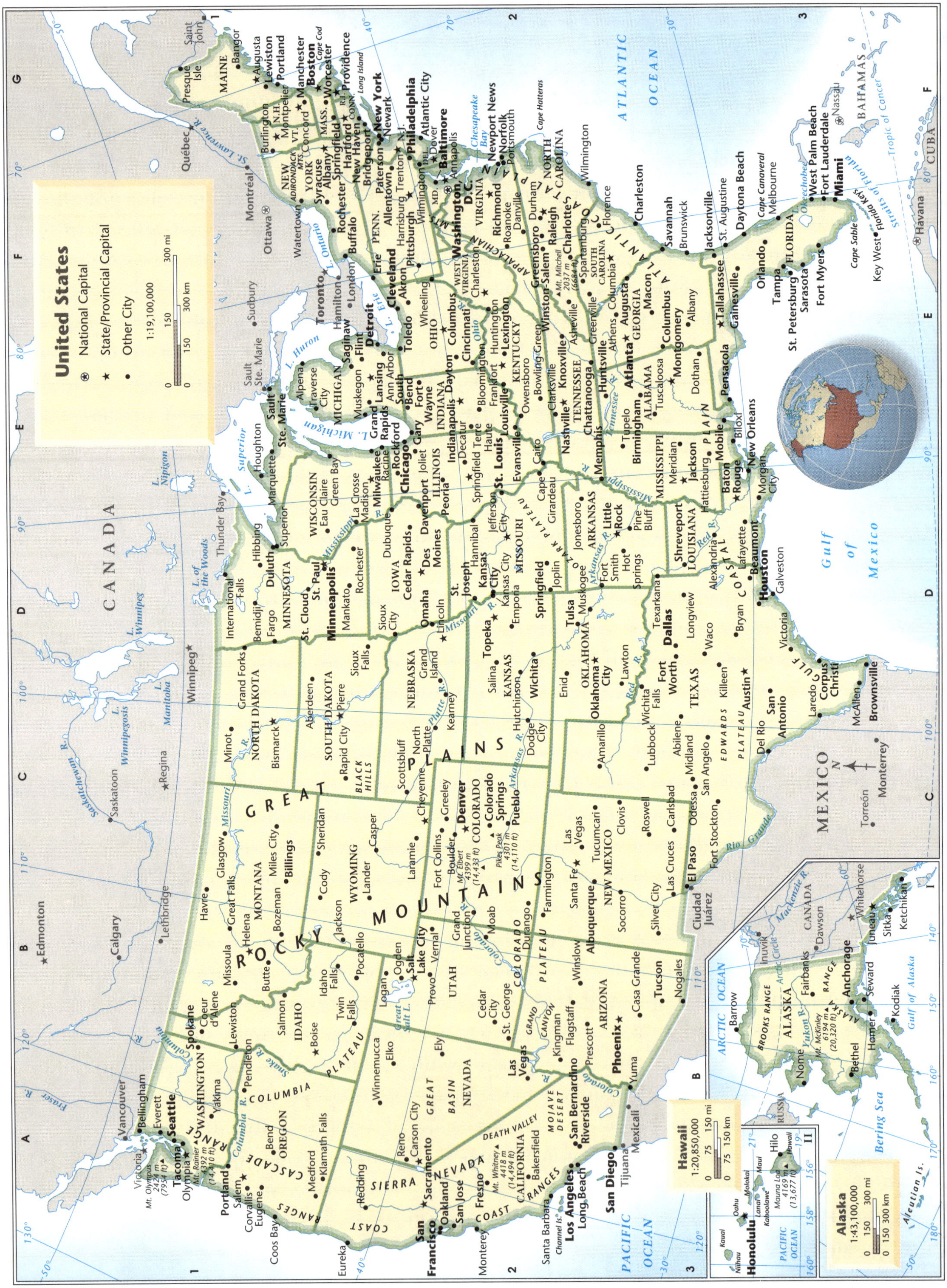

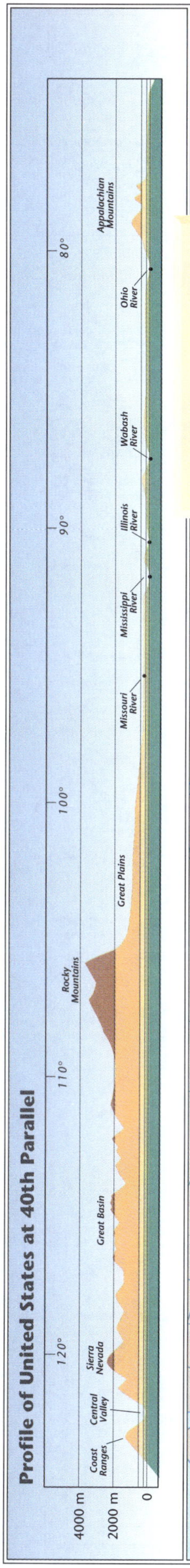
Profile of United States at 40th Parallel
4000 m
2000 m
0
120°
110°
100°
90°
80°
Coast Ranges
Central Valley
Sierra Nevada
Great Basin
Rocky Mountains
Great Plains
Missouri River
Mississippi River
Illinois River
Wabash River
Ohio River
Appalachian Mountains

Elevation in feet
Over 13,100
6600–13,100
1600–6600
700–1600
0–700
Below sea level
Elevation in meters
Over 4000
2000–4000
500–2000
200–500
0–200
Below sea level
Landforms of the United States
1:18,989,000
0 150 300 mi
0 150 300 km
Albers Equal Area Projection
CANADA
MEXICO
PACIFIC OCEAN
ATLANTIC OCEAN
Gulf of Mexico
ROCKY MOUNTAINS
GREAT PLAINS
High Plains
APPALACHIAN MOUNTAINS
ATLANTIC COASTAL PLAIN
GULF COASTAL PLAIN
Great Basin
Columbia Plateau
Colorado Plateau
Cascade Range
Sierra Nevada
Coast Ranges
Central Valley
Death Valley
Mojave Desert
Sonoran Desert
Painted Desert
Grand Canyon
Mogollon Rim
Wasatch Range
Uinta Mts.
Wyoming Basin
Wind River Range
Absaroka Range
Bighorn Mts.
Bitterroot Range
Snake River Plain
Blue Mts.
Black Hills
Badlands
Missouri Coteau
Sand Hills
Smoky Hills
Flint Hills
Ozark Plateau
Boston Mts.
Ouachita Mts.
Llano Estacado
Edwards Plateau
Stockton Plateau
Guadalupe Mts.
Sangre de Cristo Mts.
San Juan Range
Pikes Peak 4301 m (14,110 ft)
Mt. Elbert 4399 m (14,433 ft)
Mt. Whitney 4418 m (14,494 ft)
Mt. Rainier 4392 m (14,410 ft)
Mt. Olympus 2424 m (7954 ft)
Mt. Mitchell 2037 m (6684 ft)
Great Smoky Mts.
Blue Ridge
Piedmont
Allegheny Front
Great Valley
Cumberland Plateau
Adirondack Mts.
Green Mts.
White Mts.
Superior Upland
Mesabi Range
Lower Peninsula
Upper Peninsula
Isle Royale
Black Belt
Yazoo Basin
Mississippi Delta
Okefenokee Swamp
The Everglades
Florida Keys
Austin Chalk Cliffs
Denver
Dallas
St. Louis
Chicago
New Orleans
Miami
Washington, D.C.
Philadelphia
New York
Boston
Los Angeles
Cape Cod
Cape Hatteras
Cape Fear
Cape Canaveral
Cape Flattery
Point Conception
Channel Islands
Strait of San Juan de Fuca
Straits of Florida
Long Island
Gulf of Maine
Delaware Bay
Chesapeake Bay
Tampa Bay
Apalachee Bay
Mobile Bay
Galveston Bay
L. Superior
L. Michigan
L. Huron
L. Erie
L. Ontario
L. Okeechobee
L. of the Woods
Great Salt L.
L. Tahoe
L. Mead
L. Powell
Salton Sea
Niagara Falls
Finger Lakes
Mississippi R.
Missouri R.
Ohio R.
Platte R.
Arkansas R.
Red R.
Rio Grande R.
Colorado R.
Snake R.
Columbia R.
Sacramento R.
San Joaquin R.
St. Lawrence R.
Connecticut R.
Susquehanna R.
Tennessee R.
Kentucky L.
Klamath Mts.
Hawaii
Mauna Kea 4169 m (13,677 ft)
Kauai
Niihau
Oahu
Molokai
Maui
Lanai
Kahoolawe
0 75 150 mi
0 75 150 km
ARCTIC OCEAN
Beaufort Sea
Chukchi Sea
Bering Sea
Gulf of Alaska
Brooks Range
Alaska Range
Mt. McKinley 6194 m (20,320 ft)
Yukon R.
Kuskokwim Mts.
Alaska Peninsula
Kodiak I.
Alexander Archipelago
St. Lawrence I.
Bering Strait
Arctic Circle
RUSSIA
0 150 300 mi
0 150 300 km

Capital: Montgomery
Area: 52,400 sq. mi. 135,800 sq. km.
Population: 4,187,000
Largest City: Birmingham

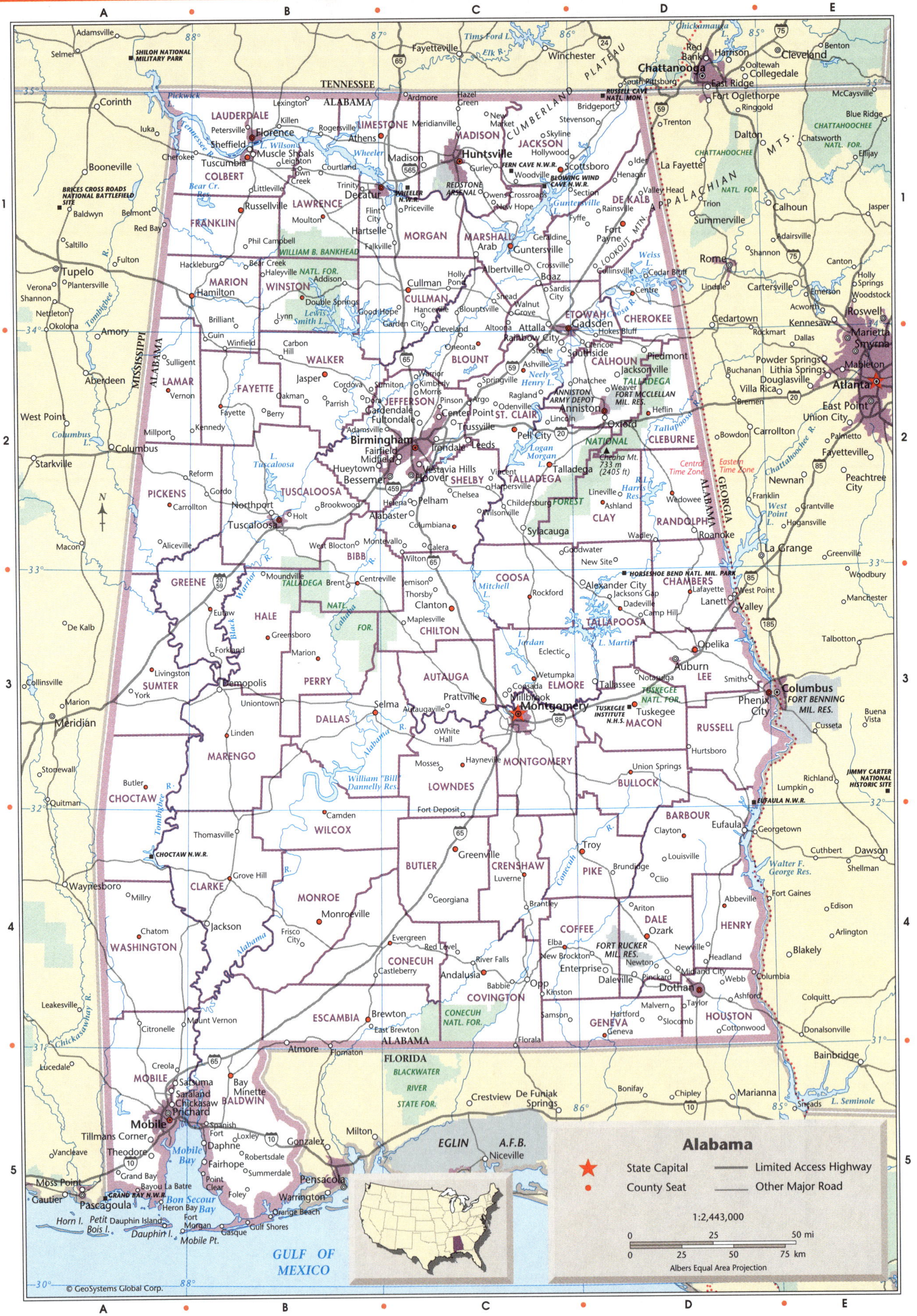

Capital: Juneau **Population:** 599,000
Area: 656,400 sq. mi. 1,700,000 sq. km. **Largest City:** Anchorage

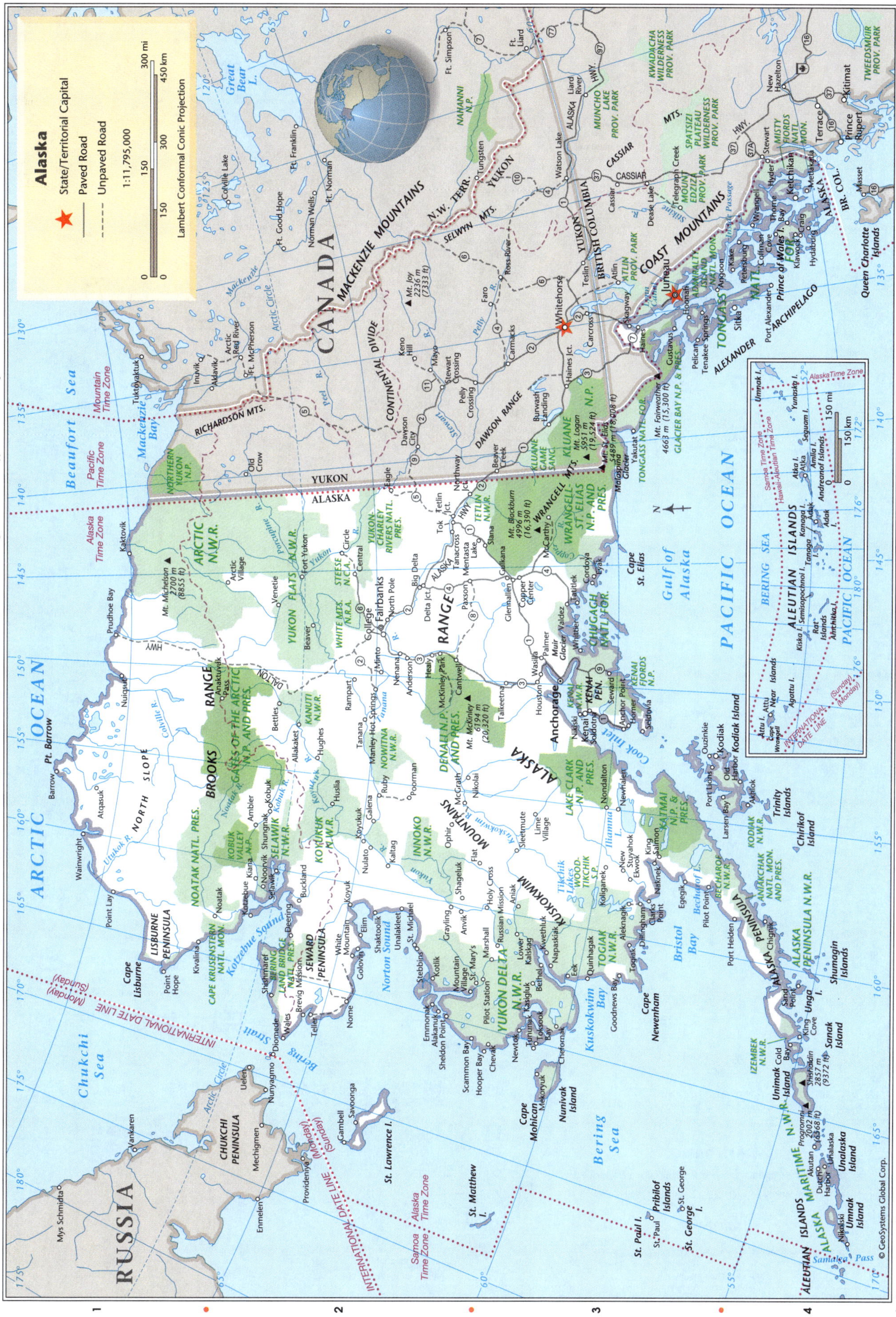

Capital: Phoenix
Area: 114,000 sq. mi.
295,300 sq. km.
Population: 3,936,000
Largest City: Phoenix

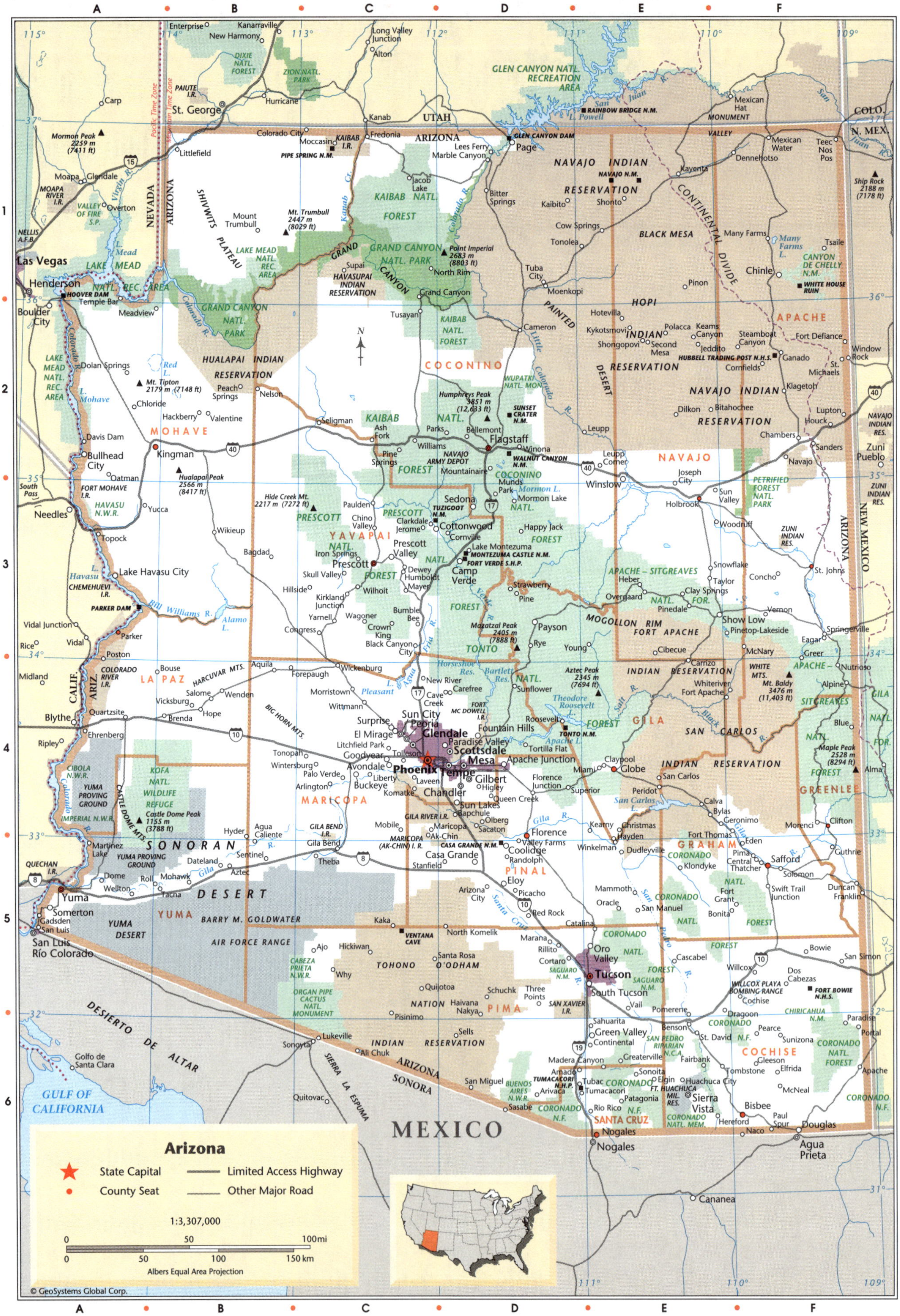

Capital: Little Rock
Area: 53,200 sq. mi. 137,700 sq. km.
Population: 2,424,000
Largest City: Little Rock

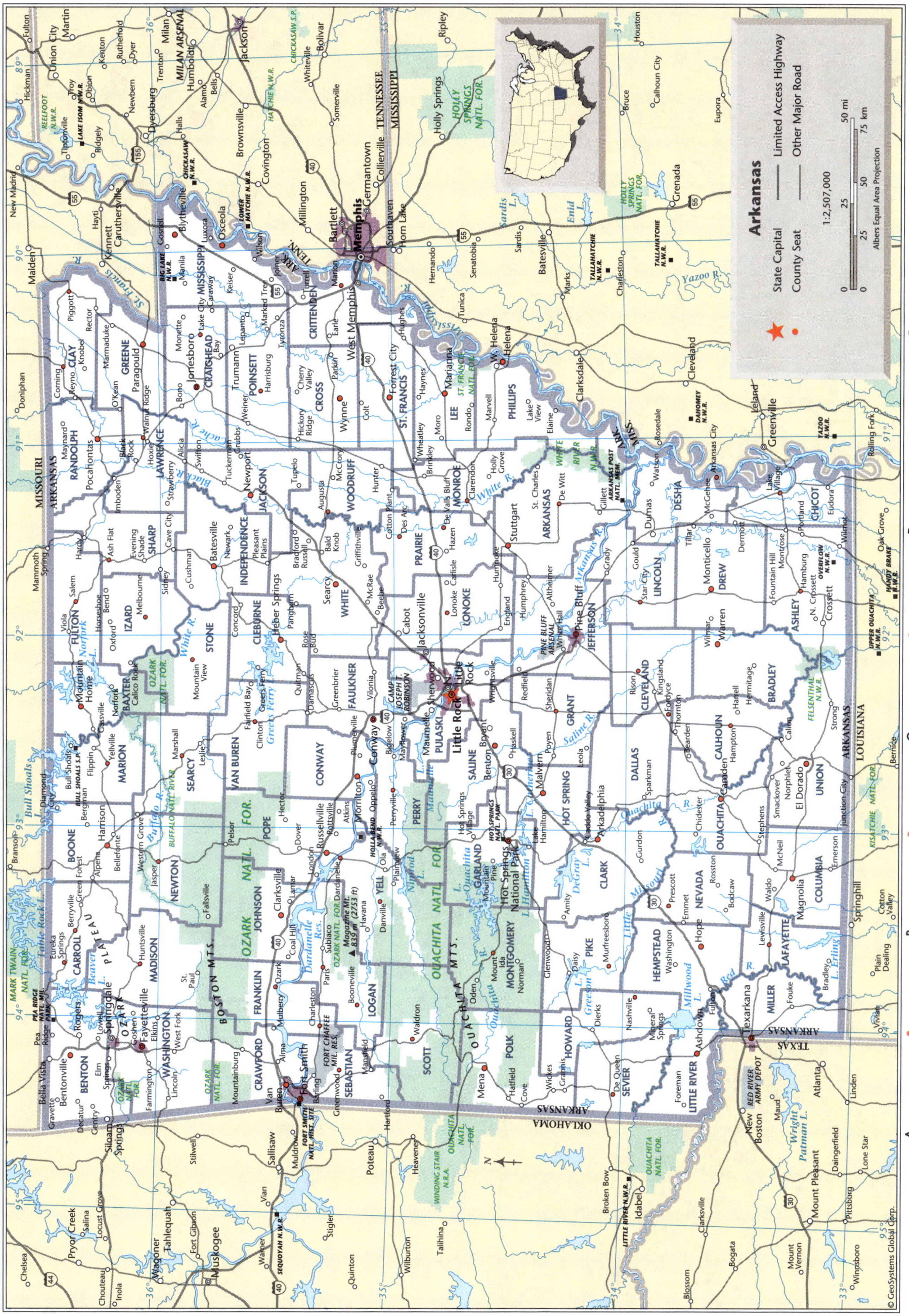

CALIFORNIA

Capital: Sacramento
Area: 163,700 sq. mi. / 424,000 sq. km.
Population: 31,211,000
Largest City: Los Angeles

Capital: Denver
Area: 104,100 sq. mi.
269,600 sq. km.
Population: 3,566,000
Largest City: Denver

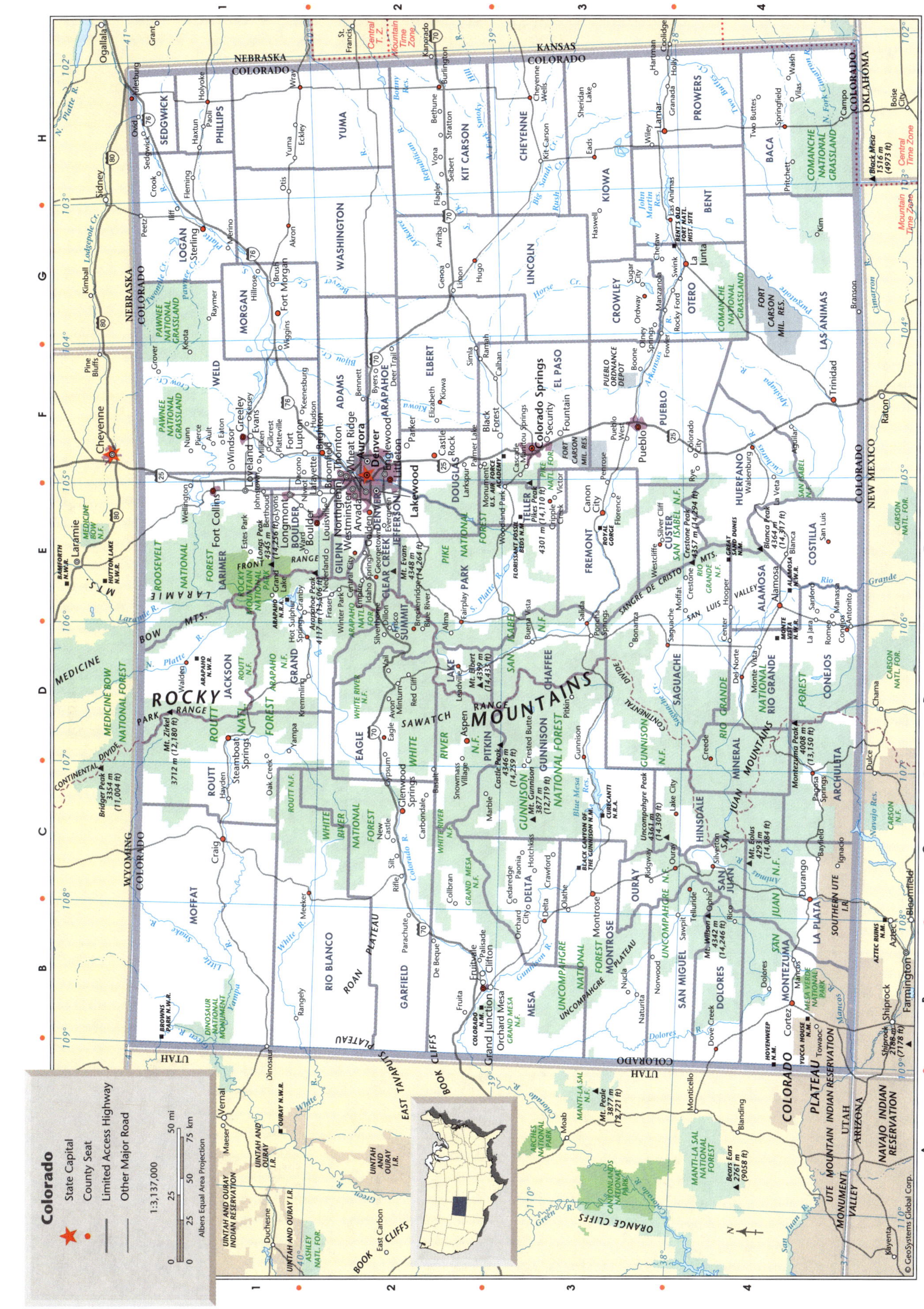

Capital: Hartford
Area: 5,500 sq. mi.
14,400 sq. km.

Population: 3,277,000
Largest City: Hartford

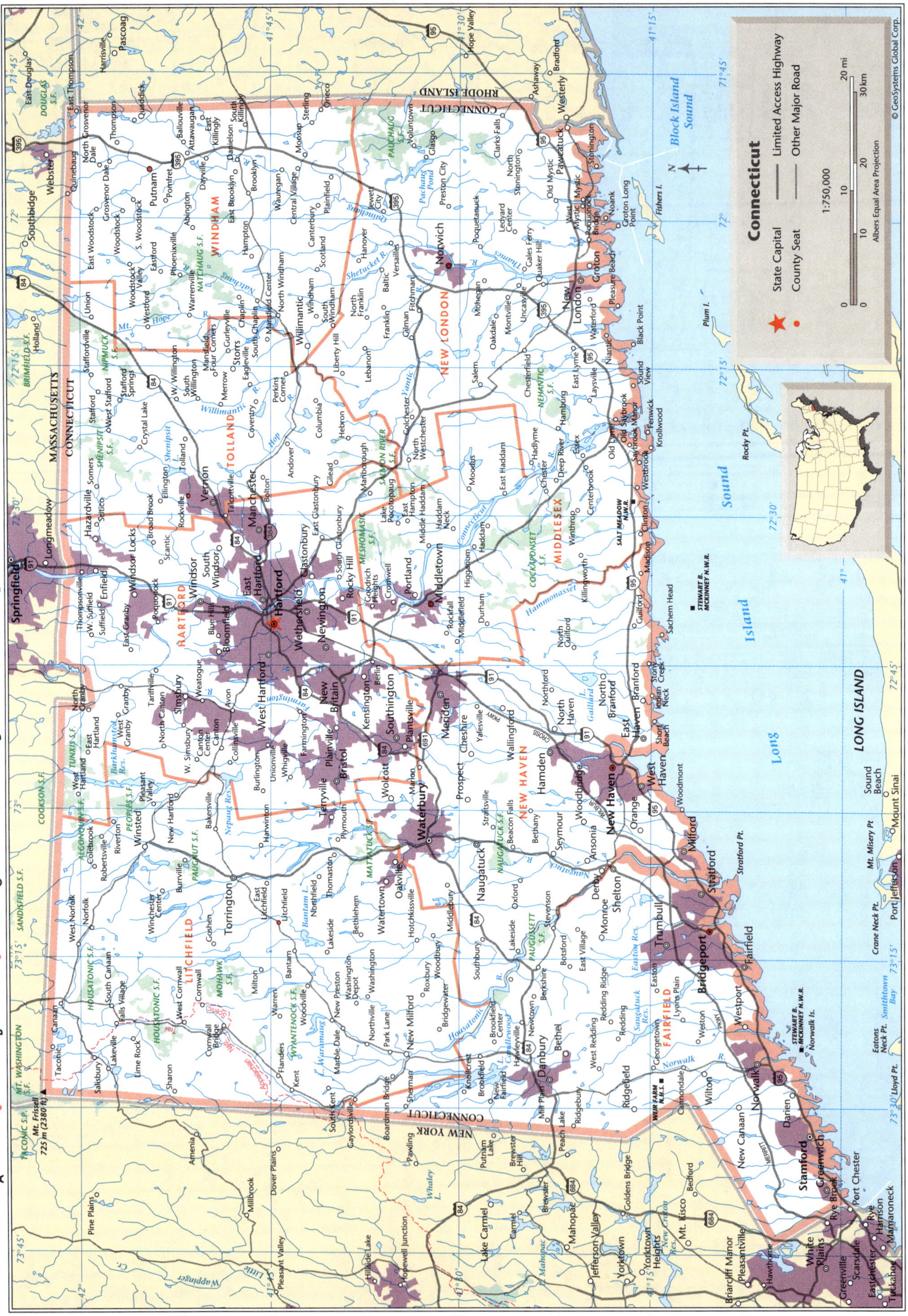

Capital: Dover
Area: 2,500 sq. mi.
6,400 sq. km.

Population: 700,000
Largest City: Wilmington

Capital: Tallahassee
Area: 65,800 sq. mi. 170,300 sq. km.
Population: 13,679,000
Largest City: Miami

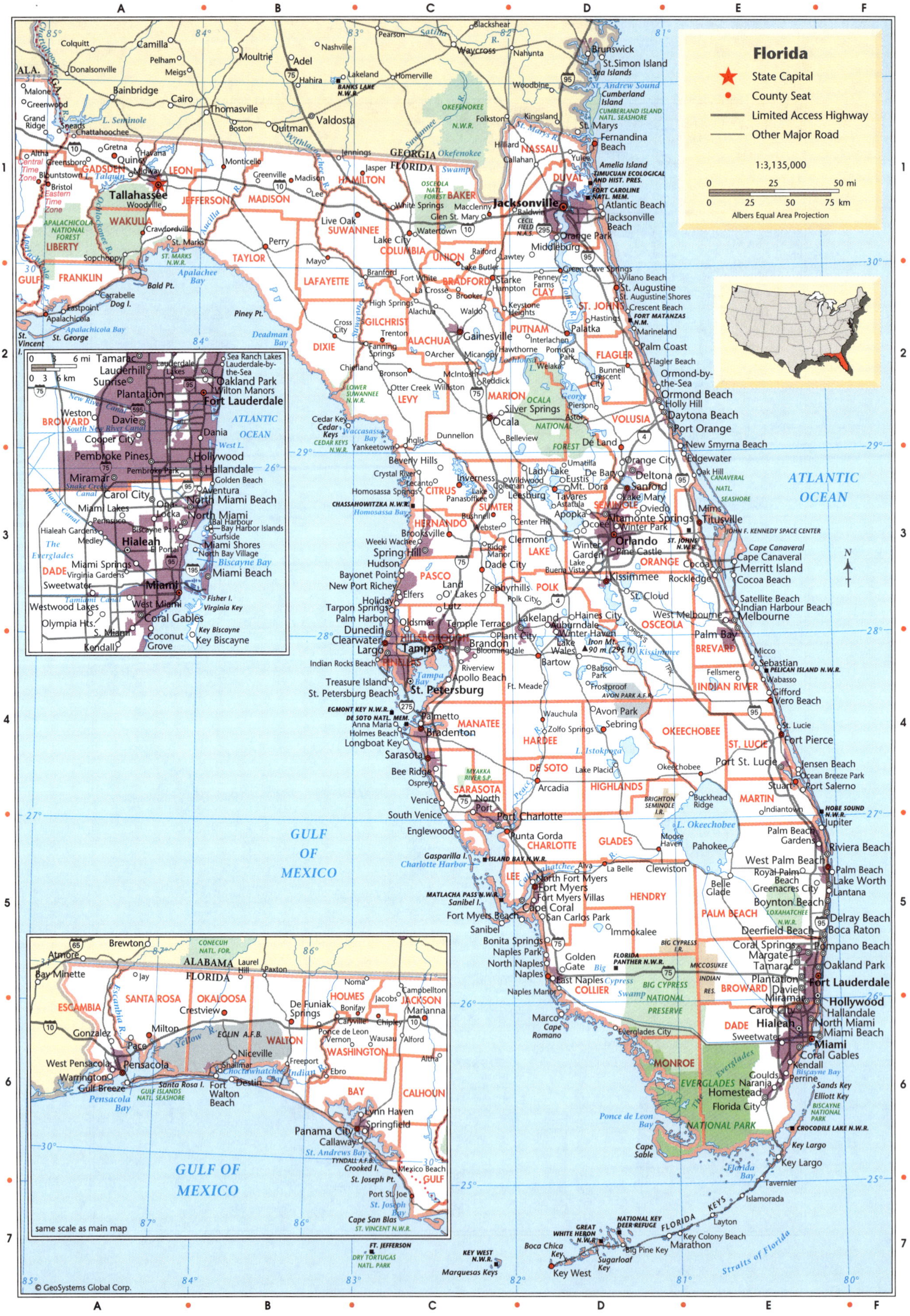

Capital: Atlanta
Area: 59,400 sq. mi.
153,900 sq. km.

Population: 6,917,000
Largest City: Atlanta

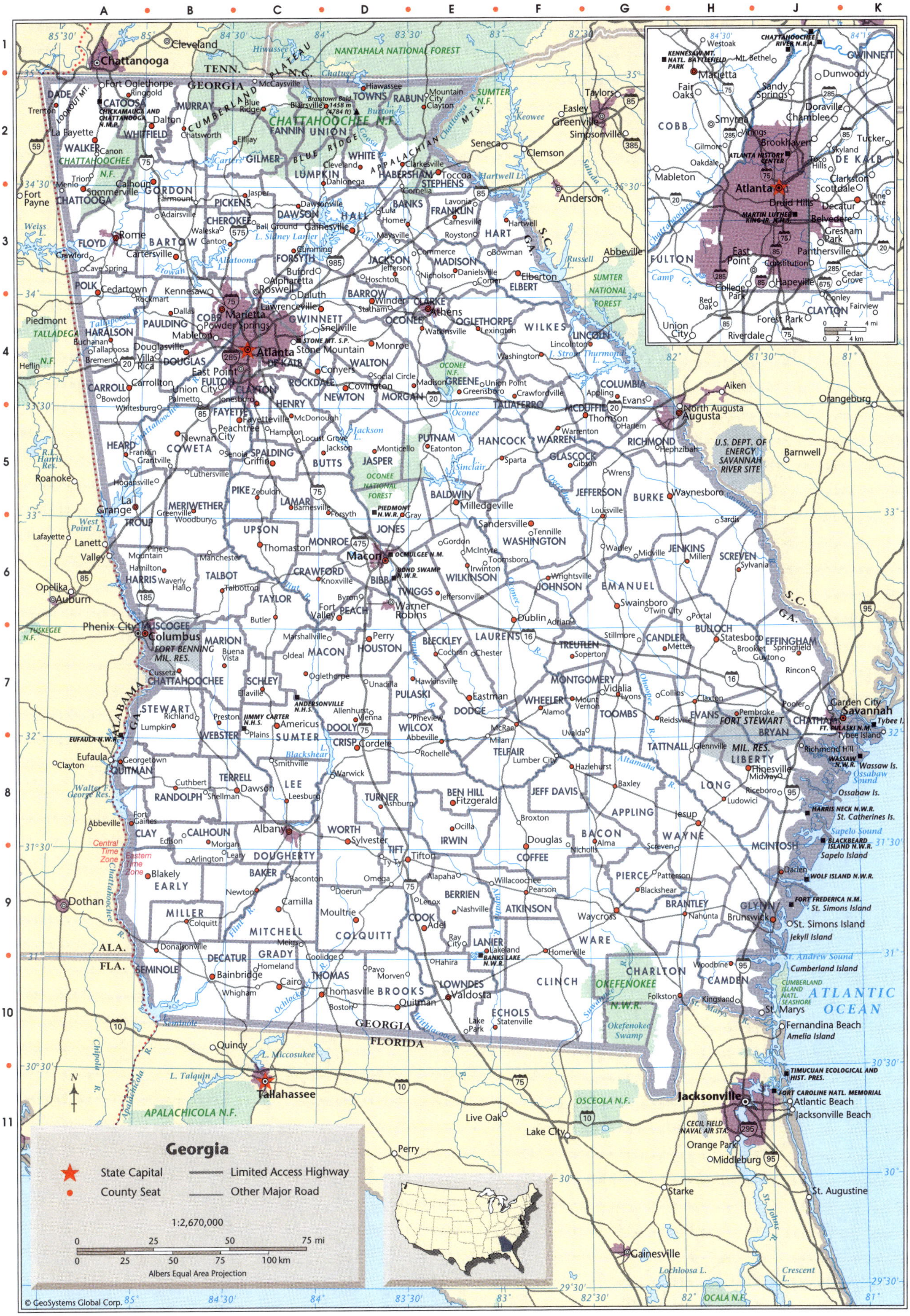

Capital: Honolulu **Area:** 10,900 sq. mi. 28,300 sq. km. **Population:** 1,172,000 **Largest City:** Honolulu

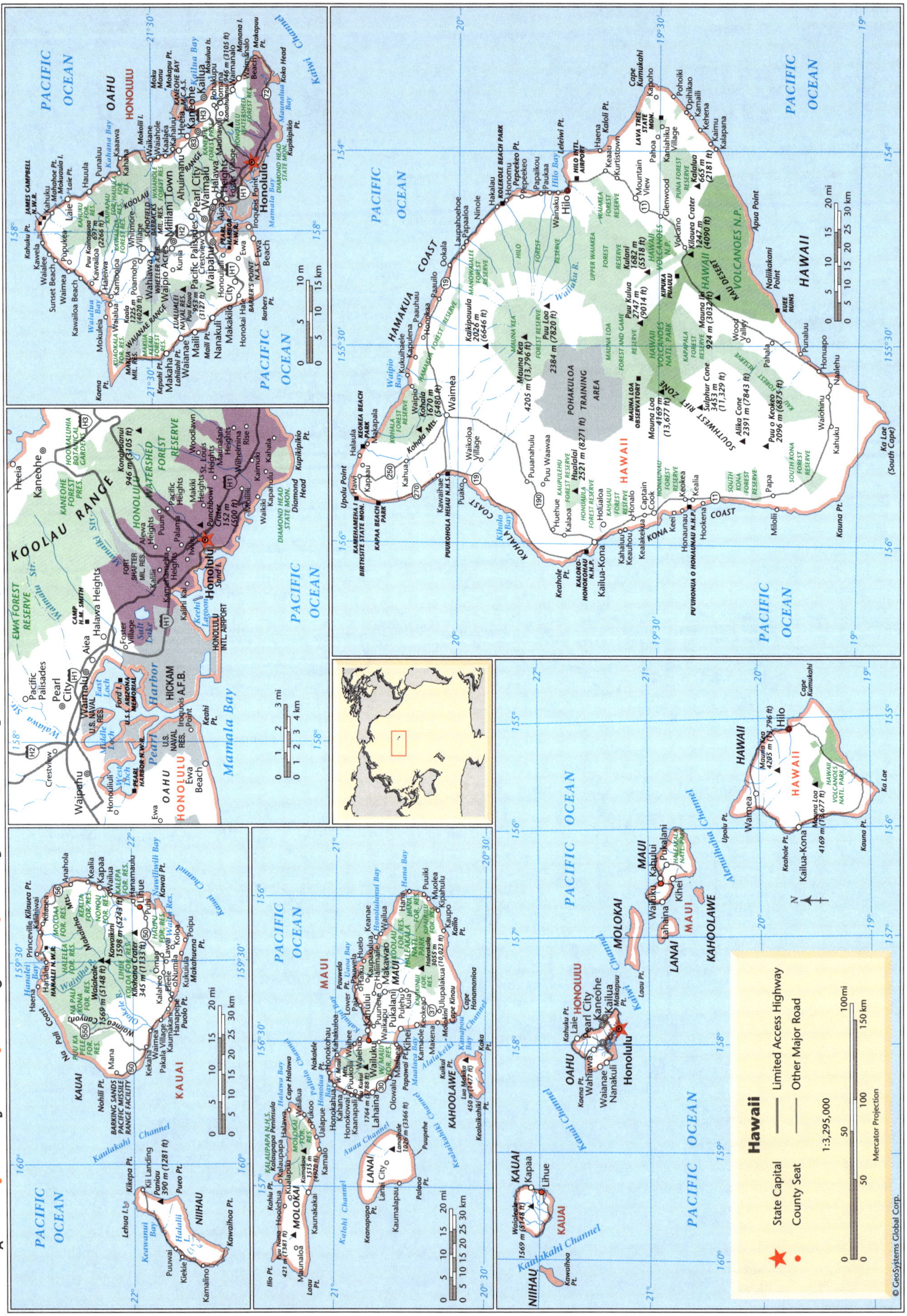

Capital: Boise
Area: 83,600 sq. mi.
216,500 sq. km.
Population: 1,099,000
Largest City: Boise

Capital: Springfield
Area: 57,900 sq. mi.
150,000 sq. km.
Population: 11,697,000
Largest City: Chicago

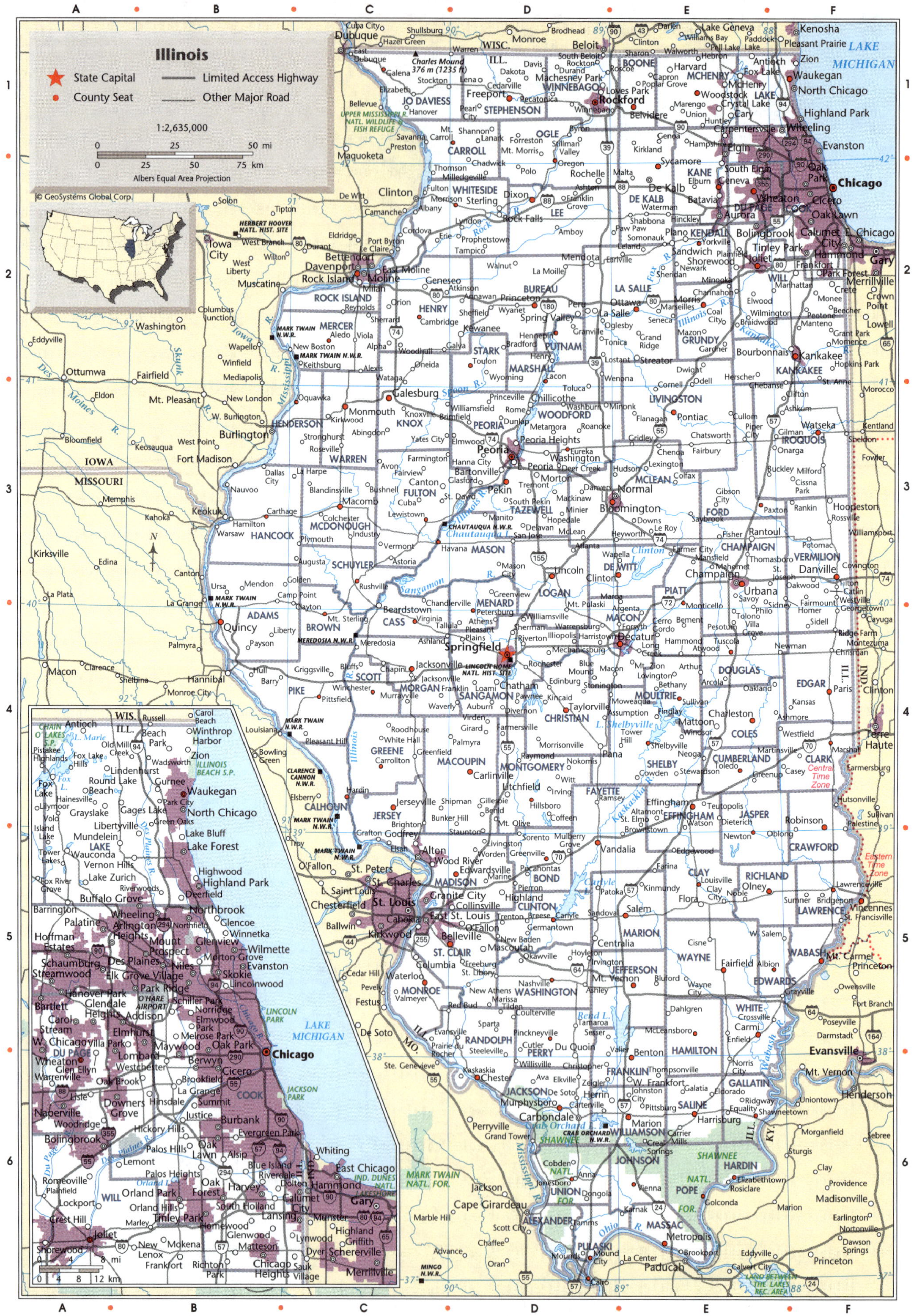

Capital: Indianapolis
Area: 36,400 sq. mi.
94,300 sq. km.
Population: 5,713,000
Largest City: Indianapolis

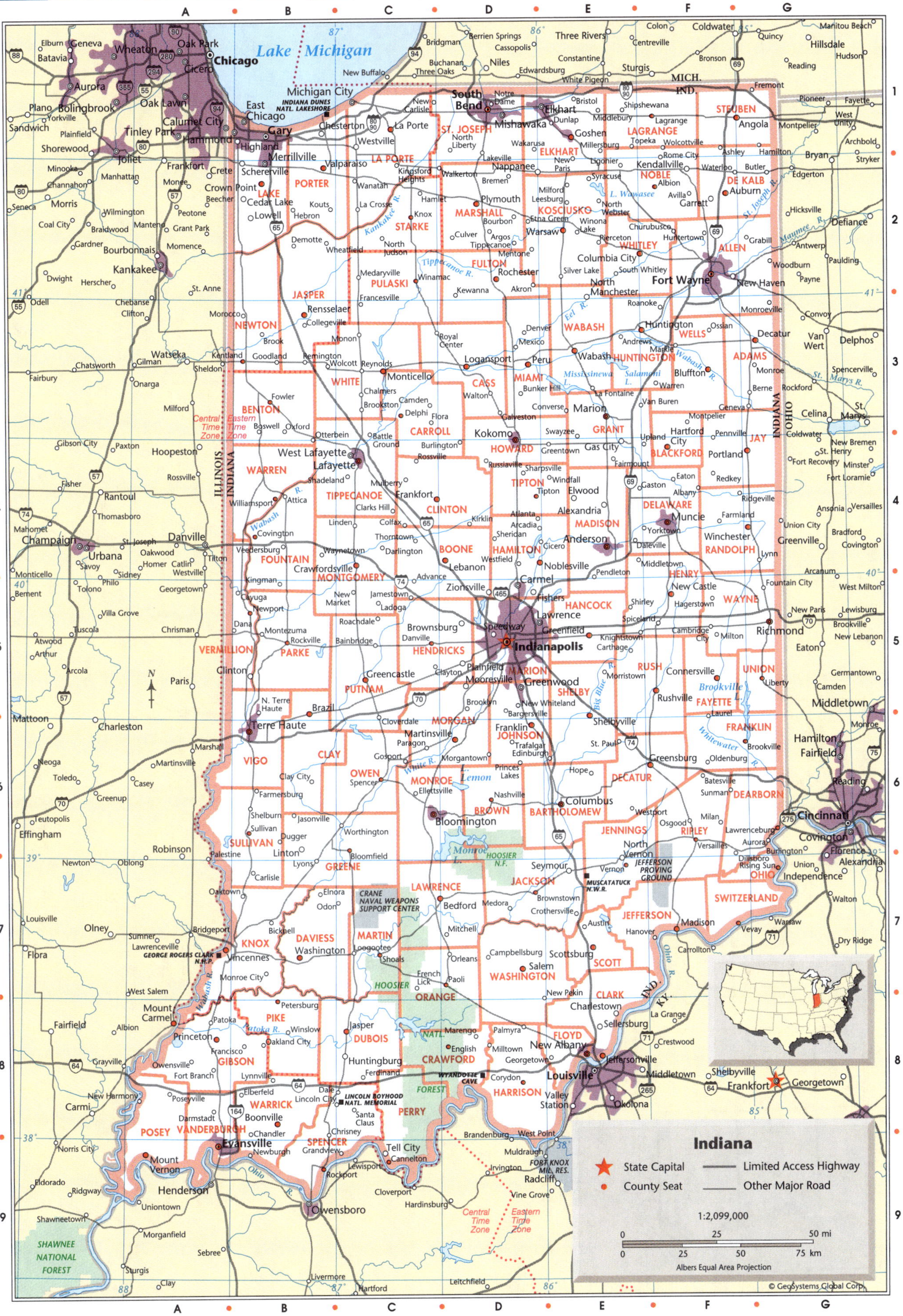

Capital: Des Moines
Area: 56,300 sq. mi. 145,800 sq. km.
Population: 2,814,000
Largest City: Des Moines

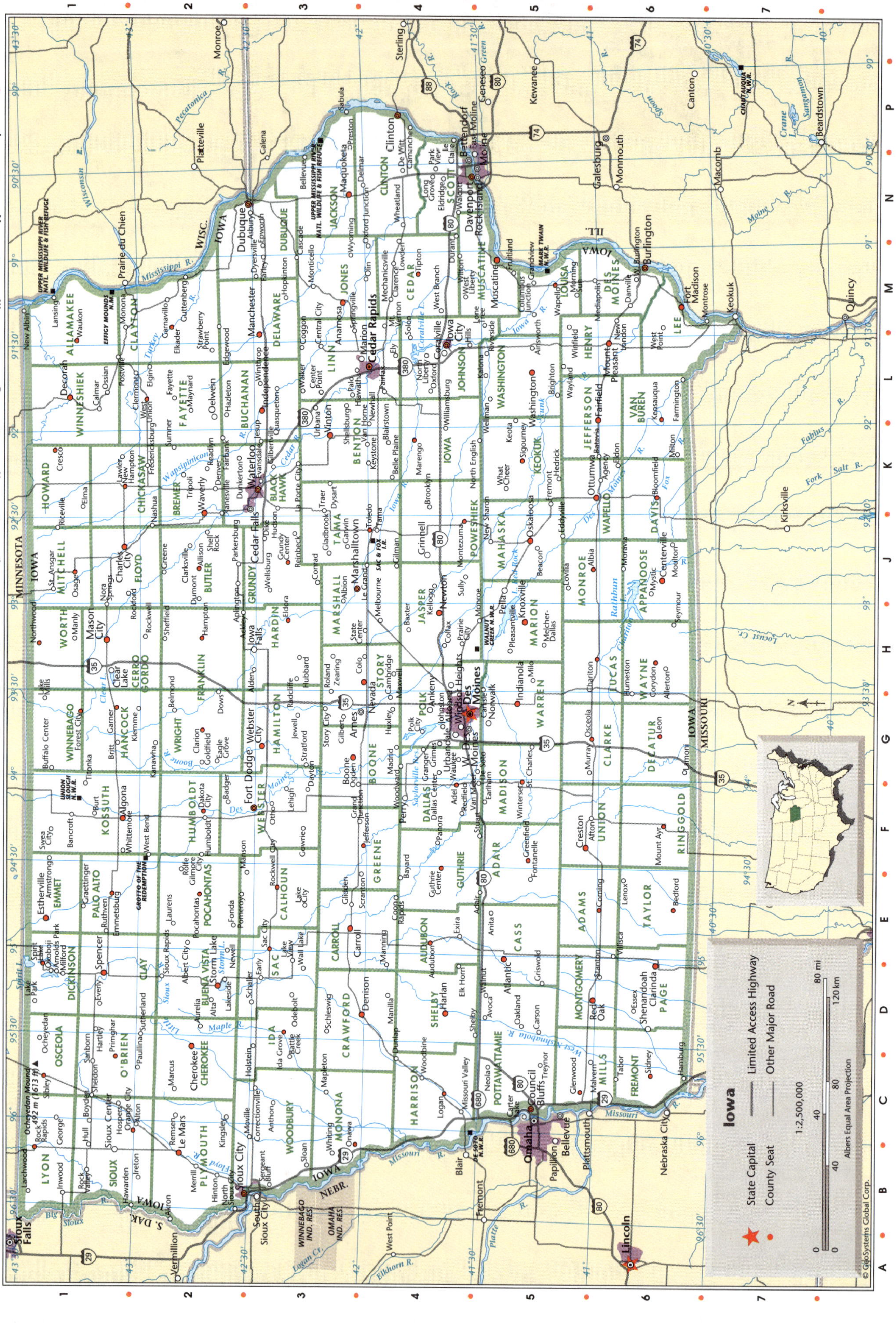

Capital: Topeka
Area: 82,300 sq. mi. 213,100 sq. km.
Population: 2,531,000
Largest City: Wichita

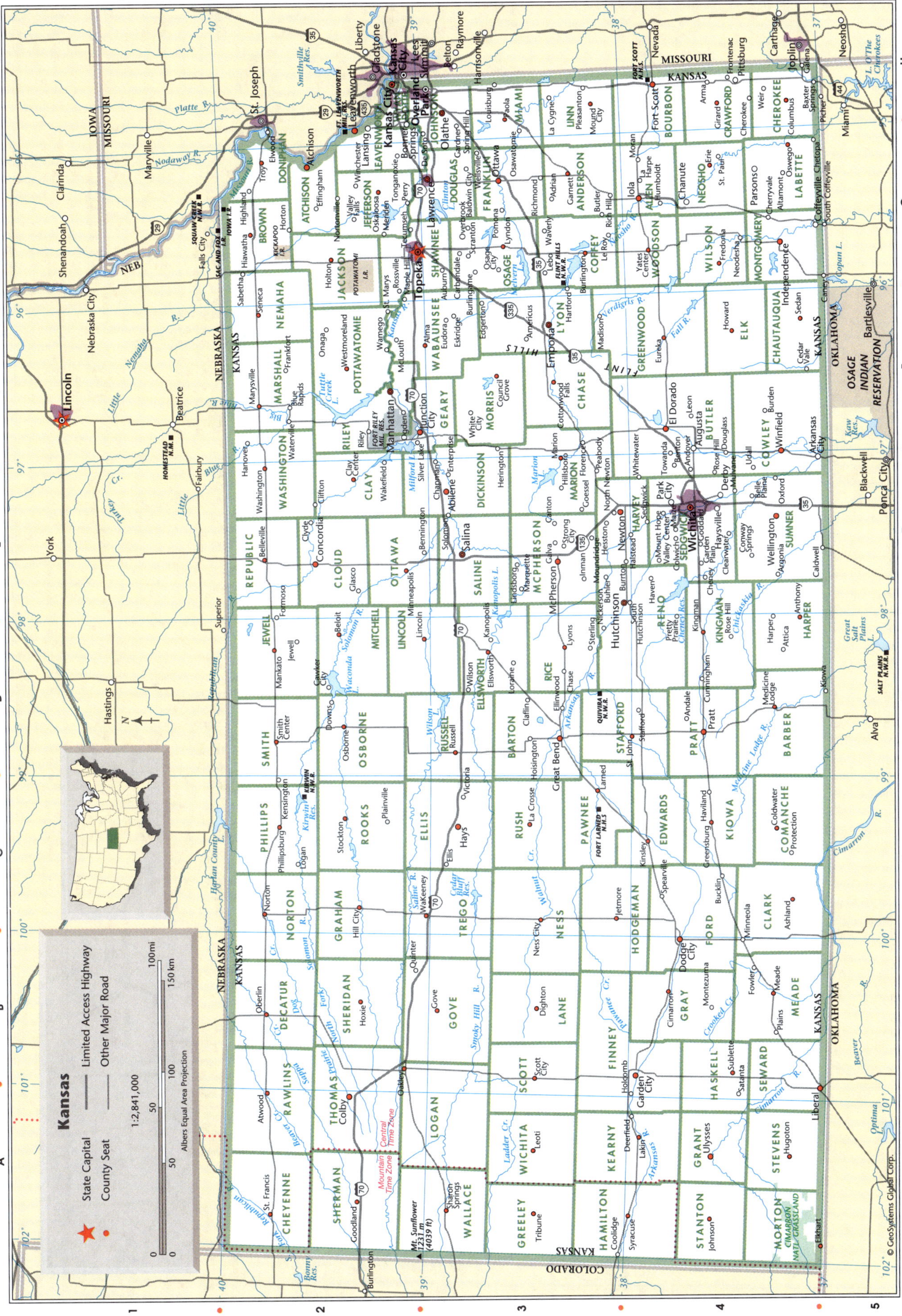

Capital: Frankfort
Area: 40,400 sq. mi.
104,700 sq. km.

Population: 3,789,000
Largest City: Louisville

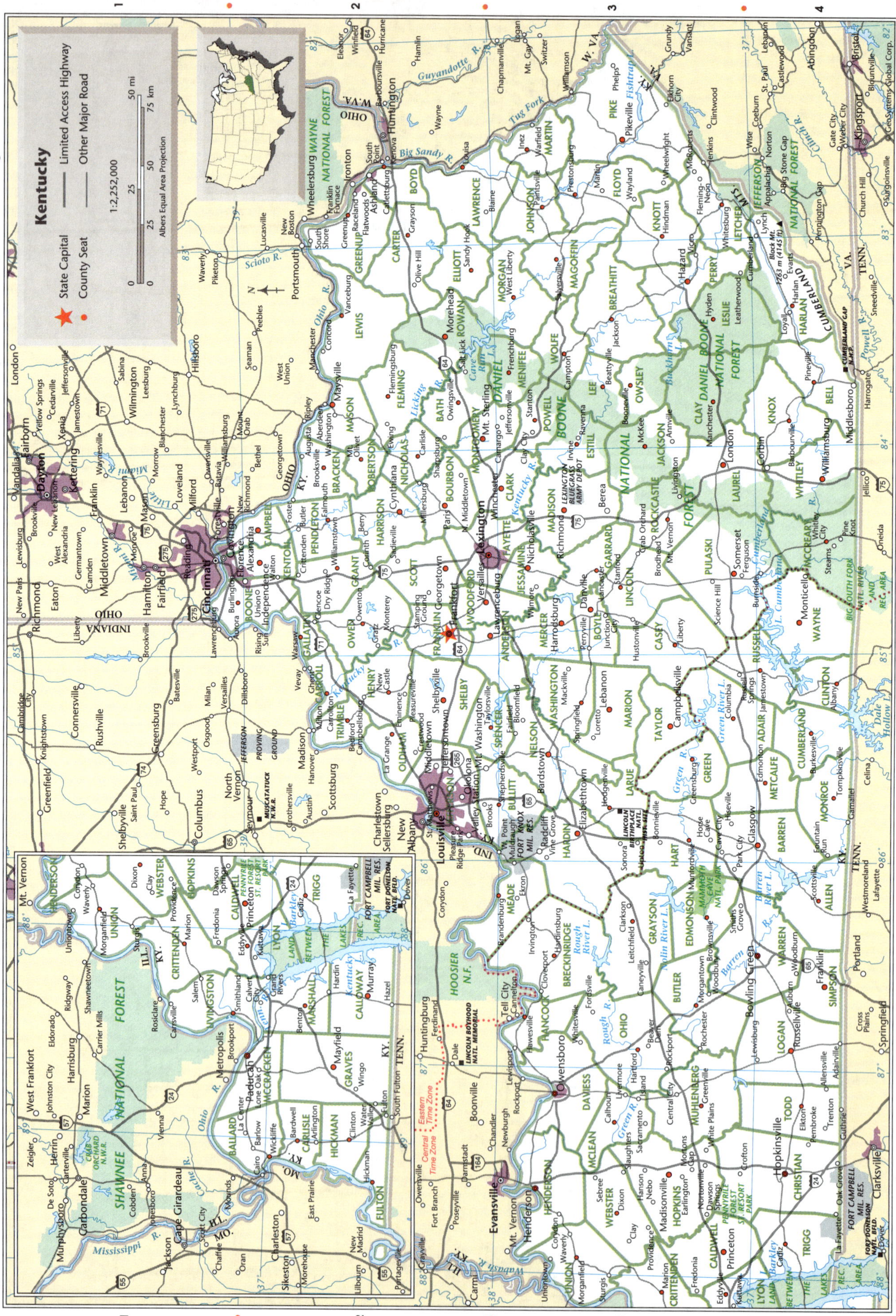

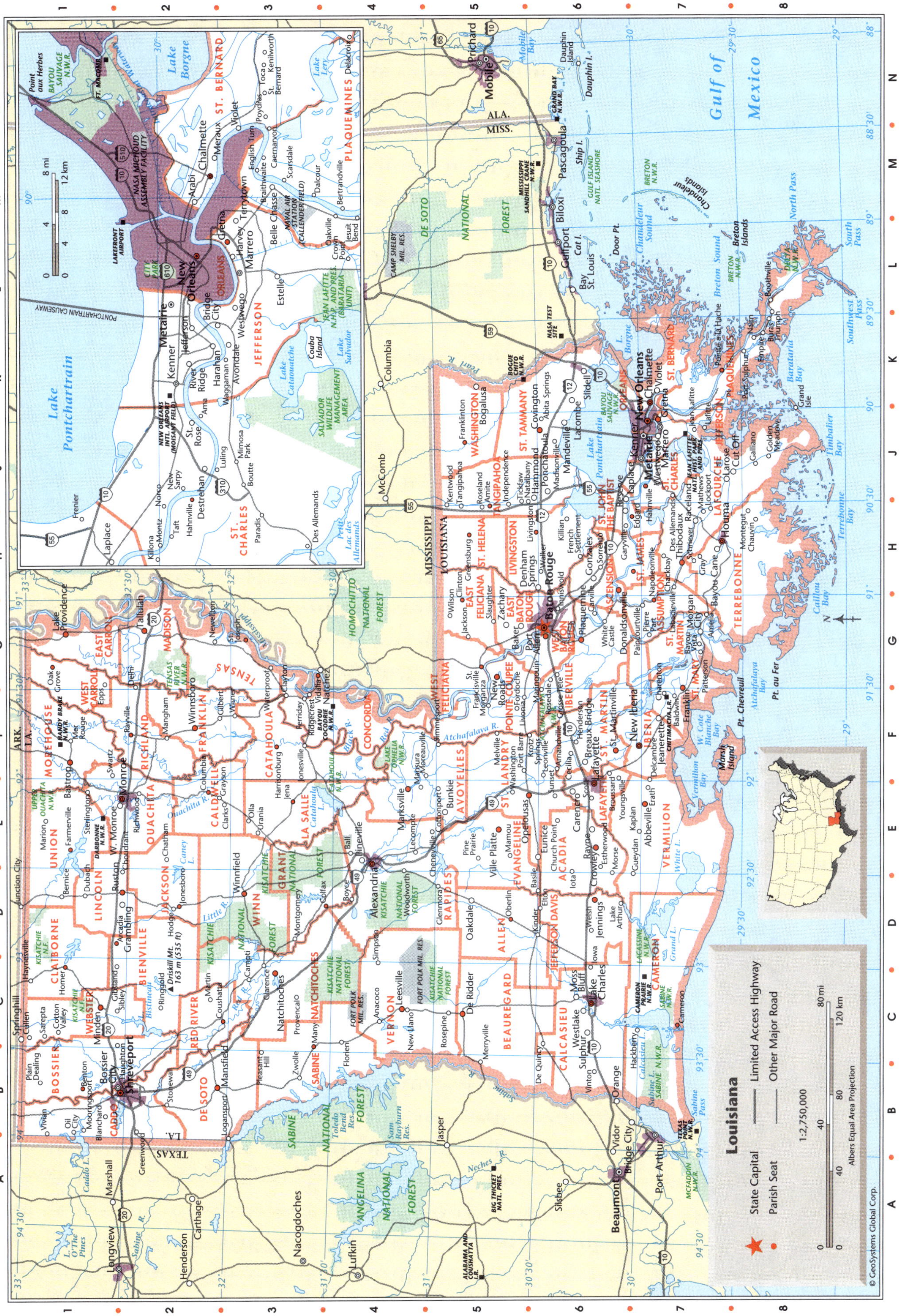

Louisiana
State Capital
Parish Seat
Limited Access Highway
Other Major Road
1:2,750,000
0 40 80 mi
0 40 80 120 km
Albers Equal Area Projection
© GeoSystems Global Corp.
Gulf of Mexico
Lake Pontchartrain
Baton Rouge
New Orleans
Shreveport
MISSISSIPPI
TEXAS
ARK.

Capital: Augusta
Area: 35,400 sq. mi. 91,700 sq. km.
Population: 1,239,000
Largest City: Portland

Capital: Annapolis
Area: 12,400 sq. mi. 32,100 sq. km.
Population: 4,965,000
Largest City: Baltimore

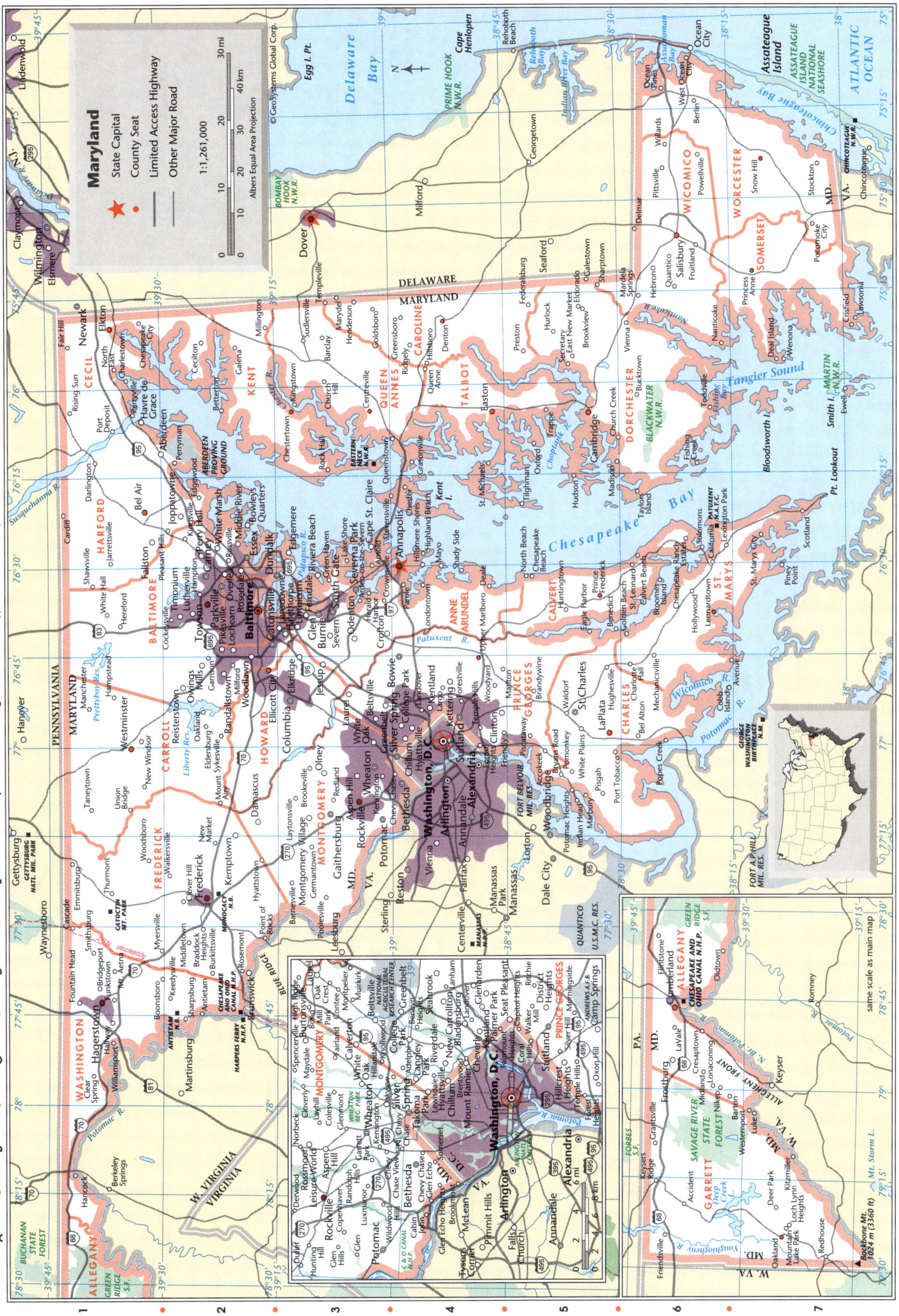

Capital: Boston
Area: 10,600 sq. mi.
27,300 sq. km.
Population: 6,012,000
Largest City: Boston

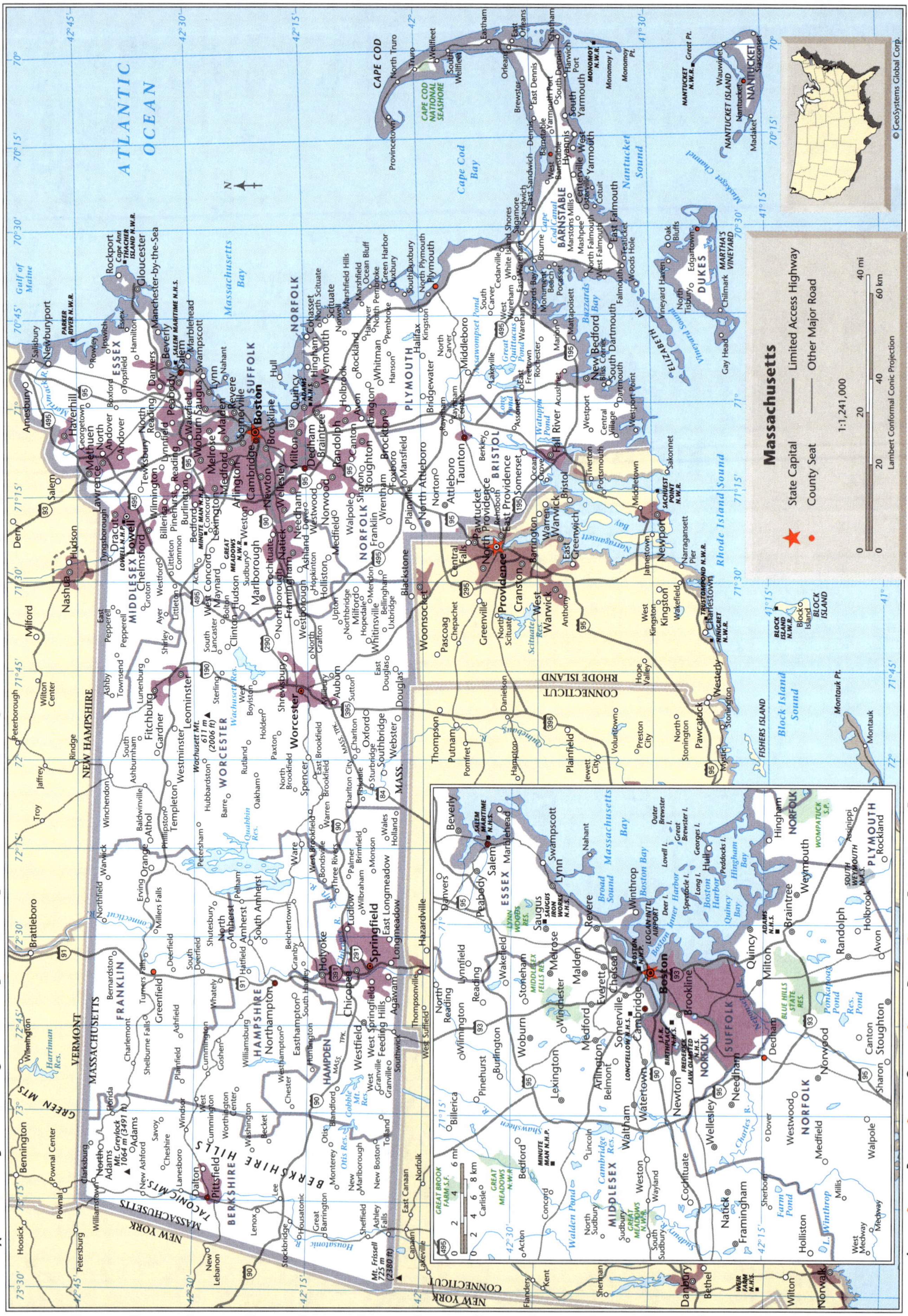

Capital: Lansing
Area: 96,700 sq. mi.
250,500 sq. km.
Population: 9,478,000
Largest City: Detroit

Capital: St. Paul
Area: 86,900 sq. mi.
225,200 sq. km.
Population: 4,517,000
Largest City: Minneapolis

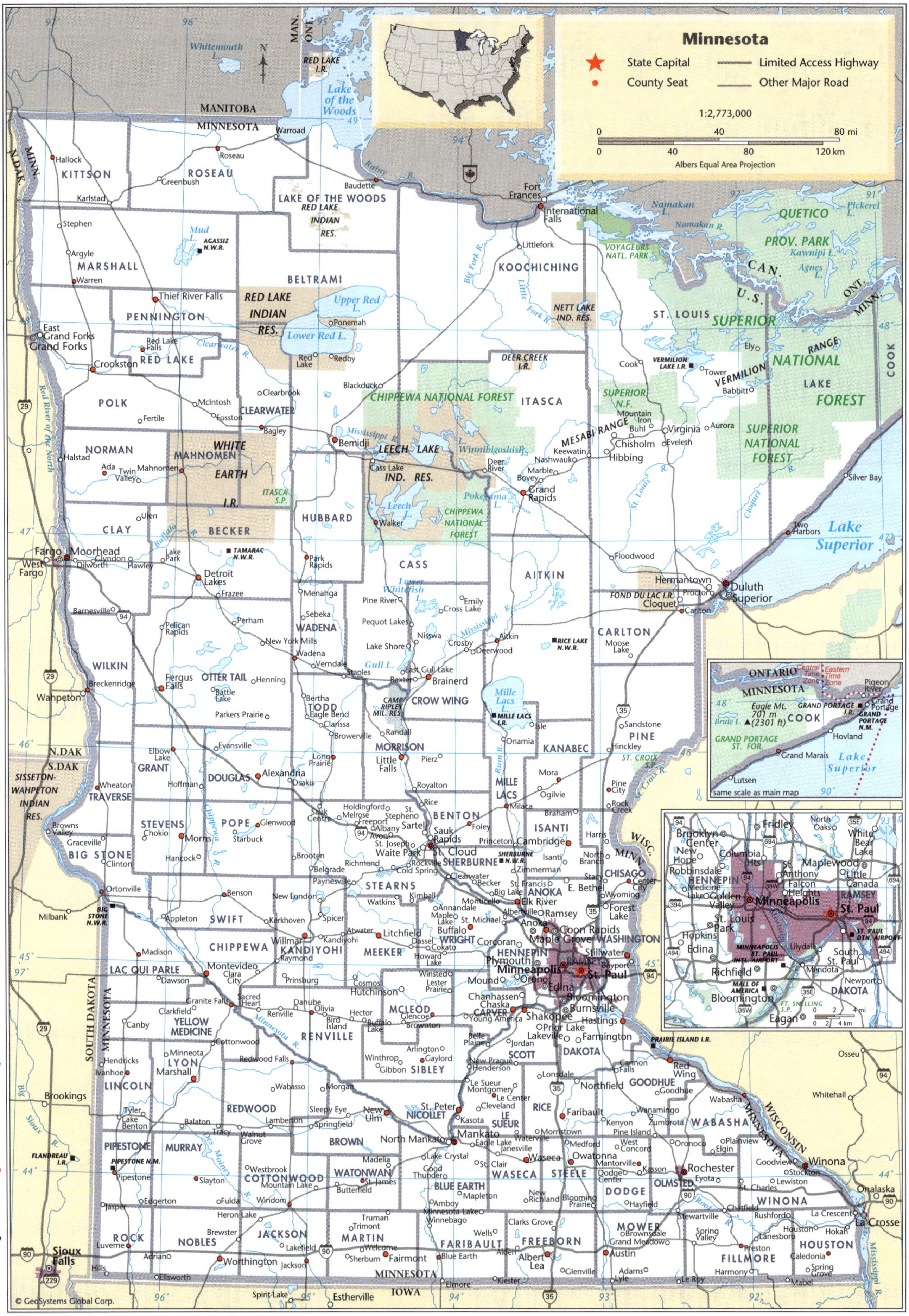

Capital: Jackson
Area: 48,400 sq. mi.
125,400 sq. km.
Population: 2,643,000
Largest City: Jackson

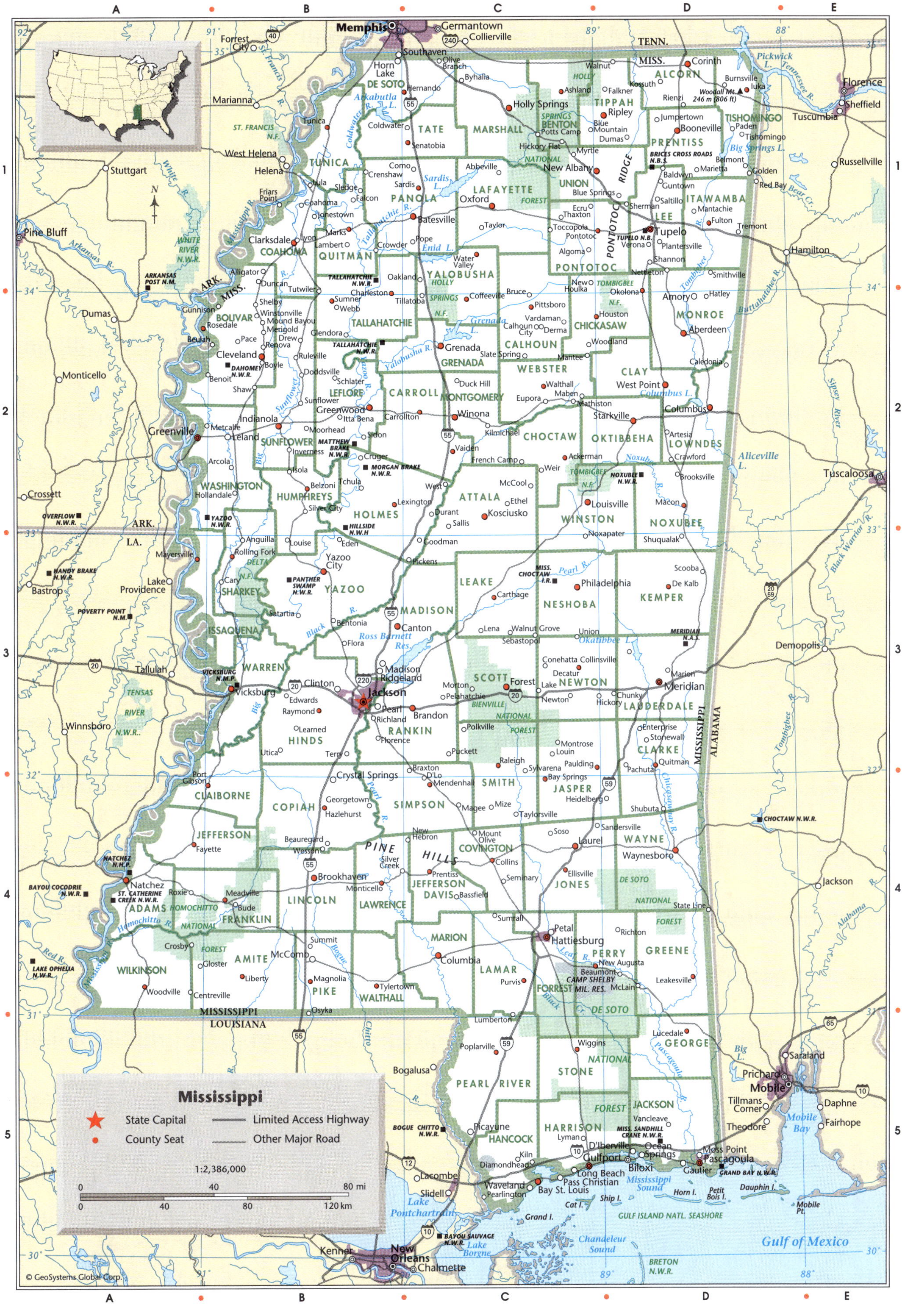

Capital: Jefferson City
Area: 69,700 sq. mi.
180,500 sq. km.
Population: 5,234,000
Largest City: St. Louis

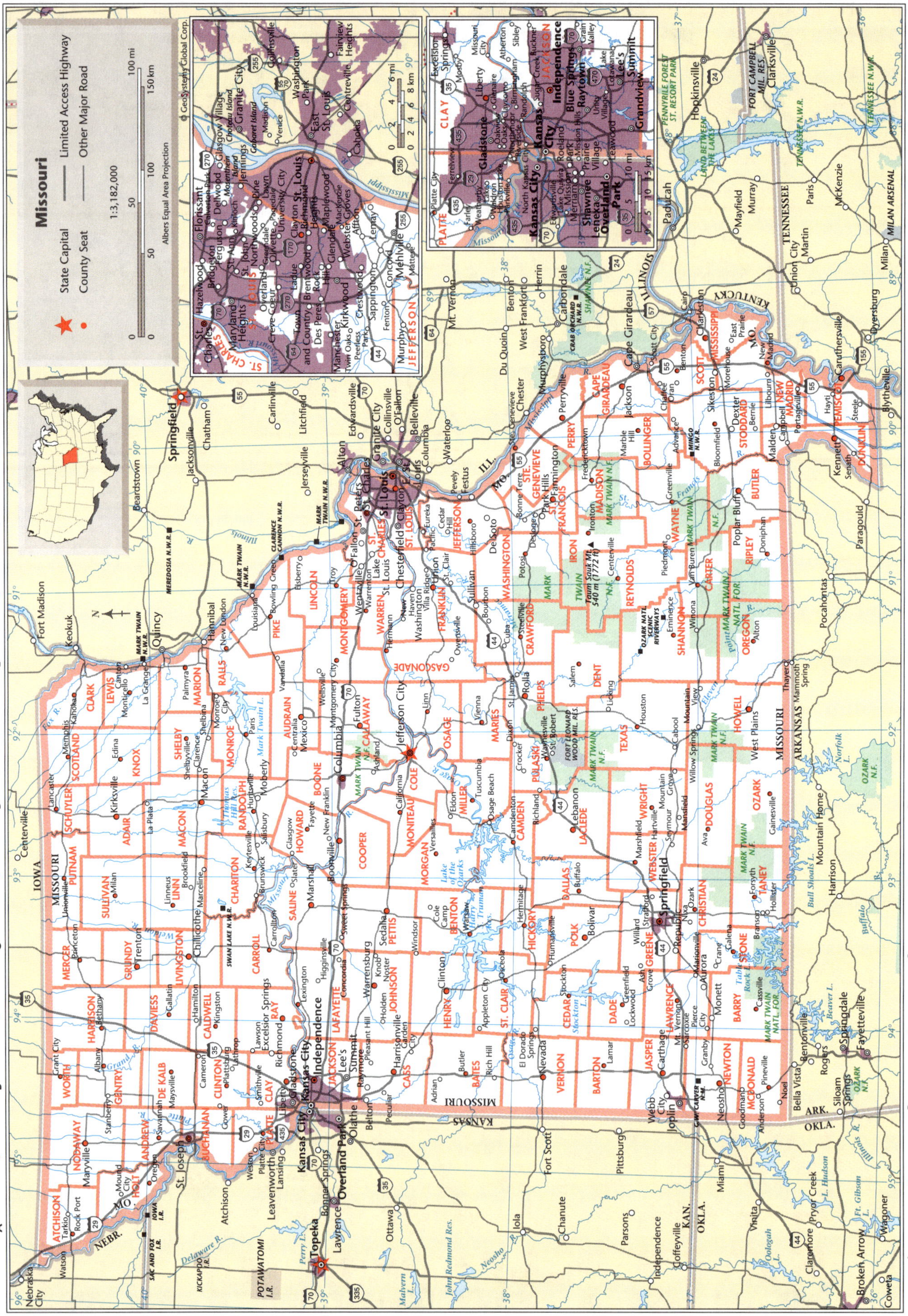

Capital: Helena
Area: 147,000 sq. mi.
380,800 sq. km.
Population: 839,000
Largest City: Billings

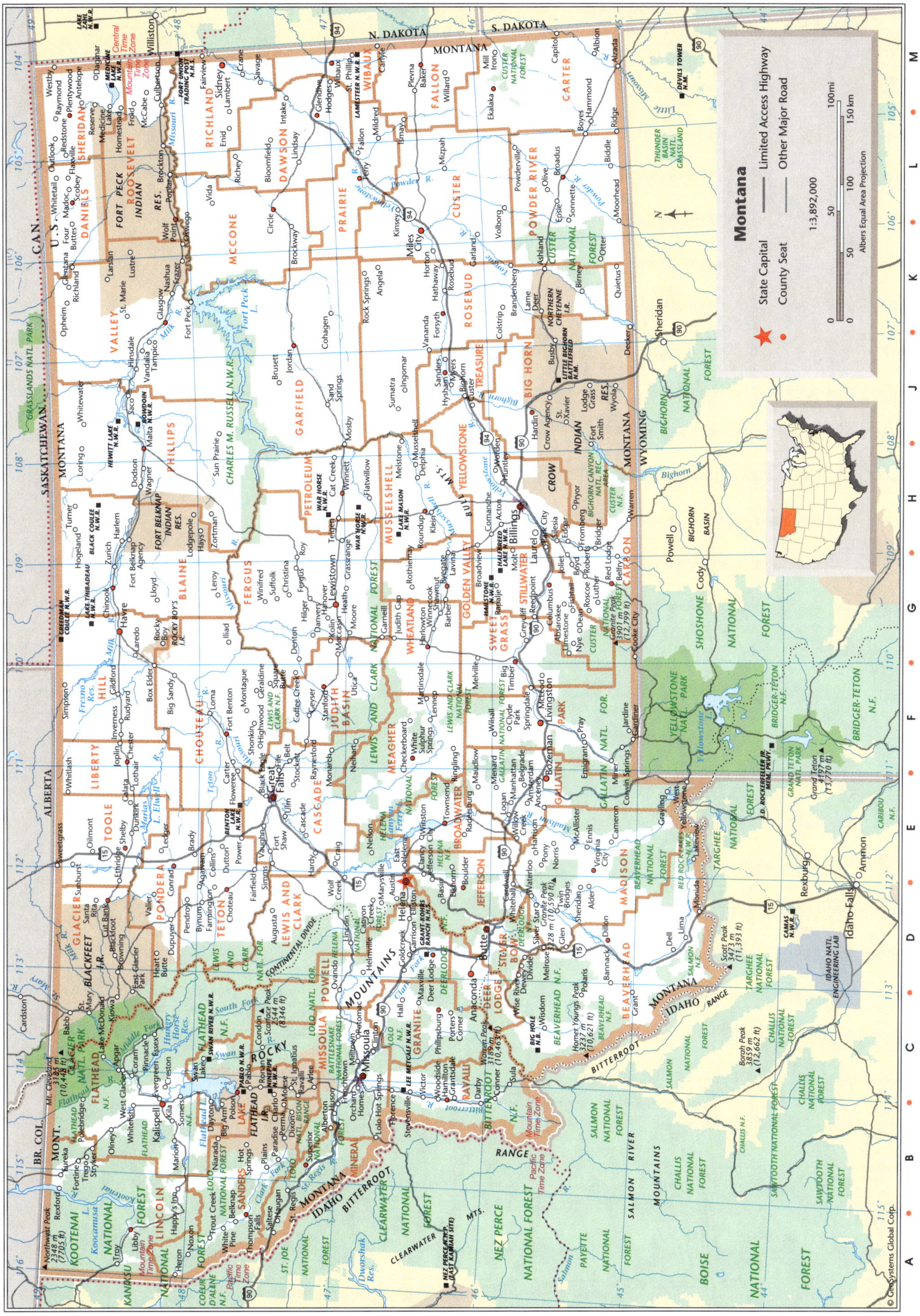

Capital: Lincoln
Area: 77,400 sq. mi.
200,300 sq. km.

Population: 1,607,000
Largest City: Omaha

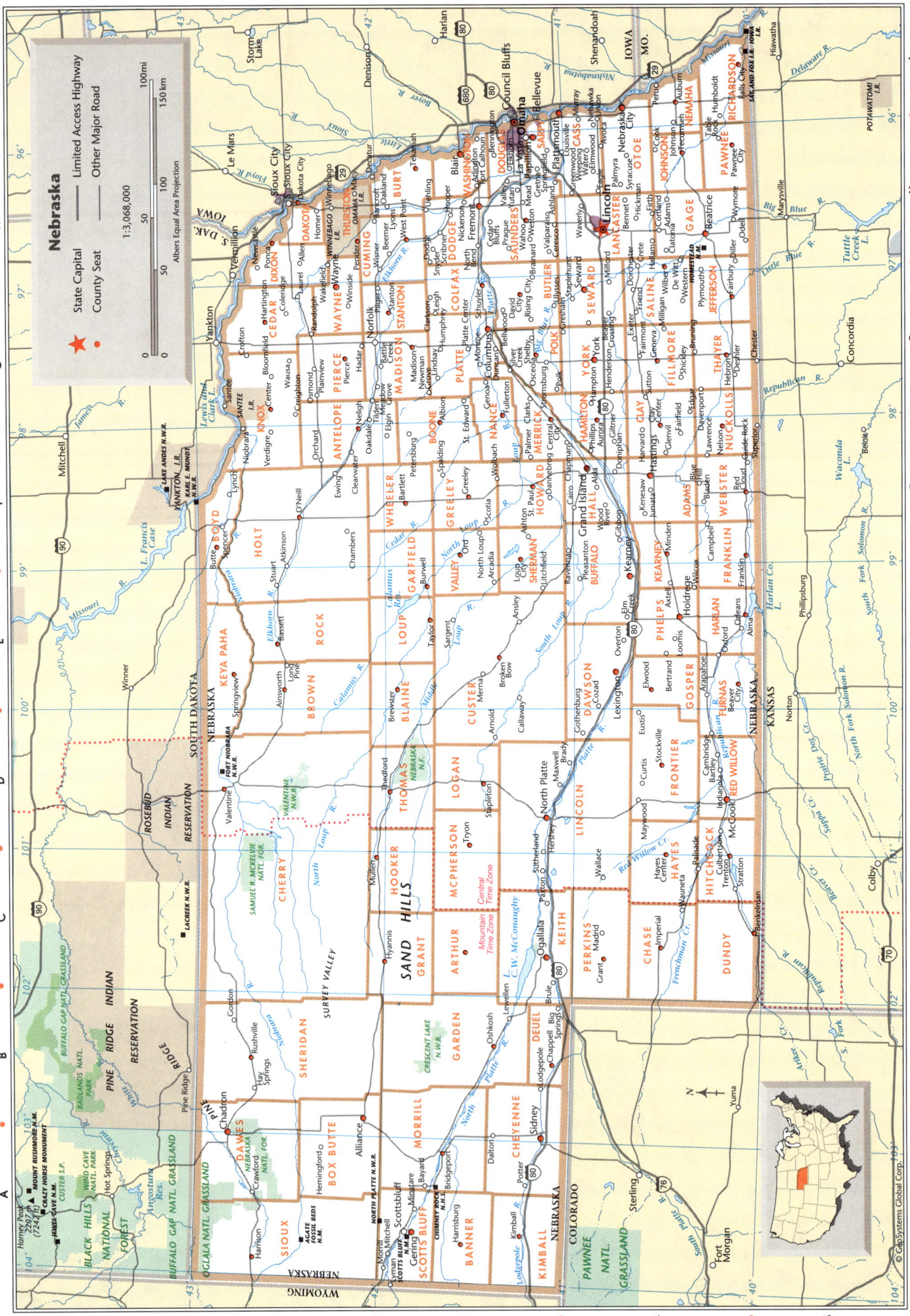

Capital: Carson City
Area: 110,600 sq. mi. 286,400 sq. km.
Population: 1,389,000
Largest City: Las Vegas

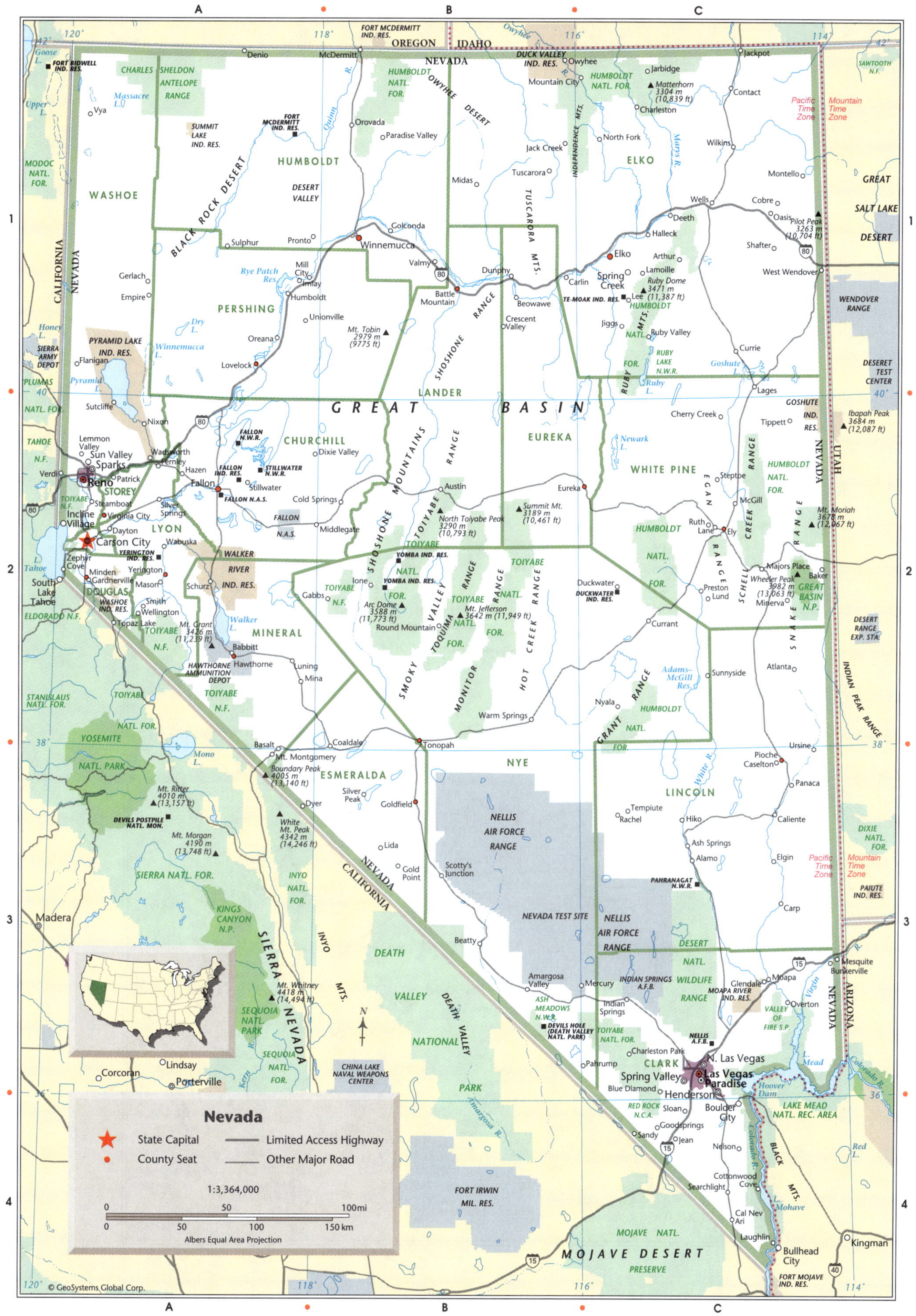

Capital: Concord
Area: 9,400 sq. mi.
24,200 sq. km.
Population: 1,125,000
Largest City: Manchester

Capital: Trenton
Area: 8,700 sq. mi.
22,600 sq. km.
Population: 7,879,000
Largest City: Newark

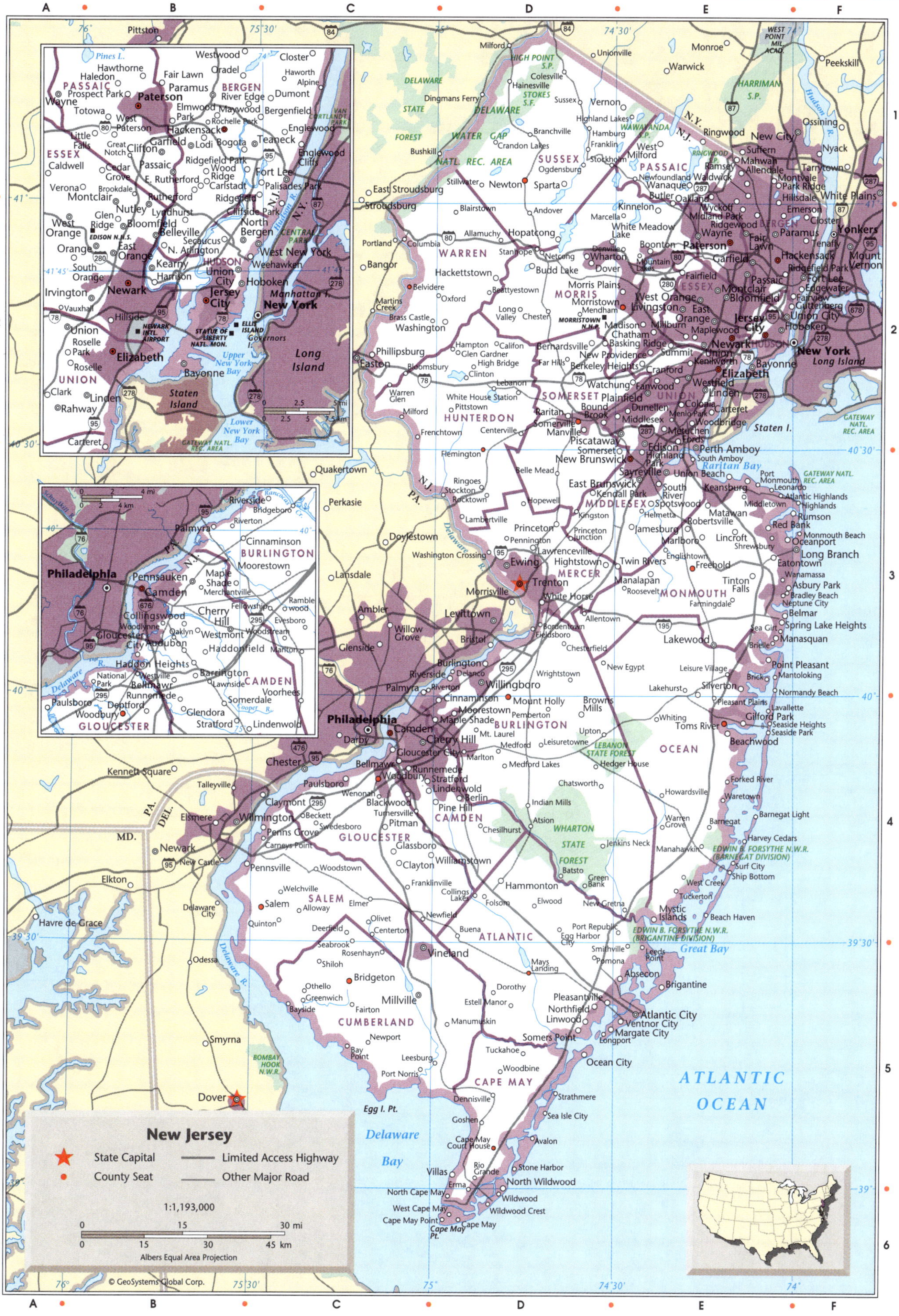

NEW MEXICO

Capital: Santa Fe
Area: 121,600 sq. mi. 314,900 sq. km.
Population: 1,616,000
Largest City: Albuquerque

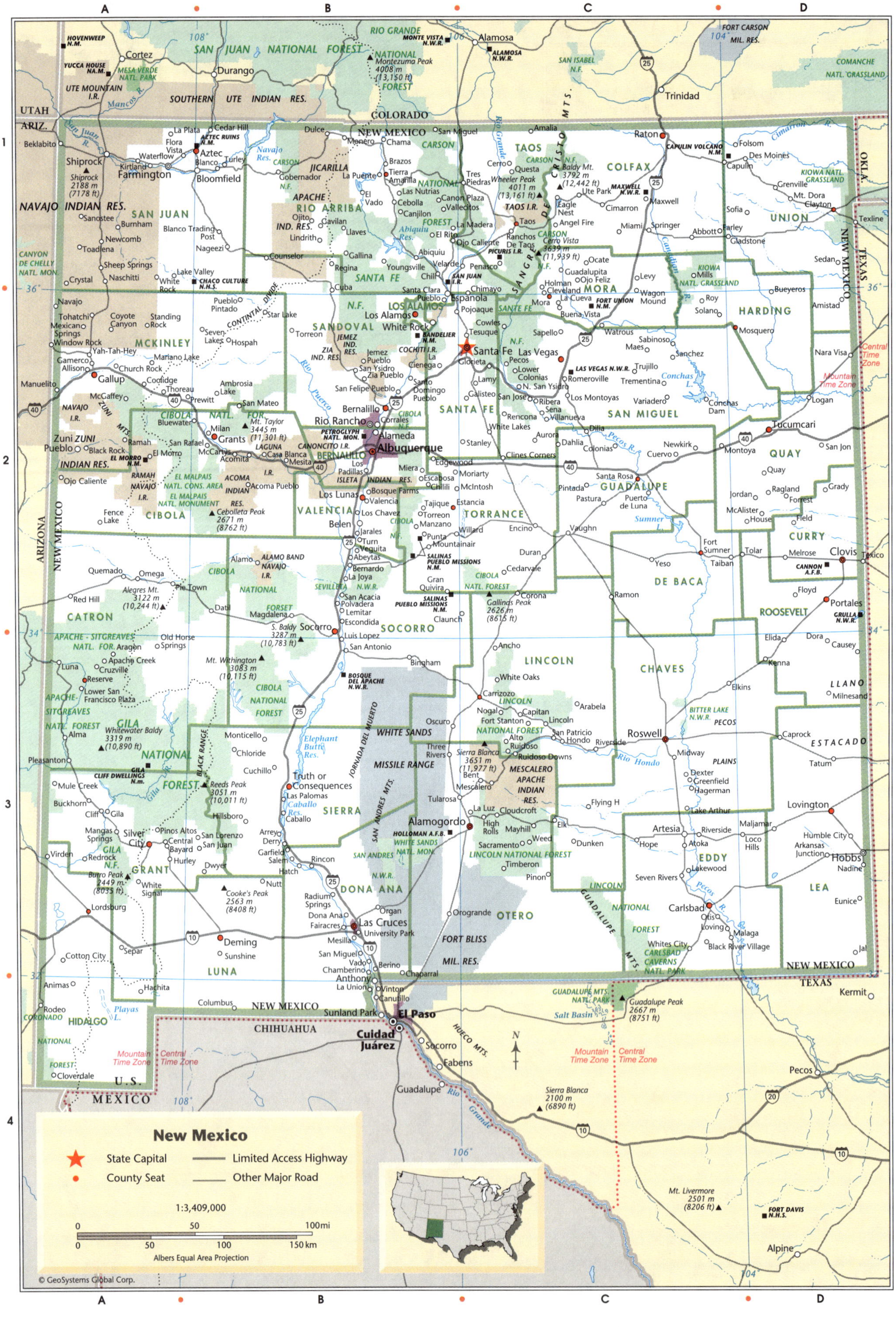

Capital: Albany
Area: 54,700 sq. mi. 141,100 sq. km.

Population: 18,197,000
Largest City: New York

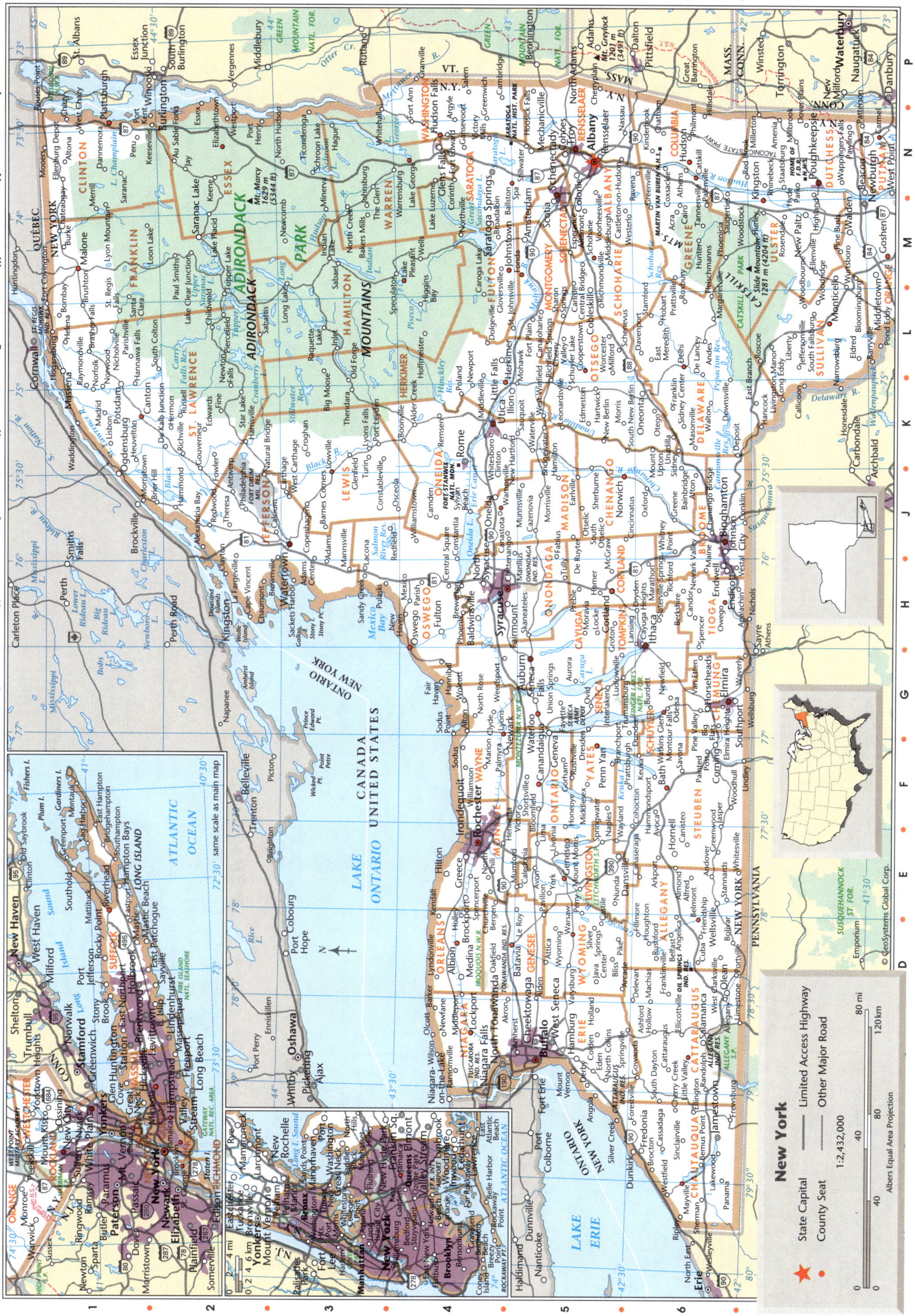

Capital: Raleigh
Area: 53,800 sq. mi.
139,400 sq. km.

Population: 6,945,000
Largest City: Charlotte

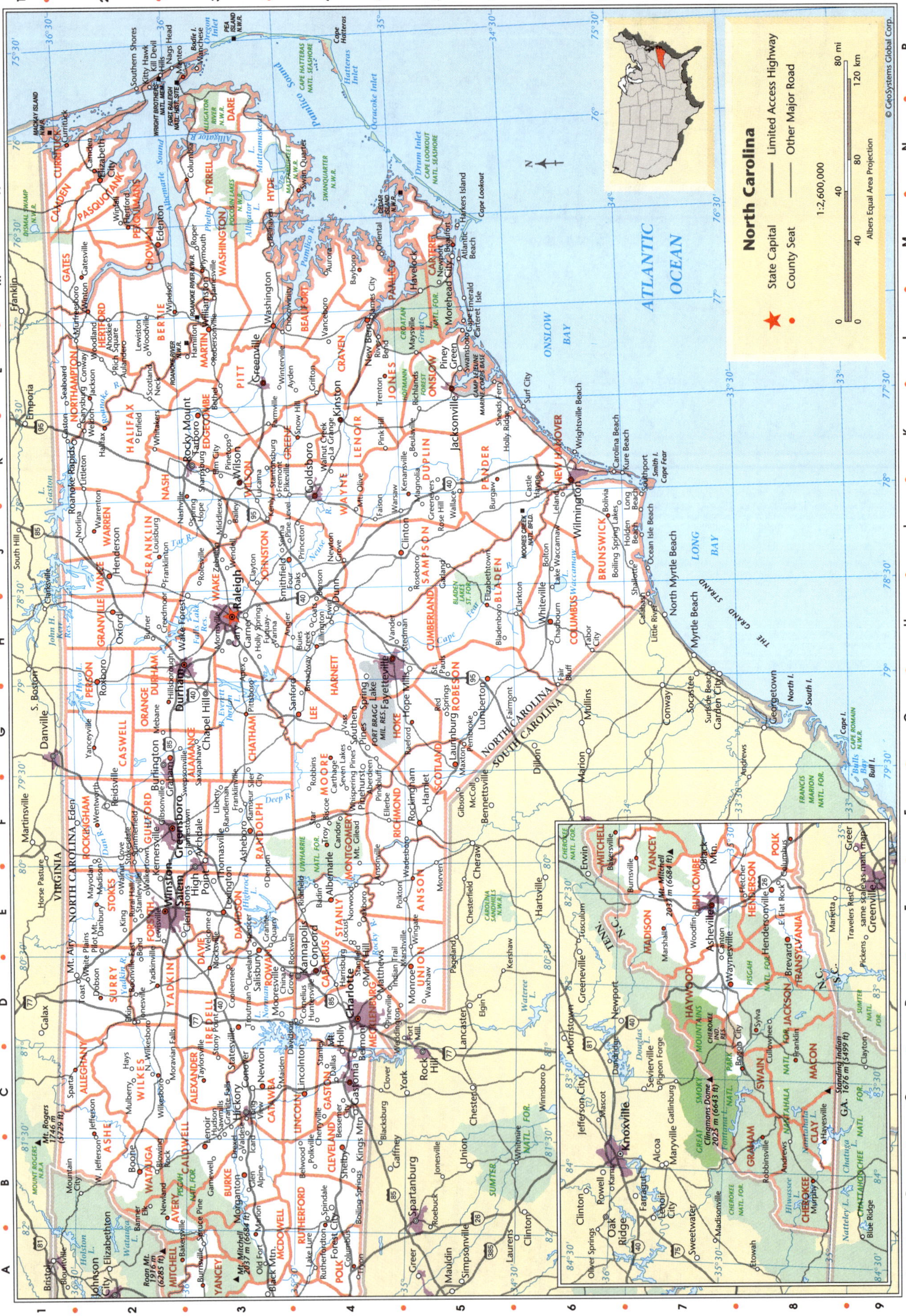

Capital: Bismarck
Area: 70,700 sq. mi.
183,100 sq. km.

Population: 635,000
Largest City: Fargo

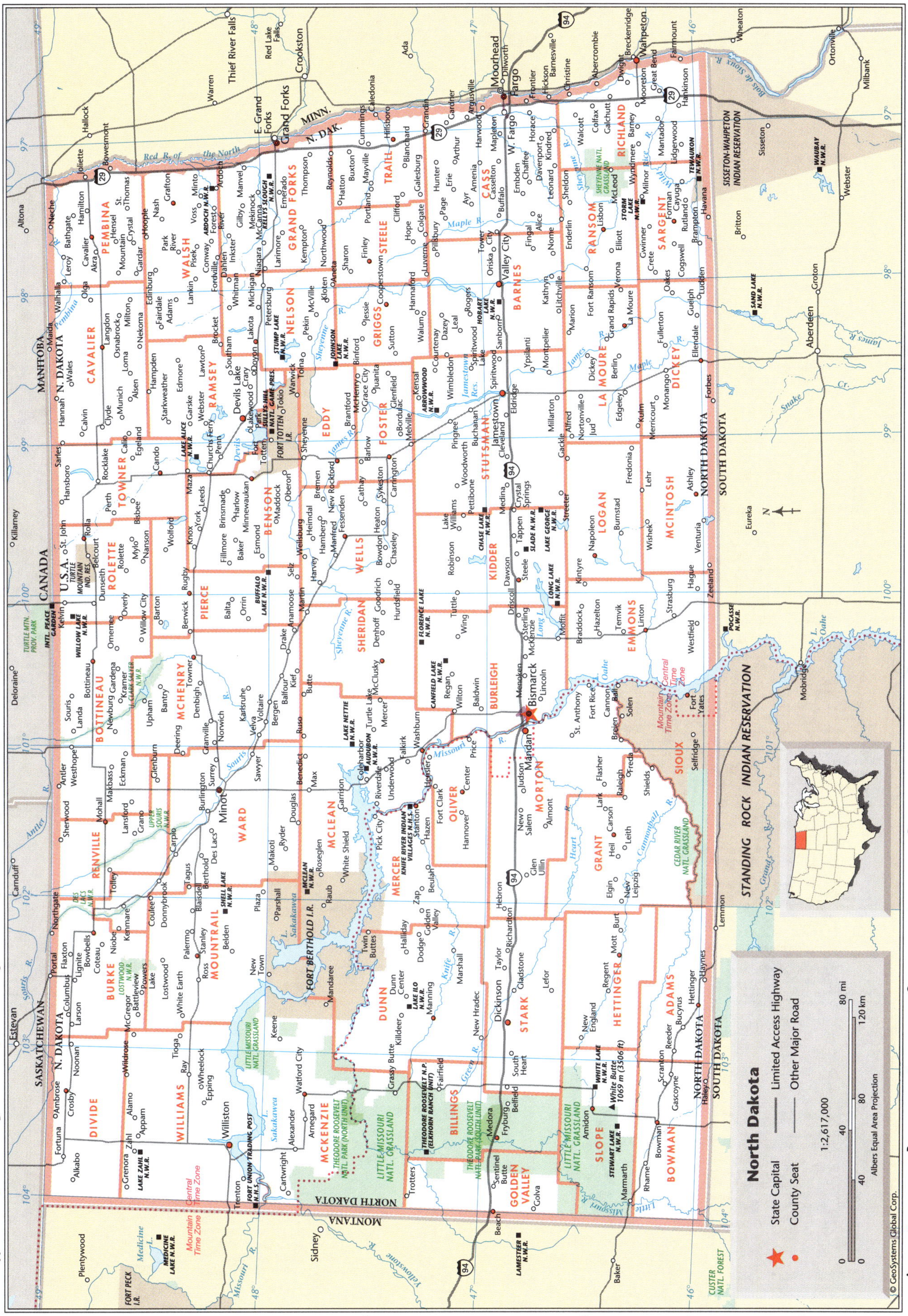

Capital: Columbus
Area: 44,800 sq. mi. 116,100 sq. km.
Population: 11,091,000
Largest City: Columbus

Capital: Oklahoma City **Population:** 3,231,000
Area: 69,900 sq. mi. **Largest City:** Oklahoma City
181,000 sq. km.

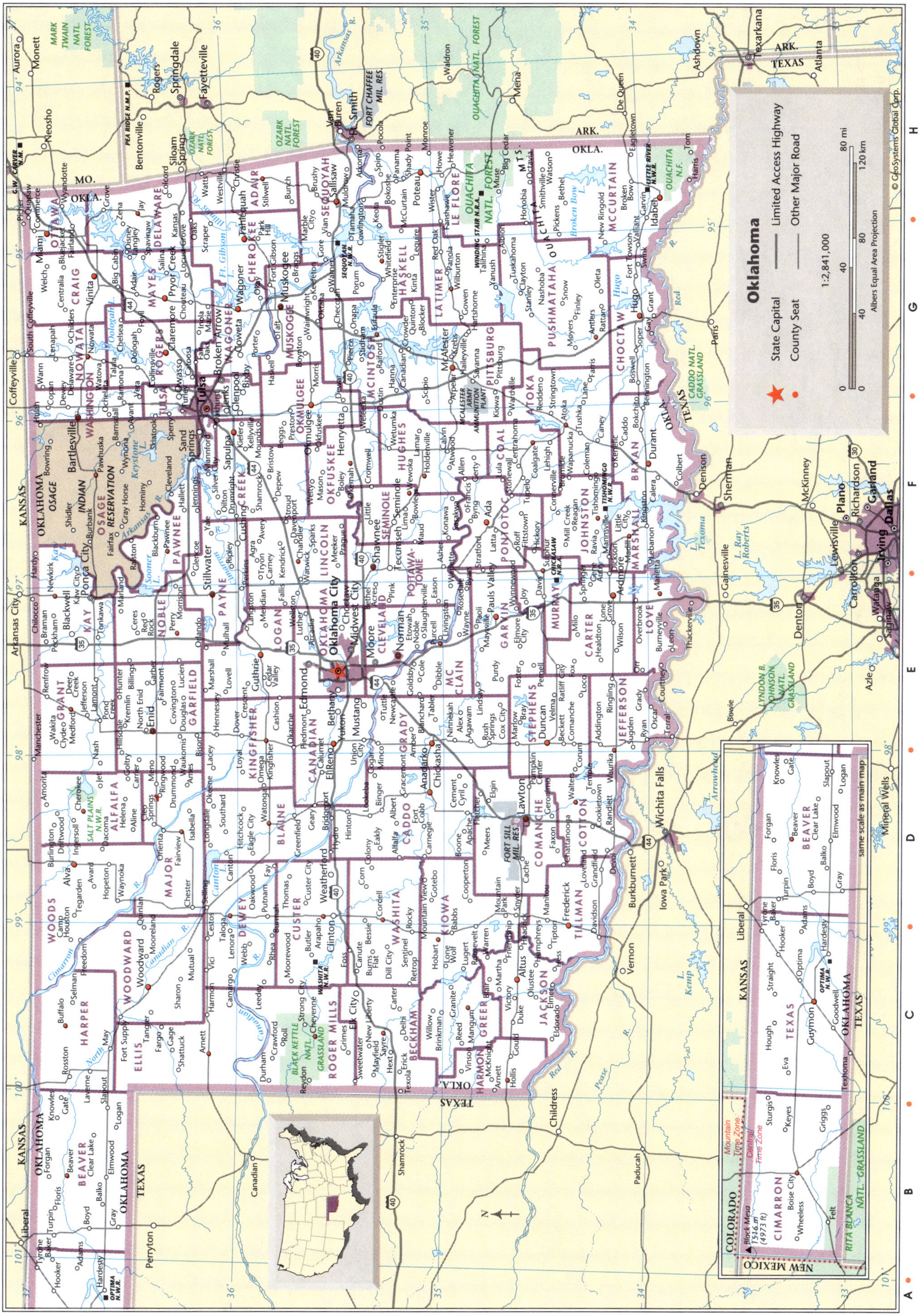

Capital: Salem
Area: 98,400 sq. mi. 254,800 sq. km.
Population: 3,032,000
Largest City: Portland

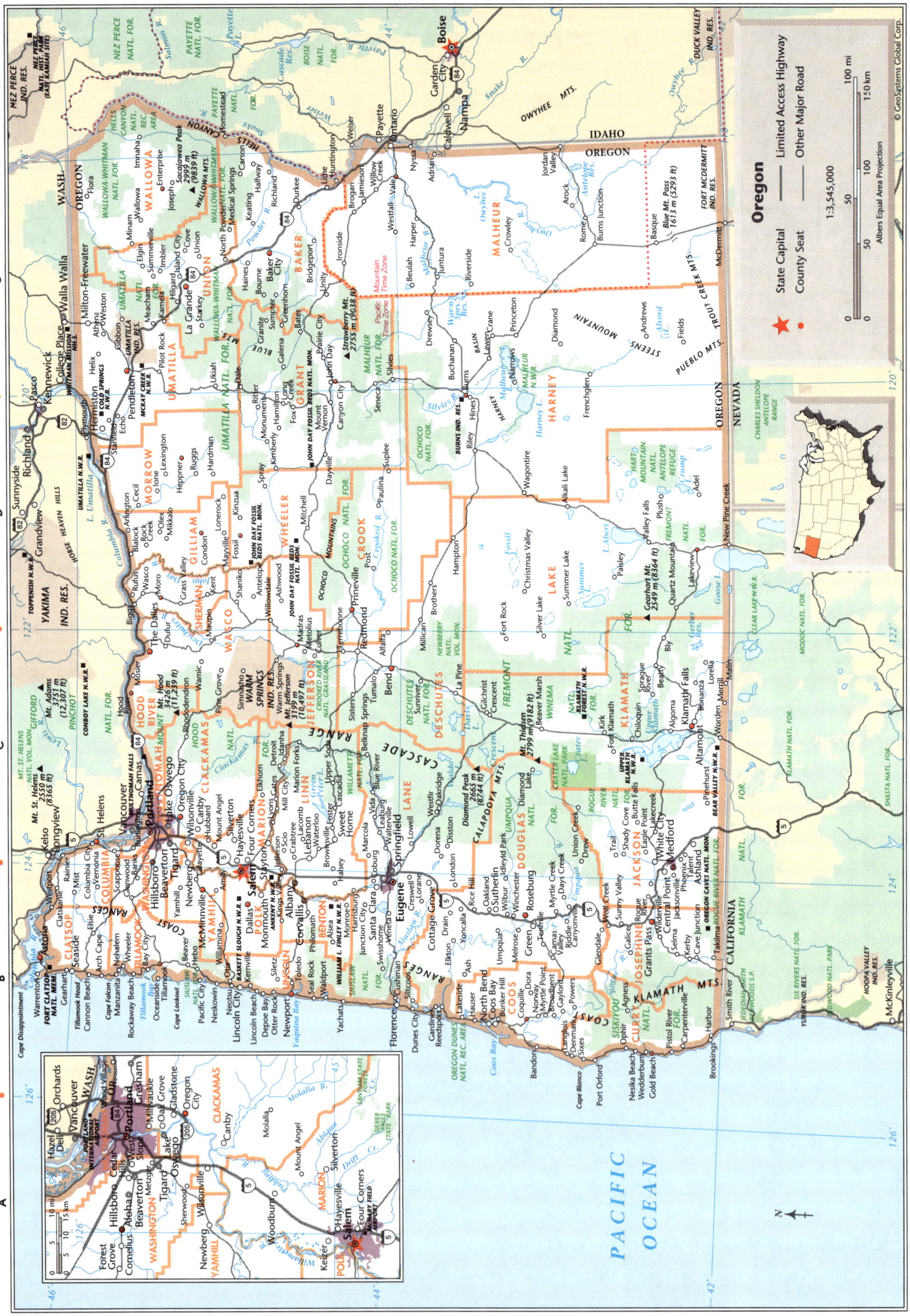

Capital: Harrisburg
Area: 45,300 sq. mi.
117,300 sq. km.
Population: 12,048,000
Largest City: Philadelphia

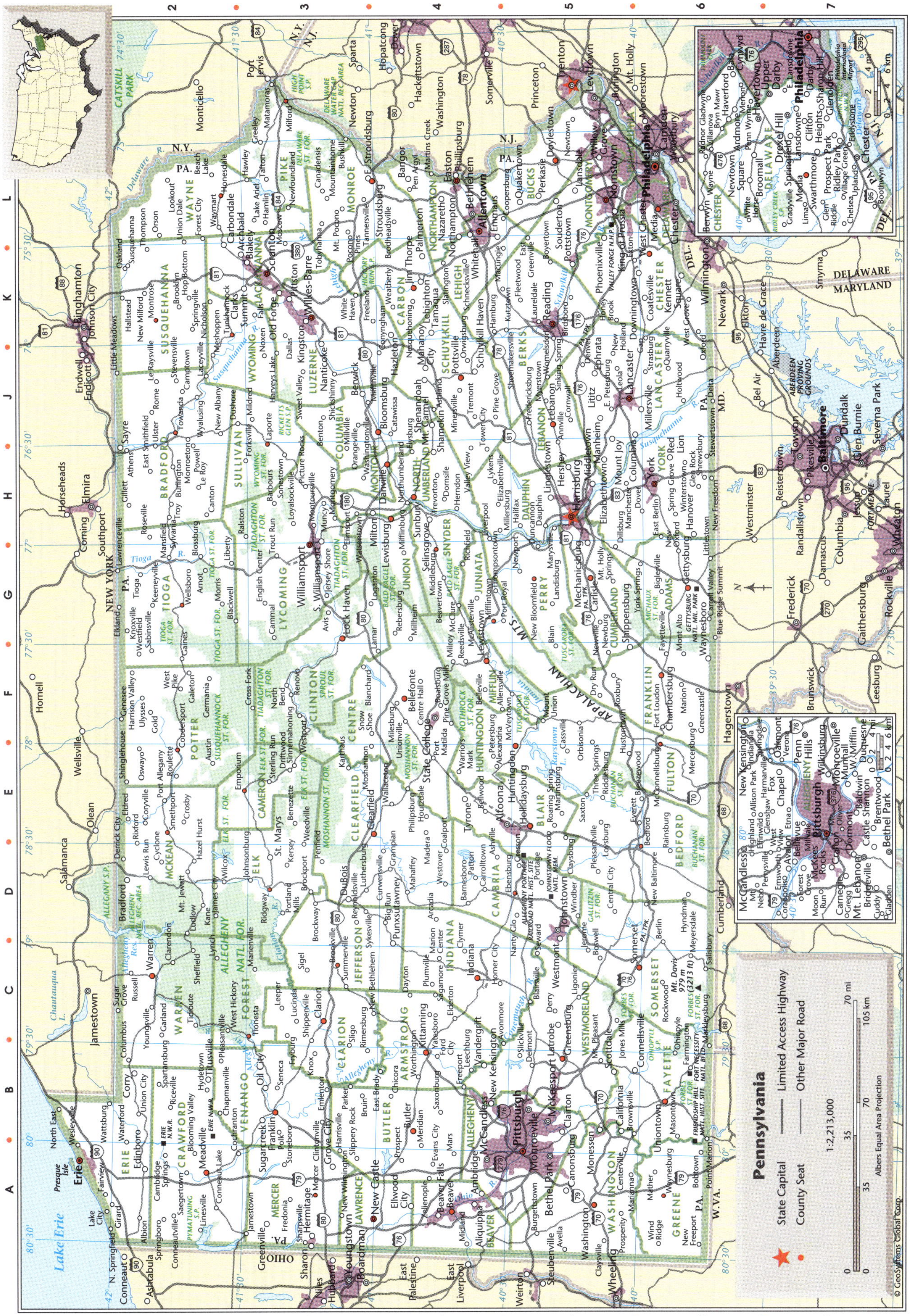

Capital: Providence **Area:** 1,500 sq. mi. 4,000 sq. km.

Population: 1,000,000 **Largest City:** Providence

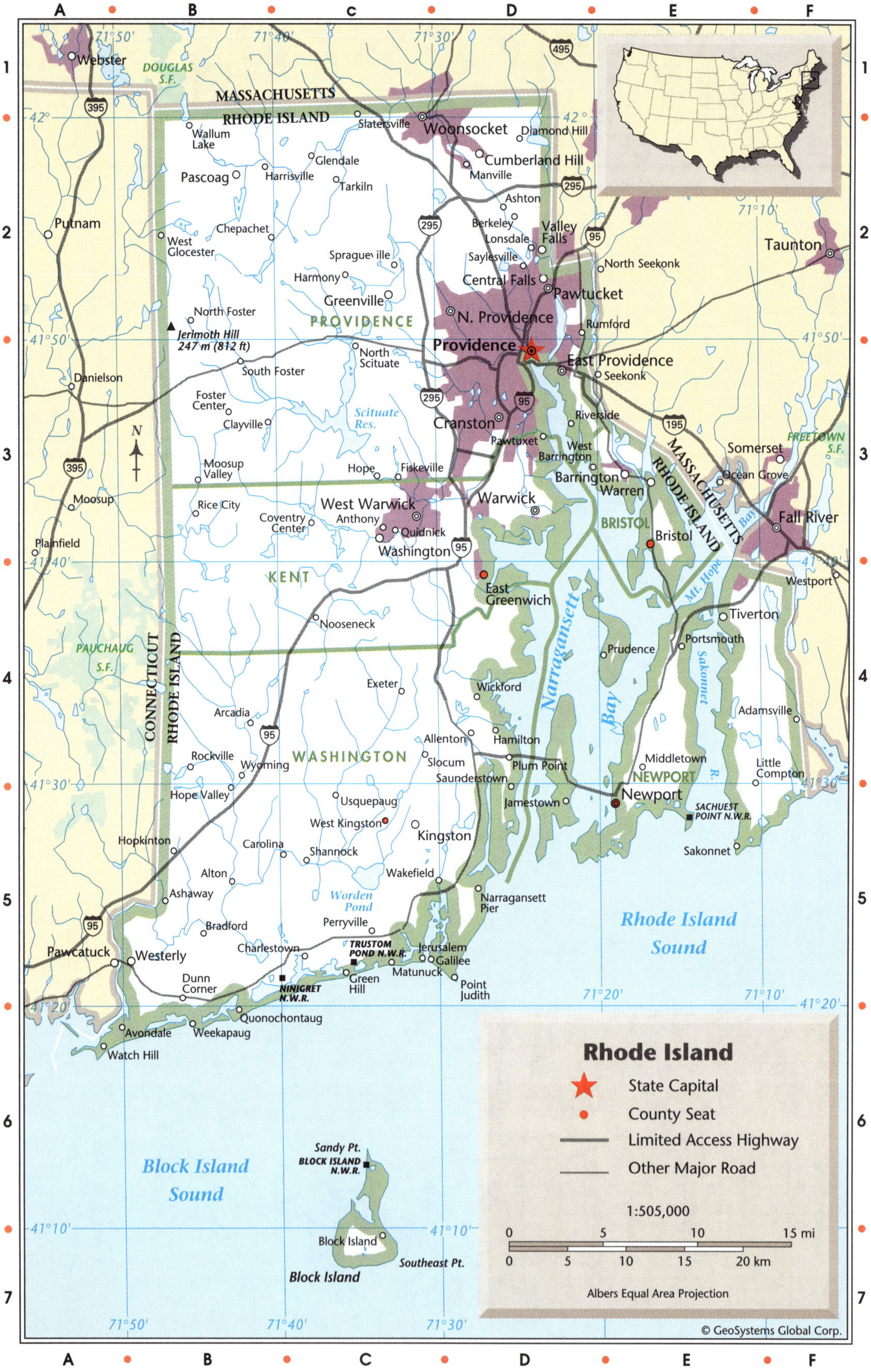

Capital: Columbia
Area: 32,000 sq. mi.
82,900 sq. km.
Population: 3,643,000
Largest City: Columbia

Capital: Pierre
Area: 77,100 sq. mi.
199,700 sq. km.
Population: 715,000
Largest City: Sioux Falls

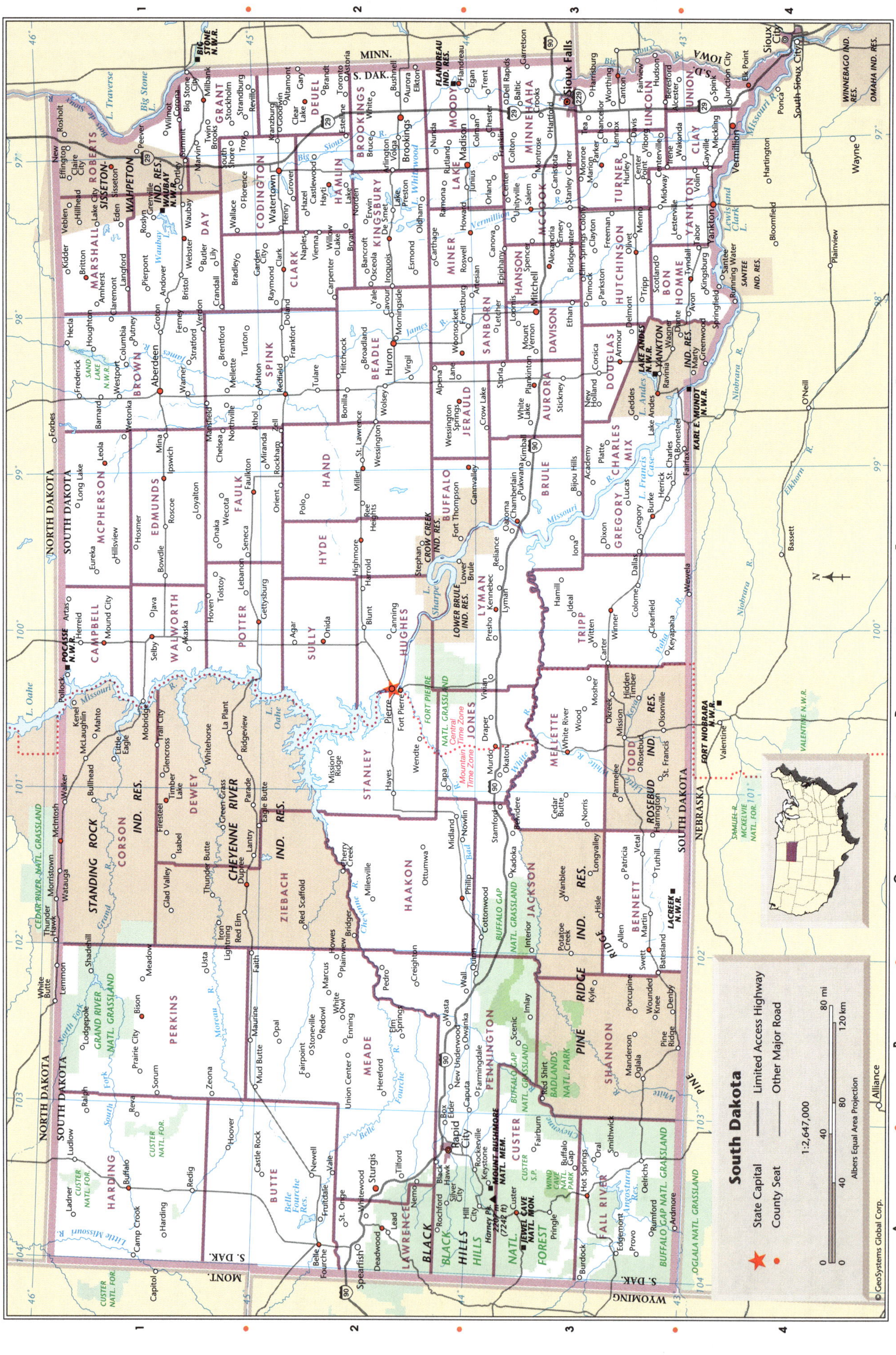

Capital: Nashville
Area: 42,100 sq. mi. 109,200 sq. km.
Population: 5,099,000
Largest City: Memphis

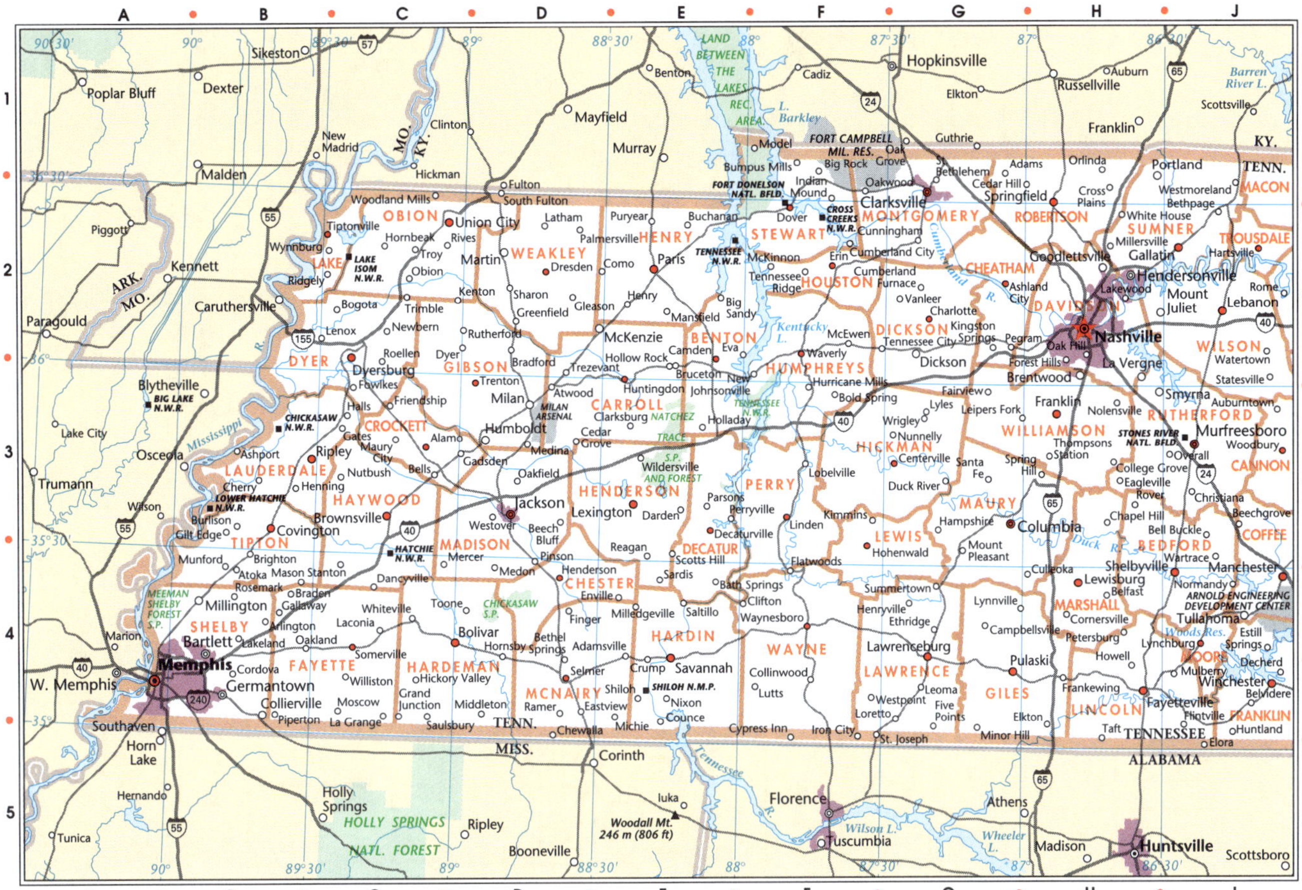

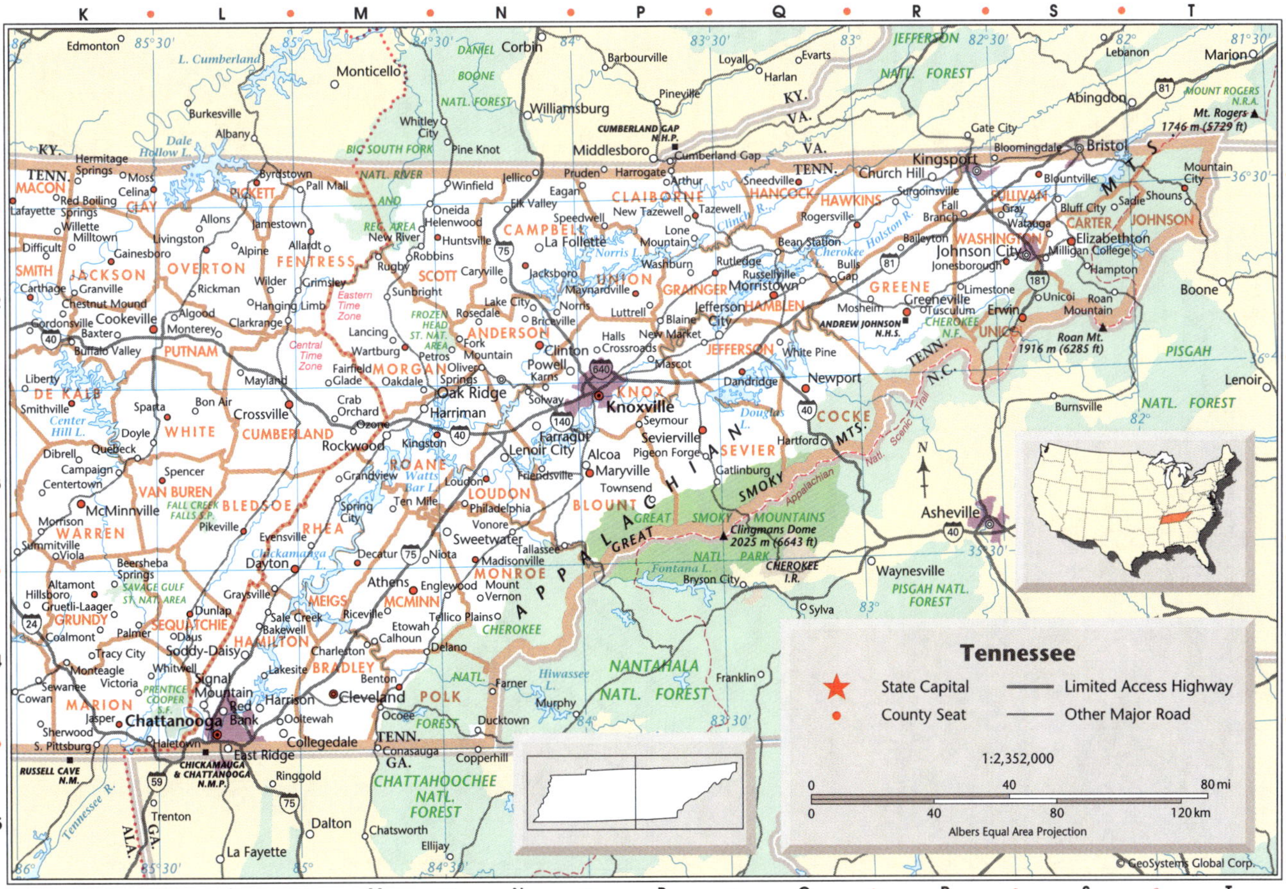

Capital: Austin
Area: 268,600 sq. mi. / 695,700 sq. km.
Population: 18,031,000
Largest City: Houston

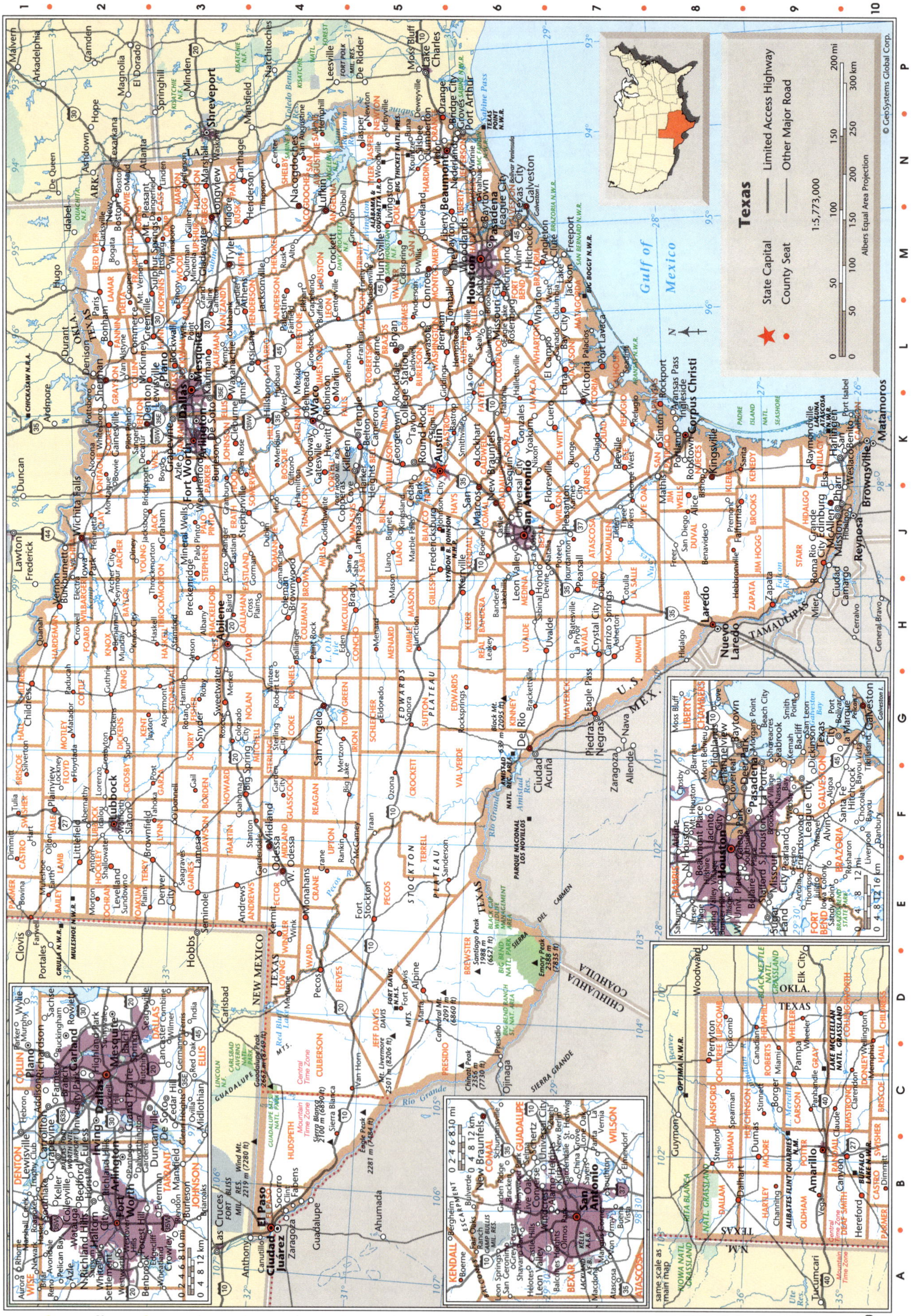

Capital: Salt Lake City
Area: 84,900 sq. mi.
219,900 sq. km.
Population: 1,860,000
Largest City: Salt Lake City

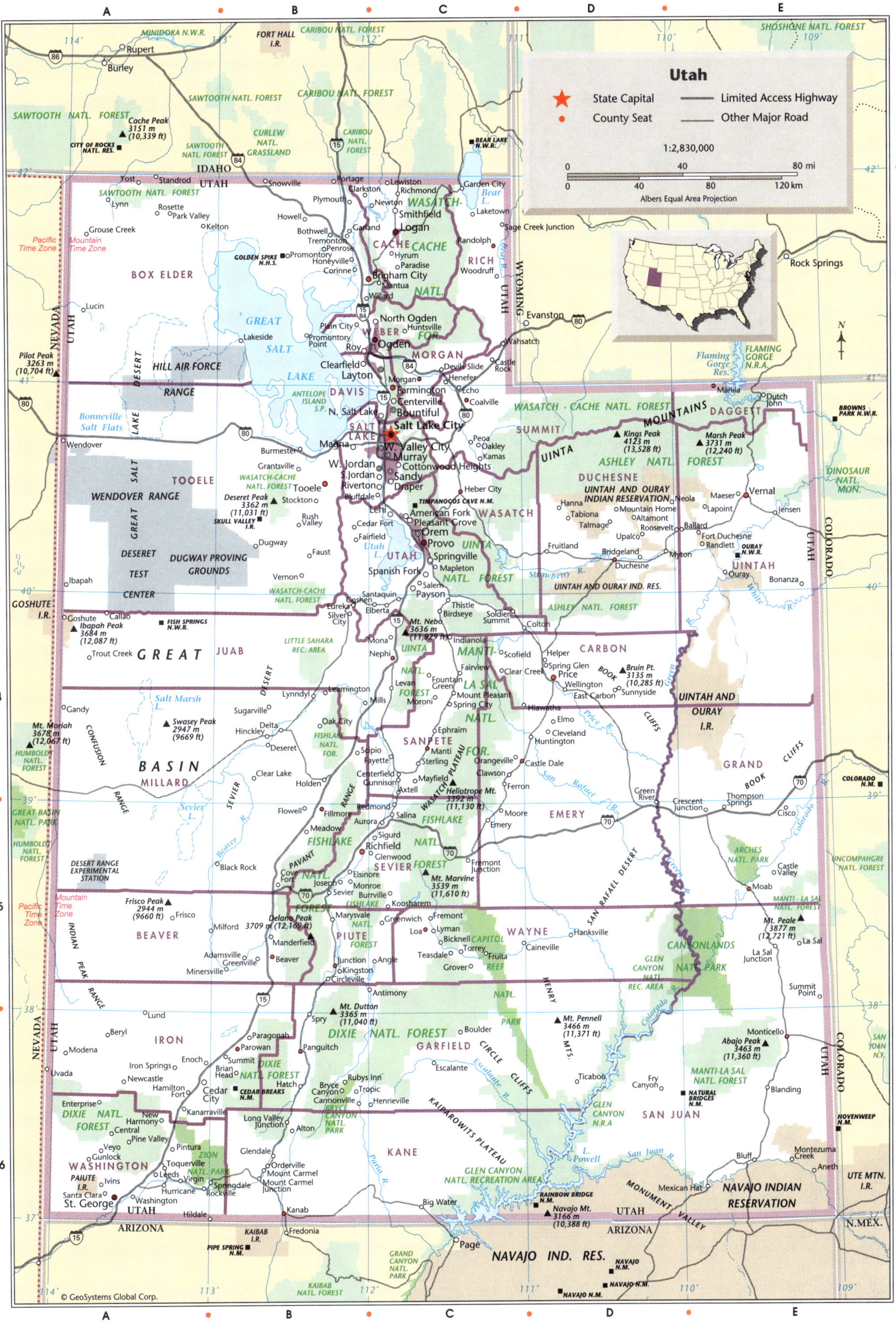

Capital: Montpelier
Area: 9,600 sq. mi.
24,900 sq. km.
Population: 576,000
Largest City: Burlington

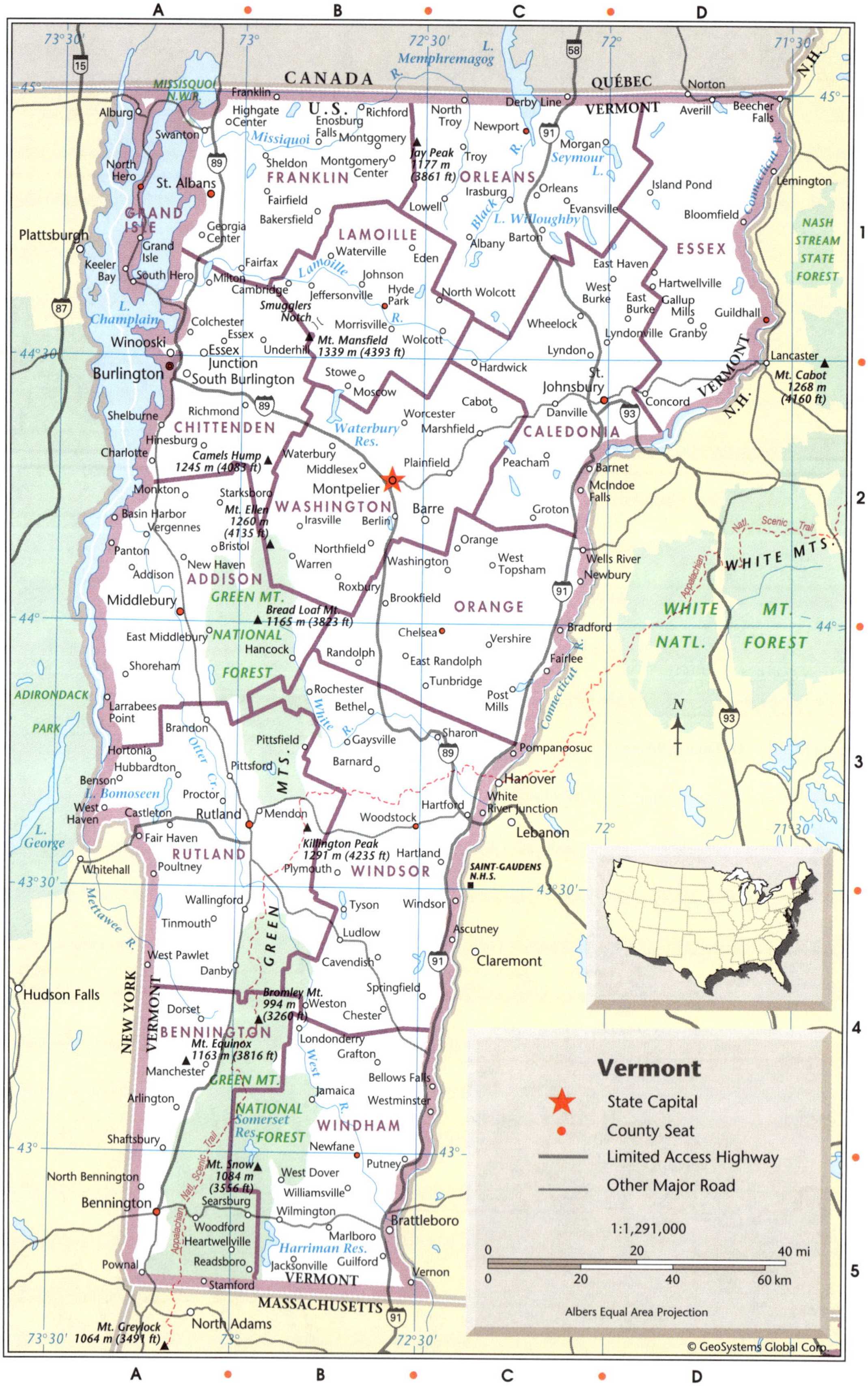

Capital: Richmond
Area: 42,800 sq. mi.
110,800 sq. km.
Population: 6,491,000
Largest City: Virginia Beach

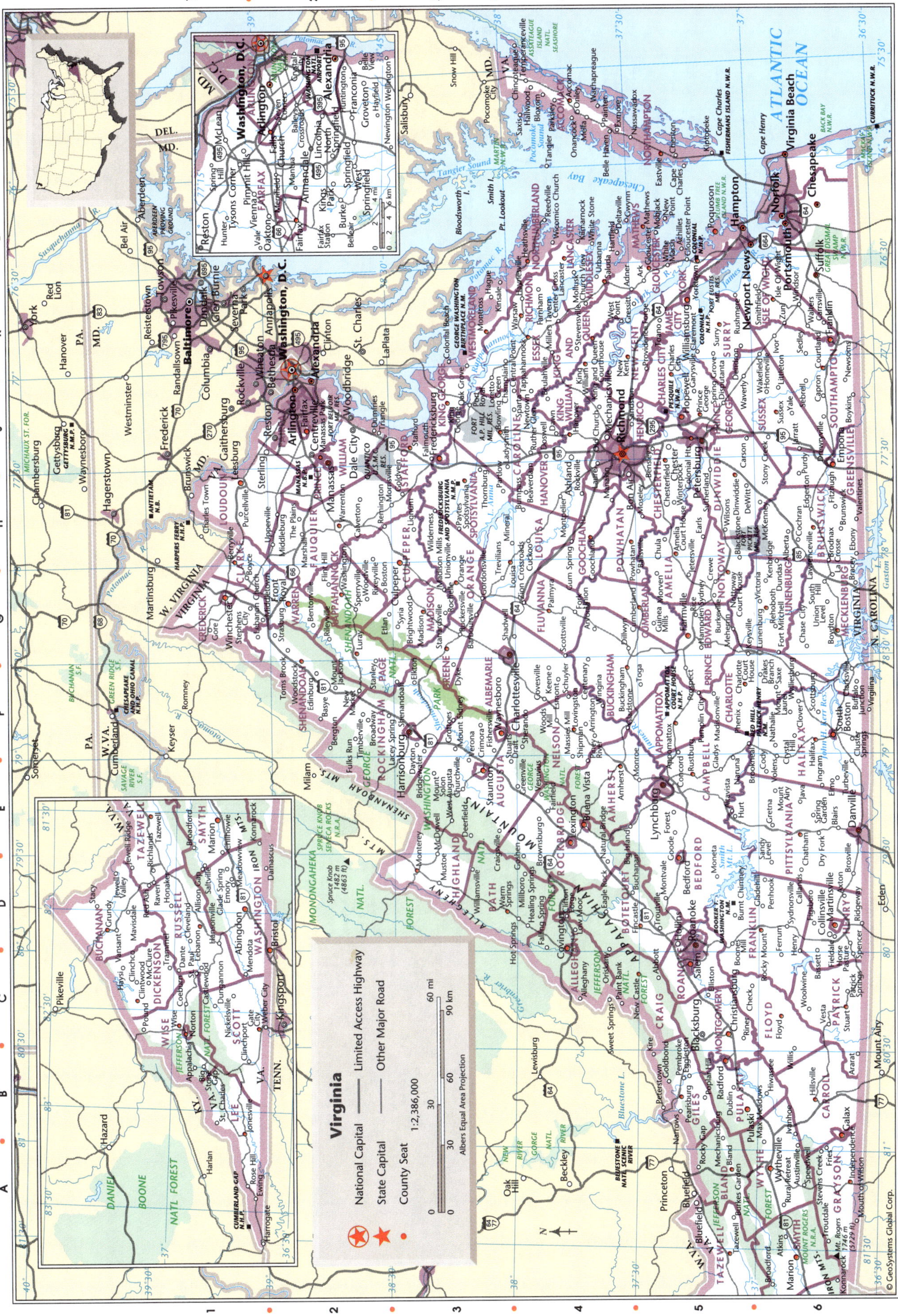

Capital: Olympia
Area: 71,300 sq. mi.
184,700 sq. km.
Population: 5,255,000
Largest City: Seattle

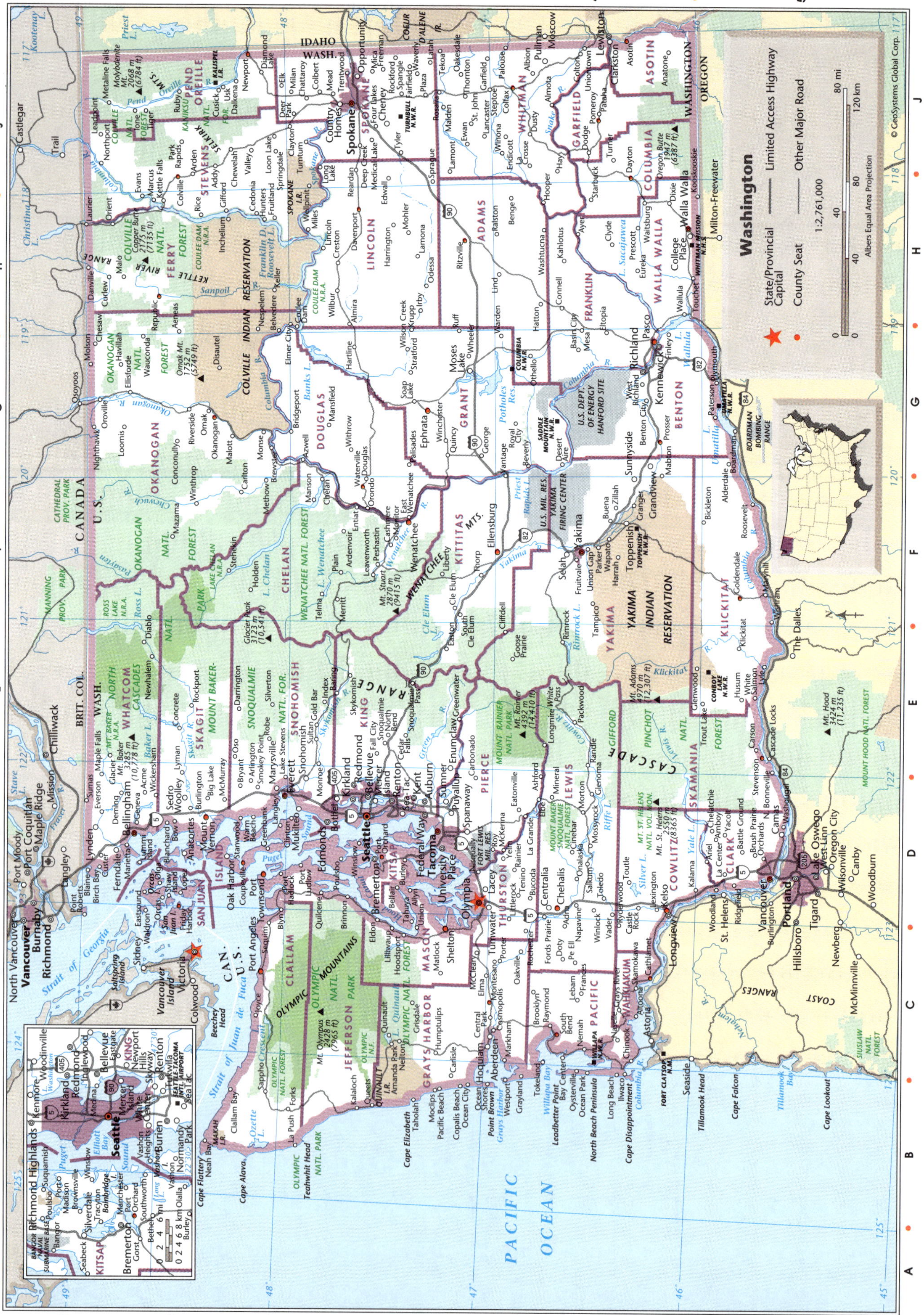

Capital: Charleston
Area: 24,200 sq. mi. 62,800 sq. km.
Population: 1,820,000
Largest City: Charleston

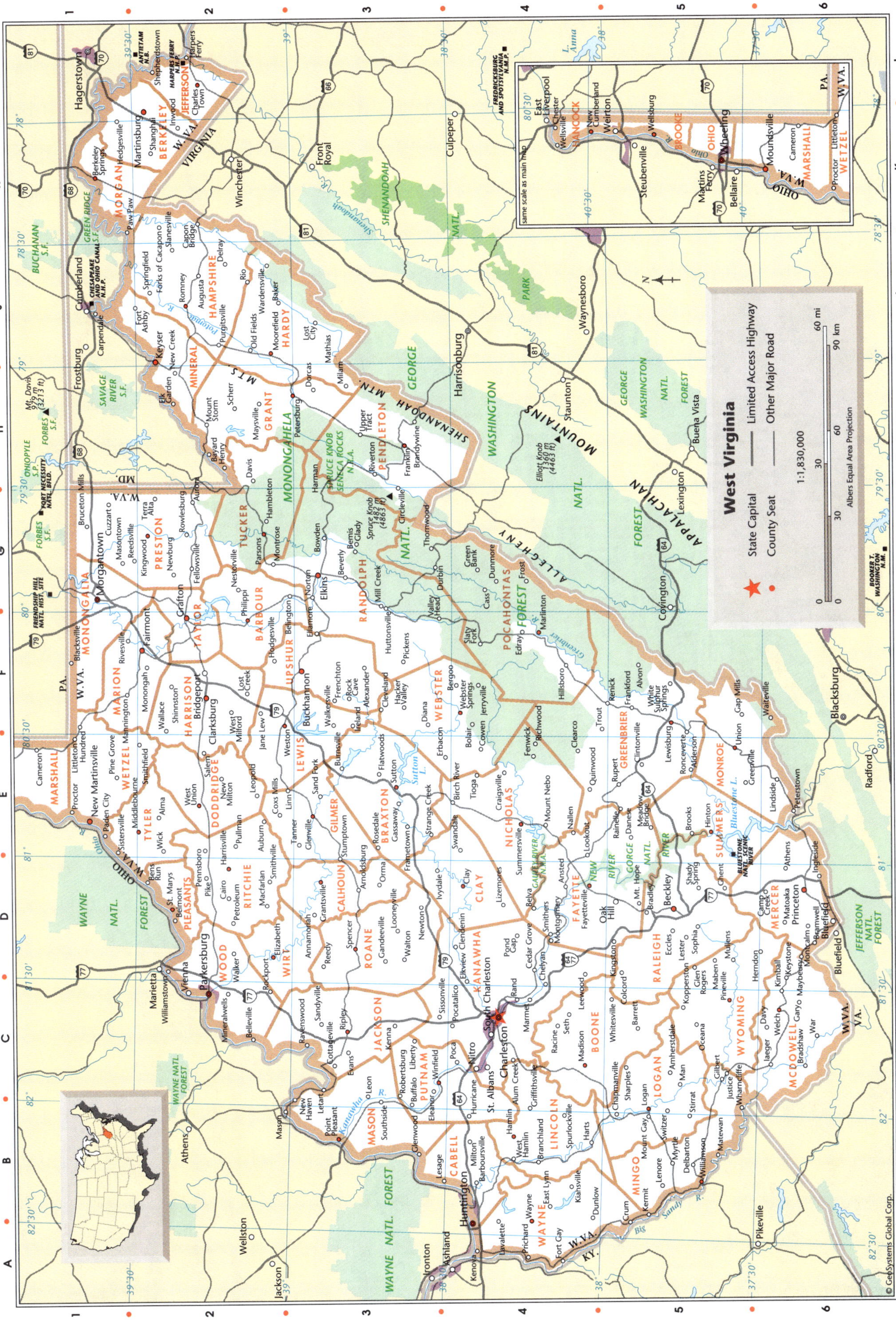

Capital: Madison
Area: 65,500 sq. mi. 169,600 sq. km.
Population: 5,038,000
Largest City: Milwaukee

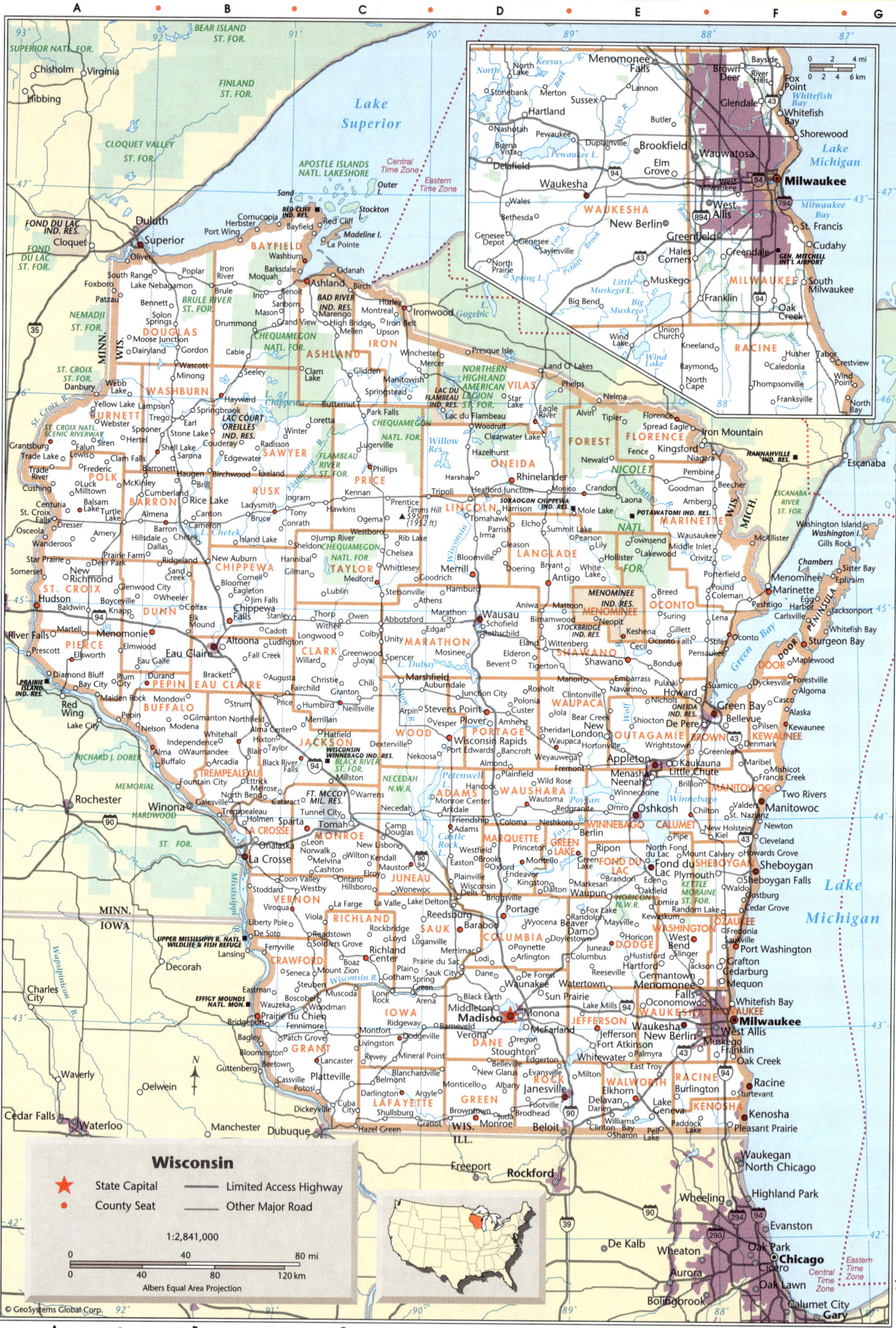

Capital: Cheyenne
Area: 97,800 sq. mi.
253,300 sq. km.
Population: 470,000
Largest City: Cheyenne

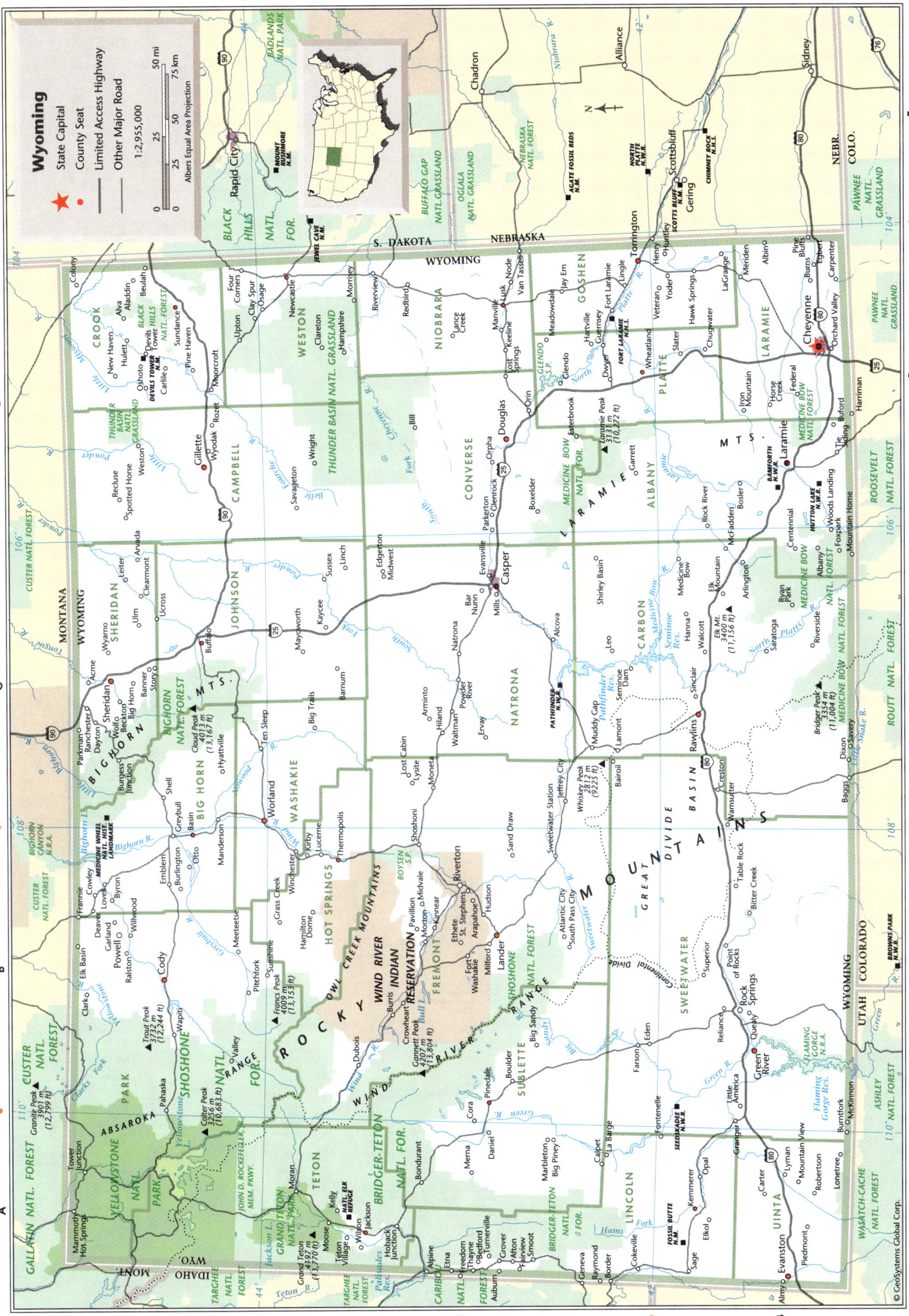

Abbreviations
N.H.P. ... National Historical Park
N.H.S. ... National Historic Site
N.M. ... National Monument
N.P. ... National Park
N.R.A. ... National Recreation Area

Other Features

Colorado ....page 133

Cities and Towns

Other Features

Connecticut ....page 134

Cities and Towns

Key

Key

Pelican Bay A2
Perryton C8
Pharr J9
Pilot Point L2
Pittsburg N2
Plains E2
Plainview F1
Plano L2
Pleasanton J7
Port Arthur P6
Port Bolivar G9
Port Isabel K9
Portland K8
Port Lavaca L7
Post F2
Poteet J6
Premont J8
Presidio C6
Quanah H1
Quitman M3
Ranger J3
Rankin F4
Raymondville K9
Red Oak C3
Refugio K7
Reno A2
Richardson C1
Richland Hills A2
Richmond M6
Rio Grande City J9
Roanoke A1
Robert Lee G4
Robinson K4
Robstown K8
Roby G3
Rockdale L5
Rockport K8
Rocksprings G5
Rockwall L3
Roma H9
Roscoe G3
Rosenberg M6
Rosharon E9
Rotan G3
Round Rock K5
Rowlett C2
Rusk M4
Sabinal H6
Sachse C1
St. Hedwig G9
San Angelo G4
San Antonio J6
San Augustine N4
San Benito K9
Sanderson E5
San Diego J8
Sandy Point E9
Sanger K2
San Geronimo A6
San Leon G9
San Marcos K6
San Saba J4
Sansom Park A2
Sarita K8
Satsuma E8
Sayers B7
Schertz B6
Schumansville C6
Seabrook F9
Seadrift L7
Seagoville C2
Seagraves E3
Sealy L6
Seguin K6
Selma B6
Seminole E3
Seymour H2
Shallowater E2
Shavano Park A6
Sherman L2
Shoreacres G9
Sierra Blanca B4
Silsbee N5
Silverton F1
Sinton K7
Slaton F2
Smith Point G9
Smithville K5
Snyder G3
Socorro A4
Sonora G5
South Houston F9
Southlake A1
Southside Place E8
Southton B7
Spearman C8
Spring Valley E8
Spur G2
Stafford E9
Stamford H3
Stanton F3
Stephenville J3
Sterling City G4
Stratford B8
Sugar Land E9
Sulphur Springs M2
Sundown E2
Sunnyvale C2
Sweetwater G3
Tahoka F2
Taylor K5
Temple K4
Texarkana N2
Texas City N6
The Woodlands M5
Thompsons E9
Three Rivers J7
Throckmorton H2
Tilden J7
Tomball M5
Trinity M5
Trophy Club A1
Tulia F1
Tyler M3
Universal City J6
University Park C2
Uvalde H6
Van Alstyne L2
Van Horn C4
Vega B9
Vernon H1
Victoria L7
Vidor N5
Von Ormy A7
Waco K4
Waskom N3
Watauga A2
Waxahachie L3
Weatherford K3
Webster F9
Wellington D10
Weslaco K9
West K4
West Columbia M6
West Odessa E4
Westover Hills A2
West University Place E8
Westworth A2
Wharton L6
Wheatland A3
Wheeler D9
White Settlement A2
Whitesboro L2
Wichita Falls J2
Willis M5
Wills Point L3
Wilmer C3
Windcrest B6
Winnie N6
Winnsboro M3
Winters H4
Wolfforth F2
Woodville N5
Woodway K4
Wylie D1
Yoakum K6
Zapata H9
Zuehl B7

Other Features

Alibates Flint Quarries N.M. B9
Amistad, *reservoir* F6
Amistad Natl. Rec. Area G6
Balcones, *escarpment* A6
Big Bend Natl. Park D6
Big Thicket Natl. Preserve N5
Black, *mt.* G6
Canadian, *river* C9
Cathedral, *mt.* D5
Chinati Peak, *mt.* C6
Dallas-Fort Worth Intl. Airport B2
Davis, *mts.* C5
Eagle Peak, *mt.* B5
Edwards, *plateau* G5
Emory Peak, *mt.* D6
Falcon, *reservoir* H9
Fort Davis Natl. Hist. Site D5
Galveston, *bay* G9
Galveston, *island* N6
Guadalupe, *mts.* C3
Guadalupe Mts. Natl. Park C4
Guadalupe Peak, *mt.* C4
Kemp, *lake* H2
Livermore, *mt.* C5
Livingston, *lake* M5
Lyndon B. Johnson N.H.P. J5
Meredith, *lake* C9
Nueces, *river* J7
O.H. Ivie, *lake* H4
Padre Island Natl. Seashore K8
Pecos, *river* E4
Pelican, *island* G9
Red, *river* H1
Red Bluff, *lake* D4
Rio Grande, *river* F6
Sabine, *pass* P6
Sabine, *river* P5
Sam Rayburn, *reservoir* N4
Santiago Peak, *mt.* D6
Sierra Del Carmen, *mt.* D6
Stockton, *plateau* E5
Toledo Bend, *reservoir* P4

Utah ....page 171

Cities and Towns

American Fork C3
Beaver B5
Bicknell C5
Blanding E6
Bluffdale C3
Bountiful C3
Brigham City C2
Castle Dale C4
Cedar City A6
Centerville C3
Clearfield B2
Coalville C3
Cottonwood Heights C3
Delta B4
Draper C3
Duchesne D3
East Carbon D4
Enoch A6
Ephraim C4
Farmington C3
Ferron C4
Fillmore B5
Garland B2
Grantsville B3
Gunnison C4
Heber City C3
Helper D4
Hildale A6
Huntington D4
Hurricane A6
Hyrum C2
Ivins A6
Junction B5
Kanab B6
Lapoint E3
Layton C2
Lehi C3
Lewiston C2
Loa C5
Logan C2
Long Valley Junction B6
Maeser E3
Magna B3
Manila E3
Manti C4
Mapleton C3
Moab E5
Monroe B5
Monticello E6
Morgan C2
Mount Pleasant C4
Murray C3
Myton D3
N. Salt Lake C3
Nephi C4
North Ogden C2
Ogden C2
Orangeville C4
Orem C3
Panguitch B6
Parowan B6
Payson C3
Plain City B2
Pleasant Grove C3
Price D4
Provo C3
Randolph C2
Richfield B5
Richmond C2
Riverton C3
Roosevelt D3
Roy B2
St. George A6
Salem C3
Salina C5
Salt Lake City, *capital* C3
Sandy C3
Santa Clara A6
Santaquin C4
Smithfield C2
South Jordan C3
Spanish Fork C3
Springville C3
Sugarville B4
Tooele B3
Tremonton B2
Vernal E3
Washington A6
Wellington D4
West Jordan C3
West Valley City C3
Willard B2

Other Features

Abajo Peak, *mt.* E6
Arches Natl. Park E5
Bear, *lake* C2
Bear, *river* C2
Beaver, *river* B5
Bonneville Salt Flats A3
Bruin Point, *mt.* D4
Bryce Canyon Natl. Park B6
Canyonlands Natl. Park E5
Capitol Reef Natl. Park C5
Cedar Breaks Natl. Monument B6
Colorado, *river* E5
Delano Peak, *mt.* B5
Deseret Peak, *mt.* B3
Dinosaur Natl. Monument E3
Dutton, *mt.* B5
Escalante, *river* C6
Flaming Gorge, *reservoir* E2
Flaming Gorge Natl. Rec. Area E2
Frisco Peak, *mt.* A5
Glen Canyon Natl. Rec. Area D6
Golden Spike Natl. Hist. Site B2
Great, *basin* A4
Great Salt, *lake* B2
Great Salt Lake, *desert* A3
Green, *river* D4
Heliotrope, *mt.* C4
Henry, *mts.* D6
Ibapah Peak, *mt.* A4
Kings Peak, *mt.* D3
Marsh Peak, *mt.* E3
Marvine, *mt.* C5
Monument, *valley* D6
Natural Bridges Natl. Monument E6
Navajo, *mt.* D6
Navajo Indian Res. E6
Nebo, *mt.* C4
Paria, *river* C6
Pavant, *range* B5
Peale, *mt.* E5
Pennell, *mt.* D6
Powell, *lake* D6
Price, *river* D4
Rainbow Bridge Natl. Monument D6
Salt Marsh, *lake* A4
San Juan, *river* D6
San Rafael, *river* D4
Sevier, *desert* B4
Sevier, *lake* A5
Strawberry, *river* D3
Swasey Peak, *mt.* A4
Timpanogos Cave N.M. C3
Uinta, *mts.* D3
Utah, *lake* C3
Wasatch, *plateau* C5
White, *river* E3
Zion Natl. Park A6

Vermont ....page 172

Cities and Towns

Addison A2
Albany C1
Ascutney C4
Averill D1
Bakersfield B1
Barnard B3
Barnet C2
Barre C2
Basin Harbor A2
Beecher Falls D1
Bellows Falls C4
Bennington A5
Benson A3
Berlin B3
Bethel B3
Bloomfield D1
Bradford C3
Brandon A3
Brattleboro B5
Bristol A2
Brookfield B2
Burlington A2
Cabot C2
Cambridge B1
Castleton A3
Cavendish B4
Charlotte A2
Chelsea C3
Colchester A1
Concord D2
Danby B4
Danville C2
Dorset A4
East Burke D1
East Haven D1
East Middlebury A3
East Randolph B3
Eden B1
Enosburg Falls B1
Essex A1
Essex Junction A1
Evansville C1
Fair Haven A3
Fairfax B1
Fairfield B1
Fairlee C3
Franklin B1
Gallup Mills D1
Gaysville B3
Georgia Center A1
Grafton B4
Granby D1
Grand Isle A1
Groton C2
Guildhall D1
Guilford B5
Hancock B3
Hanover C3
Hardwick C2
Hartford C3
Hartland C3
Hartwellville D1
Heartwellville A5
Highgate Center A1
Hinesburg A2
Hortonia A3
Hubbardton A3
Hyde Park B1
Irasburg C1
Irasville B2
Jacksonville B5
Jamaica B4
Jeffersonville B1
Johnson B1
Keeler Bay A1
Larrabees Point A3
Lemington D1
Londonderry B4
Lowell C1
Lyndon C1
Lyndonville C1
McIndoe Falls C2
Marlboro B5
Mendon B3
Middlebury A2
Middlesex B2
Milton A1
Monkton A2
Montgomery B1
Montgomery Center B1
Montpelier, *capital* B2
Morgan C1
Morrisville B1
Moscow B2
Newbury C2
Newfane B4
New Haven A2
Newport C1
North Bennington A5
Northfield B2
North Hero A1
North Wolcott C1
Norton D1
Orange C2
Panton A2
Peacham C2
Pittsfield B3
Pittsford A3
Plainfield C2
Plymouth B3
Pompanoosuc C3
Post Mills C3
Poultney A3
Pownal A5
Proctor A3
Putney B5
Randolph B3
Readsboro B5
Richford B1
Richmond A2
Rochester B3
Roxbury B2
Rutland B3
St. Albans A1
St. Johnsbury C2
Searsburg B5
Shaftsbury A4
Sharon C3
Shelburne A2
Sheldon B1
Shoreham A3
South Burlington A2
South Hero A1
Springfield C4
Stamford A5
Starksboro A2
Swanton A1
Tinmouth A4
Troy C1
Tunbridge C3
Tyson B4
Underhill B1
Vergennes A2
Vernon B5
Vershire C3
Warren B2
Washington C2
Waterbury B2
Waterville B1
Wells River C2
West Burke D1
West Dover B5
West Haven A3
Westminster C4
Weston B4
West Pawlet A4
West Topsham C2
Wheelock C1
White River Junction C3
Williamsville B5
Wilmington B5
Windsor C4
Winooski A1
Wolcott C1
Woodford A5
Woodstock B3
Worcester B2

Other Features

Appalachian Natl. Scenic Trail A5
Black, *river* C1
Bomoseen, *lake* A3
Bread Loaf, *mt.* B2
Bromley, *mt.* B4
Camels Hump, *mt.* B2
Champlain, *lake* A1
Connecticut, *river* C3
Ellen, *mt.* B2
Equinox, *mt.* A4
Green, *mts.* B4
Harriman, *reservoir* B5
Jay Peak, *mt.* B1
Killington Peak, *mt.* B3
Lamoille, *river* B1
Mansfield, *mt.* B1
Mettawee, *river* A3
Missisquoi, *river* B1
Seymour, *lake* C1
Smugglers Notch, *pass* B1
Snow, *mt.* B5
Somerset, *reservoir* B4
Waterbury, *reservoir* B2
West, *river* B4
White, *river* B3
Willoughby, *lake* C1

Virginia ....page 173

Cities and Towns

Abingdon D1
Accomac M4
Achilles L5
Alberta H6
Alexandria J2
Allison Gap D1
Altavista E5
Amelia Court House H5
Amherst E4
Annandale M2
Appalachia B1
Appomattox F5
Arlington J2
Ashland H4
Baileys Crossroads M2
Bassett C6
Basye F2
Bedford D5
Belleair L2
Belle Haven M4
Belle View M2
Bensley J5
Berryville H1
Big Stone Gap C2
Blacksburg B5
Blackstone H5
Bland A5
Bloxom M4
Bluefield A5
Bon Air H4
Bowling Green J3
Boyce G1
Boydton G6
Boykins J6
Bridgewater F3
Bristol D2
Brodnax G6
Brookneal F5
Brunswick H6
Buckingham F4
Buena Vista E4
Burke L2
Burkeville G5
Callands D6
Cape Charles L5
Castlewood C1
Centreville J2
Charles City J5
Charlotte Court House F5
Charlottesville F4
Chase City G6
Chatham E6
Cheriton M5
Chesapeake L6
Chester J5
Chesterfield H5
Chilhowie E1
Chincoteague M4
Christiansburg C5
Chula H5
Claremont K5
Clifton Forge D4
Clinchco C1
Clintwood C1
Coeburn C1
Collinsville D6
Colonial Beach K3
Colonial Hts. J5
Concord E5
Courtland J6
Covington C4
Crewe G5
Crimora F3
Crystal City M2
Crystal Hill F6
Culpeper G3
Cumberland G4
Dale City J2
Danville E6
Dendron K5
Dillwyn G4
Dinwiddie H5
Drakes Branch F6
Dublin B5
Dumfries J2
Dungannon C1
Eastville M5
Elkton F3
Emory D1
Emporia H6
Ewing A1
Fairfax J2
Fairfax Station L2
Falls Church M2
Falmouth J3
Farmville G5
Ferrum D6
Figsboro D6
Fincastle D4
Fishersville F3
Flint Hill G2
Floyd C6
Forest E5
Fort Mitchell G6
Franconia M2
Franklin K6
Fredericksburg J3
Fries B6
Front Royal G2
Galax B6
Gate City C1
Glade Spring D1
Gloucester K5
Gloucester Point L5
Goochland H4
Gordonsville G3
Goshen D4
Gretna E6
Grottoes F3
Groveton M2
Grundy D1
Halifax F6
Hampton L5
Hanover J4
Harrisonburg F3
Harrogate A1
Heathsville L4
Hollins D5
Hopewell J5
Horse Pasture D6
Huntington M2
Hurt E5
Independence A6
Isle of Wight K6
Jetersville G5
Jonesville B1
Kenbridge G6
King and Queen Courthouse K4
King George J3
Kings Park L2
King William J4
Lancaster L4
Lawrenceville H6
Lebanon D1
Leesburg H1
Lexington E4
Lincolnia M2
Louisa G4
Lovingston F4
Lunenburg G6
Luray G2
Lynchburg E5
McLean M1
Madison G3
Manakin H4
Manassas J2
Manassas Park J2
Mantua L2
Marion A6
Martinsville D6
Mathews L5
Mechanicsburg A5
Mechanicsville J4
Meherrin G5
Millboro D4
Monterey D3
Montross K3
Mount Jackson F2
Narrows B5
New Castle C4
New Kent K4
New Market F2
Newport News L6
Newsoms J6
Norfolk L6
North Springfield M2
Norton C1
Nottoway Court House G5
Oakton L2
Onancock M4
Orange G3
Palmyra G4
Pearisburg B5
Petersburg J5
Peterstown B5
Pimmit Hills M1
Poquoson L5
Portsmouth L6
Powhatan H4
Prince George J5
Pulaski B5
Purcellville H1
Radford B5
Raven D1
Reston J2
Richlands D1
Richmond, *capital* J4
Ridgeway D6
Roanoke D5
Rocky Mount D6
Rustburg E5
Ruther Glen J4
Salem C5
Saltville D1
Saluda K4
Shenandoah F3
Smithfield K6
South Boston F6
South Hill G6
Spotsylvania H3
Springfield M2
Spring Hill M1
Stafford J3
Stanardsville G3
Staunton E3
Sterling J1
Stony Creek J6
Strasburg G2
Stuart C6
Stuarts Draft E3
Suffolk K6
Surry K5
Sussex J6
Tappahannock K4
Tazewell A5
Timberville F2
Triangle J2
Tysons Corner M1
Vale L1
Verona E3
Victoria G6
Vienna L1
Virginia Beach M6
Warm Springs D3
Warrenton H2
Warsaw K4
Washington G2
Waverly J5
Waynesboro F3
Weber City C1
Wellington M3
West Point K4
West Springfield M2
Williamsburg K5
Winchester G1
Wise C1
Woodbridge J2
Woodstock F2
Wytheville A6
Yorktown K5

Other Features

Allegheny, *mts.* D3
Anna, *lake* H3
Appalachian, *mts.* C5
Appomattox Court House N.H.P. F5
Arlington Natl. Cem. M2
Assateague Island Natl. Seashore M4
Booker T. Washington N.M. D5
Charles, *cape* M5
Chesapeake, *bay* L5
Colonial Natl. Hist. Park K5
Fredericksburg & Spotsylvania Natl. Mil. Park H3
Gaston, *lake* G6
George Washington Birthplace Natl. Monument K3
Henry, *cape* M6
Iron, *mts.* A6
James, *river* K5
John H. Kerr, *reservoir* F6
Mount Rogers Natl. Rec. Area A6
Potomac, *river* K3

Key

Washington ..... page 174

Cities and Towns

Other Features

West Virginia ..... page 175

Cities and Towns

Other Features

Wisconsin ..... page 176

Cities and Towns

Other Features

Wyoming ..... page 177

Cities and Towns

Other Features